P9-AER-426

Coastal Southern California

K/H GEOLOGY FIELD GUIDE SERIES

FIELD GUIDE

Coastal
Southern
California

Robert P. Sharp
California Institute of Technology

KENDALL/HUNT PUBLISHING COMPANY
2460 Kerper Boulevard, Dubuque, Iowa 52001

K/H GEOLOGY FIELD GUIDE SERIES

Consulting Editor
John W. Harbaugh
Stanford University

Copyright © 1978 by Kendall/Hunt Publishing Company

Library of Congress Catalog Card Number: 78-51270

ISBN 0–8403–1863–4

All rights reserved. No part of this publication may be reproduced, stored in a retrieval system, or transmitted, in any form or by any means, electronic, mechanical, photocopying, recording, or otherwise, without the prior written permission of the copyright owner.

Printed in the United States of America

401863   01

CONTENTS

Appendixes

Foreword

Dr. Sharp's book is one of the K/H *Geology Field Guide Series.* The objective of this series is to provide an authoritatively written layman's guide to important geologic features in each region treated. Stress is placed on observations in the field. Each guide provides an overview of the region to which it pertains, and outlines a series of self-guiding field trips which will allow users to make their own firsthand observations on features that typify the area.

The series is directed toward diverse groups of users. It should find use in formal classes in geology, both at the college and university level, and in high schools, in which field trips form an essential part of introductory or advanced courses. Furthermore, the books in the series should be useful to professional geologists and other scientists who desire an introduction to the geologic features of particular regions. Finally, they should find use among individuals who are not necessarily trained in science, but who do have an active interest in natural history and who enjoy travel.

Authors of these books all have intimate acquaintance with their respective regions and extensive teaching experience which has stressed field trip observations. Consequently, each book represents a distillation of teaching experiences that have involved many students and numerous field trips.

John W. Harbaugh
Consulting Editor

Preface

Like its predecessor, *Geology—Field Guide to Southern California*, this booklet is designed primarily for non-professionals interested in the natural environment. Hopefully, most college-level geology students will find it useful, and mature professionals can be amused by its shortcomings, oversights, and errors.

The first booklet provided descriptive guides for field trips directed inland, primarily to Death Valley and the eastern Sierra. This volume furnishes descriptions for similar trips within the coastal belt of southern California from the Mexican border to San Luis Obispo. Focus is primarily upon features to be seen while traveling, although occasional stops and short diversions are recommended. Since most coastwise travel is on freeways, this can be a challenging exercise. Things flash by rather rapidly at 55 mph. Nonetheless, freeways are what we have, so let's make the best of them. California is lavishly endowed with geological features and relationships, and the lives of its inhabitants can be enriched through at least a passing acquaintance with some of them.

An introductory chapter provides information concerning landforms and the processes that create them. This should help in understanding the landscapes seen while traveling. A glossary, Appendix C, explains those items of geological jargon that cannot easily or conveniently be avoided. The bulk of the booklet consists of route descriptions for 18 separate field-trip segments within the southern California coastal zone.

Words cannot adequately express my appreciation to: Enid Bell for superb typing, editing, and critical servicing of the manuscript; Dorothy Coy for preliminary typing, patience, and interest; the Graphic Arts Facilities at Caltech for excellent services; the Department of Geography at University of California, Los Angeles, for aid and cooperation; John S. Shelton and Robert C. Frampton for photographs; Jan Scott for drafting; Michael P. Kennedy and Robert Sydnor for constructive criticism; and many, many others who throughout the years have observed, unlocked, and made known some of the secrets of California geology. The ready cooperation of Kendall-Hunt personnel has added to the pleasure of this task.

Chapter 1

Natural Landscapes

Some General Principles

Recognition of individual landforms composing a natural scene gives somewhat the same pleasure as meeting an old friend. This chapter aims to make you friendly with landforms in southern California coastal areas and to provide understanding of geological processes which created them. Such acquaintance and understanding will contribute to your enjoyment of road guides because landforms are among the more numerous and more easily observed features seen while whishing along coastal freeways.

Most landscapes are the product of two opposing groups of processes, the "builder uppers" and the "tearer downers." Outpouring of volcanic material to form a cone, such as Mt. Shasta, is a building-up or *constructive* process. Glaciers and streams gnawing into the flanks of Mt. Shasta are tearing-down or *destructive* agents. Both have contributed to the configuration of that landform. Volcanism is not currently active in coastal southern California, but it *was* 15 to 20 million years ago. Glaciers lay on the highest peaks of the San Bernardino Mountains only 15,000 years ago, and streams are today the most potent tearing-down agent at work in southern California, except possibly for man himself.

Building-up Processes and Their Products

A principal building-up process in southern California is the up, down, and sidewise movement of blocks of the earth's crust known as *tectonic deformation*. It is caused by forces coming from deep within the earth, driven by heat energy. Crustal blocks move past each other along fractures called faults, and fault movements cause earthquakes. Southern California is unusual, within the United States, in that tectonic deformation occurs currently. Be a little proud—we are living within a local geological revolution, an episode of marked crustal deformation. This may not be the safest place to live, but geologically it is one of the most varied and exciting.

In addition to faulting, tectonic deformation results in folding, warping, or tilting. Signal Hill near Long Beach, Camarillo Hills in Ventura County, and Wheeler Ridge in San Joaquin Valley were formed only yesterday, geologically speaking, by folding. Tectonic activity occurs in coastal southern California because it is located on the east edge of the Pacific plate. So, what is the Pacific plate and what is wrong with its east edge?

The entire earth's surface, including continents and ocean basins, is divided into seven major plates, which are in constant motion, either pushing against each other or slipping sidewise past one another. Edges of the plates take a battering. The suture separating the Pacific plate, on which coastal southern California is located, and the North American plate on which the remainder of United States lies, is the San Andreas fault. This fault borders the southwestern edge of Mojave Desert, extending south into Imperial Valley and north through the Coast Ranges, passing just west of San Francisco. San Francisco belongs to the North American plate, and Los Angeles is part of a different geological world, the Pacific plate.

Tearing-down Processes and Their Products

Weathering and Erosion.   Whenever new rock material is brought to the earth's surface by one of several geological means, it is subjected to a physical and chemical attack collectively known as weathering. Rusting of tools exposed to dew or rain is

a form of weathering. Rocks are broken by freezing of water in pores and cracks, by tree roots, and especially by expansion of mineral components as they are attacked chemically by water, gases, acids and by bacteria, fungi and other organisms. The original minerals are partly changed into new substances, such as clay, of larger volume, and the resulting expansion breaks the rock apart. It literally disintegrates into the component particles or small aggregates of particles.

Soil is a product of physical disintegration and chemical alteration of rocks. It is one of our most precious natural resources, more necessary than oil, gas, gold, copper, or coal. Without soil, you and I wouldn't be here. It is absolutely essential to life on land as we know it, so pay respects to weathering the next time you see some soil.

The weathered mantle rock (Photo 1-1), including soil, on a hillslope is not going to stay there. As it is removed, new rock is exposed and more weathered mantle is developed. That is how high-standing areas are worn down, the process being known as erosion. Erosion is the principal destructive process affecting landscapes. It involves

Photo 1-1. Weathered mantle rock derived from a basaltic lava flow. Concentric structure at hammer is a product of the weathering process.

pickup and removal (transportation) of rock materials, mostly those already loosened by weathering. Several processes produce erosion.

Mass Movements. Part of the downslope movement of weathered mantle rock occurs in mass form under the pull of gravity. Such *mass movements* occur in many varieties and probably do not get the full credit they deserve for shaping landscapes. On many slopes, a layer of weathered debris, several inches to several feet thick, moves constantly but slowly, no more than a small fraction of an inch a year, downslope by a process known as *creep.* Under abnormally wet conditions, the same material may move more rapidly a few feet a day or a mile or two an hour, as an earthflow. Occasionally, larger masses of weathered debris and some of the underlying bedrock break away and slump or

slide catastrophically downslope, at tens of miles per hour or even faster, as a landslide (Photo 1-2).

We are impressed by such sudden, catastrophic events, but slow hillside creep is probably more important in its total influence on landform development. Creep affects most slopes, works twenty-four hours a day, seven days a week, year in and year out. You sometimes see the effects of creep on hillsides in the form of tilted telephone or fence poles, distorted fence lines, bent tree trunks, and large rock fragments displaced from a parent outcropping. After exceptionally wet winters, grassy hillslopes in coastal southern California are marked by scars where the weathered mantle has moved by earthflowage (Photo 1-3). Such scars usually take many years, even decades, to heal. Large landslides leave more enduring scars, and they deposit, at the foot

Photo 1-2. Gros Ventre landslide in Wyoming occurred in 1925 damming river to form lake.

Photo 1-3. Earthflow near Gorman, California. Break-away scarp and slump block at head, protruding tongue in lower part.

of the slope, a jumbled mass of broken rock debris with highly irregular topography.

You must have noticed the little parallel paths a foot or two wide, called terracettes, running in contour fashion on near-level lines across grassy hillsides, especially where stock has grazed (Photo 1-4). These paths are fancifully attributed to the lop-sided saugus, a mystical four-legged beast with longer legs on one side than the other which enables it to run with ease and com-

Photo 1-4. Terracettes on grassy hillslope in British Columbia.

fort across a steeply sloping hillside. The saugus is doomed to travel in only one direction; he can't reverse his field. Geologists recognize this as pure myth, knowing that the terracettes are natural features. They are little benches formed by small-scale, shallow slumping within the weathered mantle rock on steep grassy slopes, which are integrated into continuous paths by animals interested in getting across the slope as easily as possible without going up or down very much. The animals find the benches helpful and simply walk from one little bench to the next at about the same level, thus integrating them into a continuous path.

Running Water.   We are used to the heavy fall of raindrops on the roof, or as the song says, "on our head," but we are less familiar with the effects of rainbeat on loose bare dirt. It is a highly effective erosive process, admittedly less efficient on vegetated surfaces, especially those covered by grass. One reason for the sharp increase in erosion following a wildfire or cultivation of a slope is the increased effectiveness of rainbeat. Each raindrop impacting bare, loose soil creates a little crater and blasts a spray of water and soil particles upward and outward. Water from neighboring and successive drops eventually gathers into little irregular threads flowing downslope, carrying some of the loosened soil. As more rain falls, the threads get larger and more numerous. Eventually, they merge to form a thin but continuous sheet of flowing water. Sheetflow can sometimes be seen on sloping lawns when too heavily sprinkled. This water sheet increases in depth and velocity downslope until it separates into small parallel streamlets or rills. Rills join farther downslope to make larger, integrated streamlets which carve gullies. Water, acting in all these modes, carries loose weathered material downslope with ever increasing efficiency because of its increasing volume and the more channeled nature of flow.

The cross profile of many grassy hills or

ridges, as seen against the sky in southern California coastal hills, can be one of the most graceful and pleasing curves in nature (Figure 1-1). The summit is normally rounded, that is, convex to the sky. It is usually succeeded downslope by a straight, uniformly sloping reach that gives way to a concave curve. Sometimes the concave and convex forms come together without the intervening straight reach. All erosive processes act on all parts of the slope, but creep seems to dominate in the upper convex part and erosion by running water dominates the lower concave part. The intervening straight reach is where these two influences are balanced.

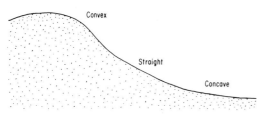

Figure 1-1. The graceful compound curve often seen in profiles of southern California coastal hills underlain by soft sedimentary material.

Material carried downslope by erosive processes would accumulate indefinitely at the base of the slope if it were not for the eager, hungry stream flowing in the canyon or valley to which the slope is tributary. These streams accept the rocky debris delivered by the hillsides and do their best to carry it to the ultimate sump, the ocean. This is no mean task in southern California where water is not overly plentiful and streams often go dry in summer. However, streams are patient, and they will continue the job next winter or during the next flood.

Streams are the principal agents of erosion that dissect and wear down land areas uplifted by tectonic deformation. They carve gullies, arroyos, barrancas, canyons and valleys into the land and transport large quantities of water and rock debris toward and into the sea. They are controlled by natural laws and variables, and behave in a generally predictable fashion.

Streams are not stupid. If you offer one the option of transporting fine dirt, sand, or boulders, it will take them in that order because the fine dirt is more easily and efficiently carried. Streams tend to leave the boulders behind as long as possible, although in times of flood their power may be so great that the boulders are also moved. The major work of transportation by most streams is accomplished during floods. If you offered a stream a certain volume of water and asked whether it would like to receive the water in small amounts over a longer time or in large amounts over a shorter time, any commonsense stream will take the second option, saying, "Don't fool around—if you want me to do the job, give me the water all at once so I can flood." We may not like streams in flood, and most southern California counties have large flood control operations, but floods in a stream are to some degree essential to its healthful existence.

Undesirable side effects usually result when the workings of natural systems are altered, as we do with flood-control programs. For example, construction of water-storage and flood-control dams on many southern California coastal streams has played hob with our prized sandy beaches. Most of the sand used by shoreline processes to build beaches has been carried to the ocean by streams during floods. Dams not only prevent flooding, but they capture sediment, so the sand supplied to the ocean is sharply curtailed. Consequently, hungry waves and currents begin eating into the existing beaches causing serious deterioration.

A few streams have relatively straight channels, and some have regular sinuous (meandering) channels (Photo 1-5), but most stream courses are just plain irregular. Furthermore, a main stream and its tributaries usually compose a pattern which resembles the trunk and limbs of a defoliated deciduous tree (Figure 1-2). In other in-

Photo 1-5. Meandering stream with cut-off meanders, Yukon Territory, Canada.

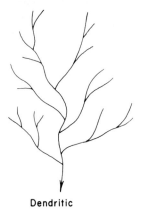

Dendritic

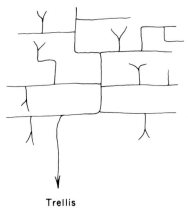

Trellis

Figure 1-2. A comparison of uncontrolled drainage dendritic) developed on homogeneous materials and controlled drainage (trellis) developed on materials with strong planar structure, such as tilted sedimentary beds.

stances, the pattern displays more geometrical regularity because of control by structures in the underlying rocks (Figure 1-2). In southern California, parts of a number of streams are aligned along faults which make them, and the canyons they carve, abnormally straight. East and west forks of San Gabriel River behind Azusa are good examples of fault-controlled stream courses.

Most people realize that a trunk stream has tributaries, like branches to the trunk of a tree, but fewer realize that some streams have distributaries which serve the opposite function. Instead of concentrating the flow of water, they distribute it. Distributaries form where streams spread out, usually on deltas at river mouths or upon alluvial fans at mountain fronts.

Composite Landscapes. Early in their development, most streams are cutting down into (dissecting) the land. This need not be a steady uninterrupted process, and in some stream valleys it is possible to see that an inner, steep-walled canyon lies below, or inside, remnants of a higher, older, wider, more open valley (Figure 1-3). The remnants of this older landscape may be preserved only as benches or flat-topped, gently sloping spurs on canyon walls. After developing the older valley by sidewise erosion, as its power for downcutting decreased, the stream has been rejuvenated, probably by tectonic uplift, and has again cut down more vigorously forming the narrow canyon within the older valley. These are called two-storied valleys.

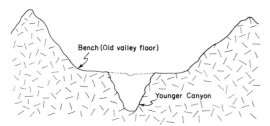

Figure 1-3. Cross section of a two-story valley, an inner canyon cut below the floor of an older, wider valley.

Most southern California landscape is complex in the sense that it includes features of earlier landscapes, but it is composite in the sense of being made up of assemblages of landforms created by different processes. This is especially true in coastal regions. The nature and structure of the underlying rocks also play a role. For instance, a sea cliff cut into hard, uniform, granitic rocks will have a configuration and character different from a sea cliff cut into layered rocks composed of beds of different resistance to weathering and erosion.

Time is an important element in landscape development. A stream that has been cutting into the land for only a short time usually flows in a steep-walled, narrow canyon, although the nature of the rocks being cut also influences canyon width and wall steepness. Soft rocks permit a widening of the canyon and a gentling of the side slopes sooner than hard rocks, but granted enough time, a stream will form a wide valley even in hard rocks. Given time and stability, landforms progress through a succession of developments from youthful to mature and eventually to old and senile, just like people. Carried to the ultimate end, weathering and erosion aim to reduce the land to a relatively smooth surface of low relief sloping gently toward the sea. Extensive plains of erosion are seldom achieved in coastal southern California because the high rate of tectonic deformation rejuvenates erosion into initiating a new cycle of dissection. Most gentle plains of any extent and recency in the southland are more likely to have been produced by deposition than erosion, the floors of San Joaquin and San Fernando valleys being examples.

Paradoxically, tearing-down processes can contribute to creation of landforms of construction. Rock debris derived from stream erosion can be laid down in the form of plains, fans, and aprons creating landforms of deposition, a constructive act. Other examples are beaches, built by shoreline processes, and sand dunes heaped up by the wind, although both are effective tearing-down agents.

Wind Work. Strong winds blow frequently in the desert, and many of us mentally associate wind, sand, and dunes with desert conditions. Yet, some of the finest dunes in California are along the coast, for example, south of Pismo (Photo J-2). Smaller dunes are seen just after takeoff at the west end of runways at Los Angeles International Airport.

Wind can be an ornery and contrary agent of transportation and deposition. Rivers spend much time and energy carrying sand downhill to the sea where waves use it to build beaches. In places, conditions are such that wind picks up sand from the beach and carries it back inland many miles, sometimes uphill. This happens where copious sand supply has enabled waves to build wide, sandy beaches and relatively strong winds blow frequently inland across the beach. In special situations, some of this sand may be dumped back into the stream which earlier carried it to the sea. The stream probably mutters under its breath, "You fool, I just carried this stuff down to the sea where it belongs."

Shoreline Processes and Features

Beaches are places of beauty and contrast, where land, water, and sky meet, and they are the site of continual activity. Although we don't usually think of it as such, the ocean is a great pool of energy. Seventy percent of the solar energy coming to Earth falls upon the sea, much of it being converted into other types of energy. Some of this huge supply is expended at the contact of sea against land, which embraces not only our beloved beaches, but also steeply cliffed, rocky shore of wild beauty. Energy is expended against the land largely through the action of waves and associated currents which accomplish much erosion, transportation, and deposition, all important to man.

Let us step back and look at just one sequence of developments in this transfer of solar energy into geological work. A large storm occurring in the Gulf of Alaska or far out in the central Pacific generates a train of swells (waves) which move outward from the storm center for distances of thousands of miles, much like waves caused by dropping a stone into a quiet millpond. These waves are of different size and travel with different speeds. Those moving most rapidly naturally get ahead of the others, and after a journey of several hundred miles the swells are separated into groups of similar size and speed. Thus, the swells from a specific storm arriving off the California coast at any one time are relatively uniform in character, although they may differ considerably from swells arriving at the same time from other storm centers.

The size of swells involves two dimensions—the distance from crest to crest (wave length), and the vertical separation between crests and troughs (height). Wave lengths of a few hundred feet and heights of a few feet are common, and travel speeds of 30 miles per hour are representative. Swells from an Alaskan storm approach the California coast from the northwest, more parallel to the coast than directly against it. However, as they move into shallower waters, swells are bent—we like to say "refracted" to face more directly toward shore. This comes about because a swell begins to "feel" the bottom in a water depth about one-half its wave length. For a wave length of 500 feet, this is water 250 feet deep. That part of the wave front moving in shallow water is slowed down and lags behind the part still traveling in deeper water. This causes the bending, or refraction, that brings the wave front more nearly parallel to shore (Figure 1-4).

Much of the sea floor near a coast is irregular, being broken by broad, flat, high areas known as banks, and by submarine ridges and canyons. These irregularities can cause local refraction which significantly

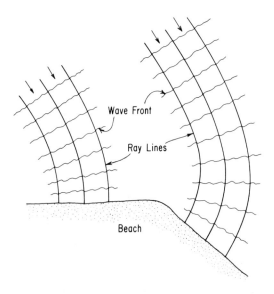

Figure 1-4. Simplified sketch showing ocean waves (swells) refracted to near-parallelism with the shoreline (beach). Ray lines are drawn orthogonal to wave lines (fronts).

modifies configuration of the swell pattern. For example, a submarine ridge extending directly outward from the shore causes the swell fronts to bend so they are concave toward the shore because the part of the swell moving along the ridge is slowed up with respect to parts on either side in deeper water. This effects a convergence, or focusing, of energy upon the shore at the head of the ridge, and the waves and breakers will be higher and more powerful there (Figure 1-5). A submarine canyon has just the reverse effect.

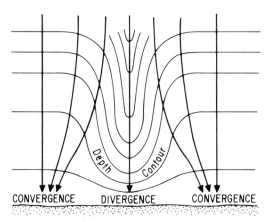

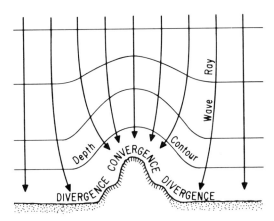

Figure 1-5. Convergence and divergence of ray lines (with arrows) caused by refraction of waves over a submarine canyon (top) and submarine ridge (bottom). Solid lines are bottom contours, not wave fronts.

As swells move onshore into ever shallower water, they drag more and more strongly on the bottom. Consequently, they slow down, wave length becomes shorter, and height increases because of energy conservation. They also become increasingly asymmetrical, with a steeper face toward shore. Eventually, they become so oversteepened that they topple and fall, forming breakers. Any swimmer or surfer caught in a breaker knows it is a locus of great power, turbulence, and energy. Sand is whipped up from the sea floor and a great deal of stress is exerted on any body, especially yours, caught in the breaker. The water of the broken waves is propelled powerfully onshore as a wave of translation that produces a swash up the sloping beach until its power is overcome by gravity. Then the water retreats down the beach forming a backwash that interferes with the next incoming swash. The so-called undertow on a beach is partly the result of a bottom current returning to the open ocean some of the water piled onto the beach by breaker-generated swashes.

On any particular day, swells impinging upon a coast may not be refracted enough to approach the shore directly head-on, so they hit the beach obliquely. This produces a longshore drift of water and of objects light enough to float, at least temporarily, such as bathers and grapefruit rinds. Most bathers have experienced this drift. It varies in strength, and even in direction, from day to day depending upon the size and obliquity of the swells.

On days when the longshore drift is strong, bathers need to be on the lookout for improperly named "rip tides." This is a misnomer because a *current* rather than the tide is involved. "Rip current" is the proper term, and such currents involve an outward flow of water piled up at a particular place on the shore, or by a head-on collision of longshore currents moving toward each other (Figure 1-6). A rip current is nature's way of returning excess water from the shore to the open ocean.

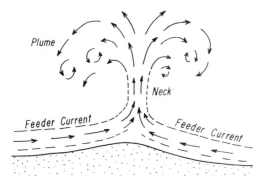

Figure 1-6. Idealized diagrammatic sketch of a rip current (after Inman and Shepherd).

Location of rip currents changes with swell pattern and other conditions, but certain places along shores tend to be favored, either because of wave refraction patterns generated by offshore bottom features, or because of special configurations of the shoreline.

Rip currents are capable of carrying an unwary swimmer out to sea. Most people caught in rip currents instinctively try to swim directly back toward shore. This is like trying to swim up a fast-flowing river. Not many swimmers can lick a rip current that way. The more reasonable response is to swim parallel to the beach and escape through the side of the rip current (Figure 1-6), or, confident swimmers can just relax, go along for the ride, and then swim back to the beach leisurely after the rip current has dumped them off into its lateral plumes where the local circulation may aid the swimmer's return toward land.

A little thought should bring realization that swells from different directions and of different characteristics will probably be differently refracted by local sea-floor features. This has been demonstrated by the breakwater at Long Beach which has been pierced by strong wave attack caused by the focusing effect of an offshore bank. This bank concentrates the energy of swells of a particular size coming from a certain direction upon one small part of the break-

water. Elsewhere along the southern California shore, unusual offshore topography refracts waves in such a way as to interrupt the longshore drift of sand, thereby creating local sandbars of abnormal size, as at El Estero near Carpinteria.

Surfers and surf swimmers are familiar with a pattern of wave behavior in which a group of four or five large waves is followed by a succession of smaller waves, often lasting several minutes before another group of large waves arrives. This comes about because swells from different storms are arriving at the shore simultaneously. Individual waves, within two or more sets of swells of different wave length and frequency, interact, alternately reinforcing or weakening each other. High waves result when waves of the two sets are in phase, or nearly so, and low waves are the product of interference between wave sets which diminishes energy because the wave motions are out of phase and partly cancel each other.

In addition to swells from remote storm centers, shorelines are subject to swells generated by local storms. In southern California, this happens mostly during the winter stormy season. Locally generated swells have, on the average, shorter wave lengths and hence break closer to shore. When waves break directly upon a beach, as some do in winter, the beach usually suffers because the high turbulence loosens beach sand which is seized by the retreating backwash and carried, with the help of offshore bottom currents, into deeper water.

Habituées of southern California beaches may have noticed that smoothly worn stones, often of considerable size, miraculously appear on normally sandy beaches in winter. Indeed some beaches, sandy in summer, become largely stony in winter. One might be inclined to think that the breakers created by intense winter storms are perhaps powerful enough to toss such stones onto the beach. Although the power and competence of breakers are readily granted, they generally cannot lay hand quickly upon stones of this type off a sandy shore. The truth is, the stones were already on the beach. In summer, sand moves onto and off of beaches, but the balance favors movement onto the beach. The stones appearing on winter beaches were simply buried by this excess accumulation of summer sand, and they become exposed when the cycle reverses in winter.

A short-term change that occurs episodically on beaches is the formation and disappearance of *cusps*. A cusp is a crescent-shaped depression on the beach opening toward the sea (Photo 1-6). It consists of two horns that enclose a lower, wider, smooth-floored indentation. Cusps range from a few tens to a few hundred feet from horn to horn and are usually on the order of a foot or so deep. They lie side by side, each sharing a horn with its neighbors. When a swash moves onto a beach, the inward penetration of white foamy water is greater in the hollow between horns, and it nicely defines the spacing and symmetry of the cusps. All beach visitors have surely seen cusps—they are that common—but may not have recognized them. They come and go on relatively short notice—a few hours— and change size and characteristics with shifts in swell conditions.

Cusps form when a regular set of swells impinges upon a beach in such a way as to create a longshore drift containing a succession of fixed cells, or centers of circulation, which erode the beach creating the cusp depressions. Since the cells are equally spaced, their symmetry is reproduced in the cusps. Once initiated, a cusp helps sustain itself by channeling the swash into the indentation between horns and by concentrating the backwash into a central (axial) current competent to carry sand from the beach. Cusps are primarily erosional features and develop most readily on sand beaches, but they also form on pebbly beaches (Photo 1-6). The symmetry of a set of well-formed beach cusps is a pleasure to behold. Watch for them.

Not all the coastline is bordered by sandy strands. In many reaches, near-vertical cliffs extend to the water's edge, and the shore is irregular and rocky. This is usually the condition where sand supply is too limited to build beaches, and the near-shore water is deep so that waves break directly against the land. The base of a sea cliff takes a pounding, not only from the water which develops huge impact pressures, but from stones that the waves pick and hurl against the cliff. At spots of favorable configuration, water often shoots high into the air

Photo 1-6. Cusps on gravelly beach, St. Lawrence Island, Bering Sea.

when a wave breaks against a cliff, and sometimes these water columns carry large stones. Stones have been thrown through lighthouse windows 150 feet above water level, and others have come down through the roof of lighthouse keepers' cottages. This rough, abrasive treatment of loose rock fragments along a rocky shore soon rounds and smooths them (Photo 1-7). People enjoy collecting beach pebbles partly because of these characteristics. Furthermore, stones

Photo 1-7. Smoothly abraded nip at base of sea cliff and well-worn shoreline cobbles, Palos Verdes Peninsula.

able to survive this treatment are tough and usually have attractive textures and colors.

A sea cliff is the product of powerful horizontal cutting by waves at its base. Cliffs along some parts of the California coast are known to have receded at average rates of many inches per year within historical times. Don't build your house too near the edge of an active sea cliff. The scenery may be great, but your longevity may be limited.

As a sea cliff recedes, a nearly flat rock platform, just a few feet below mean water level, is left in its wake (Photo 1-8). When this wave-cut bench gets wider, it becomes a marine abrasion platform. The width of the abrasion platform measures the distance of sea-cliff recession.

If the level of the sea drops for some reason, such as removal of water to form glaciers on land, or if the coastal land rises because of tectonic activity, a marine abrasion platform may suddenly find itself high and dry. At that point it becomes the tread of a marine terrace (Photo 1-8). A terrace is simply a geometrical form, a tread or step

Photo 1-8. Marine terrace (left), sea cliff, cove beach (foreground), storm-wave platform, and offshore stacks, near Rosario Beach, Baja California. Nearer stack has a sea arch (or window).

consisting of a nearly horizontal surface bounded by a steep face or riser at its inner edge (the sea cliff). Many major arteries of coastwise travel and many southern California coastal towns are on marine terraces. If you have done any traveling at all along the California coast, you have at one time or another certainly traversed the surface of a marine terrace, as, for example, going westward from Santa Barbara toward Gaviota or southeastward from San Clemente toward Oceanside.

Since marine terraces are such a common landscape feature of the California coast, let us consider them a bit further. The abrasion platform of a marine terrace slopes very gently seaward and truncates the underlying, often hard, and usually complexly structured bedrock. For most marine terraces, this platform is usually seen only in profile on the face of a younger sea cliff or along the walls of gullies which dissect the terrace. Such exposures show that the abrasion platform is mantled by rock debris, locally of considerable thickness and

of variable constitution (Figure 1-7). In the ideal example, the base of the debris mantle, resting directly on the truncated bedrock, is a thin layer of well-worn, rounded boulders, some with the little hemispherical holes made by the boring of shoreline animals (pholad borings). These stones are usually embedded in fine gravel or sand, and above may be a thicker layer of uniform, clean, homogeneous sand. The boulders and the overlying sand are shoreline deposits left on the platform as the sea cliff retreated. This shifting shoreline operated something like the gigantic cement-spreading machines used to construct highways. As it moved across the surface, it left behind a relatively uniform layer of boulders and sand. These are marine materials laid down on the abrasion platform before it became a terrace.

Overlying those layers on most California terraces, backed by hilly or mountainous inland terrain, are layers of poorly sorted rock detritus usually with indistinct bedding, only partly worn rock fragments, a

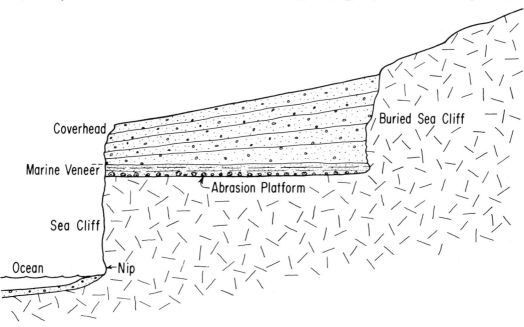

Figure 1-7. Coverhead on an emerged marine terrace.

great range of particle sizes from clay to boulders, and usually weathered, dark brown (Figure 1-7). Off the mouths of major streams, the deposit may have all the aspects of a stream gravel. This material is obviously land-laid and may be up to 100 feet thick. It creates a surface sloping outward from the hills toward the sea. The land-laid mantle is known as alluvial coverhead, or simply coverhead, and it forms in the following fashion. As sea level falls, the shoreline recedes across the marine abrasion platform, and the debris from land, formerly dumped directly into the sea, now accumulates on the surface of the abandoned abrasion platform. Streams start building alluvial fans at their mouths, and slope wash, aided by mass movements, carries debris onto the platform in the interstream areas. Large streams with adequate flow eventually build their fans out to the new shoreline position, whereupon they cease fan-building because they once again dump their debris directly into the ocean. Smaller streams may not be so successful, and may not complete the job of fan-building before something else happens.

While streams and other agents are depositing an apron of debris upon the emerged abrasion platform, ocean waves and currents are not standing idly by. Once sea level is stabilized, unless offshore waters are abnormally shallow, waves start at once to fashion a new sea cliff and drive it back into the newly emerged land, creating a new abrasion platform. As the sea cliff retreats, it eats away at the outer edge of the emerged terrace surface, making it ever narrower. Streams which have succeeded in extending their fans to the new shoreline position know what is going on, and the smaller stream also eventually gets the news. As a sea cliff forms and recedes, it creates a waterfall at the stream's mouth. Streams abhor waterfalls and destroy them by cutting down their bed. In effect, the streams are rejuvenated as the sea cliff de-

velops and recedes. Thus, a single emergence can set into motion a series of developments leading to the accumulation of coverhead on the platform and, later, to dissection of that deposit and the underlying abrasion platform as well.

The coverhead mantling an emerged marine terrace usually has an interesting geological story to tell. The basal sea-laid beds may be locally fossiliferous, and the fossil shells can be used to determine prevailing temperature, salinity, and depth of water as well as the power of the surf. The overlying land-laid beds may record episodes of cutting and filling resulting from relative movements of land and sea, and sea cliff retreat. Periods of stability are usually marked by buried soils or weathered zones that indicate the climatic environment at that time in the coastal zone. The character of the deposits themselves gives some indication of the relief and other aspects of the terrain inland from the shore.

Prehistoric Indians liked to live near the edge of a marine terrace where they were close to the abundant seashore foods, scenic views were striking, and they were safe from storm waves. Their refuse piles (kitchen middens) dot the surfaces of marine terraces and are usually rich in clam, mussel, and other shells. Other evidences of still earlier human occupations have been found buried within the coverhead on some marine terraces.

Where a succession of terraces exists, each lower terrace has developed at the expense of the next higher terrace. Thus, the width of a terrace remnant is always less than the original width of the abrasion platform, and, in some instances higher terraces have been completely destroyed by the cutting of lower terraces. Given enough time, a lower terrace will always destroy the next higher terrace. The fact that we have flights of as many as a dozen terrace levels along parts of the California coast is a reflection largely of tectonic instability. Something usually happens before the lower surface can completely destroy all the higher and older surfaces.

Whenever water is removed from or returned to the oceans, sea level falls or rises, independent of any movement of the land. These are called eustatic sea level changes, and they occurred repeatedly during the Pleistocene ice ages when water was removed from the oceans to form glaciers on land. Such glacier-controlled fluctuations of sea level amounted to only a few hundred feet. In California, Pleistocene marine terraces are more than 1,000 feet above the sea, and these terraces are tilted. Tectonic activity has clearly played a role in their formation. Eustatic sea level changes have also been involved because, just like income taxes, there is no way they can be avoided.

The configuration of a shoreline, that is, its projections, indentations, and other irregularities, can be the product of a variety of factors. If a dissected, hilly land-mass is partly submerged along its seaward edge by tectonic down-warping, or by eustatic rise of sea level, a highly irregular shoreline results. Ridges in the hilly landscape become projecting headlands, and valleys and canyons become bays and estuaries. Following submergence, shoreline processes start immediately to modify the larger aspects of this irregularity. Waves and breakers gnaw away the headlands driving them inland. Where sand supply is adequate, waves and currents build bars part way (a spit) or all the way (a baymouth bar) across the mouth of estuaries and bays.

As the projecting headlands are chewed back, they develop a cliff and a small-scale irregularity all their own, provided the rocks are not abnormally homogeneous. Soft zones or beds are eroded into little inlets or coves, and hard masses or beds are etched into projecting points (Photo 1-9). As the cliff recedes, it may leave behind small,

Photo 1-9. Marine terrace and wave-eroded coast with headlands, coves, cove beaches, and stacks, near Point Buchon, San Luis Obispo County. (Spence air photo E-13224, 9/19/47).

island-like remnants of rock rising well above water level (Photo 1-8). These are called *stacks* from their resemblance to old-fashioned haystacks. As sea-cave explorers know, differential wave erosion can create a cave, literally a tunnel, extending 100 feet or more back under the land. The roof of such a cave can be locally pierced to daylight, and there, with a strong swell at high tide, a column of water periodically shoots into the air like a spouting whale or a geyser (blowhole). Caves sometimes extend laterally through a projecting point, thus joining the inlets on both sides and forming a sea arch. Arches, or windows, sometimes form in offshore stacks (Photo 1-8).

The base of a sea cliff takes a terrific battering from waves. It is undercut to form a recessed hollow or nip. The surface of this nip, when cut into hard rock, is smoothed through abrasion by sand and rocks picked up by the waves and hurled against the base of the cliff (Photo 1-7).

The California coastline is complex for four reasons. First, the rocks composing the land are diverse in lithology and complicated in structure, so they respond to erosional shoreline processes in uneven fashion. Second, it, like all coastlines of the world, has been affected by eustatic changes in sea level caused by glaciation. Third, many parts of the California coastal zone have been tectonically active recently, moving up or down with respect to the sea. Finally, this coast is exposed to the direct attack of powerful wave trains generated by storms in the Gulf of Alaska and the open Pacific. Only locally, as along the Santa Barbara Channel, is it protected to any degree by offshore islands.

All the above is but the briefest of introductions to landforms and the processes creating them. Selected references listed in Appendix D treat these matters more comprehensively.

Chapter 2

Road Guides

General Introductory Statement

The following road-guide descriptions are designed primarily for travelers proceeding along a California coastal freeway at about 55 mph. Occasional stops at view points or turnouts and short diversions to spots of special interest are urged, but attention is given principally to features and relationships seen while on the move. Driving in the right-hand lane of a freeway can be beneficial because of the slower pace.

Following road guides on freeways is a two-person affair, one to drive and one to read. It is virtually impossible for a lone traveler to follow a guide along a freeway because opportunities to stop and read are too widely spaced. Even on back-country roads, a companion is helpful. Under any circumstances, reading ahead is always desirable because nature does not arrange her displays to our convenience. In places features are clustered, so you pass some while reading about others. Or a feature may appear so suddenly that you are not prepared to observe it unless already alerted. Reading the entire trip description before starting, and reading ahead while traveling are both sound procedures.

It is usually impossible to see everything the first time along a route, so don't be disturbed that some features are missed. Hopefully, you will be following the route again

sometime and can pick them up. Trips can be covered many times with continuing or even increasing profit and pleasure. Geologists have about as much fun as anybody while traveling, even though they may have been over the route hundreds of times. Following a road guide is something of an art. You will improve with practice, and your pleasure will increase proportionally.

Distribution of Route Segments

Descriptions of geological and other features are provided along eighteen separate route segments within the southern California coastal belt, between the Mexican border and San Luis Obispo, and inland as far as Cuyama Valley. A listing of route segments is given in the table of contents and in Table 1. Their geographical locations are shown on the maps, placed on inside covers for easy access.

Since the greater Los Angeles area is the principal center of population within the area treated, the guides are constructed for travelers outbound from the periphery of that congested area. Although this will offend and inconvenience the good citizens of San Diego, San Luis Obispo, and points between, hopefully those people will realize that a trip has to start somewhere and to proceed in some direction.

TABLE 1
Listing of Route Guide Segments

Up-Coast from Los Angeles

A. Encino to Ventura (Highway 101)

B. Santa Monica to Oxnard (Highway 1)

C. Castaic Junction to Ventura (Highway 126)

D. Santa Paula to Ojai (Highway 150)

E. Ventura to Ojai (Highway 33)

F. Ojai to Ozena (Cuyama Valley) (Highway 33)

G. Ventura to Santa Barbara (Highway 101)

H. Santa Barbara to Highway 154 (Highway 101)

I. Santa Barbara to Los Olivos (Highway 154)

J. From Highway 154 to San Luis Obispo Highway 101)

Down-Coast from Los Angeles

K. El Toro to Oceanside (Highway 5)

L. Corona Del Mar to Dana Point (Highway 1)

M. Riverside to Escondido (Highway 15E)

N. Corona to Temecula (Highway 71)

O. Elsinore to San Juan Capistrano (Highway 74)

P. Oceanside to San Diego (Highway 5)

Q. Escondido to San Ysidro (Highways 15 and 805)

R. Freeway 805 Link (San Diego) (Highway 805)

Special efforts have been made to provide for travelers following a route guide in a reverse direction, or what is termed "inbound." To do full justice to both outbound and inbound travelers, two separate, largely repetitive descriptions comprising essentially two separate books, would be required.

This was simply not possible within the scope of the present volume. What has been done is to provide a series of special inbound paragraphs, sequentially numbered I-1, I-2, I-3, . . . to supplement each corresponding outbound paragraph (or group of paragraphs) numbered O-1, O-2, O-3, . . . The outbound paragraphs are arranged in proper sequence in the first part of a route segment, and the inbound paragraphs, arranged in reverse order, are grouped in a following section. Inbound travelers should read the correspondingly numbered outbound paragraph, preferably *before* digesting the contents of their inbound paragraph which provides primarily navigational directions and notes on aspects of features as seen from the opposite direction. Outbound travelers can skip the group of inbound paragraphs, but inbound travelers must read the outbound material. This arrangement is admittedly awkward, but it is the best we could devise short of preparing two wholly separate books. The descriptions are prepared for conditions of good visbility and favorable lighting. These conditions may not attain during your trip, and distant views may be restricted.

Navigational Procedures

The traditional method of location used in professional field guides is specification by mileage (odometer readings). This is a coherent, logical procedure, but as known by anyone who has attempted to follow such guides, it has limitations. Mileages are simply not consistently measurable to the accuracy of the 0.1 mile value usually given, and one's eyes become glued to the odometer thereby missing the passing scene. Under the mileage system, once you get out of phase on either mileage or location, chaos reigns. Although you are advised herein to record an odometer reading at the start of each segment, and occasionally at some in-between point, this is done more to create a sense of scale and distance than for specific navigational purposes. Occasionally the guide says "0.5 mile down the freeway" or "1.5 miles beyond the apple-butter sign." Such comments are designed to give some sense of how far it is to the feature to be seen.

Instead of mileages, things to be viewed are related to prominent roadside features, hopefully of some permanence, such as large freeway signs, bridges, overpasses, powerlines, billboards, or recognizable urban structures. One of the virtues of this system is easy visibility, even at 55 mph, and secondly, if you get lost, it's not hard to get back on track through recognition of a subsequent navigational point. For brevity's sake, the words of a freeway or any other sign cited are simply shown in quotes ("Leucadia Exit, 1 Mile") without specifying that it is a sign. Some signs located in the center-divider strip between opposing freeway lanes are identified by (center-divider).

Most California highways are lined by small (8 × 24 inch), white, elongate, rectangular metal markers on steel posts projecting three to four feet above ground level (Figure 2-1). Many of these markers bear small, clear, or orange reflectors, but some have black printing identifying the county, highway number, and distance from some reference point, usually a county line or one terminus of that particular highway. The example shown in Figure 2-1 indicates Highway 126 in Ventura County at a point 12.79 miles from the reference datum. Mileages are commonly given to hundredths, and may increase or decrease, depending upon direction of travel. Practices differ from county to county, and in some instances county identification precedes the highway number. Frequency of signs also varies considerably, and in some places a letter precedes the mileage figure, usually a capital R, making them harder to read until you learn to blank out the R. On some highways, especially freeways, mileages are printed in bold figures. On back-country roads where other navigational aids may be sparse, considerable use is made of these highway-margin markers. They won't be used much on freeways because they are hard to see unless traveling in the right-hand lane. Bridges and overpasses also usually bear mileage figures consistent with this system. Be aware that mileage figures along a highway change upon crossing a county line or where two highways join to follow a common route.

Navigation is something of an art at which you get better with experience. It's fun when you do things right—a little like a treasure hunt. It can be practiced by both driver and reader, and it sharpens your perceptions of the roadside scene. Children become adept at the navigational game.

Some features to be viewed while traveling are further located with respect to direction by means of a clock-hour designation. Imagine the face of a big clock lying flat in front of you with 12 o'clock directly ahead up the highway. Nine o'clock is then directly left and 3 o'clock directly right. Intermediate clock hours, or fractions thereof, locate intermediate directions. The same system can be used at stopping places by designating some obvious feature as the 12 o'clock point.

Small, page-size map sketches accompany each field-trip segment, but it is desirable to carry good touring maps, particularly of the various counties, as available from auto clubs. Some of the air photos used as illustrations are vintage works, dating back several decades. They are used because geology shows better when not veneered by the works of man, because we thought you would be interested to see what far-reaching changes have been wrought in parts of southern California in just a decade or two, and finally because they were reasonably inexpensive and available.

Enough of this briefing and calisthenics. Let's get on with the game by taking some trips. Geology is of the real world and it needs to be seen, not just read about.

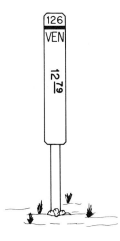

Figure 2-1. Roadside mileage marker, valued as a navigational aid.

Segment A

Encino to Ventura, 53 Miles

O-1 This segment begins, outbound, at intersection of San Diego Freeway (I-405) and Ventura Freeway (Highway 101) near Encino, and proceeds westward on Ventura Freeway. Note odometer reading in passing through the interchange. We travel along the south side of San Fernando Valley just north of Santa Monica Mountains. This flank of the Santa Monicas is composed largely of soft, punky, clay-rich shales (upper Miocene, Modelo Formation, 8-12 m.y.).

San Fernando Valley is a structural trough filled with about 15,000 feet of sedimentary rocks mantled by a considerable thickness of unconsolidated sand, gravel, and soil swept down from the bordering mountains largely by tributaries of Los Angeles River. The course of the river where it flows east has been pushed to the south edge of San Fernando Valley by the large volume of debris shed from the higher mountains north of San Fernando Valley.

(Inbound travelers see p. 32.)

O-2 Just as the Ventura Freeway clears the interchange, you get a quick view, at 12:30 o'clock, of the large Sepulveda flood-control dam, constructed by U.S. Army Engineers for Los Angeles County Flood Control District.

O-3 In another mile westward, near the center-divider sign for Hayvenhurst, Balboa, and White Oak avenues, the spacious park-like impoundment area behind the dam comes into view just to the north. The area is normally dry because no flood-control dam can function if the storage area is full of water. Making a park and recreation area out of the reservoir floor was an intelligent act. In case of flooding, damage is minimal. More damaging than the water will be rocky debris and muck. Debris deposited by a single flood has nearly filled the storage area behind some flood-control dams, making them possibly suitable for strawberry patches but not worth much for flood control. The dual task of handling water and debris causes flood-control engineers to twist uneasily in their sleep. The debris problem in the Sepulveda basin is less pressing because much of the coarser flood detritus will have been captured by debris basins and flood-control dams upstream.

Flood control is a major activity the world over. A fully satisfactory solution is probably not possible, for nature has been creating floods since time immemorial, and it's a habit she resists giving up. We suffer partly from the lack of early, farsighted zoning programs that would have prevented

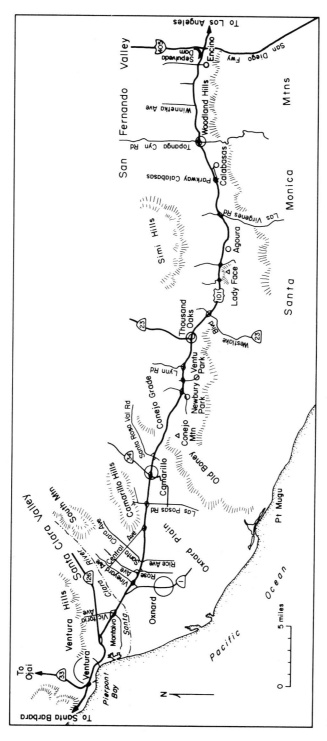

Figure A-1. Segment A, Encino to Ventura.

the building of valuable facilities in flood-prone areas which are now protected at considerable expense.

O-4 Having read all this, unless you foresightedly started before reaching the Ventura-San Diego interchange, you may now be several miles west of the dam. In places where the freeway is elevated, you should be getting fairly good views of modestly high Santa Susana Mountains (3700 ft.), on the north skyline at 2-3 o'clock, and of the lower, rough, rugged Simi Hills closing the west end of San Fernando Valley, at 12-1 o'clock. For a dozen miles, you get glimpses and views of these mountain masses, and we shall speak of them again a little later.

O-5 Watch for Winnetka Avenue signs about 6.5 miles west of the freeway interchange. Approaching Winnetka Avenue, the freeway is seen rising ahead to cross through a ridge in a deep roadcut. This ridge is known as Chalk Hills, so called from chalky shale beds (Modelo Formation). The big roadcut on the north begins about at "Warner Center, Next 3 Exits" and exposes near-horizontal layers of shale. This is an unusual attitude for Modelo strata, which in most places are severely deformed. Even in the cut just across the freeway dips are varied and steeper.

O-6 Shortly, at "Canoga Avenue Exit, ½ Mile," Simi Hills are at 1:30 to 2:00 o'clock, and Santa Susana Mountains are at 3 o'clock. Rounded ridges and summits and the generally smooth appearance of the Santa Susanas compared to the rough, rugged ridges of Simi Hills reflects a difference in bedrock. The Santa Susanas are composed largely of relatively fine, not firmly consolidated Miocene and Pliocene marine strata. Although they are folded, faulted, and refolded again, these rocks are not resistant enough for this complexity to show in the landscape. The greater height of the Santa Susanas is caused by recent tec-

tonic uplift, not by greater rock resistance or durability. The Simi Hills, although of simpler structure, are underlain by older rock, partly Cretaceous (80-100 million years), which are mostly well-consolidated, coarse sandstones, crisscrossed by two or three systems of joints (fractures). Weathering and erosion along these joints has produced the rough topography characterizing these hills.

O-7 Topanga Canyon Boulevard is crossed about 8.6 miles from the interchange. This is a good place to note an odometer reading again. If you like exploration, a drive south across Santa Monica Mountains via Topanga Canyon is geologically interesting. To make the trip, take Topanga Canyon Boulevard South, which requires you to overrun Topanga Canyon underpass, turn off north at "Topanga Canyon Boulevard Only," and come back to the south-bound lanes of Topanga Canyon Boulevard. Follow the signs; they are explicit.

Topanga Canyon Side Trip. Continue due south on Topanga Canyon Boulevard through Woodland Hills. Shortly the highway describes some curves, and a little beyond the last stoplight (Mulholland Drive) approaches the base of the hills. Just beyond Cezanne Avenue on the left is a large roadcut in tilted, well-stratified rocks, mostly shales (Modelo) which are transected by clastic dikes of sandstone. Roadcuts along the succeeding 1.5 miles of winding highway to the top are in well-bedded Modelo shales displaying various degrees and directions of dip, with the large, right-side exposures at the top being especially good. Roadside mileage markers begin with 10^{50} at the first switchback. A turnout on the left at the summit offers, on clear days, fine views of country to the north.

Taking the junction (Santa Susana Pass) between rough, cliffy Simi Hills to the left and smoother Santa Susana Mountains to the right as 12 o'clock, San Fernando Pass is the low saddle at 1 o'clock separating the Santa Susanas from San Gabriel Mountains. The San Gabriels, composed of crystalline rocks, make up the far, high skyline at 3 o'clock, with Verdugo Hills as a forelying ridge of crystalline rock at 2 o'clock. From this overlook one sometimes gets an unusual view of the atmospheric inversion beneath which Los Angeles Basin smog is trapped. On a really clear day, Topatopa and Piru mountains on the north side of Santa Clara Valley (Segment C) may be visible on the farthest skyline at 1 o'clock.

From the summit, continue south into upper Topanga Canyon. The first 1.5 miles are in the Modelo, but this basal part contains more and thicker sandstone beds. Finally, a predominance of thick, massive sandstones with some conglomerate interlayers, signals passage into the underlying Topanga Formation (middle Miocene, 12-18 m.y.). This occurs a little beyond marker 8⁵⁰, near Entrado Road. In 0.5 mile the road makes a long switchback to the east to cross a canyon, and just where it curves sharply south, about ¼ miles beyond marker 7⁵⁰, are exposures of dark-brown rock. These are volcanics interlayered within the Topanga sandstones. The next several miles are all in the Topanga Formation. You see mostly thick beds of sandstone, some dipping north, some south, and some with fossil ripple marks on exposed bedding planes. Canyon walls are steeper and closer together, reflecting greater erosional resistance of Topanga sandstones compared to Modelo shales. Sandstones become even more massive beyond 5⁵⁰, and the canyon narrows further. Approaching 5⁰⁰, volcanic rocks begin to crop out on the left. Walls and other stone structures built of dark-brown, angular, sharp-edged rock fragments (lava) are good indicators of the location of volcanic-rock exposures along the highway. Volcanic rocks, with some intercalations of sandstone predominate south to vicinity of Greenleaf Canyon Road (turns off right).

At and beyond intersection with Old Topanga Canyon Road is the main village of Topanga (post office, store, and other buildings). Beyond the built-up area, the canyon narrows to a gorge, walls are much steeper, and roadcuts are in darker, harder rocks. Some are lavas or shallow intrusives related to lavas, and some are dark-gray massive sandstones. At 4⁰⁰ massive bluffs of Topanga sandstone and conglomerate, which make up the left canyon wall for a mile or two, are well seen. Beyond "No Parking Anytime, Next 1½ Miles," the gorge gets still narrower. At 3⁰⁰ an intrusive igneous rock (diabase) makes the vertical cut and bluff on the right. Beyond this point you begin to see what looks like a good angular unconformity on the left across the canyon between near-horizontal, light brown, massive beds of Topanga (middle Miocene) sandstone above and tilted reddish Sespe (Oligocene) sandstone and conglomerate beds below. This is an illusion created by a near-vertical fault extending parallel to the base of the Topanga bluffs that separates these two sets of rocks. The Topanga and Sespe lie side by side along that fault, not one on top of the other as it looks from the highway.

Beyond marker 2⁵⁰, steeply tilted layers of about the best conglomerate anyone could hope to see make up the canyon walls. The stones, mostly of cobble size, are well-rounded and composed of a variety of resistant rock types. These conglomerates are largely of Eocene and Paleocene age (40-70 m.y.). Still older Cretaceous conglomerates and sandstones are probably represented here, but at speeds required by traffic on this highway, they are not easily distinguished. Near 1⁰⁰ the canyon opens somewhat and exposures deteriorate, although sandstone and conglomerate continue as the dominant rocks. In a mile the canyon ends, and there ahead is the wide, hopefully blue Pacific Ocean. If you choose to drive along the coast in either direction, see Segment B.

For travelers headed north up Topanga Canyon initial rock exposures are only fair, but at 1[00] the gorge narrows and good exposures of conglomerate and sandstone begin. Just above "No Parking Anytime, Next 1½ Miles," the gorge with its steep, rugged, conglomerate walls becomes spectacular. Looking ahead one sees the false angular unconformity between Topanga (middle Miocene) and Sespe (Oligocene) beds. It is best and clearest just beyond "Los Angeles City Limit." Diabasic materials are seen on the left from there to 3[00]. To the right, approaching and passing through Topanga Village are cliffs of massive Topanga sandstone and conglomerate. Beyond 4[43] are massive Topanga sandstones at highway level, and just beyond Greenleaf Canyon Road (turns off left) volcanics crop out more or less continuously on the right to a little beyond Highvale Trail (a street) and marker 5[00]. At 5[50] we are back into massive uniform Topanga sandstones. Just north of Canyon Trail (a street) are nice bedding-plane exposures on the right. To the left on a hillside about ¼ mile beyond Cheney Drive is a fresh landslide scar in Topanga sandstone. The last volcanic-rock exposure is passed at the apex of a switchback about midway between 7[01] and 7[50]. North-dipping, massive sandstones seen in a following deep, double-walled roadcut are still Topanga, but a little beyond 8[00], near Entrado Drive (separating left), the route passes into Modelo. These mixed shales and sandstones continue to the summit another mile ahead. Descending toward Woodland Hills immediate views are of hilly terrain, largely in Miocene rocks. The last large roadcut with sandstone dikes is just beyond "Los Angeles City Limit."

O-8   Continuing west from Topanga Canyon Boulevard on Ventura Freeway, the smooth, rounded ridges and hillocks on either side are rather typical of landscapes developed on soft, fine-grained beds, here Modelo shales. Slopes of this type are commonly grass-covered in the California Coast Ranges, presumably because shales provide suitable moisture and nourishment for the growth of grass, although locally, as here, such slopes can be house covered. Light green, whispy pepper trees line this sector of the freeway.

O-9   After underpassing Parkway Calabasas the freeway ascends into hills, and in about 100 yards the first of two large right-side roadcuts begins. They expose thinly bedded Modelo shales over an extended distance, and you see numerous changes in the degree and direction of bedding inclination within these cuts, indicating significant deformation. Beyond the grade crest is a double-walled cut showing similar relationships. Then the highway descends in a gently curving course through rolling, hilly country dotted by scattered oak trees and carpeted in winter and spring with green grass. The rocks seen in roadcuts are still part of the Modelo.

O-10   After nearly two miles of downhill travel, rounding a curve on the approach to Las Virgenes Road intersection, a large cut on the hillside directly ahead exposes a well-layered sequence of Miocene shale and sandstone beds dipping northeast. At this intersection, one can again elect to cross Santa Monica Mountains by turning south on Las Virgenes Road and traversing Malibu Canyon to the ocean at Malibu Beach. Initially, the journey is through open country carved in soft sedimentary rocks, but Malibu Canyon is a narrow, steep-walled gorge where older, harder sandstone and conglomerate beds, mostly middle and early Miocene, and a little Oligocene, are traversed. As Malibu Canyon Road emerges into open territory and the ocean comes to view, it enters Sespe beds and shortly crosses Malibu Coastal fault, a major structure discussed in Segment B.

O-11   Approaching, at, and west of Kanan Road overpass (with Reyes Adobe Road sign), the difference in appearance of terrains on opposite sides of the freeway is striking. To the north at 1-2 o'clock, the hills are low, rounded, smooth, and covered by grass with scattered oaks. To the south at about 9:30-10:00 o'clock, they are higher, rugged, craggy, of darker color, and mantled by dense chaparral. The prominent ridge at 9:30 o'clock is locally known as Lady Face (Photo A-1). The reason for this topographic contrast is the difference in underlying rocks. To the north are relatively soft, fine-grained Miocene sedimentary materials, to the south are volcanics. From here west, much of the ruggedness of peaks and ridges south of the freeway reflects the fact that they are composed of lava flows, other volcanic materials, and associated shallow igneous intrusive rocks.

O-12   In another mile, somewhat beyond Lindero Canyon Road, the hills fall back to the south, and we enter a wide alluvium-floored valley (Russell Valley) at the east edge of Thousand Oaks. The high sky-line to the south, 9:15-11:00 o'clock, is rugged because it is underlain by resistant volcanics and the well-cemented older sedimentary units that form part of the gorges of lower Topanga and Malibu canyons. The contrast in terrains north and south of the freeway continues (Photo A-2), and the difference in color of the rocks, whitish to the north, dark brown to the south, is apparent in vicinity of Westlake Boulevard.

O-13   Approaching separation of Highway 23, to Moorpark and Fillmore, on a clear day the distant skyline at about 1 o'clock displays high peaks of Topatopa Mountains north of Santa Clara Valley (see Segment C). West of Thousand Oaks, beginning near Conejo (Spanish for rabbit) Rancho golf course (on the left), a subtle change in topography occurs alongside the freeway. Flat-topped hills and ridges appear. We are entering a wide part of Conejo Valley which has been partly filled with young, weakly consolidated, nearly hori-

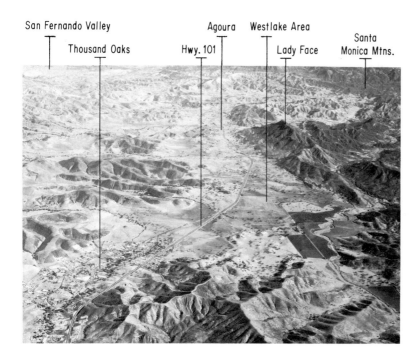

San Fernando Valley   Agoura   Westlake Area

Thousand Oaks   Hwy. 101   Lady Face   Santa Monica Mtns.

Photo A-1. View east along Highway 101 from Thousand Oaks. (Spence air photo L-18023, 11/14/61).

zontal layers of poorly sorted gravel. Glimpses of this rather nondescript material can be caught in several of the large roadcuts on the left approaching and beyond the golf course and especially in the double-walled roadcut near "Ventu Park Road, ¼ Mile." Dissection of these deposits has produced the flat-topped features.

O-14   West of Rancho Conejo Boulevard overpass (Borchard Road turnoff), knobs and ridges rise on the near skyline ahead (Photo A-2). They are composed of volcanic rocks, the so-called Conejo Volcanics. We see a good section of them descending Conejo Grade (Photo A-3). The brink of Conejo Grade is attained about three miles

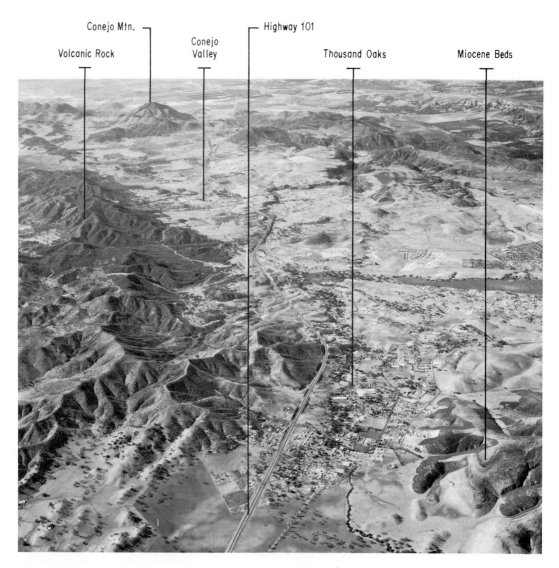

Conejo Mtn. —   — Highway 101

Volcanic Rock   Conejo Valley   Thousand Oaks   Miocene Beds

Photo A-2.   View west along Highway 101 from Westlake area. (Spence air photo E-18045, 11/14/61).

Photo A-3.   Looking west down Conejo Grade to Camarillo, top right. Newbury Park lower left, Conejo Mountain slightly left of center. Mostly volcanic rock with alluvium of Oxnard Plain beyond. (Spence air photo E-19710, 12/17/65).

west of Newbury Park. Just short of the crest, at the Weigh Station turn-in, deep roadcuts on both sides expose dark volcanic rocks. Here, and descending the 700-foot drop of Conejo Grade, you see fairly massive solid lava flows, layers of volcanic agglomerate, and dikes cutting the lava and agglomerate layers.

O-15   Be particularly alert about 1.3 miles below top of Conejo Grade at the first double-walled roadcut, just beyond "Camarillo Springs Road County Park, Next Right." Visible on both sides, but best on the left and better seen by looking back a bit, is an inclined dike about 30 feet wide cutting the volcanics. This dike is distinguished by its columnar jointing, that is, a set of fractures which causes the dike rock to break into crudely polygonal columns lying perpendicular to the dike walls, something like stacked cord wood (Photo A-4). You may not see this feature too well on your first try, but if you travel this route frequently, keep watching and eventually you will see and appreciate its unusual nature. Columnar joints form principally in

Photo A-4.   Columnar jointing in dike, south side of double-walled roadcut, Conejo Grade. (Photo by John S. Shelton, 3493).

homogeneous volcanic rocks as a result of contraction upon cooling.

A descent of Conejo Grade on clear days provides views to the north and west. On the far north and northwest skyline are high ridges and peaks of Topatopa and Santa Ynez mountains. Successively lower ridges southward include Sulphur Mountain (dotted with trees), grass- and brush-covered South Mountain still closer, and just beyond the foot of the grade are the heavily housed Camarillo Hills (Photo A-5). All these features trend essentially east and west and are part of the Transverse Ranges province of southern California.

Santa Clara River valley lies in a deep, wide trough between South Mountain and the high skyline country to the north (Segment C). The broad, flat Oxnard Plain, which opens west from the base of Conejo Grade, is a depressed area deeply filled with alluvium from the Santa Clara and other streams. It pushes westward into Santa Barbara Channel like a delta because of the large volume of this recent sediment. This is a fertile agricultural area, now heavily devoted to cultivation of vegetables, strawberries, and lawn turfs, in addition to the former principal crops of lima beans, sugar beets, and lemons. About a mile down Conejo Grade, upon rounding a curve, views open to the west giving a more comprehensive picture of Oxnard Plain and of Santa Barbara Channel and the Channel Islands, particularly Anacapa (left) and Santa Cruz (right).

O-16   Approaching the base of Conejo Grade, look across the mobile-home park and golf course (with ponds) at 9 o'clock to the steep hill base. The gray exposures there are the walls of a quarry from which large blocks of rock were taken to build local breakwaters, groins, and sea walls to protect seashore properties from wave attack. At the base of the grade to the right,

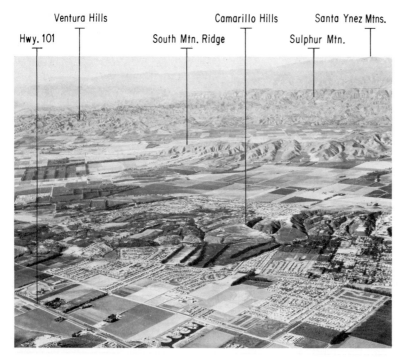

Ventura Hills   Camarillo Hills   Santa Ynez Mtns.

Hwy. 101   South Mtn. Ridge   Sulphur Mtn.

Photo A-5.   View northwestward across Camarillo Hills and lower Santa Clara River valley. (Spence air photo V-128, 1/24/68).

roadcuts in cactus-covered slopes expose good volcanic agglomerates. You should be able to see that they consist of individual fragments and to recognize that the fragments represent different kinds of rock, all volcanic however. Most of the stones are somewhat rounded, which is typical of agglomerates.

O-17 Just beyond "Camarillo State Hospital, Second Right," the old Juan Camarillo house is visible about a quarter mile north of the freeway. It is to the left of the new, low, modern house you see first. Juan Camarillo was one of the last of the Spanish grandees of this region, and a local philanthropic benefactor of note. Beyond, we enter a corridor of fine old eucalyptus (blue gum) trees lining both sides of the road. Such trees were widely planted by early settlers as windbreaks to protect crops, orchards, and buildings. In passing through Camarillo, travelers with an eye for topography will see that downtown Camarillo, on the left, is built on a low ridge that extends west parallel to the freeway. This ridge was created by recent uplift along Camarillo fault on its south side, where the character of the ridge is more sharply defined. Camarillo Hills lie more than two miles north, but they are closer beyond Las Posas Road (Photo A-5).

O-18 West of Camarillo (city), approaching and beyond Las Posas Road overpass, Camarillo Hills are only a half-mile away and are more easily visible. They are the result of geologically recent folding and faulting, the principal structures being an anticlinal fold bearing west and plunging in that direction. The hills come to an end at Central Avenue two miles ahead. The folding is so youthful that erosion has done little more than gully the flanks of the folds, and the present topographic form closely mirrors the form of the structure. Springville fault, along the south base of the hills, has helped elevate them above the adjoining alluvial Oxnard Plain.

O-19 Upon clearing Camarillo Hills westbound on a clear day, the imposing face of Topatopa Bluff on the high skyline at 3 o'clock comes into view. This massive mountain, roughly 6,000 feet high, dominates the scene and is regarded with affection by local residents as "their mountain." The banding across its face is produced by massive layers of resistant Eocene sandstone. They appear horizontal in this view but are actually inclined northward at a modest angle. You will have repeated views of Topatopa Bluff from here to Ventura.

The lower, rounded, tree-dotted, mid-distant ridge parallel to Topatopa is Sulphur Mountain. It consists largely of highly deformed but much softer Miocene sedimentary rocks. For more information on these features, see descriptions in Segment D. Also, west of Central Avenue and a little south of the freeway at about 10 o'clock, are tanks, pumps, and other facilities of Oxnard oil field. This operation pumps oil from beneath buried volcanic rocks like those seen at Conejo Grade. It also extracts tar, used in asphalt, from Pliocene and Miocene sand beds above the volcanics. The highly viscous tar can be brought to the surface only after being heated by steam pumped down drill holes to the tar sands. Watch for the extensive strawberry fields between Santa Clara and Rose avenues, a mile or two ahead.

Since passing Central Avenue, the west end of South Mountain ridge, the nearest hills to the northeast, have been in view at 2:45 o'clock. The blunt end of this ridge is composed of fine-grained, soft sediments of the Plio-Pleistocene Santa Barbara and San Pedro formations. For more on South Mountain ridge, see Segment C. The smooth, nearly flat surface of the deep alluvial fill beneath Oxnard Plain (Photo A-6) buries complex structures in older rocks. They are folded and faulted in much the same manner as rocks of corresponding age in the surrounding mountains.

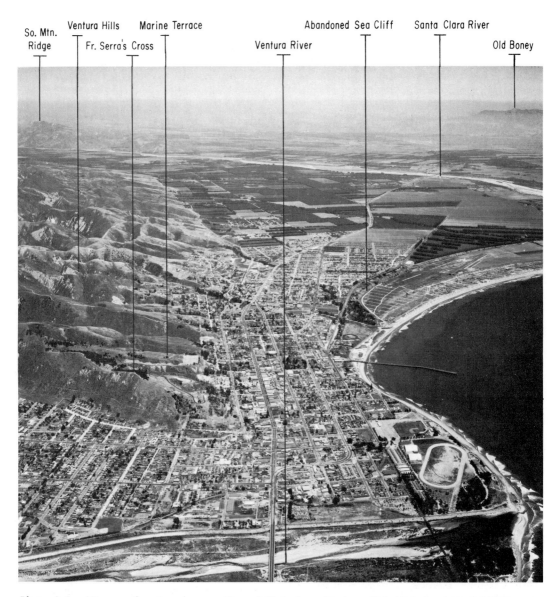

Photo A-6. View southeastward across Oxnard Plain from Ventura (Fairchild air photo 0-12800, 6/13/52).

O-20   West of Vineyard Avenue overpass, a view of Topatopa Bluff at about 1:30 o'clock is supplemented by Santa Paula Ridge at 2:30 o'clock. Also, directly ahead, the high-skyline mountain with the bare rock slope is White Ledge Peak in Santa Ynez Mountains. The rocks in this peak are essentially the same as those exposed in the face of Topatopa Bluff, but at White Ledge they are tilted south and erosion has simply stripped away overlying material down to the bedding-plane surface of a resistant sandstone layer, forming a dip slope.

O-21 About a mile west of Vineyard Avenue, the wide, sandy, and usually dry bed of Santa Clara River is crossed on a long concrete bridge. The Santa Clara is a major source of sand and gravel for Ventura County. The river looks harmless, but in times past it has flooded viciously, and occasionally still does. The old wooden bridges crossing it were routinely removed by the floods, but construction of the modern concrete structures has cured that problem. One of the greatest floods to come down this channel was that generated by the St. Francis Dam disaster of 1928 (Photo C-2) described in Chapter 4 of the earlier southern California guidebook.

O-22 In another mile we pass through Montalvo on an occasionally elevated course affording good cross-country views. Approaching Victoria Avenue underpass in Montalvo, the low hill just north is "The Mound." Like Camarillo Hills, it is the product of recent deformation, folding on Montalvo anticline and displacement on Oak Ridge fault, which have uplifted young, relatively unconsolidated sediments to create this topographic feature. Oil companies have drilled this structure without finding oil.

O-23 Between Montalvo and Ventura, on clear days, good views are seen of Santa Cruz Island (10 o'clock), the largest of the four Channel Islands, and of Anacapa (9 o'clock). Anacapa is actually three islands separated by narrow straits. If visibility is unusually good and your eyes sharp, you should be able to see the 40-foot high sea arch (Cabrillo's Arch) at the eastern tip of Anacapa.

O-24 The low Ventura Hills lie a few miles to the north beyond Montalvo. Their relatively smooth contours and rounded summits reflect the soft, unconsolidated nature of the Pliocene and Pleistocene mudstones and sandstones composing them. The subdued topographic configuration is not an indicator of simple internal structure, for the beds are steeply inclined, folded, and faulted. Gravels on terraces along this hill front have yielded the bones of an extinct Pleistocene elephant.

Approaching Ventura, the freeway descends gradually through nicely landscaped cuts backed by lemon orchards and eucalyptus-tree windbreaks. It emerges onto a shoreline flat at Pierpont Bay approaching Seaward Avenue. Look to the right at the Seaward Avenue exit to see an abandoned sea cliff, 40 to 50 feet high, a few hundred yards to the north. We approach to within 100 feet of this cliff about 0.2 mile beyond Seaward Avenue overpass, and we crossed it in the cut descending to beach level before reaching Seaward Avenue.

The flat fronting the sea cliff is underlain by beach deposits laid down by waves and currents during the last few centuries. At that time the shore received a copious supply of sand from Ventura River floods. Much of this material was carried eastward into Pierpont Bay where the shoreline was built outward at an astounding average rate of seven feet a year, as shown by comparison of maps made in 1855 and 1933.

Dams up the Ventura River now largely prevent major floods from reaching the sea, thus depriving the waves and longshore currents of their normal supply of sand. In recent years, the naturally prograding beaches of Pierpont Bay have been attacked and eroded. Thus, man, in protecting himself from floods and preventing the loss of valuable fresh water, has inflicted a curse upon a different part of his environment by causing beach erosion. It's often difficult to have things both ways, and we must be ready to make choices. However, it's important to know what those choices are, what the consequences of some seemingly desirable act may be, and what alternatives are available. Knowing all those things, we may elect to put up with beach erosion anyway, but at least it would be a conscious decision made in the light of a tradeoff between advantages (water conservation, flood control) and penalties (beach deterioration).

O-25 This segment ends at the junction of Highway 101 with Highway 33. Anyone, outbound or inbound, wishing to make an interesting little side trip to a spectacular lookout point on the hills back of Ventura can do so by wending their way to Father Serra's Cross via the following route. (The Franciscan priest, Junípero Serra, explored "Upper California" from 1769 to 1784 and established nine major California missions.) Follow Highway 33 north about one mile to the first turnoff, at Stanley Avenue. Take Stanley Avenue east 0.5 mile to Ventura Avenue and go right on same to the first stoplight. Beyond that stoplight, turn left onto any one of the following streets, Ramona, Simpson, Center, or Prospect, to the base of the hill. There turn right on Cedar Street and follow it uphill. Where Cedar starts to curve east around the point of the hill, keep a sharp lookout left for Ferro Drive which takes off steeply uphill. Follow Ferro Drive and Grant Park signs to a large parking area and picnic facilities at Father Serra's Cross. Once well up Ferro Drive, you can see your destination and follow your nose in getting there. The same spot can be reached from farther east via a very narrow, steep, alley-like street taking off from Poli Street right at the west end of the Ventura County courthouse, but that turnoff is even more difficult to locate.

On a clear day, views from this spot are simply superb. You can look north up Ventura River valley to Ventura oil field and to tree-dotted Red Mountain a bit to the left beyond. Farther back, in the right mid-distance, is Sulphur Mountain, and on the distant skyline the high ridges and peaks of Topatopa and Santa Ynez mountains. South, the view is to the Ventura River fan-delta, out into Santa Barbara Channel, and to the Channel Islands. South by southeast is the curving strand and surf along the edge of Oxnard Plain. Southeast is the western end of Santa Monica Mountains and Point Mugu. The rugged, rough northern part of the Santa Monica Mountain profile, Old Boney (Photo A-6), is underlain by volcanic rocks. Eastward, the view is directly up Santa Clara River Valley, a great synclinal downwarp bounded on both sides by mountains uplifted along high-angle thrust faults. This is a great place to eat lunch on a clear day.

Segment A— Inbound Descriptions

(The corresponding outbound material should be read first.)

I-25 Travelers headed east (inbound) for Los Angeles start this segment near the southwest corner of Ventura, at junction of Highway 101 (Ventura Freeway) and Highway 33 from Ojai. Note an odometer reading at this interchange.

I-24 For inbound travelers starting from the junction of highways 101 and 33 near the southwest corner of Ventura, the hills back of the city display sloping benches which are remnants of Pleistocene marine terraces mantled by a thick coverhead. Upon emerging from the submerged freeway course and from beneath a maze of overpass structures, Ventura beach is on the right and shortly, at Sanjon Creek crossing, the projecting groins along the shore of Pierpont Bay (Photo A-6) are visible ahead at 12:30-1:00 o'clock. The abandoned Pierpont Bay sea cliff begins on the left opposite "Seaward Avenue Exit, ½ Mile" and is good opposite the Seaward Avenue turnoff. The cliff remains in view intermittently until we cut through it beyond Seaward

Avenue as the highway rises from the Pierpont Bay flat.

I-23 Views of the islands are just as good eastbound as westbound. Approaching Montalvo, in vicinity of "Victoria Avenue-Montalvo Exit, ¾ Mile," a little knob can be seen to the right of the freeway at the industrial park. Like "The Mound" ahead, it is probably a product of recent tectonic deformation.

I-22 Eastward travelers see "The Mound" at 9 o'clock from vicinity of the Victoria Avenue overpass, which is identified by "Sherwin Avenue Exit, 1 Mile." The flat Oxnard Plain is also impressive from here to the right (Photo A-6).

I-21 Eastbound travelers see the Santa Clara River channel a little after passing Montalvo (Victoria Avenue).

I-20 This view is too hard to see for eastbound travelers. They do better to admire the local countryside.

I-19 Inbound travelers can easily drop off the freeway at the Santa Clara-Rice Avenue overpass to buy a box or two of fresh strawberries in proper season. Oxnard oil field is best seen beyond Almond Drive at 3 o'clock from "Central Avenue, Right Lane," and Topatopa Bluff, the west end of South Mountain, and the upcoming Camarillo Hills can be identified on the left.

I-18 Going east, Camarillo Hills (Photo A-5) are well seen starting at Central Avenue. Conejo Mountain at 12:20 o'clock and Old Boney at 1:15 o'clock are prominent skyline elements in the volcanic-rock terrane of the western Santa Monica Mountains, approaching Las Posas Road.

I-17 For inbound travelers the west tip of the Camarillo city ridge is easily spotted, a half-mile off, at about 12:15 o'clock beyond Las Posas Road. The Juan Camarillo house is beyond "Newbury Park 7, Thousand Oaks 10, Los Angeles 50" directly to

the left (9 o'clock) of "Pleasant Valley Road, Santa Rosa Road, Right Lane." You will have to look quickly as views are partly blocked by trees.

I-16 Inbound travelers see the agglomerates within the first roadcuts on the left, and the quarry wall is visible beyond the golf course at 1 o'clock. Upslope from the mobile-home park and just south of the freeway, was the location of the old Conejo oil field, discovered in 1892. This was a small operation, unusual because the oil was trapped in fractures in the volcanic rocks and in thin interbedded sandstone layers. Oil was obtained from depths of only a few tens of feet; most modern oil wells are thousands of feet deep. The oil had migrated upward from underlying petroliferous sedimentary beds, and its presence was revealed by surface seeps. The field was serviced by a few large central gas engines which jerked cables back and forth to operate pumps on the wells. By this means, one engine served many wells. These same volcanic rocks extend west under the Oxnard Plain where they are buried by thousands of feet of sedimentary materials. There, they also impound oil that is produced in the Oxnard oil field.

I-15 The view of the jointed dike coming upgrade is better on the right. It is in the second, and much deeper, double-walled cut encountered coming upgrade, just beyond "Weigh Station Exit, 1 Mile." Deep roadcuts on the right farther up the grade provide exposures of the various rocks composing the Conejo Volcanics.

I-14 Travelers ascending the grade see these cuts just over the crest.

I-13 Approaching Ventu Park Road exit and going under the overpass beyond, low hills on the near skyline and a higher hill on the intermediate skyline are nicely flat-topped, because they are underlain by the Conejo Valley gravels, which are exposed in the following double-walled roadcut at

"Lynn Road ¼ Mile, Moorpark Road 1¼ Mile" (center-divider). Further exposures of these deposits are seen in large roadcuts eastward on the right, as for example, at Lynn Road exit and beyond Rancho Road underpass. Knobs and ridges of volcanic rock, buried beneath the gravels, are exposed in the cores of some of the larger cuts, and a ridge of volcanic rock lies behind the gravels in vicinity of Rancho Road.

I-12 Eastbound, a similar view of the country, both north and south, is available after passing Westlake Boulevard.

I-11 Eastbound, the contrast between volcanic Lady Face (Photo A-1) and the sedimentary country to the north comes into view on the skyline at about 11:50 o'clock approaching Hampshire Road, but it is most plainly seen at Lindero Canyon Road exit.

On both sides of the freeway between Reyes Adobe Road overpass and Kanan Road are flat benches, fifty feet above freeway level, that look like they were underlain by gravels similar to the Quaternary deposits of Conejo Valley. At Liberty Canyon Road exit, to the right behind the tract houses, are dipping Topanga sandstones (middle Miocene) in a big hillside cut. Beyond, hills along the freeway are mostly grass-covered, suggesting a predominance of shale over sandstone. In passing through the Las Virgenes interchange, on the left at 9 o'clock nicely dipping strata are seen in a large cut at the hill base beyond the freeway.

I-10 Inbound travelers can easily make the diversion to Malibu Canyon via Las Virgenes Road; just follow the signs.

I-9 Ascending the grade eastward from Las Virgenes Road, cuts to the left expose thinly bedded brown shales (Modelo) with different inclinations, especially near the top in the deep, double-walled cut just short

of the summit, a little beyond "Parkway Calabasas, Calabasas Exit, 1 Mile." From the grade crest, the rugged mountains on the far skyline are the San Gabriels, made up of crystalline rocks. Going downgrade are the two big left-side roadcuts, and in the upper part of the second one you can see some nice folding of thin shale beds.

I-8 Inbound travelers see this smooth-sloped terrain east of Parkway Calabasas. Pepper trees start about at "Los Angeles City Limit," are especially lush near Fallbrook Avenue, and continue in disconnected strips to east of Desoto Avenue.

I-7 Inbound travelers will find the turn-off onto south-bound Topanga Canyon Boulevard (Highway 27) easier; just watch the signs. Ventura Boulevard exit is at the same place.

I-6 Travelers going east have to look back a little over their left shoulder to get views of the Simi Hills, but the Santa Susanas will be easily visible at about 9 o'clock on the left.

I-5 Inbounders cross this ridge beyond Desoto Avenue, entering it at "Winnetka Avenue, Exit ½ Mile."

I-4 Eastbound travelers see the Santa Susanas by looking northward and the Simi Hills by looking back over the left shoulder to the northwest and west.

I-3 Travelers from the west begin to see the park-like Sepulveda impoundment area on the left at "Haskell Avenue, 1¾ Mile, etc." (center-divider).

I-2 Eastbound travelers cannot see this dam very well approaching junction with the San Diego Freeway, although they have been able for some time to see the gate house on top. They do get a quick glimpse of the dam's east face (front) at 9 o'clock from Haskell Avenue exit.

I-1 Just read O-1.

Segment **B**

Santa Monica to Oxnard
via Pacific Coast Highway, 50 Miles

O-1   Start this segment at the west end of Santa Monica Freeway and proceed westward up Malibu Coast along the south flank of Santa Monica Mountains on Pacific Coast Highway (Highway 1). If more convenient, Highway 1 can be picked up anywhere southeast of Santa Monica Freeway, or entered farther northwest at major boulevards such as Wilshire, Santa Monica, or Sunset. Mileage markers are useful on this trip; watch for them. This is a scenic coastal drive in its western half and a nice, cool journey on a hot summer day. In combination with either segments A or C, it makes a loop trip. Record an odometer reading at the start.

(Inbound travelers see p. 49.)

O-2   At the Santa Monica end, The Palisades cliffs (Photo B-1) are immediately to the right. Their initial height of 40-60 feet is less impressive than the 90-125 feet seen a bit farther west, but the component materials are better exposed. They are alluvial sands and gravels, dark-brown, poorly sorted, of ill-defined nearly horizontal layering, and although not strongly consolidated, they are coherent enough to stand in a near-vertical face. This Pleistocene alluvium represents material swept down by streams from the south flank of Santa Monica Mountains, a mile or two north. It composes a large apron, formerly extending well beyond the present shoreline, that was built when sea level was lower

Photo B-1. The Palisades cliff just west of Chautauqua Boulevard and Santa Monica Canyon. Small recent slide on cliff face left of center. (Fairchild air photo 0-11047, 11/15/49).

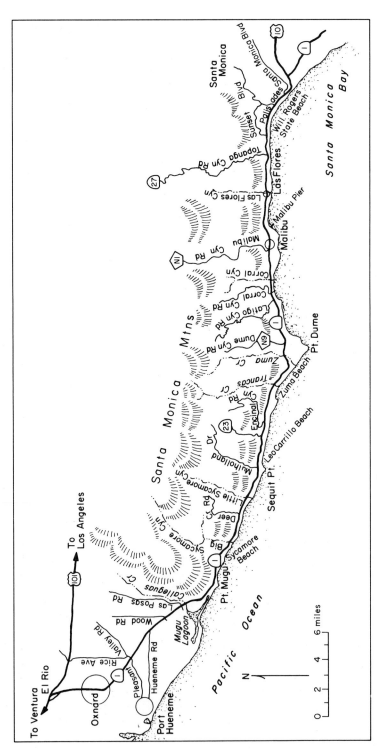

Figure B-1.   Segment B, Santa Monica to Oxnard.

and the shoreline lay a significant distance southwest. With a rise in sea level, ocean waves found these alluvial deposits fairly easy going and cut back extensively into them forming the sea cliff that constitutes the present face of The Palisades.

The smooth surface of usually blue and lovely Santa Monica Bay tells us nothing about the configuration of the sea floor below. About twenty miles offshore is a large closed basin nearly 3,000 feet deep. This Santa Monica basin, twenty miles wide and forty-five miles long, extends from Palos Verdes Peninsula west-northwest to Anacapa Island. It is a sump for rock detritus from adjacent parts of southern California. Submarine canyons run down its slopes and at times carry sand and mud, as well as water-filled beer cans, to the basin floor where they accumulate in layers, not unlike the uplifted marine strata now seen in coastal hills, *sans* beer cans.

O-3   In less than a mile, westbound, the cliffs have attained a height of nearly 100 feet. In about 0.5 mile beyond the first stoplight and marker 36⁰⁰, they give way to a steep slope with an irregular, jumbled, knobby appearance and a heavy vegetative cover of palms, eucalyptus, and sumac. Marker 36⁵⁰ is opposite this locality. The alluvial deposits yield easily to landsliding (Photo B-1), and the topographic irregularities seen here are probably the result of an old slide.

O-4   After clearing Chautauqua Boulevard stoplight, look to the top of the bluffs to see an overhanging concrete footing for someone's front-yard patio. Nobody has yet designed a method of pouring concrete into open space, so you can infer what has happened. About 0.6 mile beyond Chautauqua Boulevard, a large recent landslide is indicated by a precipitous break-away scarp deeply indenting the brink and upper face of the cliff accompanied by a lobe-shaped protruding mass of rock debris below. This is the famed slide of April, 1958 (Photo B-2).

Watch for the Sunspot Motel (1977 name) on the right where the highway starts to curve out around the debris lobe. There you can see a segment of the old highway (used now as a work area by highway crews) extending to the edge of the slide where it was buried. Beyond the slide, The Palisades bluffs are no longer composed of alluvium. Westward for a considerable distance you see mostly light-colored, fine-grained Tertiary sedimentary rocks.

Extensive measures have been taken to prevent sliding along The Palisades. A cardinal rule of slide prevention is "keep things dry." Near-horizontal drainage tunnels were driven 100-200 feet into the base of the cliff and outfitted with furnaces to dry the ground, where conditions were particularly hazardous and property values high.

O-5   West of Temescal Canyon Road, The Palisades' face is an irregular, steep hillslope rather than a cliff. Roadcut and hillside exposures show fine-grained, fractured, deformed shales (upper Miocene, Modelo). Near the big slide, we crossed an important geological structure which is related to a change in nature of the bedrock and the transition to alluvium. Santa Monica Mountains are separated from Los Angeles Basin by Santa Monica fault, which we crossed near the slide. This same line of faulting extends westward as the Malibu coastal fault and eastward as the Raymond fault, passing just south of Pasadena.

O-6   West of Sunset Boulevard (Photo B-3), complexly deformed Modelo shales continue to make up the hillslopes north of the highway. The beach narrows and the shoreline becomes locally rocky. We are too close under the cliff to see the good terrace above (Photo B-3). Just west of Coastline Drive (stoplight), the bluffs are composed of fine sandstone, but soon, beyond "Malibu 6, Oxnard 41," some darker shaly rocks appear (presumably Paleocene, 60-70 million years, Martinez Formation). Now, be alert for some striking exposures

Photo B-2.   Large slide of April, 1958, on The Palisades cliff just short of Temescal Canyon. (Photo by John S. Shelton, 987).

of conglomerate beds dipping steeply oceanward on the right at the tip of the point about half a mile west of Coastline Drive. Stones in the conglomerates are beautifully rounded and up to twelve inches in largest diameter. These are part of the oldest Tertiary rocks in the Santa Monica Mountains (Martinez). Beyond the point is Topanga Canyon up which beautiful exposures of Paleocene and Cretaceous con-

glomerates are seen by folks traveling the Highway 27 route (see special note on Topanga Canyon in Segment A).

O-7   Topanga Canyon is a good place to record another odometer reading and to note that marker 41^{00} is just beyond. Westbound travelers now start a four-mile traverse along the base of a rugged bedrock sea cliff cut into the south flank of the

Photo B-3. Marine terrace in Castellammare area west of Sunset Blvd. Santa Monica Mountains in background. (Fairchild air photo 0-9602, 1/29/47).

mountains. A variety of rocks of different ages, including Cretaceous, Paleocene, Oligocene, and early, middle, and late Miocene, all of sedimentary origin save for some middle Miocene volcanics, are exposed. Structures within and interrelationships between these rocks are complex owing to faulting, fracturing, and steeply inclined bedding, caused by proximity to the Malibu coastal fault zone lying just a little offshore. Black rocks between markers 41^{50} and 42^{00} are partly shales (Paleocene) and partly volcanics (middle Miocene).

One of the more distinctive rock units along this trek is the Sespe Formation, a land-laid deposit, which is entered beyond Big Rock Drive (stoplight) and traversed for more than two miles. It consists principally of massive beds of sandstone and conglomerate, largely gray, brown, white, pink, and red, the last two hues being distinctive. These beds trend nearly parallel to the highway and dip steeply inland. An interesting minor aspect in bluffs of massive Sespe sandstone is development of small-scale cavernous weathering. See if you can spot the large boulder pictured in Photo B-4. It lies on the right just above car level about three miles beyond Topanga Canyon Road, about 0.35 mile west of marker 43^{50}. Slices of other formations are occasionally mixed with the Sespe, and coming up on Las Flores Canyon Road is a cliff of black shales (Paleocene). For more than a mile beyond Las Flores Canyon, the rocks are largely sandstone (middle Miocene, Topanga Formation).

O-8   Beyond Las Flores Canyon, westbound travelers will note a gentling of slopes and their modest recession inland, which permit more houses to be built. This character is more marked beyond Carbon Canyon Road, and reflects the increasing softness of the bedrock.

Beyond Carbon Canyon Road, in vicinity of marker 45^{00}, the Malibu coastal fault passes inland and subsequently extends

Photo B-4. Small-scale, cavernous weathering in Sespe sandstone boulder, Pacific Coast Highway a little west of marker 43^{50}.

parallel to our route for many miles westward. It brings softer, less-resistant shales (Modelo) down to road level, and for a considerable distance west most of the bedrock we see nearby are these shales.

O-9   About 1.5 miles west from Carbon Canyon Road the highway curves out to Malibu Point, with Malibu sport-fishing pier, marked by a stoplight, on its east side. Shortly thereafter we cross Malibu Creek on a long concrete bridge and emerge onto the open flatland at Malibu (town), an area of alluvial fill. Material carried to the ocean by Malibu Creek is largely responsible for the sandbar that cuts off the flatland from the ocean. Inland, the abrupt rise of the mountain front marks the trace of Malibu coastal fault. The mountains are steep, rugged, and craggy because they are composed of older, more massive, harder Tertiary rocks (largely Sespe) compared to softer shales underlying the area south of the fault. The relief between mountains and lowlands is probably due wholly to differential erosion and not directly to fault displacement. This is what geologists call a fault-line scarp rather than a fault scarp.

Opportunity for a side trip north occurs a little ahead at Malibu Canyon Road which can be taken across the mountains to Ventura Freeway (Highway 101) at Las Virgenes Road (Segment A). The lower part of Malibu Canyon, traversed on the trip, is an impressive steep-walled gorge cut in resistant sandstones, conglomerates, and volcanics of Oligocene to middle Miocene age.

O-10   West from Webb Way (stoplight) in Malibu, the highway ascends toward a smooth, gently sloping surface seen in profile ahead. Going uphill, exposures of light-colored beds (Miocene) can be seen to the left, especially near the sea cliff. These beds are overlain by fifty feet of dark-brown alluvium, exposed in roadcuts on both sides nearing the top. The surface onto which we emerge, about 200 feet above sea level, is the top of this alluvial deposit which rests upon a smooth, nearly flat, marine-abrasion platform truncating the bedrock. This is a terrace, and each terrace level along this coast carries a similar blanket of alluvium. On some, it is fine-grained, sandy and silty, and only a few feet thick. In other instances the blanket may be 100 feet thick and, at least locally, as coarse as bouldery gravel, for example just beyond Malibu Canyon Road. Thick or thin, coarse or fine (as explained in Chapter 1), this material is known as coverhead. The surface of any coverhead deposit slopes gently seaward, because these materials were laid down by slope wash and streams flowing from higher terrain inland. Each emerged abrasion-platform will have a sea cliff at its inner edge, much like the cliff along the present shore. Usually, these old cliffs are partly or wholly buried by the coverhead (Figure 1-7).

At Malibu Canyon Road (stoplight), the buildings of Pepperdine University, hard by the Malibu coastal fault, are half a mile away on the right at about 2 o'clock. Approaching John Tyler Drive (stoplight)

Point Dume is seen, in good weather, on the low skyline 6.5 miles ahead at 11:30 o'clock. The white sea cliff curving gracefully out to the point consists of shale (lower Modelo), and the smooth surface extending inland from its brink is the Dume terrace. A higher surface seen in profile extending inland from the saddle just north of Point Dume is the older Malibu terrace.

O-11   John Tyler Drive (stoplight) is at marker 48^{50}, and somewhat less than two miles west is the Corral Canyon site of the highly controversial Malibu atomic reactor, a power-generating facility proposed in the mid-1960s by Los Angeles Department of Water and Power but never built. A coastal location is favored for atomic reactors because seawater can be used for cooling. Local residents in the Malibu area were not happy with the thought of an atomic reactor in their midst, and they challenged the safety of the site in terms of proximity to the Malibu coastal fault zone and evidences of local landslide activity. After much investigation, controversy, and extended public hearings, U.S. Atomic Energy Commission declined to grant a license for construction of the facility as initially designed. So far, the city has not elected to continue its efforts in view of the near impossibility of satisfying some of the requirements for licensing. In crossing Corral Canyon ahead, we do not see the site which is about 0.5 mile inland.

O-12   At marker 49^{50}, less than a mile beyond John Tyler Drive, westbound travelers are descending to beach level. Ahead, weather permitting, is a scenic view of the gracefully curving beach strand and sea cliff extending to Point Dume. Direct particular attention to the dark-brown cliff bordering the highway beyond the bottom of the hill, at 11:00 to 11:15 o'clock. The lower 60-70 feet is a nearly vertical face

above which is a steep slope. The transition from slope to cliff is defined by a near-horizontal plane forming a line on the face of the cut. That plane is the abrasion platform of Dume terrace truncating dark-colored, very messy bedrock (fragmented middle Miocene igneous materials). The steep slope above the cliff is equally dark, but less resistant, coverhead. We cross Corral Canyon at mileage 49^{89}, according to figures on the bridge, and pass Corral Canyon Road at 50^{36}. The cliff just described starts just beyond Corral Canyon Road and extends for nearly ¾ mile.

O-13   Westbound beyond the dark cliff, the highway ascends, passes Latigo Canyon Road, and tops out on coverhead mantling the Dume terrace. We don't stay on the terrace long as in half a mile, near marker 51^{50}, we drop into the canyon of Escondido Creek and cross a concrete bridge at 51^{80}. Sandy Escondido Beach exists partly because Escondido Creek brings sand to the ocean during floods. Starting downhill into Escondido Canyon, one catches a glimpse of Paradise Cove and its pier on the left, and ahead at 11:30 o'clock is the modern white sea cliff, 60-70 feet high.

Beyond marker 52^{00} some roadcuts, not obscured by vegetation, show the Dume abrasion platform, truncating white shales and overlain by fine brown coverhead, to be a remarkably smooth, horizontal surface. Beyond Ramirez Mesa Road (right), the highway traverses a half-mile of smooth, relatively undissected coverhead on the Dume surface. About 300 yards west of marker 53^{50}, the highway curves and starts a gentle ascent to a higher surface, the Malibu terrace.

O-14   About 0.3 mile beyond Point Dume Road, westbounders emerge onto a smooth surface about seventy feet above the Dume level. This is the Malibu terrace. Anyone wishing to visit Point Dume can turn left at the Heathercliff Drive stoplight and, by dead reckoning, intuition, and visual navigation, traverse residential streets to the point. It is at the tip of a triangle projecting into the sea. As usual, a configuration like this reflects a geological influence. The knob at Point Dume consists of hard, black, volcanic rock (lower Miocene), faulted into contact with the much softer, white, sedimentary beds seen in sea cliffs to both east and west. This igneous mass resists wave erosion so much more effectively than the sedimentary beds that it has protected the land behind, thus forming the triangle. It is no accident that the Point Dume triangle preserves the widest remnants of both Dume and Malibu terraces along the coast. The top of the knob is at the Malibu terrace level, but the saddle behind is at the Dume level. The knob must have been a little offshore island in the Dume sea.

Westbound travelers don't stay on the Malibu surface long, as steep descent into Zuma Creek canyon starts 0.2 mile west of Heathercliff Drive. In roadcuts on the left at top of the grade the Malibu abrasion-platform, truncating gently dipping white Miocene beds, is exposed between patches of iceplant. A mantle of fine, brown coverhead overlies the smooth, wave-cut surface. In preparation for construction of the buildings just to the south, a contractor bulldozed away the thin mantle of coverhead probably without realizing that the smooth bedrock surface uncovered was once the bottom of the sea.

Going downgrade good exposures of modestly tilted Miocene beds, cut here and there by small faults, continue on the left. These rocks are light-colored because they contain abundant calcareous (calcite-$CaCO_3$) and siliceous (silica-SiO_2) grains largely derived from the skeletons of single-celled plants and animals that floated about in Miocene seas in great abundance.

At the bottom, before crossing Zuma Creek, a turn left onto Westward Beach Road leads to the eastern part of Zuma Beach and eventually to Point Dume. The official entrance to Zuma Beach State Park is just beyond Zuma Creek bridge, as indicated by signs. Zuma Beach is one of the finest sand strands along this coast and owes much of its wealth in sand to material dumped into the ocean by Zuma and Trancas creeks. Point Dume also plays a role by capturing sand on its up-current side, like a gigantic groin. Offshore sea-bottom configuration may be a further factor through its influence on wave refraction patterns. A submarine canyon off the tip of Point Dume extends to within a few hundred yards of shore. The walls of the upper reach of this canyon are cut in volcanic rock.

O-15   Westbound travelers should take as close a look as possible at the face of the next roadcut on the right, about 0.5 miles west of Zuma Creek. It is opposite a restroom building in the beach park, and anyone inside the park can examine the cut with comfort and safety from behind the chain-link fence south of the highway. This cut exposes modestly dipping, cream-colored beds (upper Miocene), etched by weathering and erosion and offset by many tens of small faults, each displaying only a few feet of displacement. These faults dip either west or east, but all have the same sense of displacement; the hanging wall has moved down. This identifies a gravity or normal fault, although, in truth, it is no more normal than any other type of fault.

O-16   Near Malibu (town) the top of the coverhead on the Dume terrace is roughly 200 feet above sea level. At Point Dume, the Dume coverhead is only about 100 feet above the sea. The flat plane truncating the faulted beds in the roadcut just passed is the Dume abrasion platform, and it is only about 50 feet above the sea, although the top of the coverhead is a little higher. Clearly, the Dume surface becomes lower westward. Between here and Trancas Creek, the Dume surface appears in several roadcuts on the right. Its elevation decreases progressively westward to 10-12 feet above road level in the last exposure, a little west of marker 56[00]. The westward inclination of the Dume terrace is the result of tectonic tilting, either at the time the terrace emerged from the sea or subsequently. This tilt brings the Dume terrace to sea level west of Leo Carrillo State Beach, about six miles ahead. Don't be surprised that some roadcuts show only alluvial materials, especially approaching Trancas Creek, where the debris is notably coarser (cobbles and boulders). Such deposits fill gullies cut below the Dume surface during earlier episodes of sea-level shift and sea-cliff retreat.

O-17   Beyond Guernsey Drive and marker 56[50], roadcuts show only coverhead, some of it rather bouldery. On the left, the wide strand of Zuma Beach is giving way to the narrower, but still attractive, Trancas Beach. After crossing Trancas Creek (concrete bridge) and passing through Trancas Canyon Road stoplight, the highway starts upgrade. This ascent leads into the upper part of a thick (70-80 feet) deposit of dark-brown, pebbly coverhead burying the Dume surface. For most of the next five miles, the highway runs on or near the surface of this coverhead, with the steep hill front, of Eocene and lower to middle Miocene rocks, not far north. By watching roadcuts and gully walls carefully, you can occasionally catch a glimpse of light-colored rocks, part of the Topanga Formation. The coverhead is dissected by gullies and some of the best exposures are in gully walls. Two of the deepest and largest with bare, badland slopes are on

the right about 0.5 mile west of Malibu Riding and Tennis Club; marker 61[50] lies between them.

Remember that Malibu coastal fault has been tracing a near-parallel course. Proximity of the steep hillslopes suggests that we are here close to the fault, and we actually began cruising almost along it west of Highway 23 (Decker Canyon Road). Just before we drop into Arroyo Sequit at Leo Carrillo Beach, the fault crosses the highway and passes out to sea. We don't see its trace owing to burial by coverhead.

Refraction of swells coming into the cove at Leo Carrillo Beach makes this a spot favored by surfers. The truncated top of rocky outcrops behind Sequit Point, enclosing the cove on the west side, marks the Dume terrace level, the last you will see of it going west

O-18   Leaving Leo Carrillo Beach, westbound, Highway 1 passes Mulholland Highway (right) and ascends toward the surface of a thick coverhead mantling the Dume terrace beyond marker 62[50]. The bedrock in the mountains is largely sedimentary with local near-surface intrusions of dark igneous rock (middle Miocene). Shortly, we cross Ventura County line where a different set of markers begins, more numerous but with smaller mileage figures. If visibility is reasonable, you will shortly see ahead a spectacular rocky coast with steep mountain slopes descending precipitously into the sea. The marine terraces have disappeared beneath the sea owing to westward tilting of the land. Road construction along this rocky coast was not child's play.

O-19   Westbound, we descend close to water level a little beyond marker 1[00] at a sandy beach with a rocky point beyond. The canyon on the right at 1[32] is Little Sycamore. We now pass through a succession of small coves separated by projecting rocky points. Some of the coves sport narrow, sandy or pebbly beaches; others are nearly as rocky as the points. The points have generally good exposures of inclined sedimentary strata, largely massive sandstones (Topanga), locally cut by dikes and sills of dark, fine-grained igneous rock.

At the head of some coves are cliffs cut into coarse, bouldery, alluvial material, the first example being near marker 1^{95} extending to 2^{22}. This is coverhead laid down upon a marine terrace, probably the Dume, when it stood above sea level. Tilting has submerged the terrace and given waves opportunity to cut horizontally into the coverhead. In most places along this section of coast, erosion has completely removed the coverhead. It is preserved only locally, other examples being near Deer Creek Road and beyond marker 3^{17}. After nearly 3.5 miles of rocky points and intervening coves, we come to the attractive facilities of Point Mugu State Beach Park at Big Sycamore Canyon, just short of 4^{47}.

O-20   Massive gray Lower Miocene (Vaqueros) sandstones with interbeds of black shale, locally cut by irregular igneous dikes, are seen west from Big Sycamore Canyon to beyond Point Mugu. Within half a mile beyond Big Sycamore, after rounding a rocky point of massive gray sandstone in near-horizontal beds and passing "End of Slide Area," is a long, straight, sandy beach. At this end is a large climbing dune formed by the prevailing westerly wind which picks up sand from the beach, carries it across the highway, and piles it up against the hill face. Marker 5^{00} is near the dune's mid-point. Wind is one of the few natural processes capable of transporting material upslope. The steep rock face above the sand-mantled slope sheds large angular boulders onto the sand. Eventually they will be incorporated within this deposit through burial. We can easily understand how this happens because we have the whole setting in view, but a geologist looking at such a deposit ten million years

after it had become solidified, possibly tilted, and dissected by erosion, might be deeply puzzled by the presence of large rock fragments within a deposit of eolian sand. The straight sandy strand, at times strongly cusped, is part of Point Mugu State Park. Entrance to the beach facilities is near its west end.

O-21   Westward from this beach the coast is again rocky. We traverse several small coves and pass cliffed headlands before rounding a point, near marker 7^{00}, to a striking view of the pyramidal rock knob at Point Mugu with the deep slot-like roadcut to the north (Photo B-5). Ample parking space is available to the left just this side of Point Mugu, and it's a stop worth making, both for scenery and geology. Watch the cross-traffic as you pull off to park somewhere near the metal barrier across what was once the coastal highway rounding the tip of the point. Undercutting by powerful waves on this projecting point caused abandonment of the original highway for reasons you will see.

The rocks here are mostly massive, gray (weathered light brown), coarse sandstone and nearly black shale (Vaqueros). A good place to inspect the sandstone is in the rock face just behind the black wooden sign prohibiting overnight parking. You can see coarse, angular grains and scattered pebbles in the sandstone. Some one-inch gray interlayers are rich in broken fragments of fossil shells. Weathering has pitted the face with little hemispherical holes and etched out the bedding, which is inclined about $25°$ north. Don't be confused by the rainbow hues of spray-can markings.

In walking to Point Mugu along the old abandoned concrete highway beyond the metal barrier, you can see overhanging concrete highway slabs undercut by waves. The steep rock cliff to the right is determined by a set of joints crossing the bedding which you know dips modestly inland. On the right, 85-90 feet beyond the barrier and 15 feet above road level at the

Photo B-5. View west over Point Mugu to Mugu Lagoon. (Spence air photo E-10736, 8/19/40).

top of a small debris cone of black shale fragments, is a polished and striated rock surface streaked with brown lines. You will have to get up close to see the polish and appreciate the smoothness and striated character. This is a fault plane, and the polish and scratches made on it as the opposing blocks moved past each other are *slickenside*. Slickensiding distinguishes fault planes from other planar structures such as joints, fractures along which no movement has occurred. The orientation of scratches (striations) on the slickensided surface indicates the direction of differential movement between the two blocks.

Now stand back on the road and look higher up the face. About forty-five feet above is another exposure of slickenside. You can also see the trace of this near-vertical fault, marked by a 6- to 8-inch wide band of ground-up rock (gouge). From this vantage point, look left about fifty feet to see a well-defined, near-vertical dike of olive-brown igneous rock, about three feet wide, cutting across the gray sandstone. Dikes are abundant in this area (Photo B-6), but not all are as regular as this one.

At the tip of Point Mugu, you can inspect other coarse gray sandstone beds and see that they are poorly sorted and contain some

Photo B-6. Mid-Miocene dark igneous dikes cutting early Miocene gray Vaqueros sandstones just east of Pt. Mugu.

grains that are actually rock rather than mineral fragments. These characteristics identify this as a special type of sandstone (graywacke). Looking down to the rocks near water's edge at the tip of Point Mugu, you may conclude that the strata are nearly vertical. What you are actually seeing is a series of near-vertical dikes of different widths intruded into a thick, massive sandstone layer which dips modestly inland.

The water offshore from Point Mugu is unusually blue because of a considerable depth and clarity. This depth allows waves to deliver their full power in smashing blows against the rock. Hydraulic forces of many thousands of pounds per square inch can develop in narrow wedge-shaped cracks penetrating the rocks. In rough weather, Point Mugu is a wet place because spray shoots high into the air. Under calmer conditions, it's fun to watch the swells bend (refract) as they move toward shore and to see how they are reflected from the Mugu cliff. Interference patterns develop between incoming and outgoing (reflected) swells. Point Mugu is favored by fishermen, but a number have been drowned here when washed off the rocks below by an abnormally large breaker. It is no easy task to scramble from a heavy surf back onto the wet slippery rocks before a big wave picks you up and slams you against the rock. Stay topside—it's safer.

If the day is clear, you see two of the four Channel Islands to the west, Anacapa and Santa Cruz. These islands are essentially a westward extension of Santa Monica Mountains. At one time, not long back in geological history, they formed a westward projection of the mainland, the Cabrillo Peninsula, that converted Santa Barbara Channel into a long bay. See pages 14-15 of the earlier southern California booklet for more information on the Cabrillo Peninsula and the Pleistocene pygmy elephants of the Channel Islands.

Indians coming to the mainland from the Channel Islands used Point Mugu as a landfall. It is one of the more distinctive coastal features visible from a small boat in the channel. Indians favored the Point Mugu area as a place of residence because of abundant food (shellfish, fish, and birds) provided by the biologically rich environment of Mugu Lagoon west of the point.

Much closer at hand, looking west from Point Mugu, is Mugu Lagoon (Photo B-7). Its sandbar and installations of the Naval Guided Missile Center are better seen by walking 200 feet to the west. We will later have opportunity to see more of Mugu Lagoon and learn something of its natural history at a vista point on its north shore. The lagoon was formed as waves, supplied with copious quantities of sand, built the bar that now separates this brackish water wetland from the open ocean. Sandstone in roadcuts along this walk locally contain large fragments of thick oyster shells.

Speaking of sand, an interesting thing happened at Point Mugu Guided Missile Center a few years ago. Wave erosion began to undercut facilities which had been built years before at a seemingly safe distance from the water's edge. The cause was not difficult to find. Early in World War II, the Navy took over Hueneme Harbor, about seven miles farther west, and converted it to a major Sea Bee base. One of the first things the Navy did was to extend the breakwater at Port Hueneme to provide better protection for the harbor entrance. The extended breakwater interrupted the flow of sand normally moving eastward along the coast. Some of the sand accumulated west of the breakwater, but a lot of it was diverted offshore into the upper part of Hueneme submarine canyon where sand flows could carry it to the floor of Santa Monica Basin. Waves and longshore currents, having lost their normal supply of sand, started to eat away at the sandy beaches east of Port Hueneme. It was only a matter of time before this state of affairs extended east to Mugu Lagoon, and the beach there began to retreat inland. The Navy ultimately instituted a program of sand dredging west of Port Hueneme breakwater that supplied a slurry of sand and water pumped through pipes past Hueneme Harbor to beaches farther east. In time, this program reestablished a condition of uneasy equilibrium in the Mugu Lagoon area.

A complicating factor at Mugu Lagoon is a submarine canyon draining south into

Photo B-7. View west over Mugu sandbar and Mugu Lagoon to Oxnard Plain, just west of Pt. Mugu. Calleguas Creek in flood, Highway 1 at right margin. (Spence air photo O-9628, 11/25/46).

Santa Monica Basin. Near shore, the canyon divides into two branches both heading within a few hundred feet of the beach. This uneven sea floor topography refracts swells of various wave lengths coming from different directions in distinctly different ways. As a result, wave energy (causing accelerated erosion) is focused onto different parts of the beach under different conditions. The Navy is not always sure where trouble is likely to occur, but analyses of wave-refraction patterns by oceanographers help them anticipate likely trouble spots.

Returning to your car, the climbing dune is in view 2.5 miles east. In the roadcuts just east of the parking area, black shales are particularly abundant. The face of the cut about ¼ mile east, toward the first rocky point, displays a remarkable complex of irregular igneous dikes (Photo B-6) cutting through sandstone.

O-22 Leaving the Point Mugu parking area, westbound travelers pass through the deep cut transecting the Point Mugu ridge (Photo B-8). The rocks are sandstone with much black shale (Vaqueros). Shortly after clearing the cut, we cruise along the north shore of Mugu Lagoon. Formerly it was possible to spot, while traveling, some old Indian kitchen middens (village garbage dumps) just right of the highway because

Photo B-8. East-side view of deep cut in early Miocene Vaqueros sandstone and shale, Pacific Coast Highway, Pt. Mugu.

Photo B-9. Well stratified middle Miocene Temblor sandstones and shales behind Mugu Lagoon, between mileage markers 8³¹ and 8⁵⁰.

they were so rich in white seashells. The area has now been so reworked and regraded that these middens are no longer easy to see. Beginning about at 8³¹ and extending to 8⁵⁰, roadcuts expose regular and beautifully bedded sedimentary rocks, alternating sandstones (lighter) and shales (darker) (Photo B-9). These beds are middle Miocene, some geologists refer them to the Temblor Formation, a name that comes from the west side of the southern San Joaquin Valley.

O-23   Watch for the vista-point sign and a wide parking area left of the highway beyond 8⁷¹. This is a stop worth making. There's a little overlook platform for viewing Mugu Lagoon and a display of six panels depicting the shellfish, bird, fish and plant life of the lagoon, dedicated to Professor George E. MacGinitie and his wife for their interest in preserving the biological riches of California coastal wetlands. From this spot, facilities of Point Mugu Naval Guided Missile Station are in view, with Anacapa Island and the sea cliffs at the east end of Santa Cruz Island furnishing background on a clear day.

O-24   Upon leaving the vista point, outbound travelers cross Calleguas Creek in less than one mile and emerge onto the wide, flat Oxnard Plain across which the highway travels for several miles. This plain is an area of deep alluvial fill at the east end of the depressed Santa Barbara Channel. The area must have been downwarped in modern geological time because land-laid alluvium now extends well below sea level. However, deposition of rock debris, carried largely by Santa Clara River, has exceeded the rate of downwarping so the shoreline has been built westward (prograded) into the sea, creating the westward bulge that now exists between Point Mugu and Ventura. Beneath the alluvial fill are the same sedimentary and volcanic formations exposed in the surrounding mountains. Their structure is complex and many folds and some faults are buried by the alluvial cover.

Traveling toward Oxnard, you can see that this is fertile, pleasant country. Much of the land is devoted to cultivation of vegetables which support an extensive frozen food industry. Nearer Oxnard are some lemon orchards and some fine rows of old eucalyptus trees (blue gum) planted in the early days as windbreaks to protect crops and orchards from the prevailing westerly winds and the occasional, more devastating east winds.

If weather is clear, Santa Ynez Mountains are visible on the distant skyline ahead. The high mountain with the banded face on the skyline to the right at about 1:30 o'clock, just beyond Las Posas overpass, is Topatopa Bluff (6,367 ft.). The bands are made by massive Eocene sandstone beds. At 3-4 o'clock, is the west end of Santa Monica Mountains. The very irregular craggy skyline at 3 o'clock, locally known as "Old Boney," is composed of a thick succession of volcanic and associated near-surface igneous intrusive rocks.

0-25 The city of Oxnard and its many stoplights is not easily bypassed. The simplest thing to do is just stay on Highway 1 and endure the passage as gracefully as possible. Except at times of heavy traffic, it's not a difficult trip as the lights are well synchronized. The city was named for Henry T. Oxnard, an officer of the American Beet Sugar Company which erected a sugar factory here in 1897.

We join Ventura Freeway (Highway 101) and Segment A near Wagon Wheel Road on the north edge of the city, just short of Santa Clara River. Outbound travelers have the options of continuing on up the coast, using segments A and G, or returning to Los Angeles via Highway 101 and Segment A. They can also continue northwest on Highway 101 three miles to junction with Santa Paula Freeway and take that route east up Santa Clara Valley following Segment C to Golden State Freeway at Castaic Junction.

A return to Los Angeles by way of Ventura Freeway (Highway 101) and Segment A is best made by turning right on Vineyard Avenue, at a stoplight roughly a half-mile beyond Gonzales Road (stoplight) and about a half-mile short of Wagon Wheel junction on Highway 101. Follow Vineyard Avenue northeast a half mile to junction with Highway 101. There is no way of turning south on 101 at the Wagon Wheel junction.

Segment B— Inbound Descriptions

(The corresponding outbound material should be read first.)

I-25 Travelers headed for Santa Monica start this trip by turning onto Highway 1 (Oxnard Boulevard) from Ventura Freeway (Highway 101), a little beyond Wagon Wheel Road exit near the north edge of Oxnard. Record an odometer reading and take a patience pill for toleration of the many Oxnard stoplights.

I-24 Leaving Oxnard, travelers headed toward Santa Monica see many of these features from a slightly different aspect. The west end of the Santa Monica Mountains looms prominently ahead, and at marker 14^{00} Old Boney is in good view at about 11:30 o'clock. In rising over the underpass at Hueneme Road, a little beyond marker 13^{00}, Point Mugu comes into view at 12:20 o'clock.

I-23 Inbound travelers will find the vista point indicated by a blue/white sign near 9^{00} as they round a curve and Point Mugu looms ahead at about 12:15 o'clock.

I-22 Eastbound travelers begin the well-layered Temblor sequence (Photo B-9) at 8^{50} and see it best up to 8^{31}, with more scattered exposures beyond to the deep, double-walled cut behind Point Mugu (Photo B-8).

I-21 If eastbound travelers wish to make the Point Mugu stop, they should be prepared to turn off into the parking area immediately after clearing the deep cut (Photo B-8) that starts at marker 7^{50}. Do not elect the parking area at the west entrance to the deep cut as descriptions are not relevant to that spot.

I-20   Inbound travelers come to the straight sandy beach at marker 6^{00}, where La Jolla Canyon, probably a source for much of the sand, enters from the left. Entrance to the beach facilities is a short distance ahead on the right. The climbing dune is roughly one mile farther on the left.

I-19   Eastbound motorists come to Big Sycamore Canyon after rounding the rocky point beyond the dune. Campgrounds are on the left at 4^{53} and picnic facilities are to the right just beyond 4^{47}. East of Big Sycamore the spectacular rocky coast is traversed, roadcuts expose nicely layered sedimentary rocks, locally faulted, and local remnants of coverhead are seen starting at 3^{50} and extending intermittently for 0.3 mile. Better exposures are between 2^{22} and 1^{95}. Since the coverhead was here deposited on a rough bedrock terrain, ridges and knobs of bedrock cut through the deposit in many places. Little Sycamore Canyon (concrete bridge) and its cluster of buildings is passed a little beyond 1^{42}.

I-18   At and east of Little Sycamore Canyon the beaches become wider and sandy. Inbound travelers will sense a change in coastal characteristics as they pull away from shore beyond Little Sycamore Canyon and ascend to the surface of the Dume coverhead near marker 0^{50}. Larger houses and estates appear south of the highway where before there was scarcely room for a sea gull to perch. Directly ahead at mark-marker 0^{22}, Point Dume lies low on the distant skyline.

I-17   Eastbound travelers get a view of rocky Sequit Point at 12:15 o'clock just after crossing into Los Angeles County, and their first look at Leo Carrillo Beach comes about 0.35 mile farther east. The deep gullies affording exposures of coverhead are a lit-

tle more than half a mile east of Carrillo Beach Park entrance, near marker 61^{50}. Beyond Decker Canyon Road (Highway 23), a little beyond marker 59^{00}, the highway breaks into the open with a good view of Point Dume at 1 o'clock and of the high Malibu terrace north of it. Light-colored bedrock (middle Miocene) is seen in roadcuts approaching marker 58^{50}, where Broad Beach Road takes off right. A little farther east is an excellent view of the curving sandy strand of Trancas and Zuma beaches.

I-16   Eastbound travelers have already driven a good many miles on the surface of the thick Dume coverhead, but their first good look at the underlying abrasion platform is afforded by roadcuts 0.5 mile beyond Guernsey Drive (marker 56^{50}), between Trancas and Zuma creeks. The westward tilt of the platform is more easily appreciated going east than west.

I-15   For inbound travelers this cut is 1.4 miles east of the bridge across Trancas Creek and just a little east of marker 55^{50}. Being in the outer highway lanes, they get a better view.

I-14   Motorists headed east can easily turn onto Westward Beach Road if they wish to visit Point Dume or gain easy access to the beach. They can also exercise the option of a diversion to Point Dume from the Heathercliff Drive stoplight ahead. White shale (Miocene) beds are seen well going upgrade out of Zuma Creek, and a glimpse of the Malibu abrasion-platform comes near marker 54^{50} just short of the top. The rugged mountain front, about a mile inland, marks the trace of Malibu coastal fault zone. It is easy to get the feeling, at and beyond Heathercliff Drive, that a terrace remnant even higher than the Malibu terrace lies a short distance inland.

I-13   Descending from the higher Malibu platform, inbound travelers get a good view across the Dume surface. Marker 53^{50} is on the Dume level, and from it the Malibu surface is seen in profile on the left, 60-70 feet higher.

I-12 Inbound travelers come to this exposure about 0.3 mile east of Latigo Canyon Road. The west end of the cliff is near marker 51⁰⁰. Relationships are harder to see than from the east, but the abrasion platform is indicated by a horizontal line at the top of the vertical cliff of dark, broken, igneous rock.

I-11 Eastbound travelers will have identified Corral Canyon Road from the signs and crossed Corral Canyon bridge a little beyond marker 50⁰⁰ before climbing onto the terrace surface extending to John Tyler Drive. Once on the terrace, if weather is clear, Catalina Island may be in view at about 1:30 o'clock, somewhat beyond marker 49⁵⁰.

I-10 Inbounders have already seen many exposures of coverhead and have traversed both the Dume and Malibu terraces.

I-9 Motorists traveling east get a good view of the setting of Malibu town and beach as they drop downhill a little after passing Malibu Canyon Road stoplight.

I-8 Eastbound travelers can recognize the transition from younger, softer, sedimentary beds to older, more resistant rocks simply by watching the change from hillslopes dotted with houses to steep, bare, rocky, largely uninhabited cliffs.

I-7 Those traveling inbound get a somewhat better view of the cliffs between Las Flores and Topanga canyons by being a little farther from them. They can see the shallow, cavernous weathering in bluffs of massive Sespe sandstone to better advantage, but probably will not spot the boulder mentioned (Photo B-4). Best exposures of Sespe rocks end near marker 42⁵⁰. The usually heavy traffic and lack of places to stop along this stretch of highway are frustrating for travelers in either direction.

I-6 For inbound motorists, the conglomerates are on the left near road level in rounding the curve on the first point east of Topanga Canyon Road stoplight. Marker 40⁵⁰ is a little beyond.

I-5 Eastbound travelers see bedrock underlying alluvium in the cliff face from just east of Temescal Canyon Road to marker 37⁵⁰ beyond the slide. This rock is mostly shale (upper Miocene, Modelo), but in vicinity of the slide are some softer, more sandy Pliocene (Pico) and Pleistocene marine strata. Santa Monica fault is crossed near the slide without being seen.

I-4 Motorists traveling east come to the west edge of this slide about 0.2 mile east of Temescal Canyon Road (stoplight), and just east of marker 38⁰⁰. They get a fleeting view of the high break-away scarp and the rounded forelying lobe of slide debris (Photo B-2). They do not get a good look at the old abandoned highway section east of the slide. Beyond, Pleistocene alluvium largely replaces bedrock in the cliff face, although initially a little grayish, modestly consolidated conglomerate (Pliocene?) appears at the cliff base, beneath overlying alluvium. On a clear day, eastbound travelers catch glimpses of Palos Verdes Peninsula at clock hours from 12:30 to 2:30. It should not be mistaken for Catalina Island which is easy to do if low haze hides the intervening coast.

I-3 Travelers headed east (inbound) see this section of The Palisades, near marker 36⁵⁰, about 0.6 mile east of the stoplight at Chautauqua Boulevard.

I-2 Travelers headed east have seen higher Palisades cliffs than these, but exposures of the alluvial deposits, near and east of the ramp going to the Santa Monica business district, are better.

I-1 This segment ends at the point where Highway 1 gives way to Santa Monica Freeway on the coast at Santa Monica.

Segment C

Castaic Junction to Ventura, 41 Miles

O-1 Turn onto Highway 126 from Golden State Freeway (I-5) at Castaic Junction and note odometer reading. The route is westward down Santa Clara River (Photo C-1), an attractive drive through a verdant agricultural valley bounded on both sides by mountainous ridges.

(Inbound travelers see p. 64.)

O-2 Upon leaving Golden State Freeway westbound, Highway 126 descends to a sandy alluvial flat, the combined flood plains of Castaic Creek (northwest) and Santa Clara River (south). Castaic Creek, usually dry, is crossed on a concrete bridge in about two miles, but Santa Clara River remains to the south for the entire trip. Approaching Castaic Creek bridge, a neat little topographic bench rises about fifty feet on its far side. The bench is underlain by fine, brown, homogeneous alluvium and is a remnant of a former broad valley floor created by partial filling of Santa Clara and Castaic valleys. Approaching the turn-in for Indian Dunes (motorcycle recreation park), south across Santa Clara River at 9 o'clock, is an extensive, smooth bench sloping gently north about 125 feet above river level. To the right, opposite the turn-in, locally conglomeratic Saugus beds (Plio-Pleistocene) form steep bluffs behind the cultivated field.

Beyond mileage marker 3^{50}, the highway rises to cross some hilly spurs, the first of which bears a little bench, seemingly on alluvial fill and probably representing the same level as the remnant at Castaic Creek. These benches are part of an old Santa Clara Valley topography formed when the river and its tributaries were stabilized at higher levels. Lateral cutting by the streams, local fillings by alluvium, and erosional recession of valley sides formed wide, flat-floored valleys. Subsequent down-cutting by rejuvenated streams has partly destroyed these wide valley floors, leaving the benches as remnants.

Roads, tanks, and other facilities earlier seen on hills across the river identify Castaic Junction oil field, discovered in 1950. The high south skyline is part of Santa Susana Mountains, soon to give way westward to Oak Ridge. Between markers 3^{50} and 3^{00}, Indian Dunes running grounds are below on the Santa Clara River flats. Road-cuts through spurs beyond 3^{00} expose gently dipping, silty, sandy, and locally pebbly Saugus beds. The contact (not visible) between land-laid Saugus (Plio-Pleistocene) and marine Pico beds (upper Pliocene) is just ahead at Val Verde Park turnoff.

O-3 At Val Verde Park turnoff, a little beyond marker 2^{50}, we enter the first of a

52

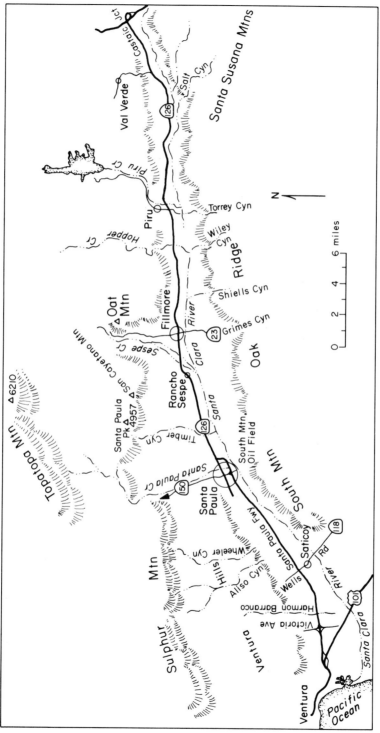

Figure C-1. Segment C, Castaic Junction to Ventura.

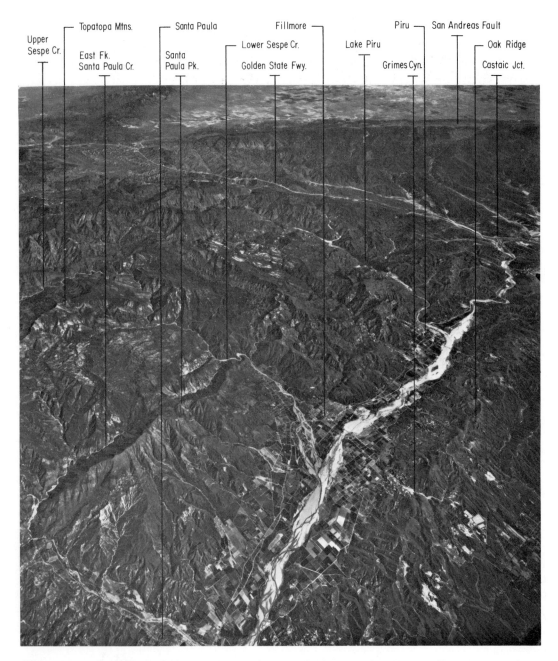

Upper
Sespe Cr.

Topatopa Mtns.

East Fk.
Santa Paula Cr.

Santa Paula

Santa
Paula Pk.

Lower Sespe Cr.

Golden State Fwy.

Fillmore

Lake Piru

Piru

Grimes Cyn.

San Andreas Fault

Oak Ridge

Castaic Jct.

Photo C-1.   High-altitude, oblique view northeastward of Santa Clara River valley. (U.S. Air Force photo taken for U.S. Geological Survey, 041-L-086).

succession of walnut groves which occupy benches at two or three levels. By looking south to 8:30-9:00 o'clock just beyond this intersection, one gets a view across Santa Clara River of eroded, gently tilted, light-colored Saugus beds making a distinctive outcrop pattern (Photo C-2). Oak trees begin to dot the crest of the skyline ridge at 10 to 11 o'clock, so it can now properly be referred to as Oak Ridge. At the county line, mileage markers shift to a Ventura County datum, the first being 34[68].

In a little less than one mile beyond Val Verde turnoff, watch for the concrete bridge across San Martinez Grande Creek (labeled). The good-sized canyon across the Santa Clara river at 9 o'clock a quarter mile farther is Potrero Canyon, a nice two-story valley as shown in Photo C-2. Unfortunately, you catch only a fleeting glimpse in passing and don't see any of the extensive workings of the Newhall-Potrero oil field farther up. Ahead the road curves left and ascends a small rise near marker 1[00] (currently reading [00] because the 1 is obscured), a roadcut on the right at the curve exposes coarse Pleistocene stream gravels containing well-rounded boulders resting upon tilted Pico beds (upper Pliocene). This is a terrace gravel, and it marks the former location of a principal channel of Santa Clara River when it flowed at this higher level. Many boulders are of crystalline rock derived from San Gabriel Mountains tens of miles east, indicating that then, as now, Santa Clara River drained that region. Large cottonwood trees on the floor of Santa Clara River here have grown since 1928 when this valley was swept clean by the disastrous St. Francis Dam flood (Photo C-3).

O-4 In another two miles we cross a railroad track, seldom used but not abandoned, so be alert! On the south, beyond marker 33[18], the bed of Santa Clara River supports a dense growth of willows and other water-loving vegetation. Watch carefully alongside the highway and you should

catch glimpses of a small stream flowing in a cress-lined channel, the best views being near marker 32[43] and beyond. This is surprising in view of the generally dry nature of the riverbed upstream. What happens is this. Just a short distance back, where the highway came uphill in a two-lane passing zone, the river describes a wide loop to the south. There it encounters impervious shales that force water, percolating along in pervious sand and gravels beneath the stream bed, to the surface where it flows for a mile or two before sinking back into the gravels.

0-5 Westbound, the valley becomes more verdant with extensive citrus orchards. In another mile is an historical marker identifying Camulos Ranch, near marker 30[64]. This property was once part of the large San Francisco Rancho Spanish grant, given in 1839 to Antonio del Valle who established his home here. It later became famed as a part-time home for Ramona, heroine of the novel by that name dealing with early California history.

O-6 Downtown Piru is bypassed, but at the first turnoff into the village (and to Lake Piru), at marker 29[31], one sees high bluffs right behind town, shifting from 1 to 3 o'clock as the highway curves south. These bluffs consist of massive sandstone and conglomerate (Pliocene, Pico) beds dipping steeply north backed by older (Miocene) shales of similar inclination. The beds are actually overturned as the Miocene overlies the Pliocene. This overturning is attributed to deformation along San Cayetano fault.

O-7 In a few tenths of a mile, Piru Creek bridge is crossed. Even in dry seasons, water sometimes runs here owing to controlled releases from Lake Piru, about five miles upstream. A little beyond the bridge, diked percolation basins are seen on both sides, between markers 28[54] and

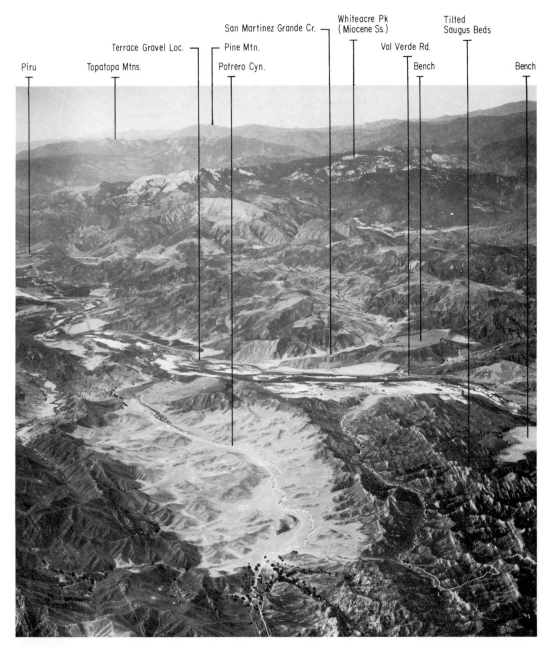

Photo C-2. View northwesterly across upper Santa Clara River valley (Fairchild air photo 0-1288, 7/29/30).

Photo C-3. Remains of St. Francis dam, as viewed upstream, following collapse and disastrous flooding of Santa Clara River in 1928. (Spence air photo E-1932, 3/13/28).

28[51]. Water emptied into these basins sinks into the underlying sands and gravels. This is a good way of storing water. It's a little hard on fish but cuts down evaporation and saves the expense of dams and reservoirs. It is recovered from pumped wells, like money from a bank.

Anyone wishing to explore Piru Canyon can turn into town and drive nearly a dozen miles north, as far as Blue Point. It is a pleasant canyon, harboring a large reservoir and displaying some spectacular geology in its upper part. Blue Point serves as a trail head for some good hikes into the back country.

O-8   Just west of Main Street turnoff into Piru, from marker 28[04] and beyond, roads, tanks, and facilities of Torrey Canyon oil field are intermittently visible well up on the north face of Oak Ridge, at about 9:30 o'clock. Oak Ridge is an uplift consisting of at least seven *en echelon* anticlinal folds, bounded at the north base by a fault dipping south—Oak Ridge thrust. Torrey Canyon oil field is on the easternmost of these anticlines.

Westward from Piru, Santa Clara Valley gradually widens and the bounding mountains become higher (Photo C-4). This valley is underlain by a deep, synclinal prism of sedimentary rocks with steep to locally overturned limbs, bounded on both sides by large thrust faults, the San Cayetano on the north and the Oak Ridge on the south (Figure C-2). Deep alluvial fill in the valley hides this structure, so it is known principally from deep wells and geophysical explorations.

Notice how irregular, disorganized and restless the topography on the north flank of Oak Ridge appears. This is most obvious at low sun angles when shadows emphasize details of relief. Little, irregularly scattered, flat benches, many backed by precipitous, usually barren, steep slopes, and the lack of well organized drainages suggest that almost every square foot of the surface has been involved in sliding or slumping, sometime in its history.

Steep-sided hills to the north are part of Piru Mountains which form an eastern extension of Topatopa Mountains lying behind Santa Paula and Ojai. Slopes are

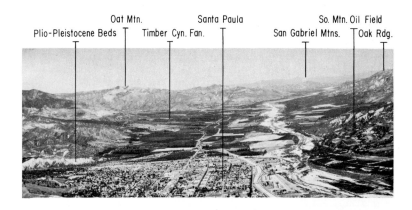

Plio-Pleistocene Beds | Oat Mtn. | Timber Cyn. Fan. | Santa Paula | San Gabriel Mtns. | So. Mtn. Oil Field | Oak Rdg.

Photo C-4. View east up Santa Clara River valley from Santa Paula. (Spence air photo E-19777, 10/14/66).

steep, and the stony nature of soil in orchards indicates that some of the bedrock in those hills is hard and resistant.

O-9   Beyond marker 27⁶², one looks at 2 o'clock into the mouth of Hopper Canyon, the steep walls of which expose structures in Miocene rocks more complex than can be appreciated at 55 mph. From just west of Hopper Creek bridge (mileage 26⁵¹), at 1:30 to 2:30 o'clock, the grassy steep valley slopes display fading scars of shallow "skin slides" or "soil slips" formed during the abnormally wet winter of 1969 (Photo C-5). Such slips involve only a foot or two of soil mantle which gets so soaked with water that a thin skin-like layer breaks away and slips downslope. Less than 0.2 mile beyond marker 26²¹, watch for the entrance to a ranch road on the right marked by two large, beautifully spherical concretions out of one of the local sedimentary formations. Opposite Hopper Creek, Oak Ridge and San Cayetano faults, or branches of them, come together under Santa Clara River. They are said to shake hands, but since the larger, more powerful San Cayetano appears to decapitate Oak Ridge, the meeting clearly involves more than a mere handshake.

O-10   West from Hopper Creek the highway climbs a little onto the valley side, and views are good southward across or-

Photo C-5. Scars of skin slides (soil slips) on north wall of Santa Clara River valley just west of Hopper Creek, formed in wet winter of 1969 and photographed in spring of that year.

ange, lemon, and avocado orchards to the restless slide topography of Oak Ridge. This terrain becomes less disorganized westward, partly because older, stronger sedimentary units are beginning to make up the north face of Oak Ridge.

Approaching Fillmore Fish Hatchery sign and road (south side), about three miles west of Hopper Creek, the large northside roadcut, starting at marker 23²², exposes fractured rocks stained brown by petroliferous material, something oil company people are always looking for. Similar brownish rock continues west in cuts along the highway and into the bluff just to the north after crossing the railroad. To the south,

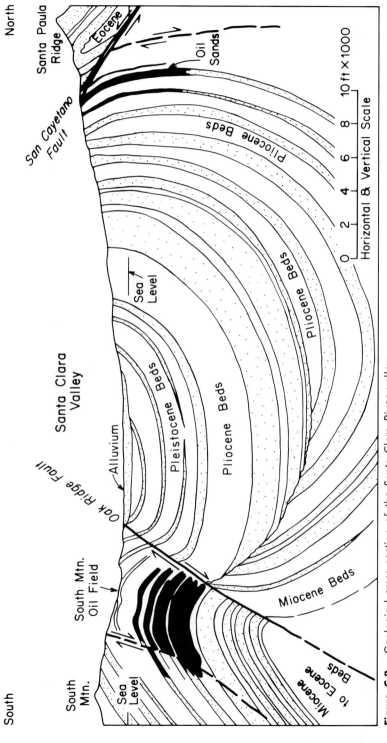

Figure C-2. Geological cross section of the Santa Clara River valley.

approaching Fillmore, roads, tanks, and other facilities low on the face of Oak Ridge are related to Shiells Canyon oil field. Bardsdale oil field lies farther west, just about south of Fillmore.

O-11   South of Fillmore, the crest of Oak Ridge looks lower. Actually, the crest retains its height, but it is displaced southward by a deep indentation made by Grimes Canyon, along which Highway 23 leads to Moorpark. In Grimes Canyon an unusual vari-colored, burned, clinker-rock (not visible from Fillmore) is quarried for decorative stone. The rock comes in combinations of red, pink, brown, white, and yellow. It is porous, broken (brecciated), and locally stringy, like pulled taffy. Although originally a shale (Miocene), it is now a partly glassy, fused mass containing an unusual assemblage of minerals. This clinker-rock was formed by the slow burning of naturally ignited petroliferous shales producing temperatures as high as 1,000°C (over 1,800°F). The principal quarries are near the bottom of Grimes Canyon, but other outcroppings of colorful clinker-rock can be spotted high on adjacent hillslopes by travelers on Highway 23.

O-12   At the stoplight in Fillmore comes opportunity for interesting side trips to the north—one short, to the mouth of Sespe Creek—one longer, to a condor lookout at

Dough Flat. To exercise this option, turn right at the stoplight on Goodenough Road (it is) and go north about four miles to a large parking area on the left near the mouth of Sespe Canyon. Goodenough Road here gives way to a narrow, bumpy, oiled road that ends in a few hundred yards at a locked gate. From the parking spot, one gets an excellent view of red, land-laid, well-bedded sandstone and conglomerate (Oligocene, Sespe Formation) composing the upstream walls of Sespe Canyon (Photo C-6). The bedding is steeply inclined because of deformation related to the several branches of San Cayetano fault crossing Sespe Canyon. Sespe Creek often carries a good discharge of water, as it drains a large area of relatively high country and is not impeded by dams.

A longer diversion can be elected by turning right from Goodenough Road onto a steeply ascending, oiled, secondary road leading to Oak Flat, Tar Creek, and other places. This turnoff occurs a few hundred yards short of the parking area, and the road goes up Little Sespe Creek into the back country east of Sespe Canyon. Initially it clings to the steep, precipitous walls of Little Sespe Canyon, affording some rather spectacular views of steeply tilted sedimentary rocks, largely of the Sespe and Lower Miocene Vaqueros and Rincon formations. Some oil wells are sited in seem-

Photo C-6. View north from over Fillmore showing, in center, dipping beds of Sespe Formation at mouth of Sespe Creek. (Spence air photo E-14424, 12/8/53).

ingly inaccessible locations. As the road reaches Oak Flat Ranger Station, it enters a gentler upland terrain that is traversed on a winding course for another eight miles to Dough Flat, a trail head into the back country and the site of a condor observation station. Although the road is locally rough, dusty, and a little breathtaking at Little Sespe Creek, experienced mountain drivers will not find it particularly challenging, and the country is wild and scenic. Fossil collectors will revel in the beds of gray, shell-rich limestone, intercalated within brown shales (lower Miocene) along Alder Creek trail leading north from Dough Flat.

Returning to Fillmore along Goodenough Road, a succession of benches, 100 to 300 feet above stream level, lies west of Sespe Creek. They were developed by erosion and deposition with respect to higher stabilized stream levels. Some of the orange, lemon, and avocado orchards traversed on Goodenough Road occupy corresponding benches on our side.

O-13   Back at the Fillmore stoplight, record an odometer reading. Heading west, Santa Paula Peak, composed of massive, tough sandstone beds (Eocene) is at 1:30 o'clock. The other large skyline peak, at 2:00 o'clock, is San Cayetano Mountain. Note the break in profile on the south face of Santa Paula Ridge where steep, precipitous sandstone bluffs and cliffs give way to a smoother, more gentle slope. That break approximately marks the San Cayetano fault trace between hard Eocene beds above and much softer Pliocene strata below. You may see some roads, tanks, and other signs of activity along the fault as we approach Santa Paula. They identify the Timber Canyon oil field operation which taps oil accumulated in steeply dipping beds cut and sealed by the north-dipping San Cayetano fault (Figure C-2).

O-14   West of Fillmore, at marker 19^{85}, is a bridge spanning one branch of Sespe

Creek and in another half mile is a second crossing. From these bridges, the well-layered, red Sespe Formation (Oligocene) rocks at the mouth of Sespe Canyon are usually visible at 3 to 4 o'clock. With good visibility, bluffs of massive, white, Miocene sandstone can be seen far back near the distant skyline at about 4 o'clock. Those bluffs are favored by condors.

O-15   West of Sespe Creek bridges, the highway ascends to a terrace, curves south, and at marker 19^{08} enters the several thousand acres of Rancho Sespe, remnant of a large Spanish grant that at one time extended to the sea. The highway is soon bordered on both sides by magnificent old eucalyptus trees.

O-16   After passing Sespe Ranch buildings, westbound, and rising at marker 18^{02} onto a higher surface, we cross railroad tracks and about 0.3 mile farther come to an historical monument at a road intersection identifying the Fremont tree, a sycamore, near which General Fremont and his men passed in 1846. Considering the subsequent vicissitudes of the general's career, he might have done better to have settled down and set up a fruit stand under his tree.

Beyond Fremont tree, the surface becomes more bouldery, as indicated by the increasing size and number of stone walls. This means we are moving onto the central part of the large Timber Canyon fan, derived in good part from the massive, firmly cemented sandstones composing Santa Paula Ridge on the north skyline.

O-17   About 0.6 mile west of the Fremont sycamore, a paved road (wide intersection) turns north to Toland Road disposal site, affording an impressive view of rugged Santa Paula Ridge on the skyline. On the south, just west of this spot is an archetypal little red schoolhouse; mileage marker 16^{00} is just beyond. Beyond the school, South Mountain looms on the Oak

Ridge skyline at about 10 o'clock. Keep your eye on this feature as we approach Santa Paula. It is the site of a major oil field and you will see much evidence of roads, rigs, tanks, and plants (Photo C-7).

O-18   The crest of Timber Canyon fan is identified by a large stone wall and a hedge of pomegranate trees, colorful in fall with yellow leaves and ruddy red fruit. The wall starts just after beginning of the passing lane for westbound cars, beyond marker 15⁵⁴. Nearing Santa Paula, one can usually see pink and white Sespe beds outcropping in bluffs on the lower slopes of South Mountain. The Sespe is of land-laid origin and would not normally be oil-bearing, but it is here. These beds define a broad anticline, and you should be able to see this fold in bypassing Santa Paula on the freeway. Oil accumulates in anticlines, if the rocks are pervious and properly confined, and if there is any oil. The puzzle here is— where did the oil come from? Deep drilling shows that South Mountain anticline lies above the south-dipping Oak Ridge thrust fault. Under the fault are steeply inclined, younger (Pliocene and Miocene) oil-bearing strata that could have leaked oil upward into the anticline. This is an unusual relationship, but experienced petroleum geologists are seldom surprised by the tricks of nature.

O-19   Westbound travelers should turn onto Santa Paula Freeway. In so doing, they head due south for a moment, putting South Mountain directly ahead. In vicinity of "126 West, Santa Paula Freeway," pink and white near-vertical to south-dipping Sespe beds can be seen at about 9 o'clock in road-cuts and river bluffs at eye level across Santa Clara River. The south-dipping beds are overturned. These exposures remain in view as the freeway curves by stages into its westward course. The overturning results from knuckling over along south-dipping Oak Ridge thrust, which lies only a short distance north of the exposures.

Junction with Highway 150 occurs at 10th

Plio-Pleistocene Beds   Telegraph Road   Aliso Cyn.
Oxnard Plain   So. Mtn. Oil Field   Ventura Hills   Santa Paula

Photo C-7. View west down lower Santa Clara River. On South Mountain ridge soft Plio-Pleistocene beds make gray slopes toward distal end and on south (left) side. (Spence air photo E-13673, 2/12/50).

Street, and those wishing to follow Segment D to Ojai should prepare to exit. It's a good trip, nice scenery, lots of geology, with particularly lovely flowers and foliage in spring.

O-20   The South Mountain anticline, an open structure with modestly dipping limbs, is exposed in bluffs about half way up the slope of South Mountain and can be seen by westbound travelers with some difficulty by looking sharply back at 7:00 to 7:30 o'clock between 10th Street and Palm Avenue, roughly one mile west.

O-21   About a mile west, a little beyond marker 8^{96}, after passing under the Briggs Road overpass, look south to 9 o'clock and observe the change in aspect of South Mountain ridge (Photo C-7). It now displays smooth inter-canyon slopes, giving way abruptly to amazingly steep canyon walls and near-vertical canyon heads. The difference, compared to Oak Ridge-South Mountain farther east, is due to a change in rocks (Photo C-4). The area viewed is underlain by homogeneous, fine-grained marine sediments of the San Pedro and Santa Barbara formations (latest Pliocene and Pleistocene), which are soft enough to erode easily but coherent enough to stand in near-vertical bluffs. To the east, older heterogeneous Pliocene, Miocene, and Oligocene rocks yield a more diversified landscape.

To the north are the low Ventura Hills backed by the steep south face of Sulphur Mountain, the tree-dotted, intermediate skyline ridge. This face is made up of steeply inclined to locally overturned Miocene beds. For more information on Sulphur Mountain, see Segment D. Features and relationships to the north are best seen rising onto an overpass across a railroad in the vicinity of Todd Barranco, near marker 8^{15}.

O-22   Descending from the railroad overpass, about 3/8 mile to the left at 9:15

o'clock from marker 7^{58}, are tanks and pumps of a small oil field. This operation taps oil accumulated in pervious beds sealed by a branch of Oak Ridge fault buried beneath the valley alluvium.

O-23   Shortly we go under Edwards overpass, at mileage marker 6^{99}, and see a line of eucalyptus trees half a mile ahead. These mark the edge of Ellsworth Barranco, crossed a little beyond marker 6^{52}. The Spanish were highly perceptive in their recognition of variety within landforms, and they gave the name "barranco" to a steep-walled, flat-floored gully cut a few tens to 100 feet or so into relatively fine, soft, coherent, alluvial materials. The view of Ellsworth Barranco is not outstanding, but it is mentioned in order to prepare you for an excellent barranco to be crossed a few miles farther west.

Approaching Wells Road (the turnoff to Saticoy), the western end of Santa Monica Mountains comes into view on the far southern skyline beyond the blunt end of South Mountain ridge. The rugged eastern part of the Santa Monicas, locally known as "Old Boney," for obvious reasons, is composed of volcanic rocks. The lower, smoother, western extension to Point Mugu is underlain by softer, more easily eroded, sedimentary formations. The broad, intervening flat is the alluviated Oxnard Plain.

O-24   West of Wells Road, trees obscure scenic views, but be alert to spot Kimball Road, near marker 2^{80}, in a little over two miles. Just 0.3 mile beyond Kimball Road, 150 feet beyond marker 2^{50}, we cross an excellent barranco, not named at the highway but locally known as Harmon Barranco. It is best seen looking north. You can anticipate it by watching for a metal railing at the freeway edge. Barrancos can be cut very rapidly; some as large as this one have developed within the present century.

O-25   In another two miles, we get our first view of the ocean and, if the day is clear, of two of the Channel Islands, Anacapa (east) and Santa Cruz (west).

O-26 A mile west of Victoria Avenue we join 101 Freeway and can follow Segment A west to Ventura. Anyone wishing to go east toward Los Angeles on 101 Freeway should turn off at Victoria Avenue and follow it south to Montalvo, as directed by the signs. There Segment A can be followed to Encino.

Segment C—
Inbound Descriptions

(The corresponding outbound material should be read first.)

I-26 Travelers headed east up Santa Clara Valley start this segment at the Santa Paula-Ventura freeways junction by taking Santa Paula Freeway (Highway 126). Note odometer reading upon leaving the interchange.

I-25 Motorists approaching Santa Paula Freeway turnoff see the ocean and the Channel Islands easily, unless visibility is poor. Rising over the interchange, and during the first mile of eastward travel to Victoria Avenue, glimpses are caught of the low Ventura Hills, two to three miles north.

I-24 Harmon Barranco is best seen by looking south, 0.15 mile east of "Kimball Road, Right Lane."

I-23 Much of the same southward view is seen approaching Wells Road from the west, with Old Boney on the far skyline at 3 o'clock, and the blunt west end of the South Mountain ridge at 1:15 o'clock. Beyond Wells Road, on clear days, are excellent views of the cliffed face of Topatopa Bluff (6,367 feet) on the far north skyline at 10:15 o'clock, and of Santa Paula Ridge with Santa Paula Peak (4,957 ft.) at 11:30 o'clock. Topatopa Bluff and

the upper part of Santa Paula Ridge consist of massive resistant sandstones (Eocene). Oat Mountain, at 11:45 o'clock, has largely Miocene rocks, and South Mountain, at 12:15 o'clock, is composed largely of Oligocene and lower and middle Miocene strata.

I-22 The little oil field is seen beyond Edwards overpass at about 3 o'clock, between marker 7^{00} and 7^{81}.

I-21 These features and relationships are seen in negotiating the railroad overpass near marker 8^{00}. In good weather, travelers also have an excellent view of rugged Santa Paula Ridge, on the high skyline at 11 o'clock. The bluffs in the upper third of its face contrast sharply with the smoother, gentler slopes below. This topographic break marks the location of San Cayetano fault, a large thrust dipping north. Silvery tanks at places along this topographic break are related to oil operations of the Timber Canyon field. Descending from the overpass, near marker 8^{40}, one sees seed-growing, flower (left), and vegetable (right) fields in season.

I-20 Traveling east on Santa Paula Freeway the South Mountain anticline is seen to best advantage on rising over the underpass at Palm Avenue (beyond Peck Road), at marker 11^{36}. At about 1:45 o'clock, bluffs on the midslope of South Mountain expose near-horizontal pink and white Sespe beds on the anticlinal crest. To the right, beds dip gently south, and north-dipping beds are visible lower on the hillsides left of the anticlinal crest. The anticline remains in view for nearly a mile. Between 10th (Highway 150) and 12th street crossings, Sespe beds dipping steeply north are visible in bluffs and roadcuts along the foot of South Mountain, at 1 o'clock. As the freeway starts to turn north, you may catch a quick glimpse at 12:30 to 1:00 o'clock of overturned Sespe beds dipping steeply south in an exposure nearly at eye level. Further glimpses of this exposure are seen beyond Santa Paula Creek crossing. These steep dips and the overturning occur just above Oak Ridge fault, a thrust dipping south and located about at the base of the hills. Along it, South Mountain block has been shoved up and over Santa Clara Valley block (Figure C-2).

Travelers not electing the Segment D trip to Ojai via Highway 150, end up headed due north just before the freeway gives way to a two-lane highway leading east to Fillmore. While headed north, Santa Paula Ridge is directly ahead on the skyline, Santa Paula Peak is at 12:45 o'clock, and tanks on the trace of San Cayetano fault, well up the mountain face, are at 12 o'clock. Massive rock outcrops and bluffs above the fault trace are made by sandstones (Eocene).

I-19   Anyone headed east can exercise the option for Segment D at 10th Street.

I-18   Motorists headed east have already had a good look at the anticline of South Mountain as they passed Santa Paula. Now they can enjoy Santa Paula Ridge, to the north, with its San Cayetano fault trace. The Timber Canyon fan, stone wall, and pomegranate trees are near markers in the fifteen mileage-marker range.

I-17   The little red schoolhouse is near the east end of the first passing lane on Highway 126 east of Santa Paula, just beyond marker 16^{00}.

I-16   The Fremont tree is about 0.6 mile east of the little red schoolhouse at the point where an asphalt road takes off northeasterly at an oblique angle. The descent to the terrace surface on which Rancho Sespe buildings are sited is near marker 17^{96}.

I-15   Motorists first enter Rancho Sespe property about two miles beyond Santa Paula and travel 3.5 miles through it to Sespe Creek.

I-14   Going east, the view up Sespe Creek and into the back country is even better, but to see Santa Paula and San Cayetano peaks one has to look sharply back to the left.

I-13   Eastbound travelers see the San Cayetano fault trace more easily than westbound travelers, and should also be able to identify Santa Paula and San Cayetano peaks.

I-12   These same options can be exercised at the Fillmore stoplight.

I-11   Passing through Fillmore, Grimes Canyon is identified by the southward displacement of the Oak Ridge face.

I-10   Going east out of Fillmore motorists see these brownish petroliferous rock exposures starting at and beyond the railroad track. The Fish Hatchery road is a little more than half a mile beyond the railroad crossing, and the best exposure of brownish rock is between markers 23^{07} and 23^{22}. Views south to Oak Ridge and to Shiells Canyon oil field are good.

I-9   The Hopper Creek area is entered near marker 25^{87}, about two miles east of the first passing lane beyond Fillmore. By craning the necks a little, travelers can see the skin-slide scars on the steep slopes west of Hopper Creek at 8 to 9 o'clock (Photo C-5). The large spherical concretions are just left of the highway, 250 feet beyond marker 26^{08}. The mouth of Hopper Canyon is seen well at 8:50 o'clock approaching the railroad crossing.

I-8   Views of the slide and slump features on Oak Ridge are usually good for those motoring east toward Piru. Nearing Piru, facilities of the Torrey Canyon oil field are seen at 2:30 o'clock. Looking east, the narrowing of Santa Clara Valley is obvious (Photo C-4), and if weather is clear the crest of Santa Susana Mountains may be visible on the far skyline.

I-7 The percolation basins are about 0.6 miles east of Main Street turnoff into Piru for eastbound travelers, between markers 28^{51} and 28^{54}.

I-6 The bluffs behind Piru are visible at, and after passing, the Main Street turnoff at marker 28^{30}.

I-5 Camulos Ranch is about 0.3 mile beyond the first passing lane east of Piru, just beyond marker 30^{64}. Santa Clara Valley narrows beyond Camulos Ranch as hillsides press in more closely from the south.

I-4 This reach of water-rich stream bed is first seen at marker 32^{18}, while in a passing lane. It extends beyond 32^{95}, where a gravel dike forms a pond. Near marker 34^{09}, the highway enters a succession of walnut groves occupying low benches and the valley becomes conspicuously less verdant.

I-3 The terrace-gravel exposure is passed 0.9 mile east of Los Angeles county line, beyond marker 0^{50}. It is on the left just around the curve identified by the unusually large yellow/black sign indicating a 90° left curve to be taken at 40 mph. The angular unconformity between tilted Pico beds and the near-horizontal gravels is best seen coming from the west. The mouth of

Potrero Canyon (Photo C-2) is across Santa Clara River at 2:30 o'clock immediately after passing the gravel exposure. The eroded, gently dipping, well stratified Saugus Formation is seen at 1:30 o'clock from opposite marker 2^{00} which is on the left side of the highway.

I-2 At Val Verde Park turnoff, eastbound travelers pass from Pico Formation to Saugus Formation. Gently dipping siltstone, fine sandstone, and locally pebbly Saugus beds are seen in the double-walled roadcuts a little beyond Val Verde Park turnoff. Beyond, on the right, are running grounds of Indian Dunes motor vehicle park (beyond marker 3^{00}), and on the far side of Santa Clara River are bluffs of gently dipping massive Saugus beds. In descending to the alluvial flat, opposite marker 3^{50}, an extensive, smooth, gently sloping bench, about 125 feet above present stream grade is in view on the far side of Santa Clara River. Indian Dunes turn-in is just beyond, and at 2 o'clock, south of the river, are facilities of Castaic Junction oil field. Large fragments of conglomeratic rock resting on steep hillslopes just left of the highway approaching Castaic Creek bridge indicate the nature of some Saugus beds composing the bluffs above. At marker 4^{00}, just before crossing the bridge of Castaic Creek, the high tower at Magic Mountain amusement park is momentarily visible at 1:30 o'clock.

I-1 This segment ends at Golden State Freeway (I-5) at Castaic Junction.

Segment **D**

Santa Paula to Ojai, 18 Miles

O-1   This is a neat little trip, especially lovely in spring after a wet winter. Start outbound from intersection of Highway 150 with Santa Paula Freeway (Highway 126) at Tenth Street near the south edge of Santa Paula. The route proceeds north via Highway 150 up Santa Paula Canyon (Photo D-1) and then goes westward up Sisar Creek, across Upper Ojai Valley, and down to Ojai Valley proper. It is a pleasant drive on a rural highway. Record an odometer reading at the start and watch the white roadside mileage markers.

(Inbound travelers see p. 75.)

O-2   In traversing Santa Paula northbound on Tenth Street, Main Street is crossed at a stoplight within the first few blocks. On the northeast corner of Main and Tenth, in an oldish stone building, is the California Oil Museum, displaying early oil field equipment and depicting historical aspects of early petroleum production in the Santa Paula area. If you like the olden days, this is worth a stop. Two blocks after crossing the railroad tracks, watch for a slightly tricky turn as Highway 150 splits right at 30° from Tenth Street.

After separation and resumption of the northerly course, Santa Paula Ridge is on the high right skyline at 12:15 to 2:00 o'clock, and the eastern flank of Topatopa Bluff is directly ahead. Both are made up largely of resistant sandstones (Eocene, 40-50 million years). Many of the boulders seen along the highway and in stone walls are derived from those sandstones. Mill Park, on the left about 0.6 mile beyond the Tenth Street separation, is a convenient picnic spot, with entrance opposite Bedford Street. Hillsides on the left for 0.5 mile beyond Mill Park expose nondescript, brown, fine, soft, south-dipping sedimentary beds (Plio-Pleistocene, 1-3 million years). Occasional glimpses are caught of the same materials in bare bluffs to the east of Royal Oaks Avenue. In another half mile, views into the country east of Santa Paula Creek become easier.

O-3   Within another mile northbound, we clear the houses of Santa Paula and shortly thereafter, beyond marker 31[36], get a view of the relatively wide, flat-floored valley of Santa Paula Creek and its steep walls. The stream channel is entrenched fifty to one hundred feet below the level of earlier valley floors which now make terraces, such as the surface on which we are traveling. Broader terrace remnants at two levels lie east of the stream providing sites for attractive orchards (orange, lemon, and avocado). The channel of Santa Paula

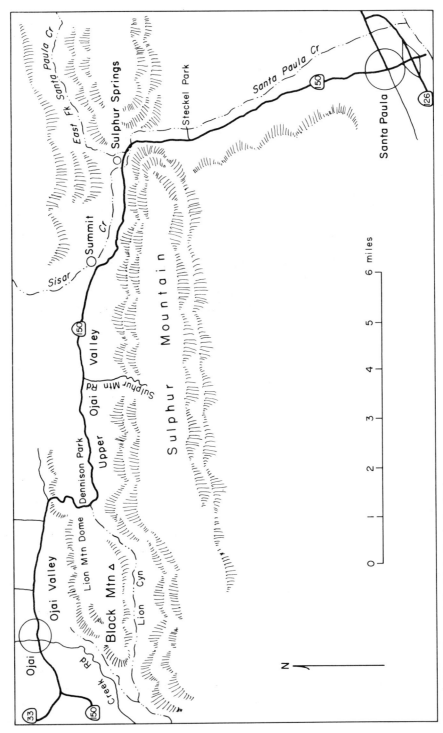

Figure D-1. Segment D, Santa Paula to Ojai.

Topatopa Bluff   Dip Slope (Eocene Ss.)   Hines Pk.   Stream Terrace   Pliocene Beds   Santa Paula Rdg.   Plio-Pleistocene Beds   San Cayetano | Flt.

Photo D-1. View north up Santa Paula Canyon from over Santa Paula. (Spence air photo E-14421, 12/8/53).

Creek just ahead provides world-famous exposures of an unusually thick (12,000 feet) succession of steeply inclined Pliocene sandstone, mudstone, siltstone, and shale beds. This is one of the greatest thicknesses of marine beds of this age and character known anywhere, and it is much visited by geologists who usually start their inspection from a little turnout ahead on the right at 30^{95}, just beyond marker 31^{01}. Mileage figures on these markers decrease outbound. At this turnout are a dam and diversion weir. Sedimentary structures in the beds exposed along the stream channel are indicative of deep-sea turbidity current activity. In the far bank of the stream, beyond 30^{86}, one sees the very steep, 70°-80°, southward dip of these beds.

O-4   In vicinity of 30^{30}, northbound travelers get their first good look at the steep south face of Sulphur Mountain, directly ahead on the near skyline. On the more distant skyline slightly to the right, Eocene beds dipping gently northeast shape the profile. The entrance to stone-walled Steckel Park, another picnic stop, is on the right one hundred and fifty feet beyond marker 30^{00}. At 9 o'clock, west of the entrance, is a nicely preserved terrace, about thirty feet above road level, planted to oranges. A half-mile beyond Steckel Park, the highway ascends onto a terrace, with orchards, nearly seventy-five feet above Santa Paula Creek. Large sycamore trees along the stream bottom are here heavily infested with mistletoe.

O-5   Beyond 29^{26} at about 2 o'clock is a high alluvial-fan surface on the far side of Santa Paula Creek, now planted to oranges. It features an impressive vertical bluff in bouldery debris along its west edge where truncated by Santa Paula Creek. Near marker 29^{08}, Santa Paula Canyon narrows, and at 28^{89}, after rounding a curve, highly deformed, brownish shales (upper Miocene, Santa Margarita Formation), crop out on the left. For the next 0.3 mile, the narrow gap between Sulphur Mountain and Santa Paula Ridge is traversed. In vicinity of markers 28⁸³ and 28⁷⁷, you learn whence comes the name, Sulphur Mountain, when hydrogen sulphide gas given off by road-side springs assaults your nose. About two hundred and fifty feet beyond the 28⁷⁷ marker is an irregular, light-brown, pro-jecting knob of travertine on the left, a little above car level. It was formed by a spring formerly active on the slope above. Most of the rock at this eastern tip of Sul-phur Mountain is Santa Margarita, but at the bridges across Santa Paula Creek we have passed into the Monterey Formation middle Miocene), which features shales of lighter color. The extreme contortion and deformation displayed by the strata com-posing Sulphur Mountain reflect their in-competence as well as the intense squeez-ing of the mountain into a fan-like anti-cline with overturned beds on both limbs. On the north flank is Sisar fault, a thrust dipping steeply south in opposition to north-dipping San Cayetano fault, which lies less than a mile to the north. Opposing thrust faults are usually indicative of strong tectonic stresses.

Shortly, at 28⁶¹, we cross three bridges in rapid succession, the first and second spanning Santa Paula Creek, with the third, at 28⁴⁷, crossing Sisar Creek. The cliff face to the left (now south) between these bridges exposes severely contorted, white, shaly beds (Monterey) reflecting deforma-tion related to the Sisar thrust fault. The parking areas here are used largely by hik-ers and backpackers going into the rugged country along upper Santa Paula Creek north of Santa Paula Ridge.

O-6   Outbound travelers are now headed west along the north side of Sulphur Moun-tain, ascending the canyon of Sisar Creek. You will never guess how local residents pronounce Sisar. They say "Seesaw" and mean it. A group of buildings, beginning

at 28²⁸ and extending to 28¹¹, is Sulphur Springs, at one time the site of a hot sul-phur-water plunge.

We don't see much geology on the north face of Sulphur Mountain owing to the heavy vegetative cover, primarily oaks with a sprinkling of lighter green native black walnut and scattered California bay trees. Occasional roadcuts will reveal dark sur-ficial debris containing fragments of white shale, suggesting that Sulphur Mountain's north flank is underlain largely by Mon-terey beds. Just north of Sisar Creek, within the next mile or two, is a spread-out oil operation, the Silverthread Field, involv-ing very complex structural relationships along San Cayetano and Big Canyon fault zones. Outbound travelers catch only fleet-ing glimpses of drill rigs, pumps, or tanks on the steep slopes to the north, for ex-ample near 27²³ as the canyon opens out a bit.

O-7   Beyond 26⁵⁰, brea deposits compose banks left of the highway. They are formed by oil that seeped out of fractured white Miocene shale, and in a few places fresh streams of tar (Photo D-2) are fed by cur-rently active seeps. Brea deposits extend beyond Koenigstein Road to about 26¹², and some are associated with bouldery gravels. Just right of the highway at 1 o'clock, from 26⁰² to 26⁰⁰, are pumps of the old Ojai (or Sisar) oil field, started in 1895. The wells were very shallow, some less than 100 feet deep, and a number of pumps were oper-ated by a single cable jerked back and forth on an eccentric driven by a large combus-tion engine. Currently (1977) some of these cable-driven pumps (Photo D-3) are still in slow operation, motivated presumably by a central electrical motor. The oil is heavy, having migrated from fractured Miocene shales into overlying Pleistocene sands and gravels with a considerable loss of volatiles. Still earlier, in the 1860s, oil was "mined" on the south face of Sulphur Mountain by means of tunnels, dug for hundreds of feet

Photo D-2. Recent oil seeps alongside Highway 150, in canyon of upper Sisar Creek about opposite Koenigstein Road.

Photo D-3. Old cable-activated pump on shallow well in Upper Ojai oil field, developed in 1895.

into the mountainsides, from which oil and water trickled in a gutter on the tunnel floor.

O-8   After climbing the short grade out of Sisar Creek and passing through the settlement of Summit, outbound travelers emerge into the open flatland of Upper Ojai Valley (Photo D-4). This is basically a fossil landscape, a leftover from acts of piracy committed by Santa Paula Creek against Ventura River. At one time Ventura River had a long eastern branch extending into the country north of Santa Paula Ridge. A goodly amount of water drains from there, and this well-fed stream had created a wide valley with gently sloping floor through the area north of Sulphur Mountain which we are traversing. At that time, Santa Paula Creek was just a small north-side tributary of the Santa Clara River, but it was an eager little stream with great hopes, ambitions, and a penchant for exploration. It kept gnawing away at the highly factured rocks near the east end of Sulphur Mountain until it cut through and discovered, to its delight, the well-fed eastern branch of Ventura River flowing unsuspectingly along at a somewhat higher level because it had a longer and gentler route to the ocean. It was no trick at all for Santa Paula Creek to behead the east fork of the Ventura River, near the present location of the three bridges, and divert the water into its own channel. Not satisfied, a branch of Santa Paula Creek then started working headward to the west behind Sulphur Mountain. In time it extended to Sisar Creek, the principal north-side tributary of the east branch of Ventura River, which it quickly diverted, thus depriving the old east branch of Ventura River of essentially all its water. The floor of this old, dried up, and abandoned drainage system is now Upper Ojai Valley (Photo D-4). It has been left high and relatively dry as the canyon of Sisar Creek was cut deeper to the east, and the main Ojai Val-

Topatopa Bluff   Overturned Coldwater Ss.   Ojai Valley   Upper Ojai Valley   Santa Paula Ridge   Sulphur Mtn.   Dennison Grade

Photo D-4. View eastward to Upper Ojai Valley from over Ojai Valley. (Spence air photo E-8083, 11/2/37).

ley area was eroded and structurally depressed to the west.

We travel some four miles westward along the axis of this abandoned valley, currently drained by Lion Creek, a tributary of San Antonio Creek which flows into Ventura River well south of Ojai. From this open valley, we get a good look at Sulphur Mountain to the left and directly ahead on the far skyline to Santa Ynez Mountains. The high country directly north is part of Topatopa Mountains, but Topatopa Bluff (Photo D-4) is not easily seen from this angle.

O-9 Outbound, nearly 0.5 mile beyond 24^{50}, a paved road (Sulphur Mountain Road) takes off south. If the day is clear, and you would like a superb view over Ventura Hills and Oxnard Plain to Santa Barbara Channel and the Channel Islands, turn off on this side road and follow it about three miles to the top of Sulphur Mountain. Then go westward a short distance along its crest to one of several view

points. In going upgrade, you will see numerous roadcut exposures of the strongly deformed, light-colored Monterey shales composing Sulphur Mountain.

O-10 The floor of Upper Ojai Valley is planted to orchards of apricots, almonds, and peaches in its eastern part and largely to English walnuts and grain fields farther west. The heavy cover of oaks on the north flank of Sulphur Mountain brings considerable verdure to the area. The setting of this intermontane valley is scenically attractive, the major lack being water. The narrow barranco-like gully, crossed by the highway several times, is the drainage of Lion Creek.

At marker 22^{50}, the prominent ridge ahead at about 12:30 o'clock on the near skyline is Black or Lion Mountain. It is a structural dome, or anticline plunging both east and west, and the topographic shape reflects the structural form. The highway turns north shortly and traverses the east nose of this structure. Oil accumulates in such structures, if the underlying rocks happen to contain oil. Small amounts have been produced from Lion Mountain dome. You will see some of the pumps descending Dennison Grade on its north flank.

O-11   In another half-mile the highway curves into a northerly course, Lion Creek is crossed at 21^{71} for the last time, and we make a gentle ascent of the east flank of Lion or Black Mountain to Dennison Park, at 21^{45}, a fine place for a picnic lunch. The coarse-grained, pinkish sandstone boulders and outcrops seen here are Sespe Formation (Oligocene). They have been brought up to this level by the folding of Lion Mountain dome. It is the attitude of these relatively resistant Sespe beds that determines the shape of the mountain, the generally softer, less resistant, overlying Miocene strata having been largely stripped away by erosion.

O-12   Immediately beyond Dennison Park, descent of Dennison Grade to the floor of Ojai Valley begins. This is a short but winding and modestly steep grade. Turnouts on the left afford excellent views of Ojai Valley and its inclosing mountains. A stop at one of them is worthwhile; perhaps the best is the large turnout with stone wall, labeled "Ojai Valley," just beyond 21^{17}.

Ojai Valley is low relative to its surroundings because it is a structurally downwarped area, essentially a stubby syncline. It is filled with several hundred feet of bouldery Pleistocene sands and gravels derived from bordering mountains. Bouldery alluvial fans seen along its north edge and east end are just the frosting on this alluvial fill.

From the stone-wall vista point, taking the powerline as 12 o'clock, the south face of that part of Topatopa Mountains known as Nordhoff Ridge is particularly prominent at 10 to 11 o'clock. Nordhoff Peak (4,485 ft.) at 11 o'clock rises nearly 4,000 feet above the floor of Ojai Valley. The city of Ojai was once named Nordhoff in honor of writer Charles Nordhoff, grandfather of C. B. Nordhoff, co-author of *Mutiny on the Bounty*. The smoother foothills along the north side of Ojai Valley, near the base of this steep face (Photo D-5), are underlain by red Sespe beds (Oligocene, 26-37 million years). The lower part of the mountain face behind the red beds is actually a forelying ridge held up by light-colored, massive Coldwater Sandstone beds (upper Eocene, 37-40 million years). Behind that ridge is a vale underlain by softer Cozy Dell Shale (older upper Eocene). The steep face behind consists of still older upper Eocene, resistant, massive cliff-making Matilija Sandstone layers, and the higher, less precipitous and less cliffy slopes are underlain by beds of shale and sandstone belonging to the Juncal Formation (middle Eocene). The unusual aspect of this succession is that these beds dip *north*. They are upside down, being part of the Matilija overturn, a striking feature of this part of the Topatopa Mountain front. Farther west in vicinity of White Ledge Peak, at about 8:45 o'clock, in Santa Ynez Mountains, these same massive sandstone beds are steeply but normally inclined southward. The Matilija overturn dies out near the mouth of Matilija Creek, which has cut the prominent canyon faintly visible at about 9:15 o'clock. This canyon is the arbitrary line of separation between Topatopa and Santa Ynez mountains, which are actually a continuous geological feature. Don't feel sorry for Santa Ynez Mountains; they have their own overturn farther west near Montecito.

The westernmost part of Ojai Valley drains directly into the Ventura River, but the eastern part is drained southwestward by San Antonio Creek, a downstream tributary of Ventura River. Formerly, all the valley drained westward, but that was before San Antonio Creek worked headward and captured much of the drainage. Part of the ancient channel of the old westward

Ojai Valley   Sespe Fm.   Coldwater Ss.   Matilija Overturn   Cozy Dell Sh.   Matilija Ss.   Juncal Fm.

Photo D-5.   Looking west along Matilija overturn in Nordhoff Ridge behind Ojai Valley. Beds dipping right (north) are overturned. (Spence air photo E-13901, 12/6/50).

drainage, Long Valley, is traversed and described in Segment E.

O-13   Proceeding downgrade, roadcuts afford exposures of red Sespe sandstones and mudstones almost to the bottom. The seeming change in inclination of these beds from cut to cut is more a function of differences in cut orientation than any change in attitude of bedding. Near bottom of the grade, beyond marker 20^{39} and opposite a house on the left, exposures of massive, olive-brown sandstone begin. These are Vaqueros (lower Miocene, 20-25 million years) beds of marine origin which overlie the land-laid Sespe, and in places they contain fragments of oyster shells. Turnouts are narrow here, so if you wish to explore for fossils park with caution, on the right near 20^{39} or a little beyond on the left. The fossiliferous beds tend to be grayish and more resistant, and one of the better layers is just short of 20^{32}.

O-14   The course to Ojai heads nearly due west from the bottom of Dennison Grade. Stone walls along the highway reflect the bouldery nature of the coarse alluvial deposits flooring Ojai Valley. Stones are largely from Eocene formations. Black (Lion) Mountain is prominent on the south skyline, and Topatopa Mountain front is to the north, featuring Nordhoff Ridge at 1-2 o'clock with overturned, north-dipping, massive Matilija sandstones in its face. At about 11:50 o'clock on the far skyline is White Ledge Peak in Santa Ynez Mountains. In about a mile, at Gorham Road, light-colored Coldwater sandstones are prominent low on the face of the mountains to the north. Right at the mountain base you may be able to make out some red Sespe beds. Near marker 18^{59}, just about where heavy habitation begins, the west end of Black (Lion) Mountain is directly south at 9 o'clock. Sulphur Mountain appears as the high, tree-dotted ridge behind Black Mountain.

O-15   After negotiating the central part of Ojai, Highway 150 takes a more southwesterly course toward junction with Highway 33 and the end of this segment. This orientation provides a clearer view of Sulphur Mountain but of little else of geological interest. From the 150-33 highways junction, one can follow Segment E southward to Ventura, or turn right on Highway 33 and follow Segment F to Cuyama Valley, a journey rich in geological phenomena.

Segment D— Inbound Descriptions

(The corresponding outbound material should be read first.)

I-16   For travelers from Ojai to Santa Paula (inbound), this segment starts near the southwest corner of Ojai at the stoplighted separation of highways 33 and 150. Follow 150 eastward into and through Ojai and note an odometer reading at the start.

I-15   A half-mile beyond the 33-150 junction, past the road to Ojai Valley Inn, Ojai Ford, and California Oaks Realtors, inbound travelers negotiate a curve into a more northeasterly course and then may see, lighting and visibility being favorable, a gracefully curving outcrop pattern of massive sandstone beds near the high skyline at 10:30 o'clock. These beds are turning over into a reverse dip as they become part of the Matilija overturn. In morning light, shadows emphasize this gracefully curving pattern so it catches your attention. It is harder to see at other times of day.

I-14   Going east out of Ojai, Nordhoff Ridge, composed of north-dipping, overturned Eocene beds, is impressive to the north, and Sulphur and Black mountains lie to the south. Ledges of whitish sandstone (upper Eocene, Coldwater) near the base of Nordhoff Ridge dip north and are overturned to lie upon Sespe (Oligocene) red beds, glimpses of which can be caught in places at the very base of the slope. The view ahead is dominated by Topatopa Bluff on the skyline rather than White Ledge Peak.

I-13   Travelers ascending Dennison Grade make a switchback at 20²⁴, and the fossiliferous Vaqueros exposures are near the point of the curve beyond, a wee bit short of marker 20³². Sespe beds, largely red, are seen the rest of the way up Dennison Grade, which climbs three hundred and seventy-five feet.

I-12   Ascending Dennison Grade, inbound, this turnout with stone wall comes at 21¹⁷.

I-11   Inbound travelers come to Dennison Park just beyond the crest of Dennison Grade.

I-10   After crossing Lion Creek, south of Lion Mountain dome, the route for inbound travelers turns east and continues up the gently sloping floor of Upper Ojai Valley. Views of Topatopa Bluff on the north skyline, initially at 11:45 o'clock and ultimately at 10 o'clock at the far end of the valley approaching Summit, are good.

I-9   Headed east one comes to Sulphur Mountain Road a little beyond marker 24⁰¹.

I-8   Inbound travelers headed for Santa Paula have already traversed several miles of the wide, gently sloping floor of Upper Ojai Valley. Their views of Sulphur Mountain to the south and of Topatopa Mountains to the north and especially of Topatopa Bluff, featuring near-horizontal cliffs of massive Eocene sandstone (Photo D-4), are far superior to outbound views.

I-7   Descending from Summit, inbound, Ojai oil field remains are seen to the left from 25⁹³ to 26⁰². The first brea deposits are near 26¹² and extend to 26⁵⁰, being par-

ticularly good opposite Koenigstein Road. This descent is into the drainage of Sisar Creek, now a tributary of Santa Paula Creek. As explained in the O-8 out-bound section, downcutting by Sisar Creek below the level of Upper Ojai Valley was caused by its capture and diversion eastward into Santa Paula Creek. Formerly, Sisar Creek was tributary to the Ventura River, and it flowed westward through Upper Ojai Valley by way of the ill-fated east fork of the old Ventura River.

I-6   Starting at marker 26⁹⁰, travelers descending Sisar Creek get a better look at Silverthread oil operations which produce from fractured Miocene and Eocene sedimentary beds along San Cayetano fault zone. Approaching the junction of Sisar and Santa Paula creeks, beyond 28²⁸, inbound travelers see the west end of Santa Paula Ridge and can discern the topographic break between steep slopes above and gentler slopes below, marking the trace of San Cayetano thrust.

I-5   Inbound travelers cross Sisar Creek bridge at 28⁴⁵ and then the two Santa Paula Creek bridges. They get only an oblique view of the highly deformed Monterey beds in the cliff to the right in negotiating the bridges. They see some cemented, bouldery stream gravels (Quaternary) in a bluff just across Santa Paula Creek almost directly ahead beyond the second Santa Paula Creek bridge. The projecting knob of travertine comes about one hundred yards beyond the last bridge, just after the orange—black sharp-turn sign. In another one hundred yards is the hydrogen sulphide smell, and then come the strongly deformed shale beds (upper Miocene, Santa Margarita). Miocene exposures end at 29⁰⁰, after which the route heads nearly due south. To the left is the high bluff of Quaternary fan deposits.

I-4   Travelers headed south see Steckel Park and terraces with citrus orchards but not the other features.

I-3   Those traveling south come to this turnout (on the left) beyond 30^{89}, nearly a mile south of the entrance to Steckel Park. Coming from Steckel Park they have a good view of orchard-covered terraces on both sides of Santa Paula Creek.

I-2   Inbound travelers have a good view of South Mountain at about 11 o'clock, the center of a large, productive oil operation. For more information on the South Mountain area, see descriptions in Segment C. As inbound travelers enter Santa Paula, evidences of slumps and slides westward along the north slope of South Mountain ridge are impressive. Not all the flat benches on those slopes need be the product of slumps, as some may be remnants of earlier stages of normal landscape development. Coming into Santa Paula at and south of Royal Oaks Avenue, on the far (east) side of Santa Paula Creek, are bare bluffs in soft, south-dipping Plio-Pleistocene beds.

I-1   This segment terminates inbound at the intersection of Highway 150 with Santa Paula Freeway (Highway 126).

Segment **E**

Ventura to Ojai, 13.5 Miles

O-1   This short segment extends directly north across the structural grain of the hills between Ventura and Ojai, a route yielding maximum geological diversity per mile of travel. It starts from the southwest corner of Ventura, at interchange of highways 33 and 101, and follows 33 up Ventura River. Note odometer reading upon leaving the interchange.

(Inbound travelers see p. 83.)

O-2   Upon emerging from the interchange, near "Main Street Undercrossing," at 9 o'clock across Ventura River is a wide, smooth surface where stream and sea terraces merge (Photo E-1). In a few tenths of a mile is "Stanley Avenue Exit, 1 Mile." Directly ahead across the river is a terrace about seventy-five feet high, and a smaller remnant of another terrace lies fifty feet lower (Photo E-1). The upper terrace remains in view to "Stanley Avenue, Right Lane," where it makes an even profile from 9 to 11 o'clock, and opposite "Ojai 11, etc." an intermediate terrace appears about thirty feet lower. These surfaces were cut by Ventura River when it graded wide valley floors at higher levels. Were the present river to start cutting down rapidly, the present flat valley floor would become such a terrace.

Remnants of stream terraces extend up Ventura River to Ojai Valley, and we traverse a good example of a still higher terrace at Oak View, 8.5 miles ahead. Southward the old abandoned valley levels merge into marine terraces cut by ocean waves and currents when the sea stood higher against the continental edge.

The steep hillslopes east of lowermost Ventura River are underlain by steeply dipping, soft Pleistocene and Pliocene beds, but one would hardly surmise that by inspection from Highway 33.

O-3   At Stanley Avenue and beyond, operations of Ventura oil field (Photo E-2) become apparent on the river flat and on the skyline at 10 o'clock. Facilities become more numerous on both sides as we travel northward. The first wells are on the south flank of Ventura anticline, the principal structure of the field.

Just beyond Stanley Avenue, in the hill face to the east at 3 o'clock, is a large gray scar which marks the site of extensive excavations into the Mudpit Member of the Pico Formation (Pliocene, 5-8 million years). Initially, this fine-grained sediment was used principally to make drilling mud designed to float drill cuttings upward and to help contain gas and fluids under high pressure in deep oil wells. Recently the material has also been used to make lightweight pellets through heating in kilns.

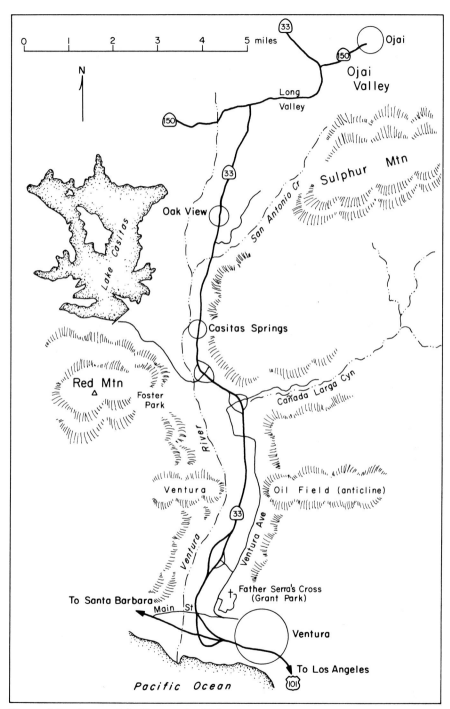

Figure E-1. Segment E, Ventura to Ojai.

Rincon Mtn.—
Fluvial-Marine Terrace—
Santa Ynez Mtns.
Pierpont Bay—
River Terraces
Ventura Oil Field—
Red Mtn. Dome
Abandoned
Sea Cliff

Photo E-1.   View west-northwestward across Ventura and Ventura River valley. (Spence air photo E-6197, 8/10/35).

O-4   Beyond Stanley Avenue, watch river bluffs to the west and soon you will see bedding planes inclined 25°-35° southward. At "Shell Road, Right Lane" (center-divider), bluffs and roadcuts in the hill base at 3 o'clock show beds still dipping south, but more gently. In another 0.1 mile, at "Shell Road Exit," beds in bluffs to both east (3:30 o'clock) and west (9 to 10:30 o'clock) dip gently *north.* Beyond "North Ventura Overpass," another 0.6 mile, beds in bluffs to the west dip even more clearly north. We have crossed the crest of the anticline and are now on its north limb.

This structure was recognized at the turn of the century by Ralph B. Lloyd, a Ventura County resident who had received some geological training at University of California, Berkeley. He knew that oil and gas accumulates in anticlines, and it was through his faith, perseverance, and unremitting efforts that a successful commercial oil well was finally drilled on the structure in 1918. Ventura has been one of the more productive of California oil fields, standing fourth in the State with a cumulative production near eight hundred million barrels; Wilmington tops the list. Deeper drilling, discovery of new productive zones, improved techniques of recovery, and extension of the field westward, have all contributed to long life and productivity in this field.

O-5   Any good anticline deserves a companion, which had better be a syncline, unless there is some extenuating structural complication. The north-side companion of Ventura anticline is a large syncline extending up the valley of Cañada Larga east of Cañada Larga Road overpass. Unfortunately, you can't see this structure from the freeway, although you get a good view up Cañada Larga from the overpass.

O-6   Beyond "Cañada Larga Road, Right Lane" (center-divider), on the left skyline, at 10-11 o'clock, the tree-dotted crest of

Pitas Pt.   Ventura Oil Field   Punta Gorda   Rincon Pt.   Trace of Red Mtn. Thrust   Red Mtn. Dome   Cañada Larga

Photo E-2.   View westward across lower Ventura River valley. (Spence air photo B-1395, 1/2/33).

Red Mountain (Photo E-2) is in view for the next two miles. Geologically, Red Mountain is a structural dome (a short, stubby anticline) with a bowed-up axis plunging outward at opposite ends. This structure is bounded at its south edge by Red Mountain thrust fault. If light is good, you may be able to see red rocks on the upper slopes. Low on the south flank of the dome are red soils in an orchard just across Ventura River at 9 o'clock, opposite "Casitas Vista Road, Right Lane" (center-divider). Owing to doming, faulting, and considerable erosion, uplifted red Sespe beds (Oligocene) are exposed over a large part of this dome.

O-7   The valley narrows where the free-way ends, as we pass from softer Pliocene rocks into older, more resistant Miocene and Oligocene formations. In 0.2 mile, a roadcut on the right exposes light-colored, thinly bedded Monterey shales (Miocene). These beds are separated from the older Sespe in Red Mountain by Red Mountain thrust (Photo E-2), which lies a little west on a course curving north around the east nose of Red Mountain dome. Ventura River terraces appear to be arched here suggesting the possibility that Red Mountain thrust and dome have been active in relatively recent times.

O-8   About half a mile beyond the freeway end, just after passing an electrical substation (left), the settlement of Casitas Springs is approached. Some steep bluffs on the high skyline directly ahead are worth attention. They remain visible on the right at 1 o'clock after making the turn into town. The severely distorted beds in these bluffs are part of the thin-bedded Miocene sequence, and this type of contortion is fairly typical of these weak, incompetent beds. Near the north edge of town, an excellent exposure of northward-dipping, darker Miocene shale beds is seen at the viewers' level in bluffs across Ventura River at 9 o'clock.

O-9   About one mile after leaving Casitas Springs, the bridge across San Antonio Creek is approached, and a little before crossing, beyond marker 7^{50} and just right of the highway, is an isolated knob of Miocene rock with a stately older house (pink of color in 1977) on top. The bedding in these rocks is particularly good; look sharply right to see it in passing. San Antonio Creek is a major east-side tributary of Ventura River and carries much of the drainage from Ojai Valley. It is a larger stream than formerly, because it has captured much of the Ojai Valley drainage that earlier flowed west directly into Ventura River. Farther along, we will traverse an interesting by-product of this diversion.

O-10   Beyond San Antonio Creek, we pass Rancho Arnaz (apples and cider in season) and ascend a short grade that climbs two hundred feet to Oak View. Roadcuts, largely on the left (west), afford good exposures of deformed, light-colored Miocene beds, largely thinly layered shales. In a few tenths of a mile, Creek Road takes off right to follow up San Antonio Creek to Camp Comfort (a county park) and eventually to Ojai by a direct, pleasant, and

lightly used route. Miocene beds continue to appear in roadcuts until near the top of the grade, where the last two or three cuts are in bouldery stream gravels that mantle the terrace upon which Oak View sits. The Oak View surface is one of the larger and better preserved terrace remnants of the Ventura River system. Although not easily perceived, the terrace actually slopes about 3° upstream, which is the reverse of its original inclination. It has been tilted north by recent deformation.

O-11   Shortly after leaving Oak View northbound is the stoplight at junction of highways 33 and 150. The latter comes in from the west, having traversed the Casitas Pass route from Carpinteria and skirted the shores of Casitas Lake. On this route one sees red rocks of the Sespe, the Sespe, and more Sespe, but it's a scenic drive across two divides and through newly planted avocado orchards.

O-12   Beginning at Tico Road, 0.2 mile around the curve eastward from the 150-33 junction, we enter an interesting bit of landscape. Our route is along the south side of a 0.25-0.5 mile wide, smooth-floored trough, Long Valley by name (Photo E-3), bounded on the north by a prominent ridge, Krotona Hill. The floor slopes gently westward, and the eastern part is an open, grassy flatland. The railroad that once ran to Ojai followed this trough as the easiest means of access. This is an abandoned stream course through which much of the drainage from Ojai Valley once passed to Ventura River. It was left high and dry, perhaps one or two hundred thousand years ago (a guess), when San Antonio Creek working headward captured much of the Ojai Valley drainage. We travel along the south edge of this abandoned valley for more than a mile. Upon emerging from Long Valley and turning north, the abandoned railroad embankment is just left of the highway and Nordhoff Ridge in Topatopa Mountains is directly ahead on the skyline.

Black Mtn.   Dennison Grade   High River Terrace   Long Valley   Hwy. 150   Ojai   Matilija Overturn   Overturned Coldwater Ss.

Photo E-3. Looking west across Ojai Valley. (Spence air photo E-13671, 2/12/50).

O-13 Northbound travelers approaching Ojai see the western end of Sulphur Mountain as a tree-dotted ridge on the right skyline. It incloses Ojai Valley on the south and is basically an anticlinal structure steeply asymmetrical to the south. Sulphur Mountain is made up almost wholly of severely deformed Miocene sedimentary rocks, as better seen and described in more detail in Segment D, Santa Paula to Ojai.

O-14 This segment terminates at the southwest corner of Ojai. One can take segment F north along Highway 33 to Cuyama Valley (Ozena) or stay on Highway 150 and follow Segment D in reverse to Santa Paula.

Segment E— Inbound Descriptions

(The corresponding outbound material should be read first.)

I-14 Travelers headed for Ventura from Ojai start this segment at the southwest edge of town where highways 33 and 150 join. Note odometer reading at this junction.

I-13 Upon leaving Ojai southbound, views of Sulphur Mountain are on the left skyline and of the Santa Ynez Range on the right skyline. Note odometer reading at the junction of highways 33 and 150 at the southwest edge of Ojai.

I-12   Travelers headed for Ventura enter this abandoned valley about one hundred yards beyond marker 16^{00}. The view westward down the valley is better than the view eastbound. Also seen, in favorable weather, is the crest and south face of the Santa Ynez Mountains on the high skyline at 12:30-1:30 o'clock, featuring massive sandstone beds (Eocene), especially in dip slopes on the upper part of White Ledge Peak at about 12:30 o'clock.

I-11   Southbound travelers wishing to go to Santa Barbara may elect to turn onto Highway 150 which passes north of Rincon Mountain while Highway 101 passes south of it. The 150 route saves considerable distance but not so much time because of its up and down, winding course.

I-10   Approaching Oak View, about a mile south of the stoplight at the highways 33-150 separation, at marker 9^{50} (Highway 33 datum), a look at the Ventura River floodplain, nearly one hundred feet below, is obtained down a gully locally known as Devil's Gulch. Steep dip slopes in shales (Miocene) are seen in the gulch. Leaving Oak View southbound, stream gravels on Oak View terrace are exposed in the first roadcuts, but they shortly give way to underlying Miocene shales dipping 45° to 50°, which are seen all the way downgrade to Rancho Arnaz with its red barn and apples.

I-9   Southbound travelers have a particularly good view of the little knob of well-bedded Miocene rocks south of San Antonio Creek after passing Rancho Arnaz and crossing the bridge.

I-8   Southbound, the high bluff face with contorted Miocene shales is on the left skyline at 8:30-9 o'clock passing through Casitas Springs, and the eye-level exposures to the west are at 3 o'clock.

I-7   Inbound travelers have already seen much Miocene rock, so this exposure will not thrill them. They are now down on the level of Ventura River floodplain.

I-6   Those traveling south need to look back over their right shoulder to about 4 o'clock approaching Cañada Larga Road to see the outline of Red Mountain dome (Photo E-2) on the skyline. They have already seen craggy exposures of steeply dipping, massive red Sespe beds to the west across Ventura River upon entering the freeway.

I-5   Southbound travelers get an easier view of the Cañada Larga country crossing Cañada Larga Road, but even they cannot see the attitude of beds defining the syncline.

I-4   After passing Cañada Larga Road, southbound travelers begin to see activities attending the Ventura oil field, including a large petrochemical plant on the right near 4^{00}. Beyond, by watching bluffs on both sides, they see north dips in Pliocene beds which gradually become gentler and eventually give way to south dips at "Stanley Avenue, 1 Mile" after crossing the anticlinal axis between "North Ventura Overpass" and "Shell Road Exit."

I-3   Inbounders have seen the main part of Ventura oil field (Photo E-2) and crossed the anticlinal axis. At "Stanley Avenue, Left Lane" (center-divider), large excavations in the Mudpit Member of Pico Formation are visible on the valley wall to the east at 10 o'clock. Under favorable lighting one should be able to make out the 30° southward dip of beds exposed there. If the day is clear, views should be good out over Santa Barbara Channel to Santa Cruz (right) and Anacapa (left) islands.

I-2   Southbound travelers see these terrace relationships approaching Ventura beyond Stanley Avenue exit.

I-1   This segment terminates inbound at the junction with Highway 101.

Segment **F**

Ojai to Ozena (Cuyama Valley), 38 Miles

O-1 This segment follows Highway 33 north from intersection with Highway 150 at the southwest corner of Ojai. Locally known as the Maricopa Road and leading to that town in San Joaquin Valley, this route crosses rugged mountainous terrain in the western Transverse Ranges essentially at right angles to the structural and topographic grain (Photo F-1). This makes for interesting scenery and provides opportunity to view a variety of geological features. Although the road winds up hill and down dale, it is well paved and presents no problems, except for occasional winter snows. It climbs to 5,084 feet in crossing Pine Mountain ridge, skirts the condor refuge, and is particularly attractive in spring when the native lilac (Ceanothus) blooms within chaparral on hillsides, or in fall when trees along stream courses turn color. This is not a trip to be made in a hurry. Do it leisurely and enjoy the turnouts, picnic spots, and campgrounds. Record an odometer reading at the 33-150 junction. Highway 33 is well furbished with roadside mileage markers (Figure 2-1). On a two-lane, back-country road they are easy to see, and we will use them extensively.

Among features seen is a sequence of Eocene (40-50 million years), marine, sedimentary rocks, roughly 12,000 feet thick, which is divided into four units; Coldwater, Cozy Dell, Matilija, and Juncal (youngest to oldest). We see them all. The first three names are from the local area, and Juncal comes from upper Santa Ynez River, just eighteen miles west. Geologists find this sequence interesting for the sedimentary features displayed. Many of the strata are thought to have been laid down by huge gravity flows of turbid, muddy waters (turbidity currents) capable of carrying large quantities of material of abnormally coarse grain, long distances into deep water. Such flows are believed active on the present-day sea floor. Their deposits are *turbidites*, a full-value 75-cent term, and *turbidites* display a variety of characteristics distinguishing them from sedimentary layers deposited by water currents or from suspension.

(Inbound travelers see p. 100.)

O-2 Ojai Valley (Photo E-3) from which this trip starts, northbound, is a structurally depressed area partly filled with and extensively mantled by bouldery stream deposits swept down from high mountains to the north. It is inclosed on the south by oak tree-dotted Sulphur Mountain and drained by branches of Ventura River. We ascend one of its tributaries, North Fork of Matilija Creek, for many miles. Entrance

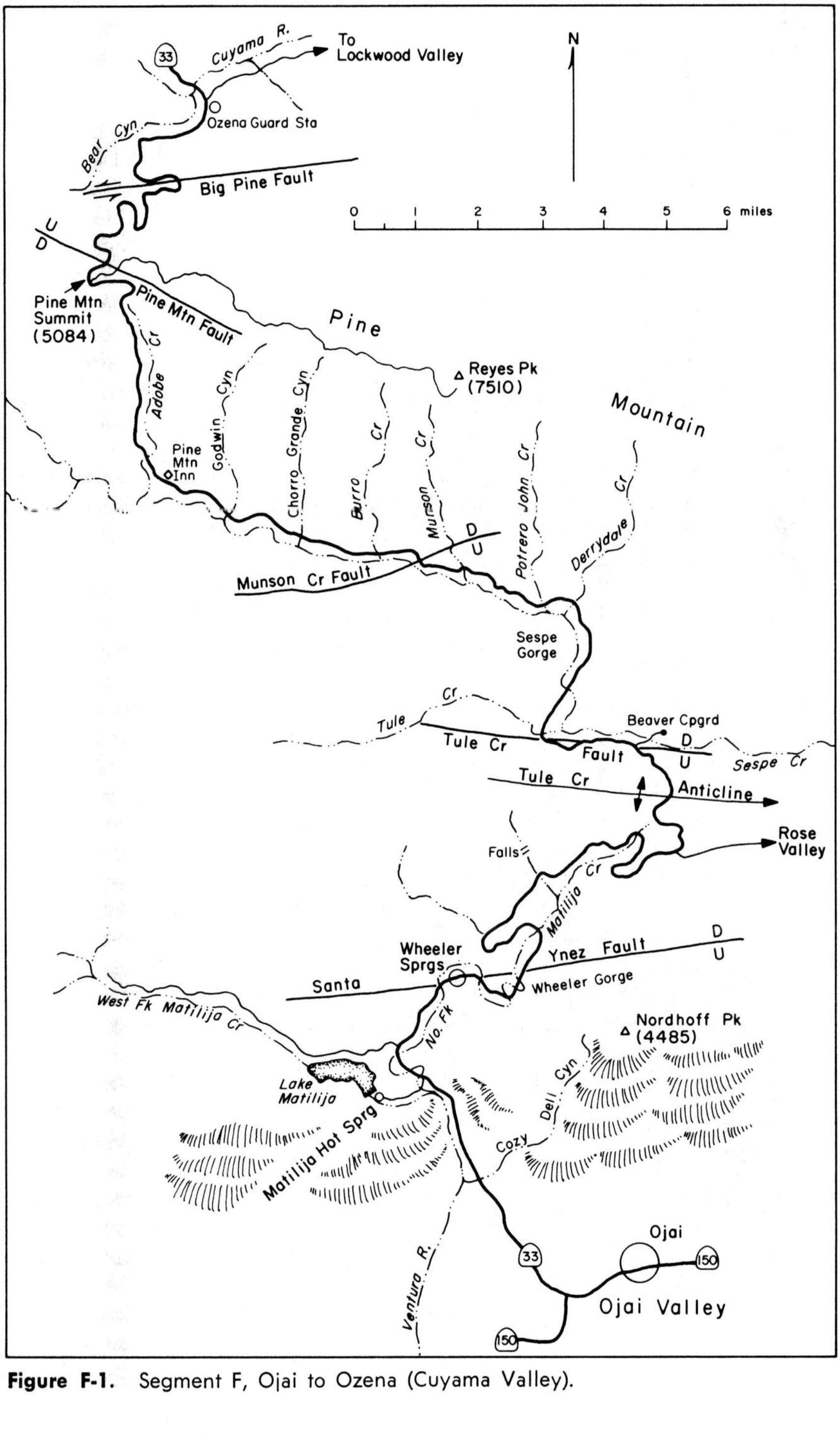

Figure F-1. Segment F, Ojai to Ozena (Cuyama Valley).

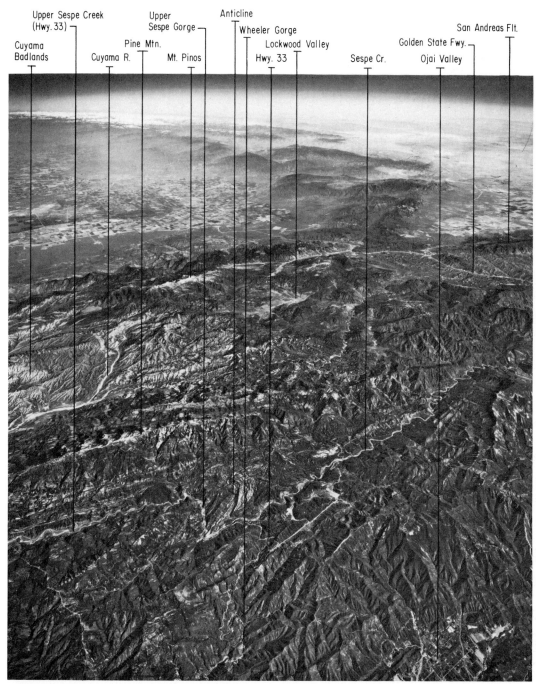

Photo F-1. High-altitude, low-oblique photo of Transverse Range country of interior Ventura County. (U.S. Air Force photo taken for U.S. Geological Survey, 041-L-084).

to Matilija Creek canyon is usually visible at about 11:45 o'clock from the first boulevard stop coming out of Ojai.

Upon leaving the 33-150 intersection, Santa Ynez Mountains and White Ledge Peak are directly ahead on the high skyline. In about 0.6 mile, the highway curves to a more northerly course, and Nordhoff Ridge, culminating in Nordhoff Peak (4,485 ft.), of Topatopa Mountains comes into view on the right from 12:30 to 1 o'clock. The town of Ojai was formerly named Nordhoff.

The first three miles are across bouldery alluvial deposits of the type exposed in roadcuts along Highway 33. Directly ahead, in the steep face of the mountains is the famed Matilija overturn (Photo D 5), so called because sedimentary beds have been tilted through the vertical into a steep northward dip, thereby becoming overturned. Thus, older beds lie on top of younger strata, just reverse of the relationship in which they were deposited. Approaching the mountain front, low hills east of the highway are underlain by our old friend the Sespe red beds (Oligocene, thirty million years). A capping of much younger, bouldery stream gravels has shed so much debris down the slopes that the bedrock is largely obscured. The first bridge, at mileage marker 13⁷³, spans Cozy Dell Creek.

O-3   The first bedrock exposed in a roadcut since leaving Ojai is on the right about two hundred feet beyond Cozy Dell Creek bridge. This brown, relatively thinly bedded, fine sandstone (Coldwater) dips north, which means it is upside down. The marker beyond the cut is 13⁹⁵, and just a little farther, in the vicinity of marker 14¹⁰, more massive layers of Coldwater Sandstone (upper Eocene, forty million years) crop out on the right as the road encircles a point. The strata seen for the next mile dip south, but then we get back into north-dipping, overturned beds. The coarse-grain and cross-lamination of this massive sandstone indicate shallow-water, near-shore deposition. The Sespe, normally lying stratigraphically next above the Coldwater, is a land-laid deposit, and from that you could properly infer that the Coldwater probably reflects a time of generally shallowing seas. Ultimately the sea vacated the land to permit accumulation of Sespe red beds. It is characteristic of many natural processes, moving with a certain trend, not to do so as a steady irreversible progression. Just like the stock market, a changing sea level experiences minor ups and downs even though the general trend may be in one direction. As a result, the uppermost Coldwater Sandstone includes intercalations of land-laid or near-shore lagoonal red beds, formed when the Coldwater seas were temporarily withdrawn.

Exposures of the Coldwater continue almost to the fruit-packing shed of Friends Ranches, at 14⁵⁹. However, a stop in one of the turnouts left of the road before that, near marker 14⁴⁶, is worthwhile. This location is at the top of a thick sequence of fine, red Coldwater sandstone and mudstone beds centered on marker 14³⁶. In the roadcut opposite 14⁴⁶, where a small gully enters a drain, are some resistant grayish beds within the brown shale-sandstone sequence. These gray beds contain abundant fragments of thick oyster shells. Don't expect to collect a whole oyster shell—they have all been broken by the pounding of a heavy surf in the old Eocene seas—but you can see something of the thickness and internal layering of the shell fragments.

O-4   North of the fruit packing shed, roadcuts are in the Cozy Dell Shale, a marine unit (Eocene), normally stratigraphically underlying the Coldwater. An increase in shale within the lower Coldwater approaching the packing shed heralded the transition to the Cozy Dell. The Cozy Dell itself contains occasional sandstone layers and clusters of sandstone beds, especially near its top and bottom where it is transitional into formations composed principally of sandstone. The Cozy Dell is regarded as having accumulated in deeper water, under quieter conditions, and farther from shore, than the Coldwater. The shoreline in Cozy Dell time was presumably a considerable distance to the north and east.

O-5   Approaching the bridge and turn-off (left) to Matilija Hot Springs, roughly 4.3 miles out, sandstone beds become thicker and more frequent, marking the transition from Cozy Dell Shale to the underlying Matilija Sandstone (Eocene). The contact is close to marker 15^{40}, but the Matilija is best seen ahead between the two bridges across North Fork of Matilija Creek. These bridges, incidentally, are the first of ten crossings of this stream to be made in the next nine miles. Huge road-cuts on the left, near 15^{63}, and a quarry wall across the stream, opposite 15^{75}, provide excellent exposures of thick, massive, coarse-to-fine-grained Matilija sandstones, some of which have a greenish cast. These sandstone layers represent a shallowing of the ocean compared to conditions during Cozy Dell time.

O-6   Beyond the second bridge, northbound, we are on the east side of Matilija Creek, and the increasing abundance of shale between thinner and fewer sandstone strata heralds a transition to the oldest Eocene formation seen on this trip, the Juncal. A northerly dip indicates that these beds are overturned. Within 0.2 mile, a third crossing of Matilija Creek at 16^{12}, returns us to its west bank, and within one hundred and fifty feet the road to Lake Matilija separates. The lake is a flood-control and water-conservation reservoir. Roadcuts beyond expose Juncal shale, mudstone, and siltstone with intercalated clusters of sandstone beds. Native lilac (Ceanothus) is a major component of the dense chaparral on neighboring hillsides, and in the spring these slopes have a delicate blue-

to-purple hue. Sycamores and oaks are abundant along the stream.

O-7   Shortly, at 17^{41}, Matilija Creek is crossed for the fourth time, and Wheeler Springs is reached a little beyond 17^{52}. Approaching this resort the highway bears east-northeast. On a parallel course to the left across the creek is one of the major faults of the western Transverse Ranges, the Santa Ynez. Deeply circulating groundwater that has been warmed and mineralized comes back to the surface along this fault in the form of springs that supply the warm sulphur-water swimming pool at Wheeler Springs. The fault is not easily discerned because it lies wholly within Juncal rocks. If the large sycamore trees at Wheeler Springs are in a defoliated state, you will be impressed with the abundant clusters of mistletoe infesting them.

O-8   After a fifth crossing of Matilija Creek, at 17^{81}, an Eocene-Cretaceous sedimentary contact is approached. If you care to make a close inspection, stop in a turn-out just beyond the large yellow/black "13 ft. 6 inch" sign at 17^{92}. The contact is ahead about opposite 18^{00}. The Cretaceous is mostly a black, fractured, angular-edged outcropping of fine-grained, hard rock, and the basal Eocene (Juncal) is a brownish and more heterogeneous assemblage of sandstone, siltstone, and shale layers. The contact is conformable here, although it may represent a significant time hiatus. In describing the broad curve beyond marker 18^{00}, the highway swings into the Cretaceous and then passes back into the Eocene just before entering the tunnel at 18^{24}. These strata dip steeply north, so they are overturned with the older Cretaceous lying structurally above the younger Eocene.

O-9   After negotiating the curving course of this first tunnel, northbound travelers follow essentially along the strike of a group of overturned, steeply dipping, massive sandstones in the Juncal Formation for

0.25 mile before reentering the Cretaceous as the road curves left approaching the sixth bridge (No. 52-69) across Matilija Creek. The double-walled roadcut just before that bridge is in typical, black, hard Cretaceous rock. This bridge marks the start of Wheeler Gorge, a narrow, winding defile. A stop is recommended for inspection of the gorge a little farther along, but small turnouts on either side just beyond this sixth bridge permit a stop here if desired. About one hundred and fifty yards upstream from the bridge, near the portal of the first of two upcoming tunnels, brown and gray rocks forming a projecting rib (Photo F-2) at about 11:45 o'clock consist of coarse sandstone and beautiful roundstone conglomerate (Cretaceous).

Roadcuts approaching the first of the two tunnels expose principally beds of well lithified, dark shale or mudstone with thin interlayerings of fine, light-colored sand displaying structures suggestive of turbidity-current action. Between the tunnels, the

Photo F-2. Looking north to south portal of double tunnel in Wheeler Gorge, Highway 33. Light-colored rock, center and left, is Cretaceous sandstone-conglomerate sequence.

stream is crossed for the seventh time and another crossing, the eighth, comes just beyond exit from the succeeding tunnel. About two hundred feet farther, on the right, is a small turnout in a nook shaded by a grove of aromatic California bay trees. A larger turnout is on the left another two hundred feet ahead, at 19⁰⁰. A stop in one or the other is urged. At the first one, crush one of the long, willow-like, shiny green bay leaves in your fingers and smell it.

With care for passing cars, walk back to the bridge past a weeping cliff on the left decorated with ferns and a light-brown coating of travertine. Stop before or near the north end of the bridge and study the rock face that rises steeply above the tunnel portal. This face displays a geological feature which you are quite capable of observing and appreciating. You are looking at the bottom of a steeply inclined sandstone layer which has been overturned so it dips north, toward you. The shale layer upon which this sandstone once rested has been stripped away by erosion. After a little study you should recognize a linear pattern of asymmetrical, elongate knobs, a foot or two in length and a few inches high, projecting from the exposed bedding surface of the sandstone. They define lines inclined about 10° downward to the right (Photo F-3).

These knobs are flute casts and are thought to have formed in the following way. Some time after the shale bed, now eroded away, was laid down and compacted to a firm condition, the sea floor was inundated by a powerful turbidity flow. Initially this current carved shallow, blunt-ended, elongate depressions known as flutes in the sea floor, but as its strength ebbed, deposition of sand filled the eroded flutes and built up the overlying bed. The flutes served as molds for the fillings of sand; hence the term *flute casts*. The alignment of the casts shows the linear course of the current, and their asymmetry, blunt end up-current, indicates the direction from

Photo F-3. Looking south to north portal of double tunnel, Wheeler Gorge. Linear streaking inclined to the right on rock face rising above tunnel is made by flute casts on bottom bedding plane of a massive Cretaceous sandstone layer.

which the flow came, in this instance the east. This is consistent with what is known about the location and configuration of the Cretaceous shoreline and sources for the sediment deposited here.

Walk to the tunnel portal, and on the right side observe that the gray sandstone contains small, angular fragments of black, shaly rock. This is called an intraformational conglomerate, or, if the fragments are mostly angular, it is an intraformational breccia, meaning that the fragments have been derived from the formation itself. This sandy bed with the black fragments is the layer with the flute casts on its bottom. The dark fragments were presumably derived from somewhere up-current through scouring of the underlying black

shale by the powerful turbidity current that made the flutes.

Continue on foot through the first tunnel for a view of the narrow winding gorge between tunnels. The narrow concrete curbing provides safe passage. Active scramblers can descend to the bottom of the gorge on the left (east) side of this in-between bridge. They will be rewarded by seeing some of the finest conglomerate any geological heart could wish. The pebble- and cobble-size stones are well rounded and composed of a wide variety of hard, resistant rocks, mostly fine- to coarse-grained igneous types, some metamorphic gneiss, a wide variety of quartzites, and fragments of quartz and cherty material. If the water is not high, one can work downstream through the gorge and regain the highway below the southern tunnel. It's a fun trip—rather short. Wheeler Gorge exists because the hard, resistant Cretaceous rocks can stand in near-vertical cliffs and because Matilija Creek has been able to cut only a narrow slot through them. The riparian (stream-side) vegetation includes considerable alder, and on the banks are some big-leaf maple that turns a nice golden-yellow in the fall.

O-10 Northbound, Wheeler Gorge Guard Station is passed (east side) a little beyond 19[10], and opposite 19[21], on the left, is the entrance to Wheeler Gorge Forest Service campground. You may have noted that Wheeler Gorge ended abruptly and that the valley beyond is much wider and more open. The reason for both is that we crossed the Santa Ynez fault at the north end of the gorge and passed from the relatively hard, tough, upper Cretaceous rocks into softer, brown Cozy Dell Shale. The fact that the Cretaceous and Cozy Dell are in contact along the fault means that all of the Matilija and Juncal formations, totaling many thousand feet of beds, have been cut out by relative upward movement of the block on the south, bringing up older beds on that side.

O-11   A quarter mile north of the Forest Service guard station, the channel of Bear Creek is crossed on a concrete bridge, at 19^{36}, and shortly thereafter Matilija Creek is crossed for the ninth time, at 19^{72}. The highway then ascends a west-side tributary with sycamore trees and then at 20^{79} makes a big switchback to the southwest before taking off northeasterly on a 3.6-mile winding traverse along the flank of the high ridge northwest of Matilija Creek. All you are going to see in roadcuts during this traverse are shales of the Cozy Dell with some interbedded sandstones. Watch for the cute little debris cones of small, fractured shale fragments that accumulate along the base of roadcuts ahead (Photo F-4).

In places, and especially at the upper end of the traverse, bedding inclination is parallel to the hillslope and to roadcuts, so exposures of bedding-plane surfaces are fairly common. Some of the bedding surfaces may appear shiny, being smooth enough to reflect light (Photo F-4), and others, as at

Photo F-4.   Exposed bedding-plane surfaces in thinly layered Eocene Cozy Dell Shale along Highway 33 in uppermost North Fork of Matilija Creek canyon, between mileage markers 23^{48} and 24^{00}.

21^{81}, display ripple marks. There's a large turnout on the left at marker 22^{27}, with drinking fountain, trash cans, and a little waterfall encrusted with travertine. The changing orientation (attitude) of bedding planes along the traverse shows that the Cozy Dell is deformed, but with exception of an open syncline two hundred feet beyond 23^{13}, you won't see folds within individual roadcuts.

In the last mile of the traverse, prominent sandstone layers crop out on hillslopes well above road level. There are Matilija-type sandstones inclined steeply to the southwest, parallel to the slope. Stripping away of overlying shale layers has exposed large areas of bedding-plane surface on the sandstones. When such exposed bedding-plane surfaces are notched by cross-cutting canyons or gullies, the remnant looks not unlike the bottom of an old-fashioned, tilted-up flat-iron; hence the term *flatirons* applied to such features. As you might suspect, if bedding planes within interlayered competent sandstones and incompetent shales are inclined parallel to a steep slope, landslides are likely to occur. Sure enough, some roadcuts near the northeast end of the traverse, as between markers 23^{42} and 23^{75}, expose masses of jumbled rock-slide debris. Between 23^{48} and 24^{00} bedding planes exposed in roadcuts are striking (Photo F-4). Eventually, the road switches back, crossing the head of Matilija Creek by means of a culvert for the tenth time, at 24^{17}.

O-12   Northbound, at 24^{83}, about 0.65 mile beyond the final crossing of Matilija Creek, a dirt road loops off to the right around a little rock knob. A vista point at the apex of the loop affords views of the valley of upper Matilija Creek, of the Matilija flatirons, and of the route just traversed. Time available, it's a good stop to make, and the dirt road comes back to the highway 0.1 mile ahead.

O-13   Back on the highway, outbound, Cozy Dell Shale continues to dominate roadcuts, albeit with more sandstone, because this is the basal phase of the formation transitional to the Matilija Sandstone. In places, dips are parallel to roadcuts, so some nice bedding-plane exposures are seen, for example beyond 25¹².

A little less than a mile from the turnout loop, we pass over a ridge and drop into Sespe Creek drainage. Just beyond, a secondary road takes off right to Rose Valley and Piedras Blancas (white rocks). Half a mile farther is a double-walled roadcut through a ridge exposing large concretions (cannonballs) in Cozy Dell Shale, and there we pass back into the Matilija Creek drainage. In roughly another half mile, just beyond 26⁸⁰, is a large turnout and vista point on the left affording distant views of Matilija Creek drainage, Santa Ynez Mountains, and, on clear days, of Santa Barbara Channel and the islands. Just beyond, we pass through a saddle and start downgrade into the valley of Sespe Creek.

Initial rock exposures, starting downgrade near marker 27⁰⁰, are in massive Matilija Sandstone beds dipping south, but in subsequent exposures the dip of these beds changes to north, for example, opposite the second turnout on the right and in the double-walled roadcut beyond 27⁴³. We are crossing the nose of Tule Creek anticline which here plunges east. At 27⁵⁴, the road reenters Cozy Dell Shale on the north limb of the fold, and we continue in Cozy Dell, with sandstone intercalations, to the bottom of the grade.

O-14   Going downgrade toward Sespe Creek, good views are seen of high, rugged Pine Mountain ridge on the distant skyline to the north and of the open Sespe Creek valley to the east (Photo F-1). A stop is recommended for a better look at details near grade bottom. Near 27⁷⁷, some unusually thin, regularly bedded shales of the Cozy Dell are seen in roadcuts on the left. Just a mile from the summit, the highway starts to swing from its northerly course into a more westerly trend, and two hundred

feet beyond marker 27⁸⁷, where the floor of Sespe Creek first comes into view ahead, is a small turnout on the right. It's a good stop to make.

Below is Beaver campground. The light-colored, locally pinkish, ridges just across Sespe Creek are Sespe sandstones and conglomerates. The Sespe is a land-laid deposit named from dark-red sandstone exposures at the mouth of Sespe Creek behind Fillmore, far downstream. The more brownish ridges behind are Coldwater Sandstone beds faulted into that position. On the north skyline is Pine Mountain ridge with bluffs of massive sandstone (Eocene, Matilija). Reyes Peak, the highest point, 7,510 feet, is out of sight to the west. Along the south base of this ridge is a major fault separating Eocene beds on the north from Miocene strata on the south. We will see aspects of this Pine Mountain fault farther along.

O-15   Back on the highway outbound, the dirt road to Beaver campground (USFS) takes off right at 28⁰⁷. The highway continues to curve and shortly is headed nearly due west up Sespe Creek. If you'd like to play geologist, stop in the turnout at 28⁹¹ or one of the other nearby turnouts. We are here in Eocene Cozy Dell Shale beds dipping northward, but only a short distance away across the creek are Oligocene Sespe beds dipping toward us. Clearly something is wrong. The Sespe beds, being younger, cannot normally pass beneath the Cozy Dell as their southward dip would seemingly require. Besides, a considerable thickness of strata, including parts of the Sespe, Coldwater, and Cozy Dell, known to exist elsewhere, are missing. There's just not enough room to turn the Sespe back up in a fold and accommodate all those missing strata. So, as geologists, we suspect a fault, a suspicion confirmed by relationships westward near Tule Creek. This is Tule Creek fault, and we travel close to it for nearly a mile. The actual relationship is more complex than outlined, but this simplified version illustrates a principle of geological analysis.

O-16   To Tule Creek, the highway remains in Eocene rocks, largely Coldwater sandstones and shales, including some red mudstones, between 28^{62} and 28^{77}, like those seen earlier entering Matilija Creek canyon. Rocks show considerable twisting and fracturing, reflecting proximity to Tule Creek fault. The road into Hartman Ranch turns off right at 28^{91}.

As the highway curves north approaching Tule Creek, we cross Tule Creek fault in the neighborhood of 29^{33}, but the fault is hard to see as it is wholly within Coldwater shales and sandstones. Approaching Tule Creek bridge, on the left at 29^{54}, one gets a quick view left up a small canyon showing a southward-dipping bedding-plane surface on a massive sandstone bed (Coldwater) exposed by the stripping of overlying shale.

O-17   Beyond Tule Creek bridge, outbound travelers head north toward Upper Sespe Gorge. Rocks on both sides are shales (mostly Cozy Dell) with frequent intercalations of sandstone. Ease of erosion in shale accounts for the openness of the valley. Within a mile, Sespe Creek is crossed, at 30^{52}, for the first and only time. There the mouth of Upper Sespe Gorge is visible at 12:30 o'clock, and it is entered in another 0.3 mile. Rocks making the gorge walls are involved in a steeply plunging anticline, the crest of which is indicated by oppositely dipping beds seen to the left a little before entering the gorge. The gorge itself lies on the northeast side of the anticinal nose (Photo F-5), but this is not easily realized from the highway.

O-18   Sespe Gorge, entered at about 31^{10}, is a narrow defile cut into steeply dipping beds of Matilija Sandstone. The lower part of its course parallels the strike of these beds and the left wall is a bedding-plane surface dipping steeply toward the stream. This rock face is favored by rock climbers

for testing of equipment, techniques, and skills. Near marker 31^{18}, just upstream from the stream-gauging station (platform, cable, and vertical cylindrical pipe), at a slightly lower level, is a display of small-scale cavernous weathering.

In the next few miles, we cross six streams tributary to Sespe Creek and ascend a seventh. They all drain south off the steep face of Pine Mountain ridge. Five are crossed by bridges, which we shall use as navigational checkpoints. The first bridge is over Derrydale Creek, at 31^{72}, just about where we leave Sespe Gorge. You get a quick glimpse of Pine Mountain ridge up Derrydale Creek. About two hundred feet beyond Derrydale on the right is a bedding-plane slide in massive Matilija Sandstone. Ample turnout space is available on the left for a stop to observe the bared bedding-plane surface and large angular blocks of broken sandstone.

O-19   For better than seven miles beyond Derrydale Creek, the highway runs westward up the generally widening valley of Sespe Creek. At first, sandstones are abundant, mostly Matilija or Matilija-like beds in the Cozy Dell, and the canyon walls are steep, close in, and ragged. Potrero John Creek is crossed at 32^{10}. Creek names are given on the horizontal guard rail of the bridge at the approach end. Sandstones continue abundant. North-facing slopes south of Sespe Creek sport scattered big cone spruce trees near 33^{00}, and cottonwoods are scattered along the stream. Shales become progressively more abundant, and the valley becomes more open in the vicinity of marker 33^{50}. Munson Creek is crossed at 33^{80}. Changes in attitude of beds along this traverse reflect large folds, hard to make out from traveling cars. A long roadcut in near-horizontal shales (Cozy Dell) is passed between 33^{95} and 34^{11}. Massive sandstones (Matilija) are exposed between 34^{40} and 34^{50}. The shearing and fracturing of these beds near 34^{42} reflects the crossing of Munson Creek fault.

Photo F-5. Plunging anticline in Eocene beds east of upper Sespe Gorge. Highway 33 along Sespe Creek just entering mouth of the gorge at lower left margin. (Spence air photo E-8085, 11/2/37).

Between 34^{50} and 34^{80} on the near right skyline, and occasionally seen ahead as the highway swings through curves, is a high hogback ridge underlain by Sespe sandstone and conglomerate beds, aided and abetted by massive gray-brown sandstone beds (Coldwater) cropping out lower on the face toward us. We see a lot of this ridge in the next few miles. At 35^{10} is a deep, double-walled roadcut and just beyond is the canyon of Burro Creek, crossed on a culvert and fill. A little farther on the left, opposite 35^{30}, is Ortega Ranch (house). Beyond it, the Sespe-Coldwater hogback is prominent on the near skyline at 3 o'clock.

By looking back over the left shoulder to 8 o'clock, beyond 35^{97}, one sees a spur in shale beds on the far side of Sespe Creek just above stream level. The face of this spur displays an unusual pattern of linear markings. One set reflects the steeply inclined sedimentary bedding; the other linear markings are little rills cut by erosion straight down the face of the spur. The two sets of linear marks intersect, producing the curious pattern.

O-20   Approaching and beyond Chorro Grande Creek, at 36^{13}, the massive Sespe-Coldwater bluff begins to dominate the near skyline ahead and on the right. These beds are dipping north, away from us, and they conformably overlie the Cozy Dell shale exposed in highway cuts. Gray-brown Coldwater Sandstone composes the lower part of the south-facing bluff, but it is abnormally thin. White, pink, and light-brown sandstone and conglomerate layers of the Sespe compose the upper part of the bluff. In places ahead, huge chunks of Sespe conglomerate have broken loose and fallen to road level.

Just beyond Chorro Grande Creek, deposits of coarse Quaternary stream gravels, containing large, well-rounded boulders, are exposed in roadcuts near 36^{18}. In another half-mile, watch for a small Forest Service sign fifty feet right of the highway. It identifies a trail into upper Chorro Grande Creek where considerable exploration for phosphate rock in the Santa Margarita Formation (late Miocene) has been carried out. Marker 36^{75} is a little beyond the trail head. This is an interesting hike of about three miles roundtrip, that carries you from the Cozy Dell, through and over the Sespe-Coldwater ridge into Miocene rocks, including a thin section of Vaqueros Sandstone (early Miocene), a thicker section of thinly bedded Monterey shales and sandstones (middle Miocene), and into a whitish Santa Margarita (late Miocene) siltstone, mudstone, and shale sequence. All Miocene formations contain fossil marine shells.

The roads and bulldozed pits seen on the hike are part of phosphate explorations made on behalf of the U.S. Gypsum Corporation which would like to mine this rock to supply about sixty-five percent of California's need for phosphatic fertilizers. The project is hotly contested by environmentalists because of possible ravages to the country and proximity to the condor refuge. Most phosphate fertilizer currently used in California is shipped from Idaho or Florida. The supply of phosphate available here would last an estimated forty-five years.

Beyond Chorro Grande trail head, the Sespe-Coldwater bluff dominates the near north skyline. Cavernous weathering is extensive in some parts of the bluff face. Highway cuts are in Cozy Dell Shale for the next 1.5 miles. Across the flat floor of Sespe Creek to the south, the lower hillslopes have a disheveled appearance suggestive of landsliding, which would be expected in view of the shaly nature of the rocks, their northward dip parallel to the relatively steep hillslope, and undercutting by Sespe Creek.

In a mile, Godwin Creek is crossed at 37^{52}, and directly ahead are bluffs of massive gray-brown sandstones (Coldwater). At 37^{76}, the Sespe bluff is prominent again ahead on the near skyline, and at 38^{10}, large, fallen fragments of Sespe conglomerate lie alongside the highway. At 38^{45} the highway is turning up into Adobe Creek, the seventh and last of the tributary canyons. In entering Adobe Creek, we pass through roadcuts in shales and thin-to-massive sandstones of the Coldwater, dipping relatively gently to the northeast. Some massive sandstones display cavernous weathering, and at 38^{57} the near skyline ridge ahead displays little knobs and pinnacles (called hoodoos) carved in sandstone. The buildings at Pine Mountain Inn (on right) are passed two hundred and fifty feet beyond marker 38^{81}, and bluffs of massive sandstone (Coldwater) with cavernous weathering flank the highway on both sides one hundred feet beyond 38^{93}. A concrete bridge at 39^{03} provides passage to the west side of Adobe Creek.

O-21 In ascending Adobe Creek, our course has shifted from west to nearly due north, and we are climbing toward Pine Mountain ridge which is to be crossed nearly four miles ahead. Conglomerate beds on the right, opposite 39^{12}, just beyond the crossing of Adobe Creek, are Sespe, and farther up the side valley to the right more thinly bedded Miocene deposits are visible. Sespe conglomerates again crop out on the left between 39⁴⁹ and 39⁵⁹, and beyond 39⁵⁵ Sespe red beds are exposed directly ahead on the hillside. Looking to the steep head of an amphitheater at 10 o'clock from 40¹¹ gives a view of Monterey beds (middle Miocene). A thin section of massive Vaqueros sandstones (early Miocene) is seen in the roadcut one hundred feet beyond 40¹¹, and one hundred feet beyond 40²⁰ a roadcut exposes Monterey shales. For the next mile roadcuts expose Monterey beds, largely shales, with various degrees of inclination. Some gentle, open folds (Photo F-6) are seen between 40⁶⁶ and 40⁷⁵, but more severe contortion is visible in other cuts. To the right at 1 o'clock from 40⁸³, part way up the canyon wall, the bluff of massive, light-colored sandstone is in the upper part of the Monterey. At 41¹², the canyon of Adobe Creek begins to widen, and the upper Monterey sandstones are again to the right. At 41¹⁷ these sandstones are exposed in hillslopes immediately to the right. Higher on the near skyline, at 1:30 o'clock, the whitish rocks are **Santa Margarita** (late Miocene).

Photo F-6. Shallow, open syncline in Monterey shale beds along Adobe Creek, Highway 33.

Ahead is an offshoot from Pine Mountain fault zone, Potrero Seco fault, which brings south-dipping Sespe rocks up on the north against the northeast-dipping Miocene rocks just traversed. The fault is crossed between markers 41⁵⁰ and 41⁵⁸, and the brownish ridge on the right beyond is underlain by Sespe. Shortly the highway describes a switchback, apexing at 41⁹⁰, and starts an oblique ascent of the face of Pine Mountain ridge. The two-walled roadcut at 42⁰⁰ is in Sespe conglomerate. An exposure of overturned (north-dipping) shale (Cozy Dell) is seen at 42¹⁸, but the remaining cuts to Pine Mountain Summit are in steep, south-dipping Sespe beds.

O-22   Approaching Pine Mountain Summit (5,084 ft.), near the top of the grade a dirt road turns eastward onto Pine Mountain ridge and to Reyes Peak. This is just before entering the deep, two-walled roadcut at the summit which exposes shale and sandstone beds (Cozy Dell). No Coldwater is recognized here between Sespe and Cozy Dell. Just beyond the deep cut is a small turnout on the left affording a first view into Cuyama Valley and the Cuyama Badlands. Other turnouts farther downgrade afford more comprehensive views, and stops in them will be recommended.

Downgrade on the north side of Pine Mountain Summit, between markers 42⁹⁴ and 43⁰⁰, are two high, steep exposures on the right. The first shows sandstone and shale beds dipping modestly southward, and the second shows principally shale beds in near-vertical attitude. This contrast reflects proximity to Pine Mountain fault which is crossed about two hundred feet ahead, beyond 43¹². Fault relations are more easily seen by inspecting the hillslope 3/4 mile to the west. The fault passes through the skyline saddle, and truncation of beds dipping north, especially a white sandstone, indicates the trace of the fault up the slope to the saddle. Rocks north of the fault are Matilija, and to the south is the Cozy Dell. The large coniferous trees on the north side of Pine Mountain ridge are big cone spruce.

O-23   Beyond Pine Mountain fault, the highway continues in beds of massive, light-colored sandstones (Matilija) with thick intercalations of brown shale that strongly resemble Cozy Dell. However, the rocks are all Matilija to 44^{29} where the route reenters Cozy Dell as it rounds a projecting point. Just beyond the point tip is a large, partly macadamized turnout on the left, opposite marker 44^{34}. This is a good place to stop for a comprehensive view of Cuyama Badlands and the encircling mountains (Photo F-7).

O-24   The basin seen from this turnout has been filled with many thousand feet of Miocene to Pleistocene coarse gravels, sands, and muds—all land-laid. These beds have been highly deformed by folding and faulting and deeply dissected by fluvial erosion to produce the terrain extending north and east from the broad, sandy floor of Cuyama River below. Intricate dissection, particularly within highly colored beds of the Caliente Formation (Miocene), has produced local badland areas as picturesque and as interesting, on a small scale, as much of Bryce Canyon or Cedar Breaks in Utah. On the far skyline to the north and extending east is the high, heavily timbered Mt. Pinos ridge composed

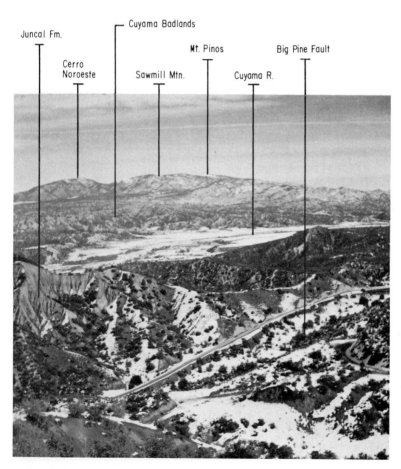

Juncal Fm.

Cerro Noroeste

Cuyama Badlands

Sawmill Mtn.

Mt. Pinos

Cuyama R.

Big Pine Fault

Photo F-7. Winter-time view north-northeast into Cuyama Basin from large turnout near mileage marker 44^{34} on Highway 33.

largely of older crystalline igneous and metamorphic rocks. The San Andreas fault lies behind that ridge, which extends from Cerro Noroeste (8,286 ft.) at its northwest end, through intermediate Sawmill Mountain (8,800 ft.), to Mt. Pinos (8,831 ft.) near its southeast end, the highest point in Ventura County.

O-25 Rock exposed in the roadcut opposite the large turnout is Cozy Dell Shale, and we continue in this formation to 44^{61} where the Matilija Sandstone takes over again. The highway describes a long, hairpin-like loop to the south in order to negotiate a canyon, all in sandstones and shales of the Matilija. Small-scale faulting in this section is not important enough to warrant a stop for inspection. Cozy Dell is entered again at 45^{04}, and we remain in that unit until crossing into the Juncal Formation at the Big Pine fault in the next valley ahead. Just beyond a curve around a point, starting near 45^{27}, is a small turnout on the left opposite marker 45^{37}, that affords an excellent view of the Big Pine fault trace. If you miss that turnout, two larger ones follow quickly on the left which are nearly as good, the first at 45^{49}.

O-26 From the little turnout you get views of Cuyama Badlands and the surrounding terrain, but the principal focus of interest is the canyon below. The highway makes a long loop east and a traverse back west on its north side opposite our view point. This canyon is unusual in its east-west orientation. Most canyons drain northward into Cuyama Valley. Our view point is in Cozy Dell and rocks exposed along the road on the north wall of the canyon are Juncal, the first time we have seen this formation since leaving it away back below Wheeler Gorge, south of Santa Ynez fault. The orientation of the canyon and the unorthodox juxtaposition of Cozy Dell and Juncal rocks should tell you that you are looking at the trace of a major fault. This, the Big Pine fault, extends for many

miles west-southwest and east-northeast. It is argued by some geologists that the course of Bear Canyon, which the highway descends when it once again heads northward, is offset 0.5 mile laterally here along the Big Pine fault. From other evidence, geologists have also argued for a total of nine to twelve miles of left-lateral displacement on Big Pine fault. The final word on this matter is not yet in, but you are looking down upon a prominent and anomalous topographic feature along a major fault trace.

O-27 Upon leaving the small turnout headed downgrade, the Big Pine fault is crossed at the northeast corner of the large horseshoe curve just about at marker 46^{00}, and then the north side of the fault canyon is traversed in Juncal Formation for roughly half a mile to marker 46^{57}. Upon Leaving the fault canyon we follow a winding route, first north, then east, and again north along Bear Canyon to the flat floor of Cuyama Valley. Roadcut exposures are all in Juncal mudstones, shales, and sandstones. Resistant sandstone layers in the generally south-dipping beds make ribs and bluffs on adjoining steep hillsides.

Shortly after reaching the valley floor, Ozena Ranger Station is passed east of the highway, and in 0.3 mile comes intersection with the Lockwood Road and the end of Segment F. The roadcut between the ranger station and this intersection exposes colorful, land-laid deposits of the Quatal Formation (Pliocene). To the north, in Quatal Canyon, gypsum is mined from this formation. The rocks of this last roadcut are separated from the Juncal to the south by Ozena fault which runs north-north-westward along the floor of Cuyama River.

From the intersection, one can turn east on Lockwood Road, a paved highway, and follow it on a scenic drive through Lockwood Valley to Golden State Freeway just beyond Frazier Park on San Andreas fault, a distance of thirty-three miles. Or, one can continue a northerly course on Highway 33, first down the Cuyama River and thence over the hills to Maricopa on the west edge of San Joaquin Valley. In spring, following a wet winter, wildflower displays in the hills going to San Joaquin Valley are often spectacular.

Segment F— Inbound Descriptions

(The corresponding outbound material should be read first.)

I-28   South-bound travelers start this segment at intersection of Highway 33 with Lockwood Road at the south edge of Cuyama Valley near Ozena. Besides noting their odometer reading here, they should be alert for roadside mileage markers (figure 2-1). Along much of this route, markers are matched on opposite sides of the highway, so mileage values cited for the outbound trip are applicable inbound.

I-27   Southbound from the Lockwood Road intersection the first roadcut almost immediately on the left exposes Quatal (Pliocene) sands and gravels, rather highly colored. Beyond Ozena Ranger Station, we enter San Rafael Mountains going upgrade and ascending Bear Canyon, first west, then south, and then east. All rocks exposed in roadcuts or on hillsides are of the Juncal Formation (Eocene), mostly shales, mudstones, siltstones, and sandstones in various admixtures. These beds dip southwesterly at modest degrees and are separated from the Quatal by Ozena fault which lies under alluvium about at the ranger station and extends north-northwestward along the Cuyama River. Some big cone spruce trees are scattered through the chaparral on the steep hillsides here.

I-26   Travelers ascending from Cuyama Valley find the small turnout with the best view of the fault canyon about one hundred and fifty feet beyond marker 45^{43}, opposite marker 45^{37}.

I-25   After leaving the small turnout at 45^{37}, travelers headed inbound pass from Cozy Dell into Matilija rocks at 45^{04} and out of the Matilija back into Cozy Dell at 44^{61}. Shales at the head of the hairpin loop up the canyon look much like Cozy Dell but are actually Matilija.

I-24   Inbound travelers find this large turnout two hundred feet beyond marker 44^{50}.

I-23   After leaving the big turnout at 44^{34}, southbound travelers return to north-dipping Matilija beds at 44^{29}.

I-22   Ascending the grade north of Pine Mountain ridge, the double-walled cut at the summit is in view, and the two large exposures, one hundred yards beyond 43^{12}, are also well seen. The trace of Pine Mountain fault on the hillside to the west is described in O-22. Pine Mountain fault is crossed near 43^{27}.

I-21   Southbound travelers descending from Pine Mountain Summit see the roadcut exposures of Sespe beds with ease, and other exposures and relationships described are not hard to spot. The fine growth of piñon trees in upper Adobe Valley attracts attention. The upper Monterey sandstones are well seen ahead on the skyline at 11 o'clock from 41^{28}, and the bluff made by these beds is near the skyline on the left at 41^{12}, shortly after entering the narrow section of Adobe Creek canyon. Open folds in the Monterey (Photo F-6) are passed between 40^{75} and 40^{66}. The Vaqueros is seen in the cut two hundred feet beyond 40^{20}, Sespe conglomerates reappear near 40^{11} and are more extensive on the right starting at 39^{68}. The bluffs ahead on the near skyline at 39^{49} are also Sespe conglomerate, and the beds dipping steeply northward directly ahead at 39^{26} are Sespe conglomerate and sandstone. The Adobe Creek bridge is crossed at 39^{06}, and the roadcut two hundred feet beyond exposes Coldwater

Sandstone. Pine Mountain Inn is two hundred feet beyond 38^{93}.

I-20   Using Pine Mountain Inn as a reference point, inbound travelers should have little trouble spotting the navigational points, mileage markers, and the various geological features to be seen traveling east down the open, flat-floored valley of upper Sespe Creek. Coming out of Adobe Creek, roadcut exposures are in Coldwater sandy, silty, and shaly beds, a good example being opposite the highway department hopper and turnout at 38^{50}. Good views of the Sespe-Coldwater bluff north of the highway are seen on the near skyline at and beyond 38^{36}. Large, angular fragments of Sespe conglomerate lie near road level on the steep hillslope near 38^{17}, and again between 37^{10} and 36^{99}. By the time Godwin Creek is reached, at 37^{53}, we are well back into brown shales (Cozy Dell). Chorro Grande trail head is about one hundred yards beyond 36^{75}, just past the two-walled roadcut. Coarse stream gravels are seen in roadcuts about one hundred and fifty feet beyond 36^{33}, approaching Chorro Grande Creek.

I-19   Inbound travelers see this pattern to better advantage at about 1 o'clock approaching and crossing Chorro Grande Creek at 36^{14} and again at about 3 o'clock opposite marker 35^{97}. Coming through the double-walled cut just beyond Burro Creek at 35^{25}, they get a nice view of Pine Mountain ridge directly ahead on the high skyline. At 35^{10}, Reyes Peak (7,510 ft.) is at 11:50 o'clock. Massive exposures of Matilija Sandstone are one hundred feet beyond 34^{50}, and the sheared zone of Munson Creek fault is crossed at 34^{42}. Munson Creek is bridged at 33^{82}, and a broad, open syncline in massive sandstone beds is seen on the canyon walls ahead between 32^{97} and 32^{83}. Potrero John Creek is at 32^{10}.

I-18   Inbounders see the bedding plane slide approaching and beyond marker 31^{93},

cross Derrydale Creek at 31^{73}, and enter Sespe Gorge at 31^{63}.

I-17   Having traversed the narrows of Sespe Gorge, inbound travelers will probably be struck by the openness of the shale country beyond. The large concrete bridge across Tule Creek is easily recognized, 1.3 mile beyond Sespe Gorge.

I-16   After crossing Tule Creek bridge, the highway turns east for inbound travelers. A quick look to the right up the side canyon 100 feet beyond the bridge will reveal the sandstone dip slope. Tule Creek fault is crossed between 29^{41} and 29^{33}. Farther along, rock and structural relationships are as described in O-16. Occasional views of Pine Mountain ridge are seen on the north skyline.

I-15   Travelers headed east down Sespe Creek can make the stop at 28^{91}, if they wish, or the basic relationships can be observed in driving the mile east from Tule Creek crossing.

I-14   Inbound travelers will find this small turnout just a mile beyond Tule Creek bridge on the left between markers 27^{97} and 27^{87}.

I-13   Inbound travelers coming upgrade first see good exposures of thinly bedded Cozy Dell Shale, near 27^{77}, and should have little trouble spotting the north-dipping Matilija Sandstone beds in the double-walled roadcut at 27^{54}. They see south dips in sandstone at 27^{20} and are out of the sandstone by 27^{07}, having completed the traverse of the nose of the Tule Creek anticline. The large view point turnout is a little beyond 27^{02}.

I-12   Inbound travelers can take this loop in reverse direction near 25^{02}, one mile after passing the secondary road turning left to Rose Valley.

I-11   Travelers going inbound have had good views of the Matilija flatirons while descending the grade to Matilija Creek. On the long southwesterly traverse, slide debris is seen at 23^{75} and between 23^{48} and 23^{42}. Other features mentioned are at the indicated markers. The large turnout at the drinking fountain locality is approached beyond 22^{44}.

I-10   After completing a switchback and crossing bridges over Matilija Creek, at 19^{73}, and Bear Creek, at 19^{37}, inbound travelers are headed toward Wheeler Gorge. The high ridge directly ahead is on the far side of the Santa Ynez fault. It is underlain by the tougher Cretaceous rocks which have been raised by upward movement of the block south of the fault. The contrast of open valley north of the fault and the narrow defile in Wheeler Gorge south of it, is more vivid inbound. The rich brown color of Cozy Dell Shale in the open valley contrasts with the nearly black Cretaceous rocks in the gorge.

I-9   Those traveling south will find the fairly large turnout, which provides good parking for the gorge-inspection trip, about 0.1 mile south of Wheeler Gorge Guard Station and roughly two hundred feet beyond marker 19^{10}.

I-8   Travelers inbound have seen better exposures of Cretaceous rocks in Wheeler Gorge, but they may wish to inspect the Eocene-Cretaceous contact at marker 18^{00} by parking in the small turnout at 17^{92}.

I-7   Inbound travelers can identify Wheeler Springs by the signs as they enter it near 17^{77}.

I-6   Traveling south one sees the Juncal Formation between Wheeler Springs and the Matilija Sandstone exposures.

I-5   Southbound travelers pass these Matilija exposures between the third and fourth bridge crossings, after leaving Wheeler Springs. This is 0.5 mile beyond the Lake Matilija turnoff.

I-4   Southbound travelers enter the Cozy Dell Shale shortly after passing the bridge and road to Matilija Hot Springs and stay in it all the way to the fruit-packing shed. They have already seen so much Cozy Dell that these exposures will not increase their pulse rate. However, if they look up and ahead at the east canyon wall between markers 15^{40} and 15^{24}, beyond Matilija Hot Springs bridge, they will see a nice, angular unconformity between steeply tilted Cozy Dell (Eocene) sandstone beds and some near-horizontal bouldery gravels (Pleistocene).

I-3   Instead of traversing the Coldwater from the top down, inbound travelers see it from bottom up, starting a little beyond the fruit-packing shed of Friends Ranches, at 14^{59}. The fossiliferous beds are opposite marker 14^{46}. Massive, light-colored sandstone near the top of the Coldwater outcrops on the curve at 14^{10}, and north-dipping (overturned) beds are seen in the next roadcut, a little beyond 13^{95}.

I-2   People traveling south see these same features at the indicated mileages, except that the Santa Ynez front and Nordhoff Ridge are hard to view without craning one's neck backwards. The southbound view of Sulphur Mountain directly ahead on the skyline is much easier.

I-1   This segment ends at the intersection of highways 33 and 150 at the southwest edge of the city of Ojai.

Segment **G**

Ventura to Santa Barbara, 26 Miles

O-1   This segment begins for westbound travelers at separation of highways 101 and 33 west of Ventura. Note odometer reading at the Ojai turnoff (Segment E), but continue on Highway 101 westward up the coast (Photo G-1). Rincon is the Spanish geographical term for an inside corner or cove defined by a point projecting into the sea, a plain, or other low-relief surface. Along the coast ahead, a rincon is a gracefully curved reentrant or indentation of the seashore between projecting points (Photo G-2). The coast between Ventura and Rincon Point thirteen miles ahead, known as The Rincon, would be better termed "The Rincons" because there are three such indentations separated by Pitas Point and Punta Gorda (fat point).

(Inbound travelers see p. 115.)

O-2   About 0.4 miles west of Ventura, the usually dry bed of Ventura River is crossed on James J. McBride bridge. Most runoff from this drainage is now impounded behind Casitas and Matilija dams. Control of floods on Ventura River and the accompanying decrease in sand normally delivered to the ocean have upset the equilibrium of beaches down the coast. Waves and currents, formerly fed by Ventura River floods, are now eating away at those beaches to satisfy their hunger for sand. In cross-ing the bridge, a glance right to the mid-distance at 3 o'clock provides a glimpse of tanks, plants, rigs, and other facilities of Ventura Oil Field (Photo E-1), more details on which are given in Segment E.

O-3   Across Ventura River, westbound, we descend to the floodplain and see ahead at 12:30-1:00 o'clock the profile of a gently sloping, smooth terrace surface about sixty feet high (Photo E-1). This is but one of several such surfaces at different levels near Ventura. This particular terrace remnant is unusual in that it is transitional between a stream-cut surface extending along Ventura River and a sea-cut surface extending along the coast. The stream-cut part is a remnant of the wide floor of an older and higher Ventura River valley, and the sea-cut part is the marine-abrasion platform created at the same time.

O-4   About 0.7 mile west of separation from Highway 33, the highway rises over the large underpass for Main Street, and just beyond well-rounded cobbles and boulders appear on slopes and in roadcuts on the right. These roundstones are derived largely from a thin bouldery deposit covering the terrace. They are smooth and well-rounded because they have been through the mill several times. Since having been

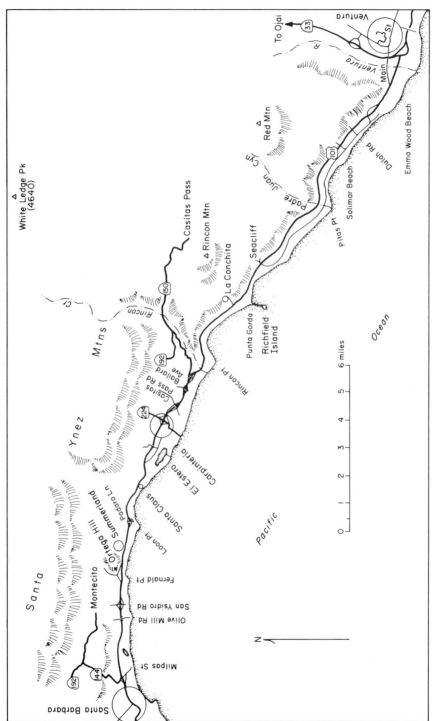

Figure G-1.   Segment G, Ventura to Santa Barbara.

Photo G-1. High altitude, oblique view east downcoast from west of Goleta. (U.S. Air Force photo taken for U.S. Geological Survey, 041-R-052).

broken as angular chunks from outcrops of resistant sandstone (largely Eocene) in the Santa Ynez and Topatopa mountains to the north, they have been transported, deposited, and reworked and redeposited several times into formations of increasingly younger age, each such episode contributing to wear and rounding of the stones. They are what geologists call third- or fourth-generation roundstones.

Scattered roundstones continue in large roadcuts north of the highway for the next mile westward, but many of them come from steeply tilted conglomerate beds in lower Pleistocene deposits (two million years, San Pedro Formation) exposed in these cuts. When the cuts were fresh, steep inclination of individual conglomerate beds within the sequence could be easily recognized, but it's now hard to see from a fast-moving car owing to weeds and weathering.

O-5   Westbound motorists can exercise the option of forsaking the freeway for a half-dozen miles of more relaxed touring on a parallel and less heavily used highway closer to the beach by turning off at "State Beaches" exit just ahead. After a short section of narrow highway and an old railroad overpass, you come out close to water level on a wide highway.

O-6   Beyond the "State Beaches" exit and after rounding an unnamed (let us call it Emma Wood) point, we enter the first of the rincons (Photo G-2). Looking ahead you can see that the lower part of the hillslopes at and somewhat above highway level have a jumbled, disorganized appearance compared to the smoothly and more steeply sloping upper part of the hill face. This relationship becomes more apparent beyond Dulah Road ahead and beyond San Miguelito Road still farther west. The irregular, mostly gentler, lower slopes display small benches at various levels, rounded projecting lobes, rounded knobs,

and a disorganized, disintegrated drainage pattern. The cause is slumping and sliding which has moved material from the higher slopes and deposited it in jumbled fashion lower down. Slumps and slides are so numerous along this reach of coast that it is hard to find any part of the lower hill face that has not been affected. Probable causes are three: first, the underlying rocks are relatively weak and incompetent marine mudstones and fine sandstones (late Pliocene to early Pleistocene Santa Barbara Formation); second, slopes have been oversteepened through undercutting by powerful waves; and, finally, the inclination of bedding planes is steeply toward the ocean, about parallel with the hill face. This is a recipe for mass movements, and they have occurred prolifically. At Dulah Road, the rocks change to an older, somewhat more competent formation (Pliocene, Pico), but slides and slumps continue beyond Punta Gorda.

O-7   Approaching Dulah Road, westbound motorists get a view of the surf and strand curving out to Pitas Point, 1.5 miles ahead at 11:30 o'clock, and of a low, modestly wide terrace extending inland to the base of the hills. Pitas Point defines the western limit of the first rincon (Photo G-2). Kelp beds growing abundantly a few hundred yards offshore indicate a rocky or stony bottom.

O-8   At San Miguelito Road, 0.7 mile west of Dulah Road, the smooth rock face just behind the light-brown water treatment plant with the vertical cylindrical tank on the right is an exposed bedding surface of a steeply inclined sandstone layer (Pico). This is what geologists call a dip slope, and it confirms the earlier statement about a steep southward inclination of strata in these rocks. The view is actually best just after passing over San Miguelito Road. Beyond, at 12:00 to 12:30 o'clock, slide and slump masses are promi-

So. Mtn. Ridge | High Terrace | Tilted Pliocene Beds | Rincon Oil Fld. (Seacliff) | Low Terrace | Kelp Beds | Santa Clara R. | Pitas Pt. | Ventura R.

Photo G-2. Looking eastward along The Rincon from near Seacliff (Spence air photo E-5266, 11/2/33).

nent on the lower part of the hill face with steep, smooth dip slopes above extending to the crest.

O-9 Approaching Pitas Point, westbound, extensive flower fields occupy at least two low terrace surfaces on the right. The white flowers blooming in summer are Marguerites. Inland from San Miguelito Road and from Pitas Point are oil fields on anticlinal structures. Some of the derricks and pumps can be seen by looking up the canyons. San Miguelito field is on a western extension of Ventura anticline (Photo G-3), and Padre Canyon field, behind Pitas Point, is on a smaller anticline to the south.

O-10 Half a mile west of Pitas Point, the shore and surf zone come into view left ahead. Beaches are narrow and stony

Photo G-3. Looking west to crest of Ventura Avenue anticline as exposed near San Miguelito. Folded beds are Pliocene. (Spence air photo E-8679, 6/21/38).

because of the reduction in sand supply from the west, largely owing to the artifices of man. In another half-mile, fields of flowers appear on the left and continue for nearly a mile, providing a dazzling display of colors in proper season. They occupy a low marine terrace (Photo G-2) mantled by fine, fertile alluvium carried down from hills to the north.

O-11   At and beyond "Sea Cliff, Next Right," if the day is clear, offshore platforms (seven in 1977) are seen in Santa Barbara Channel at about 11 o'clock. Nearer is Richfield Island and the pier to it from Punta Gorda. This artificial island, with its ornamental palm trees, provides a site for many oil wells drilled into the Rincon anticlinal structure. This same structure extends west into the Santa Barbara Channel, and the oil at the Carpinteria and Dos Cuadras offshore fields has accumulated in it. Drilling platforms are located

along its trend, and one, in the Dos Cuadras field, was the source of the ill-famed Santa Barbara Channel oil spill of 1969. The Rincon oil field, passed at Sea Cliff (Photo G-2), has extensive operations north of the highway as well as a number of actively pumping wells on short piers near Mobil Pier bridge, this side of Richfield Island.

O-12   In traversing the graceful curve of this second rincon, a high sea cliff (Photo G-4) lies directly ahead about 0.4 mile west of "Sea Cliff Exit." The smooth skyline along the upper edge of the cliff is a marine terrace. Just a little below the top of this 500-foot cliff is an angular unconformity between Pliocene beds (4-6 million years, Pico Formation) dipping 35°-40°, and nearly horizontal Pleistocene (less than one million years) terrace deposits. The Pleistocene materials make up a near-vertical uni-

Photo G-4. Bluff west of Seacliff exposing tilted Pliocene beds overlain at top by near-horizontal Pleistocene materials mantling terrace on south slope of Rincon Mountain. Additional, steplike terrace remnants seen on higher slopes. (Spence air photo E-8682, 6/21/38).

form cliff about thirty feet high right at the top, and the Pliocene beds underlie the rest of the steep, gully-riven face extending to highway level. The Pliocene sequence contains beds of stony conglomerate, seen on close approach to the cliff base near apex of the rincon. These beds were laid down in near-horizontal attitude in the ocean, then uplifted, tilted and subjected to terrestrial erosion. Later they were submerged beneath the sea and smoothly truncated by wave erosion following which the wave-cut surface was lifted to its present position as a terrace. While a new sea cliff was being cut, fine alluvial material from the hills to the north accumulated on the emerged terrace surface. It is these younger alluvial deposits that make up most of the 30-foot vertical face at the top of the cliff.

O-13   After passing directly under the unconformity, a little more than a mile west of Sea Cliff, the highway curves south and in about 0.5 mile rounds Punta Gorda at Mussel Shoals, a seashell (mussels) encrusted projection of resistant rock.

Beyond Punta Gorda is the third rincon (Photo G-5), possibly the most symmetrical and best defined in the sequence and nicely enclosed by Rincon Point to the west. The cluster of houses passed in half a mile on the right is La Conchita. The smooth surface at top of the cliff backing this rincon is a marine terrace, which slopes gently westward because of tectonic tilting. The large, light green tank beyond La Conchita is near the trace of Rincon fault, and beyond it shales (Miocene) make up the cliff face.

Photo G-5. Sea cliff behind rincon east of Rincon Point. First bare scar extending from top to base of cliff marks location of clinker-rock seen from Highway 101. Marine terrace tilted down to west (left) lies above and behind cliff. (Spence air photo E-13072, 8/29/47).

O-14   About 1.3 miles west of La Conchita turnoff on the right is "Bates Road, Exit 3/4 Mile." Just behind it, in the cliff face, is a fresh exposure of reddish rock with a pile of similar broken material at the cliff base (Photo G-5). This is what geologists call "clinker-rock," a shale (Miocene), which has been fused and discolored by long, slow, near-surface burning of naturally ignited oil-bearing shales. This is the site of a so-called "volcano" which Southern Pacific Company spent many years and much effort extinguishing because slump related to the burning caused stones to break from the cliff and roll onto their tracks. Trains do not generally run well over stones. Before extinction, and under proper atmospheric conditions, a column of white steam occasionally formed over this spot, giving the illusion of volcanic activity. For more details on the nature and formation of clinker-rock, see the material on the Grimes Canyon occurrence south of Fillmore, in Segment C.

We passed from Pliocene rocks in vicinity of Sea Cliff to Miocene rocks at the clinker-rock locality because Rincon fault brought them up on its north side. These steeply dipping beds are upside down, older

(Monterey) above younger (Santa Margarita), because of overturning close to the fault. The fault itself is hard to see, but a discerning eye can recognize the difference between the thinly bedded, platy, often white shales (Miocene) in the sea cliff here compared to the more massive, light-tan, softer mudstones, sandstones and conglomerates (Pliocene) near Sea Cliff.

O-15   Beyond the clinker-rock exposure, ahead at roughly 11 o'clock is Rincon Point. Under proper conditions, the ocean surface east of the point will be dotted with surfers taking advantage of the long, oblique ride afforded by swells refracted around the point. Rincon Point is made by the fan-delta built into the ocean at the mouth of Rincon Creek, on the Santa Barbara-Ventura County line. This is not a big stream, but it descends steeply from the mountains and at times of flood carries bouldery debris to the ocean. Much of this debris is too coarse for the waves and longshore currents to handle, so it accumulates residually to make a projecting rocky point. Other points west from here, Loon and Fernald for example, appear to be of similar origin. The tilted terrace surface has accompanied us on the near right skyline (Photo G-5).

O-16   West of the Santa Barbara County line, the freeway ascends through a deep roadcut in highly deformed beds largely shale (upper and middle Miocene). Details of the deformation are too complex to be discerned at 55 mph. At any speed, however, one can see that rocks in the core of the cut are an unweathered, light bluish-gray. The transition to a weathered (by oxidation) brown and tan coloration is visible toward the top. Upon emerging, the high skyline of Santa Ynez Mountains appears directly ahead.

O-17   A few tenths of a mile beyond the deep roadcut, westbound travelers emerge onto the wide, low-relief floor of alluvially mantled and sediment-filled Carpinteria Basin. The slightly higher ground south of the freeway near Bailard Avenue marks the trace of an east-west fault. South and a bit west were the Carpinteria tar pits (Photo G-6), a brea deposit similar to Rancho La Brea in Hancock Park, Los Angeles. The Carpinteria brea was not as extensive nor as rich in fossil bones of large mammals, but it is of comparable age and contained remains of many of the same animals, including the great dire wolf, giant cats, camels, horses, and bison. Plant remains were abundant and representative of a floral environment about like that now found in the pine forests of Monterey Peninsula, two hundred miles north. The Carpinteria pits are especially renowned for the number and variety of fossil bird remains, representing some sixty species, about thirty-five percent extinct. Curiously, most of these were woodland birds rather than the shoreline or wading birds one might have expected in view of the present setting.

A brea deposit can be seen by driving to the parking area at the east end of the road within Carpinteria State Beach Park (offramp ahead) and walking two hundred yards farther east. There, in the present beach cliffs, are old tar deposits and fresh oil seeps.

O-18   From Rincon Creek to Summerland, Santa Ynez Mountains have a forelying ridge, separated from the main Santa Ynez mass by east-west Arroyo Parida fault. We get particularly good views of the south face of this foreridge, with brown

Photo G-6. Excavated tar pit on terrace at Carpinteria. Source of many fossil bird remains. (Spence air photo E-8685, 6/21/38).

sandstone beds (Eocene) dipping steeply south toward more subdued lower slopes composed of Sespe red beds, as we approach, pass, and continue beyond Carpinteria. Well up on the main front of the Santa Ynez farther west, bedding surfaces of hard sandstone layers inclined southward are exposed as bare ledges and slopes. Still farther west, these same beds are inclined (dipping) to the north so they structurally overlie the reddish rocks near the mountain base. This is not the normal situation, for the brown sandstone is Eocene, on the order of 40-50 million years old and the reddish rocks are Oligocene, about thirty-five million years old. They should normally lie over, not under, the Eocene beds. These north-dipping beds are overturned. They compose part of a large structure locally making up the south face of Santa Ynez Mountain, known as the Montecito overturn. The tectonic push from the north was so powerful that it caused the anticlinal fold forming Santa Ynez Mountains to lay over onto its south side so that beds on that limb are upside-down.

Red rocks and soils derived from the Sespe Formation are seen on the lower slopes of the forelying ridge beyond Carpinteria, especially well at 1:30 to 2:00 o'clock rising on the overpass across Santa Claus-Padaro lanes. Much of the red-rock area is currently (1977) newly planted in orchards. Also from here, the overturned, north-dipping Eocene beds can be seen ahead high on the face of the mountains at 1:00 to 1:30 o'clock.

O-19   Beyond Carpinteria, look south as well as north so you don't miss the swampy wetlands (El Estero) a little beyond Santa Monica Road exit. Although small, El Estero is reputed to be one of the least spoiled tidal wetlands of southern California. One often sees large flocks of sea birds on its surface. It is separated from the ocean by a sandbar, the site of a number

of houses. This bar is thought to be due to a shallow offshore shoal which refracts incoming swells in such a way that they caused longshore currents moving eastward to drop much of the sand they were carrying at this place. Storm waves seized this sand and piled it above normal tide level, forming the bar. In clear weather, offshore drilling platforms are in view.

O-20   Upon approaching the western exit to Padaro Lane, marked by an overpass and "Evans Avenue Exit, 1 Mile," note that the freeway passes through a small vale between hills to the north and a small hillock to the south. This south-side hillock owes its existence to uplift on a fault at its north base which parallels the freeway. The Pleistocene beds (Casitas Formation) composing the hillock are folded into an anticline, possibly also contributing to the topographic relief.

O-21   Beyond Padaro Lane overpass, we approach the settlement of Summerland, with the knob of Ortega Hill, at 11:30 o'clock beyond on the near skyline. Summerland was once renowned for its "oil wells in the ocean" (Photo G-7). Summerland oil field, discovered in 1887, had over three hundred wells pumping small quantities of oil from Pleistocene rocks at depths of only one hundred to eight hundred feet, a trivial depth by today's standards. The unusual aspect of this operation, for that time, was the location of wells on piers projecting into the ocean. The field has long been exhausted, and nearly all traces are gone.

O-22   West of Summerland, the freeway ascends in a broad curve around Ortega Hill (Photo G-7). In bare bluffs on the east face of the hill and in roadcuts near the top, one catches glimpses of tilted, coarse, sedimentary beds (Pleistocene, Casitas Formation), representing a local, land-laid deposit of the Carpinteria-Summerland area.

Photo G-7. Oil wells on piers at Summerland in 1929, looking east. Loon Point upper right with vale through which highway and railroad pass just to north. (Fairchild air photo 0-365, 11/19/29).

Overlying these strata are near-horizontal layers of coarse, bouldery material containing large fragments of sandstone derived from Santa Ynez Mountains. The angular discordance between these two deposits is exposed in roadcuts on the right beyond "Sheffield Drive, Exit 3/4 Mile," but it's hard to see at freeway speeds. Even if you can't see it, we want you to know it exists.

O-23 Upon completing the curve around Ortega Hill and starting descent toward Montecito, westbound observers looking left at about 10 to 11 o'clock, near the Sheffield Drive turnoff sign, see a pretty little cove. It is bounded on the far side by Fernald Point, probably another fan-delta, this one built at the mouth of Romero Creek.

O-24 Westward from Sheffield Drive, views are partly obstructed by dense growths of trees and shrubs characterizing Montecito. Occasionally the higher part of Santa Ynez Mountains is glimpsed on the north skyline. Watch for the north-dipping, overturned beds of sandstone in that face.

Anyone wishing to go to the waterfront at Santa Barbara should watch for the *left* turnoff onto Cabrillo Boulevard. Beyond the exit to Hermosillo Drive, a modest ridge rises about a mile north of the freeway. This is the east end of the southern prong of Riviera Ridge. It is underlain largely by highly deformed shales (middle Miocene, Monterey and upper Miocene, Santa Margarita) and is bounded on its south side by a family of short overlapping faults of the Sycamore Canyon fault system, a canyon more noted for its devastating fire of July 26-27, 1977 than its faults. These faults define the north edge of a down-dropped block (a graben) in which downtown Santa Barbara lies. More details of this structure and The Mesa, bounding its southern margin, are given in Segment H. The face of The Mesa is seen ahead on the near skyline approaching and beyond Salinas Street exit. The Channel Islands, especially Santa Cruz, have been in view most of this trip, if weather is clear (Photo G-8). This segment terminates at the State Street stoplight on Highway 101 (locally no longer a freeway) in Santa Barbara.

Photo G-8. High-altitude oblique view of Santa Barbara coast, Santa Barbara Channel, and Channel Islands. (U.S. Air Force photo taken for U.S. Geological Survey, HA-041-R.)

Segment G—
Inbound Descriptions

(The corresponding outbound material should be read first.)

I-25   Going east from Santa Barbara, this segment starts at State Street stoplight on Highway 101 where an odometer reading can be noted.

I-24   Eastbound travelers get reasonable views of Riviera Ridge after passing Milpas exit and catch glimpses of the Santa Ynez Mountains face on the left skyline, once they have cleared the east end of Riviera Ridge. At "Olive Mill Exit, 3/4 Mile," one can see at 9:30 o'clock overturned, north-dipping beds (Eocene) in the Santa Ynez face and again at 11:40 o'clock upon emerging from Olive Mill overpass. The mountain front is in clear view opposite "Sheffield Drive, Left Lane."

I-23   Traveling east this cove and Fernald Point are seen only by looking sharply back over the right shoulder to about 5 o'clock in ascending Ortega Hill beyond Sheffield Drive, about at "Summerland, 3/4 Mile."

I-22   Inbound travelers don't get very good views of the tilted beds composing Ortega Hill, but they can see on down the coast to Loon Point and to the little knob and vale behind it (Photo G-7).

I-21   The sandy beach at Summerland is well seen descending from Ortega Hill. This beach often displays evenly spaced, nicely symmetrical indentations known as cusps (Photo 1-6), ephemeral features created by certain patterns of waves. At the east end of the beach is a prominent, brown, cliffed headland (Loon Point) and a knob (Photo G-7). A short distance offshore are beds of kelp. Farther out, one can count ten (late 1977) drilling platforms in the Santa Barbara Channel.

I-20   The vale and hillock are visible just south of the freeway at 12:30-12:45 o'clock approaching Padaro Lane turnoff and overpass. The railroad and freeway both go through the vale.

I-19   The western tip of the Carpinteria foreridge of the Santa Ynez Mountains is at 9 o'clock beyond Padaro Lane overpass, and it remains prominently in view to well beyond Carpinteria. Polo fields are immediately left of the freeway at and beyond "Santa Claus Lane, Right Lane" (center-divider). Looking across the polo fields to 10 o'clock, reddish slopes underlain by Sespe beds and newly planted to avocados, are well seen. Behind are the steeper dip slopes in massive brown sandstones (Eocene, Coldwater Sandstone).

On the Santa Claus Lane overpass near "Carpinteria Exit, 1 Mile" and beyond, the ocean and shoreline are in view. Large rocks are piled along this shore to prevent wave erosion caused by the decreased sand supply from the west. The wetland and the sandbar of El Estero are seen well at 1 to 3 o'clock just beyond Santa Claus, near "Carpinteria, Next 4 Exits."

I-18   From "Carpinteria Avenue, Exit 3/4 Mile" east to Linden Avenue, the freeway is straight, and eastbound travelers have Casitas Pass at 11:30 o'clock, and Rincon Mountain at 12:10 o'clock, ahead on the skyline (Photo G-9) for some distance. If visibility is good, White Ledge Park can also be seen near the distant skyline at 10 o'clock as a large dip slope of light-colored sandstone (Eocene).

I-17   Eastbound travelers can easily take the same offramp and follow signs south through Carpinteria to the State Beach Park, if they care to make this little side trip. Camping and picnicing are encouraged in the park, as well as brea inspecting.

I-16   Approaching Bailard Avenue exit on a clear day, eastbound travelers see Rincon Mountain (2,161 ft.) particularly well at 11:50 o'clock. Its south face sports a sequence of marine terraces, a few of which can possibly be identified as gently sloping benches. The old wagon road between Ventura and Santa Barbara went through Casitas Pass (Photo G-9), at 11 o'clock, before a road was constructed along the shore. Highway 150 now follows that route and provides a scenic drive from Carpinteria to Ojai Valley. The unweathered gray rock and some of the complexity of structure in the deep cut, mentioned in O-16, are visible as the freeway starts downhill, about 0.3 mile east of the Ojai-Lake Casitas (Highway 150) exit. An angular unconformity at the very top of the cut between steeply inclined (up to 60°) shale beds (Miocene) and a thin, near-horizontal layer of brown coverhead (Pleistocene), may be glimpsed.

I-15   The tilted terrace, left of the highway and about one hundred feet above (Photo G-5), is in good view upon rounding Rincon Point. Travelers will have to look back over their right shoulder to about 4:30 o'clock to see the surfers and the tip of Rincon Point. They can see how closely the ocean approaches the freeway in this reach, especially at high tide when waves break directly against the protecting embankment. In earlier days this section was a wooden-plank causeway on piles above the beach. At high tide waves broke under the causeway and columns of water occasionally shot into the air through cracks and holes in the boards, startling passing motorists. Regrettably, this interesting experience has been eliminated by the solidity of our modern freeway. It afforded great amusement to children, although distracting to drivers.

I-14   The clinker-rock locality is just left of the relatively small black/white "End Freeway" sign which is on the right not quite one mile after rounding Rincon Point. Pinkish cinder rock is visible nearly directly ahead and also on the left for half a mile before you get to the sign.

I-13   The sandy beach, surf zone, and offshore kelp beds of this rincon are easily seen. Richfield Island, its pier, and Mussel Rock (or Shoals) are ahead. The large green tank on the left before getting to La Conchita is about on the trace of Rincon fault. Between La Conchita and Punta Gorda, the lower hillslopes to the left display striking evidence of slumping in the form of little benches backed by steep slopes.

I-12   The unconformity comes into view directly ahead after rounding Punta Gorda. It becomes clearer and moves to the left as we traverse this intermediate rincon.

I-11   Most of the offshore features mentioned in O-11 are recognizable to inbound travelers once they have rounded Punta Gorda at Mussel Shoals. Eastbound travelers wishing to exercise the option of following the old four-lane highway close along the beach should turn off at Sea Cliff as directed by the sign "State Beaches and County Parks."

I-10   After crossing the railroad tracks on an overpass eastbound from Sea Cliff, the flower fields begin on the low terrace (Photo G-2) to the right. Through this entire stretch, and particularly approaching Pitas Point, the hillslopes on the left display benches and lobes indicative of slides and slumps, with steep dip slopes in bedrock above.

I-9   Inbound travelers see this easternmost rincon (Photo G-2) nicely upon rounding Pitas Point at Padre Juan Road. On the skyline at 11:50 o'clock are some rigs of the San Miguelito oil field. Traveling in this direction, one sees to better advantage the slide and slump blocks piled up at the foot of the steep, planar, bedrock, dip slopes making the upper one-half of the hill face ahead. Such features occur all around this rincon but are particularly prominent approaching its apex. The flower fields on the left appear to occupy at least two terrace levels. Surfers sometimes seen far offshore from the cluster of houses at

Santa Ynez Foreridge   Ortega Hill   Summerland Oil Fld.   Loon Pt.   Beach Robbed by Groins   Casitas Pass   Rincon Mtn.

Photo G-9. Old photo looking east from Santa Barbara. (Spence air photo H-1604, 12/12/36).

Solimar are riding swells enhanced by a shallow offshore reef, sometimes exposed at lowest tides.

I-8   Eastbound travelers see the exposed bedding plane best as they approach the water processing plant on the left at San Miguelito Road (mileage marker 35[42]) about 1.5 miles east of Pitas Point. South-dipping beds are also apparent high on the hill face north of the highway near Dulah Road bridge. Slumps and slides are responsible for the irregular topography through which the freeway takes its course on the lower one-third of the hill face east of Dulah Road. Smooth, planar hillslopes above are bedrock dip slopes from which the slides came.

I-7   Frequent views of the kelp, surf, strand, and ocean are obtained from the more favored outside freeway lanes.

I-6   Eastbound travelers have already seen many examples of these slumps and slides.

I-5   Travelers who exercised the option of abandoning the freeway at Sea Cliff, come back to the freeway near Emma K. Wood State Beach. Motorists who stayed on the freeway get a good view beyond Dulah Road of the complex surf and current pattern caused by offshore shoals at projecting Emma Wood Point (our name), forming the east side of the easternmost rincon. Surfers far out from shore are trying to take advantage of the swell enhancement caused by these shoals.

I-4   These roundstones are seen in barely perceptible, steeply dipping beds starting at "Main Street, Ventura, 1¼ Miles." In vicinity of "Downtown Ventura, Right Lane," is an excellent view at 1 to 2 o'clock of the projecting fan-delta of Ventura River. The pattern of surf and waves along the stony beach extending to the delta is unusually scenic.

I-3   Inbound travelers pass a little below the level of this terrace but see it in profile on the left beyond "Main Street, Ventura, Exit" before dropping toward Ventura River floodplain. Roadcuts on left expose roundstone gravels underlying the terrace.

I-2   Persons traveling east have a good view of Ventura River valley and the oil field at 9:15 o'clock before they drop to floodplain level approaching the bridge. If the day is clear, they may also see tree-dotted Sulphur Mountain on the intermediate skyline at 10 o'clock and the high Santa Ynez Mountains on the far skyline at 8:45 o'clock. Crossing the James J. McBride bridge over Ventura River, a quick look right at about 3 o'clock should reveal the ponded estuary at the river mouth. Approaching Ventura, the discerning eye will recognize that gently sloping benches on the hills north of the city are remnants of marine terraces mantled by coverhead. Travelers wishing to visit Father Serra's cross, as described at the end of Segment A, can turn onto Highway 33 toward Ojai just beyond the bridge and follow directions.

I-1   This segment ends at intersection of highways 101 and 33 at the southwest edge of Ventura.

Segment H

Santa Barbara to Highway 154 West of Los Olivos, 50 Miles

O-1 Start this excursion by heading west on Highway 101 from State Street stoplight in Santa Barbara. The route proceeds to Gaviota Creek and thence north to Highway 154 (Photo H-1). Much of this scenic journey is on marine terraces along the shore, with foothills and the imposing Santa Ynez Mountains on the north. As the route turns inland those mountains are crossed to Santa Ynez Valley through a thick section of middle and lower Tertiary sedimentary rocks. In summer, the climatic contrast between warm interior valleys and the cool coast is impressive. Record an odometer reading at the start.

(Inbound travelers see p. 130.)

O-2 The part of Santa Barbara initially traversed lies in a trough between a block 300-400 feet higher immediately to the south, The Mesa (Photo H-2), and Mission (or Riviera) Ridge about two miles north. At Bath Street offramp, the steep linear face of The Mesa is directly ahead. The trough, a down-dropped fault block (graben), trends west-northwest, and Highway 101 quickly curves to a corresponding course. It is bounded by Mesa fault to the south and by branches of Sycamore fault system on the north. The Mesa contains rocks as old as the continental Sespe Formation (Oligocene), but the unit most

widely exposed is the marine Santa Barbara Formation (Plio-Pleistocene). Mission (Riviera) Ridge consists principally of shales (Miocene, Monterey), locally capped by bouldery fanglomerate (Quaternary). Lagoonal facies of the Santa Barbara Formation are richly fossiliferous, and collections of small shells can be made from exposures in the cliff along Shoreline Drive (a westward continuation of Cabrillo Boulevard) one hundred yards west of Castillo Street behind the boat harbor. The harbor area is most easily reached, outbound, by turning left (southeast) on State Street to Cabrillo.

Santa Barbara Harbor affords a good example of what can happen when man interferes with natural processes. Under normal conditions, a considerable mass of sand was moved eastward along the Santa Barbara-Carpinteria shore maintaining the nice sandy beaches of the region. In 1926, Santa Barbara built an offshore breakwater to provide a small-craft anchorage west of Santa Barbara pier. This structure interfered to some degree with the longshore transport of sand by refracting the waves in such a way as to cause some sand deposition and widening of the beach inland of the breakwater (Photo H-3, top), but the results were not disastrous. Since the structure was not attached to land, consider-

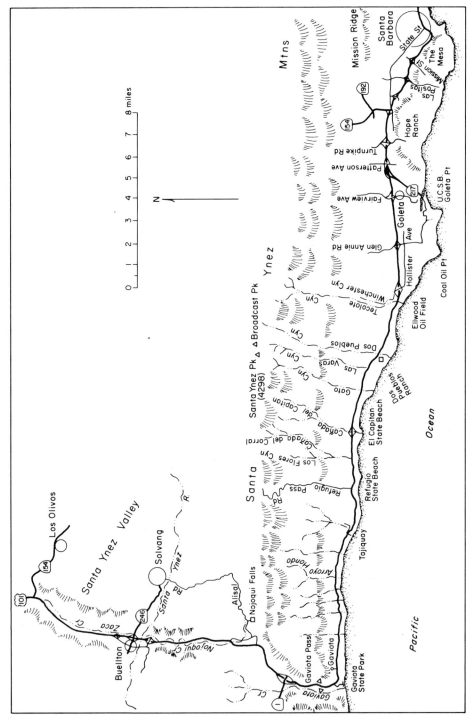

Figure H-1. Segment H, Santa Barbara to Highway 154.

Santa Ynez R.
Santa Ynez Val.
Hwy. 101-154 Jct.
Diatomite Pit
Highway 101
Lake Cachuma
Goleta Pt.
Santa Barbara
Hwy. 1
Coal Oil Pt.
Gaviota Gorge
Gaviota Beach
Tilted Strata
Anacapa Isl.

Photo H-1. High altitude oblique view of coastline eastward from over Point Conception to the Malibu coast. (Note seaward-dipping beds on both sides of Gaviota Pass. (U.S. Air Force photo taken for U.S. Geological Survey, 041-L-069).

Photo H-2. Santa Barbara looking northwest. Hilly area on left is The Mesa, Santa Ynez Mountains in background. (Fairchild air photo 0-4255, 2/16/35).

able sand continued east along shore. However, in 1930 the structure was extended to land, closing off the longshore drift and setting off a succession of events. First, as might be expected, much sand accumulated west of the breakwater creating a much wider beach (Photo H-3, bottom). This in itself was not bad, but eventually it permitted accumulation of sand outside the breakwater which shallowed the bottom so that waves and currents were able to carry sand to the east end of the structure. There, waves refracted by the breakwater tossed sand back into the boat harbor to form a bar that constricted the harbor entrance (Photo H-3, bottom). While this was

Photo H-3. Santa Barbara Harbor; top—in 1929 when offshore breakwater, constructed in 1926, was being extended to shore; bottom—35 years later (1964) showing sand accumulations caused by completion of breakwater in 1930. Arrow marks same point in both photos. (Top—Fairchild air photo 0-139, 10/31/29; Bottom—Spence air photo E-18971, 4/8/64).

going on, waves farther east along the coast, having been deprived of their natural supply of sand and being hungry, started eating away at the sandy Santa Barbara beaches. The water's edge moved inland as the beach sand disappeared, and the beaches became rocky and uninviting.

Eventually structures on land were threatened by wave erosion. This erosion and deterioration of beaches worked gradually eastward to the Carpinteria area, much to the displeasure of that community.

Since the sandbar constricting the harbor entrance needed to be removed, and the beaches to the east required sand, a reasonable solution was to dredge sand from the bar and pump it, as a slurry mixed in water, through a pipe to the beach east of Santa Barbara pier. This was done and the renewed supply of sand eventually stabilized the beaches eastward down the coast, although it did not restore them fully to their original state. Dredging is continuing, at considerable expense, to preserve the small-boat harbor and to prevent erosion of the shore farther east. The effects of such erosion are still visible, especially in the Santa Claus-Carpinteria area. Hopefully, we learn from such occurrences and should proceed more intelligently in the future as we try to modify natural dynamic systems to satisfy our needs and desires.

O-3   Beyond Carrillo Street, the high crest of Santa Ynez Mountains will be prominent ahead and to the right, in clear weather. Rugged La Cumbre and Cathedral peaks at about 2:30 o'clock display sandstone beds (Eocene, Matilija) dipping steeply south. Approaching Arrellaga turnoff, bouldery gravels and overlying finer debris (Quaternary) are seen to the right in the wall of a drainage channel. The highway bends to a more westerly course near Mission Street, and on the left opposite Las Positas Road turnoff comes the first significant roadside exposure of rock materials in a cut across the railroad tracks. There, an upper layer of coarse gravels (Quaternary) with well rounded sandstone (Eocene) boulders, rests on top of finer, rather nondescript-looking beds of Santa Barbara Formation. Approaching La Cumbre Road offramp, a bedrock knob is in view left of the highway beyond the railroad tracks. Brown, homogeneous material composing the hill is shale (lower Miocene), although Sespe beds (Oligocene) are also reported. The tree-covered hills to the south, approaching and beyond Cachuma Lake-San Marcos Pass (Highway 154) turnoff, are within the noted Hope Ranch residential area. Segment I describes features along Highway 154, a shorter, more rural route to Los Olivos for those interested in getting away from the freeway.

Approaching El Sueño Road, the hills south of the highway are diverging to the southwest because they are now bounded by More Ranch fault with a west-southwesterly trend. Beyond El Sueño, on the left across the railroad, are more exposures of bouldery gravel on Santa Barbara Formation, and we soon enter a hilly area made up of these units, as shown by deep right-side roadcuts. The course of the freeway is now essentially due west.

O-4   Beyond Turnpike Road, outbound travelers emerge onto the alluviated flat of Goleta Plain. A wide expanse of flatland extends to the left beyond Highway 217. Beyond Fairview Avenue, low hills press in more closely from the right, backed by south-dipping sandstones in the face of Santa Ynez Mountains, at 2:30 o'clock. To the left against the sea, at 9 o'clock, profiles of University of California, Santa Barbara, buildings on Goleta Point are usually visible, particularly opposite Los Carneros Road. The worked-out La Goleta (or More Ranch) gas field lies along shore east of the campus. It continues to be useful, serving as one of the first underground geological structures used in southern California for summertime storage of gas to meet winter demands. Beyond the overpass for Los Carneros Road, the smooth slopes, gentle contour, rounded divides, and lack of outcrops in foothills pressing in more closely from the north indicate that they are underlain by shales (lower Miocene, Rincon).

The highway starts a gentle ascent beyond Los Carneros, and approaching Glen Annie Road we rise above Goleta Plain into a slightly more varied topography cut in old alluvium, possibly a coverhead on a low marine terrace. Beyond Glen Annie Road-Storke Road intersection, Coal Oil Point (Photo H-1) lies nearly due south. The point gets its name from nearly 250 known, active, natural gas and gas-oil seeps on the nearby ocean floor. At Winchester Canyon Road-Hollister Avenue offramp, we are just north of Ellwood oil field (derricks at 10 o'clock) into which a Japanese submarine lobbed a few shells during World War II. Just beyond this intersection, after rising gradually from Los Carneros Road, we top out on the smooth surface of a coverhead mantling a marine terrace. Higher foothills, composed of soft brown Rincon shales, are now only about 0.5 mile north. Dissection of the terrace by drainage from the mountains create the following area of rough topography before we once again come onto a fine flat terrace. At "Buellton 25, etc.," a fleeting glance of a pier with derricks in the Ellwood field can be caught at 9 o'clock.

Although we won't see the results until we get to Gaviota Pass, some interesting stratigraphic changes are beginning in the higher foothills and lower slopes of the mountains to the north. The Coldwater Sandstone, a dominating member of the upper Eocene group of rocks in the south face of the Santa Ynez Mountains to the east, starts to pinch out dramatically, being replaced by the Sacate Formation, largely shale and siltstone. This suggests that the Eocene seas were getting deeper to the west. A massive, brown, marine sandstone unit also begins to develop within the basal part of the normally red continental Sespe Formation (Oligocene). It is the Gaviota Formation, and it thickens westward toward Gaviota Pass as the Sespe gets thinner. The Vaqueros Sandstone (lower Miocene) also thins westward from a thickness of several hundred feet here to a few tens of feet at Gaviota Pass.

O-5   On the left, opposite "Buellton 30, etc.," a railroad cut exposes Pleistocene coverhead resting unconformably on truncated Miocene rocks. Within a mile, a large gully (Eagle Canyon) is crossed, the terrace narrows, oil tanks and pumps are seen

to the left, and a lemon orchard graces hillslopes to the right. Within another half mile, the terrace widens and the highway starts a gradual descent to Dos Pueblos Creek. Dos Pueblos Rancho ahead at 11 o'clock (red tile roofs) has attractive orchid displays open to the public during reasonable daylight hours. To visit the ranch, turn off on Dos Pueblos Canyon Road and follow signs.

O-6   At and westward from Dos Pueblos Canyon the terrain is modestly rough owing to intimate stream dissection. Foothills become more rugged, and the high Santa Ynez face gets closer. Although shale (Rincon) still composes the grassy foothills, near 31^{00} you can see a sharp contact between the grassy area and rougher, brush- and tree-covered slopes on Vaqueros sandstones which underlie the Rincon shales a short distance inland. This sharp contact is made by Dos Pueblos fault, upthrown on its north side. In the next 2.5 miles, three deep canyons are crossed in which this same relationship can be seen to the right. Farther west, the highway rises a little onto the hillside so we look down upon a terrace surface. A big roadcut in this reach exposes brown, homogeneous shales (Rincon) and views up gullies inland show oak trees and brush growing on the Vaqueros, which dips steeply south. Near 32^{00} is a good view at 11:40 o'clock of El Capitan Point (Photo H-4) and a bit of the sea cliff curving out to it. At "El Capitan Ranch Road, Next Right" the highway drops to a narrow terrace, shortly El Capitan Ranch Road exits, and soon a large sign announces the approach of El Capitan State Beach. During this traverse, the highway passes from brown, soft shales (lower Miocene, Rincon) into largely white, tougher, siliceous shales (middle Miocene, Monterery). You will see fragments of white shale in hillside soil mantles, and eventually good exposures of such beds in roadcuts. The foothills continue to press in on the right. In railroad cuts left of the highway before

Photo H-4. View east across El Capitan Point (mid-photo), showing white sea cliffs in Monterey beds, terrace, foothills largely of Rincon shales, and facilities of El Capitan oil field, lower left. (Spence air photo E-7997, 10/5/37).

the bridge across large Cañada del Capitan, at mileage marker 33[85], interlayered fine and bouldery materials can be seen to compose the coverhead on the terrace being traversed.

O-7   Beyond El Capitan Creek bridge, foothills on the right display whitish rock debris derived from the underlying Monterey and a sprinkling of large boulders derived from older sandstone formations (lower Miocene to Eocene) outcropping to the north. Just before getting to the big white tank and oil well pumps on the right, part of El Capitan oil field operations, a view of a long sea cliff extending west for miles can be seen in good weather.

Sea cliffs are steep because they are constantly being cut back by wave erosion at their base. Sea cliffs in the Santa Barbara area have receded three to ten inches **per** year, or roughly fifty feet per century, within recent historical time. Sea cliffs in other parts of the world, for example the White Cliffs of Dover in England, have receded at still faster rates. Don't build

your house too close to a sea cliff, if you intend to remain in it for very long.

At the west edge of El Capitan oil field, less than half a mile beyond the large tank, is unusually large Corral Canyon. Highly deformed, light-colored shale beds (Monterey) are seen in its west wall. Beyond Corral Canyon the highway-level terrace is narrow, and a second terrace remnant lies about 35-40 feet higher on the right. The steep Santa Ynez Mountain front is now only about three miles inland. Opposite "Refugio State Beach, 1 Mile," kelp is abundant just offshore. If a light breeze is blowing, kelpless areas are rippled, but areas with kelp are smooth. As the highway curves beyond Refugio Beach exit, a fleeting view develops to the left of the cove, palm trees, and camp area at the beach.

O-8   Beyond Refugio Creek bridge, the highway curves and ascends through a large double-walled cut in light-colored contorted shales. Upon clearing the cut, at 10 o'clock, is an offshore drilling platform. Terraces are still narrow, and at least two levels are present, the second one 15-20 feet higher than the road. A sea cliff extending spectacularly far upcoast comes into view about 1.5 miles beyond Refugio Creek, near 38⁰⁰. A terrace extends inland from the cliff to smooth-sloped foothills (underlain by shale) which border the steep rugged face (sandstone) of Santa Ynez Mountains. The highway shortly starts dipping into gullies and rising to terrace remnants between. Roadcuts show mostly coverhead. About 0.5 mile beyond "Gaviota 7, Santa Maria 50," and just beyond "End of Freeway," directly ahead is a good view of the massive, steeply dipping sandstones (Oligocene and Eocene) making up the steep, rugged, rocky face of Santa Ynez Mountains to Gaviota Pass and beyond (Photo H-1). Similar views continue intermittently most of the remaining several miles to Gaviota Pass. Lower foothills south of the mountain face form a narrowing belt. White shale beds are exposed in gullies, in bluffs and secondary roadcuts on the near foothills, as well as in freeway cuts descending into and climbing out of the deeper gullies.

Approaching blue/white "Rest Area, 7 Miles," is a close-up view of the sea cliff. In this reach the terrace is narrow, and the thin coverhead is fine-grained. Beyond the canyon with an old concrete highway bridge and a steel railroad trestle (to the left), about 0.5 mile beyond the rest area sign, hillslopes on the right become smoother, grassier, more rounded, and the material exposed in roadcuts is uniformly brown. We have reentered the Rincon shales. Views up side canyons to the north approaching and just beyond the Mobil gas station show massive Vaqueros sandstones not too far upstream, with still older Oligocene and Eocene beds farther up, all dipping steeply toward the ocean. As we advance into the Rincon Formation, near 43⁰⁰, the terrace widens because the brown, soft shales have yielded more easily to wave erosion. Foothills become lower and the foothill belt narrower until finally steeply dipping, massive sandstone beds of the Santa Ynez front rise directly from the terrace surface—an impressive sight. The more resistant rocks of the mountains produce a coverhead containing many large sandstone boulders. Ahead, an early vintage jet fighter plane resides in the front yard of Vista del Mar Union School, and a little beyond are the tanks, dock, and other installations of Getty Oil Company Gaviota Marine terminal. Then comes Gaviota (population 94, elevation 150 ft.) with service stations and restaurant (closed in late 1977) situated upon a marine terrace of modest width.

O-9   Beyond Gaviota the highway continues on the terrace surface and once more crosses into white shales (Monterey). Beyond "Gaviota State Beach, Left Turn ½ Mile", the route curves into a northerly course toward Gaviota Pass. The first rock in cuts on the right as we start to curve and descend toward Gaviota Creek is light-colored shale (Monterey), but beyond "Rest Area, 3/4 Mile" we pass into brown shales (Rincon). The Monterey-Rincon contact can be seen on the far wall of Gaviota Canyon, where slopes underlain by the Rincon display considerable slumping. Gaviota State Beach turnoff comes shortly on the left, and canyon walls steepen and the canyon narrows as large dip slopes in massive sandstone rise spectacularly ahead. A brownish sandstone, about fifteen feet thick, outcropping on the right below the Rincon is the greatly thinned remnant of the Vaqueros Sandstone, which behind Santa Barbara is hundreds of feet thick. Just beyond the brown sandstone are some finer-grained, reddish beds of Sespe character, but they quickly give way to underlying brownish shales and sandstones of the marine Alegría Formation (Oligocene).

A pause at the rest stop is desirable in order to inspect the precipitous walls and steeply dipping sandstone beds of Gaviota Gorge, negotiated by the highway tunnel ahead (Photo H-5). Rest stations on both sides of the freeway are in the Alegría Formation, the western marine equivalent of the continental Sespe to the east. The large spur west of the east-side rest stop is made by massive, resistant, steeply dipping sandstone beds at the base of the Alegria. Looking north, the vales on both canyon walls this side of the gorge and tunnel are underlain by shales in the upper Gaviota Formation (Oligo-Eocene). The gorge and tunnels are in the middle member of the Gaviota, a massive resistant sandstone unit, dipping steeply (60°) south and making a dip slope as well as forming projecting ribs on the hillsides. The stone in the restroom building and other structures at the rest stops is the Pelona Schist, quarried largely in the Bouquet Canyon area of the westernmost San Gabriel Mountains. As you can see, Gaviota Gorge would make a fine place to "head 'em off at the pass." In the early days outlaws supposedly frequented this spot to hold up stagecoaches and travelers. The Spanish gathered here to stop General Fremont from bringing his brigade to Santa Barbara in 1846, but the wily general, forewarned, took the San Marcos Pass route

Photo H-5. Looking north to Gaviota Gorge from west-side rest stop. Dipping sandstone beds behind east-side rest stop (lower right) are Alegria Formation (Oligocene) and massive sandstone face at tunnel is middle Gaviota Formation (Eocene). Dips are steeply south.

and reputedly marched into Santa Barbara unopposed.

Beyond the tunnel, the canyon opens somewhat as it enters shaly beds and thinner sandstones in the lower part of the Gaviota and underlying Sacate Formation (Eocene), which has replaced the Coldwater Sandstone so prominent in Santa Ynez Mountains behind Santa Barbara. Somewhat beyond "Lompoc, Highway 1, Exit 1 Mile," materials on hillslopes to the right will look like a mess, and small wonder! They are part of a large landslide of mixed Eocene sandstone and shale beds. You are well into the slide mass at 48°°. The south branch of Santa Ynez fault crosses the road 0.5 mile beyond the tunnel, about at the edge of the slide debris, but it can't be easily recognized from the freeway. The slide mass extends almost to Highway 1 (to Lompoc and Vandenberg Air Force Base). To the left through this reach the hillslopes are underlain by south-dipping beds of sandstone and shale, principally of the Alegria (Oligocene) and the underlying Gaviota (Oligo-Eocene) formations.

Lompoc is the center of a large diatomite mining and processing operation (Photo H-1). Diatomite (or diatomaceous earth) is a sedimentary accumulation composed largely of siliceous skeletons of small, single-celled plants (diatoms) that live in the ocean. The skeletons, of highly complex geometrical configurations, consist of pure silica and are thus chemically inert. Processed diatomite is about ten percent solid matter and ninety percent open space. Diatomite is said to have over three hundred uses, but it is employed principally as a filtering medium for a wide variety of fluids from syrup to oil, as a filler in paints and other such substances, and as an insulator. The diatomite deposits of Lompoc are among the largest and purest in the world. They are largely in the Sisquoc Formation (upper Miocene-lower Pliocene) and locally in the uppermost part of the Monterey.

O-10   After passing under Highway 1 and starting upgrade toward Gaviota Pass, the hills ahead on the left, extending to the skyline, are largely smooth-sloped, round-crested, and grassy, suggesting a shaly bedrock, although sandstones are not wholly lacking. Approaching "Buellton 8, etc.," at 9 o'clock are the scars of slides, slumps and earth flows as well as faint terracettes. Slopes to the right (east) of our north-trending highway are heavily covered with oak and chaparral. The rocks there are mostly Gaviota Formation, except toward the top of the grade where some dark, locally reddish shales (Eocene, Anita) appear in roadcuts on the right. The rock at the summit is Rincon Shale, and the cut is deep enough so that much of the shale is dark, not having been oxidized to its usual, near-surface, brown color. Fracturing and contortion in shale beds approaching the summit indicate proximity to the main branch of Santa Ynez fault which crosses the highway near the grade crest.

Starting downgrade, the view to the right up Nojoqui Valley is pleasantly pastoral, with farms, fences, grain fields, and grassy slopes dotted with oaks. Shales are seen going downgrade, but near the bottom is a cut in light-tan to bluish gray, massive sandstone (Vaqueros). At foot of the grade, the highway levels onto the valley floor of Nojoqui Creek which is deeply filled with fine alluvium as shown by the exposure in vertical gully walls to the left, locally plastered with the mud nests of many swallows. We proceed due north down Nojoqui Creek toward Buellton.

For much of this traverse, rocks underlying the immediate hillslopes on both sides are mostly Oligocene to Eocene marine beds, largely shales, but locally sandstones which make projecting ribs. Try to spot roadside marker 53⁰⁰. About 0.8 mile beyond, at a ranch with large oak trees and cattle sheds at 10-12 o'clock, is a massive outcropping of gray rock. It supports trees and brush which contrast with the neighboring grassy hillslopes. The gray rock is unusual for this region because it is a limestone (Sierra Blanca), which marks the base of the Eocene sequence. Limestones are abundant in the eastern Mojave Desert, but they are rare in the coastal Cenozoic sequence. This is the Live Oak Ranch locality, and the Sierra Blanca Limestone is particularly prominent here because of a wider than normal outcrop breadth caused by exposure on the nose of a plunging anticline.

Within a mile beyond Live Oak Ranch, after crossing a concrete bridge, the highway and Nojoqui Creek enter a narrow winding gorge, with older (Cretaceous, eighty million years) harder rocks making up the walls. The first strata seen are of the Jalama Formation, and they shortly give way (near 55⁰⁰) to darker, tougher, fine-grained, greenish strata of the Espada Formation, both marine. The Espada continues until we come into the valley of Santa Ynez River. The river is approached across a flat, near-flood plain surface and crossed on a concrete bridge before intersecting Highway 246. Buellton occupies a terrace across Santa Ynez River.

O-11   Beyond Santa Ynez River and Buellton, the character of the country changes, largely because the rocks are different. We pass Buellton in a depressed freeway course and start gentle ascent of the alluviated floor of Zaca Creek. In about 0.5 mile a gravel-mantled Santa Ynez River terrace, 50-60 feet above highway level, is visible in profile on the flanks of the bare hills at 12:30 to 2:00 o'clock. Terrace remnants continue on both sides to and beyond "Los Alamos 13, San Luis Obispo 62." Besides Pleistocene terrace gravels, the hills beyond Buellton also contain marine sandstones (Pliocene, Careaga) and land-laid silts, sands, and gravel (Plio-Pleistocene, Paso Robles Formation) of which we see a lot shortly. These rocks are relatively soft, unconsolidated, and do not form strong outcrops. The first good bedrock exposure, on the left about 0.5 mile beyond the terrace views, is light-colored, thinly bedded shale (Miocene, Monterey). We continue through such shale nearly all the way to junction with Highway 154. Modest exposures are seen in stream and gully banks, and occasionally in roadcuts and hillside bluffs. Attitude of bedding changes from place to place as these strata are folded. We cross the axes of several anticlines and synclines in the next four miles. This is pretty country in the spring with a nice blanket of green grass, scattered oak trees on slopes, both live and deciduous varieties, and a modest relief of 200-250 feet. Beyond 62^{00}, just before getting to the Highway 154 junction, we pass into an overlying formation (Mio-Pliocene Sisquoc), but you can hardly tell the difference except that the rocks are possibly more light-colored and more massive. They are rich in diatomaceous materials, and most of the diatomite mined near Lompoc is in this unit. Light-colored sands (Pliocene, Careaga) are also exposed on adjoining slopes right at the junction. This locality is also at the south edge of an extensive sheet of Paso Robles Formation (Plio-Pleistocene). Continue north on 101 via Segment J, or return to Santa Barbara on Highway 154 via Segment I.

Segment H—
Inbound Descriptions

(The corresponding outbound material should be read first.)

I-12   Travelers headed toward Santa Barbara start this trip at highways 101 and 154 intersection, two miles west of Los Olivos and eight miles south of Los Alamos. Note an odometer reading at the start.

I-11   Southbound travelers start from this complex of Miocene to Pleistocene formations at the 101-154 intersection. The white exposures on the left opposite "Buel-

lton 5, Santa Barbara 49" are Sisquoc, but the thinly bedded shales seen the rest of the way down Zaca Creek, almost to Buellton, are Monterey. Exposures descending Zaca Creek are, if anything, better than for outbound travelers and changes in bedding inclination from horizontal to steeply dipping are particularly obvious. Approaching Buellton the hills become lower and Zaca Creek valley widens, displaying more cultivation. Good terraces lie on both sides near "Buellton Exit, 3/4 Mile." The high crest of the Santa Ynez Mountains dominates the skyline ahead.

I-10   After crossing Santa Ynez River beyond Buellton and traversing the flat south of the river, the highway enters the narrow winding gorge of Nojoqui Creek. The first rock exposures near "Gaviota 11, Santa Barbara 43," are dark, greenish gray, hard shales (Cretaceous, Espada). Similar rocks, with thin interbeds of light-colored sandstones, continue for nearly 1.5 miles. Canyon walls are steep, and the stream is bridged repeatedly. The gorge opens somewhat beyond the bridge at mileage 54^{74} as we penetrate overlying brownish, softer shales and sandstones (Cretaceous, Jalama). These beds are locally concretionary, and, in places, as approaching marker 54^{00}, the slopes on the left are contoured by little, parallel, trail-like terracettes (Photo 1-4). Terracettes are also seen on the left opposite blue/white "Rest Area, 7 Miles."

By now the gorge has given way to a more open valley with a wider alluviated floor, and hillslopes to the left are underlain by brown shales (Eocene, Cozy Dell). Massive sandstones on the right make dip slopes. Just a little beyond marker 54^{00}, watch for the Live Oak Ranch locality on the right with the exposures of gray, massive Sierra Blanca Limestone. Beyond the Nojoqui Park turnoff, fine alluvium, at least 25-30 feet thick, is exposed in near-vertical stream banks right of the highway. Look for the cluster of swallow nests on the face of the stream bank, one hundred and fifty feet to the right near the foot of the grade ahead. The big roadcut at bottom of the grade exposes massive sandstone (lower Miocene, Vaqueros). Going upgrade, the Santa Ynez Mountains crest is directly ahead. Shales at the top of the grade are Rincon (lower Miocene). Going downgrade on the south side of Gaviota Pass (Nojoqui Summit), a complex of shales and sandstones ranging from Eocene to Miocene make up the adjacent hillsides all the way to the Highway 1 intersection. Massive sandstones (Eocene, Matilija) near the crest of Santa Ynez Mountains are particularly impressive during this descent and merit a look or two.

I-9   Inbound passengers headed south on Highway 101 easily identify the Highway 1 junction by means of the large signs. Beyond that intersection, the large slide is to the left, and hills on the right expose sandstones and shales (Oligocene to Eocene, Alegria and Gaviota). The freeway splits and curves southeasterly about 1/4 mile before leaving the slide mass and crossing the south branch of Santa Ynez fault, beyond which shales and sandstones (Eocene, Sacate) make up the left wall of the canyon. The highway crosses a bridge and straightens into a due south course to negotiate the narrows of Gaviota Gorge which cuts through massive, south-dipping, resistant sandstones (Gaviota Formation). Good cavernous weathering is seen on the right. A pause at the rest stop a little beyond Gaviota Gorge is advised so you can inspect relationships more leisurely. Looking back to the north, the large dip-slope facing you just left of the highway is the lower sandstone unit of the Alegria Formation (Oligocene). By walking to the south end of the rest area, you can inspect, from a modest distance, the roadcut to the east showing steeply dipping beds of reddish Sespe-type (Oligocene) materials overlain by a thin layer of brownish Vaqueros (lower Miocene) Sandstone. A near-horizontal layer of bouldery Pleistocene stream

gravel truncates the steeply dipping Vaqueros with an angular unconformity.

After leaving the rest stop, beyond the turnoff into Gaviota State Beach, the freeway climbs from Gaviota Canyon and curves into an easterly course. Miocene shales, first Rincon and then Monterey, are seen going upgrade. At the top, we emerge onto a terrace and to the left we can see flat reaches on spurs indicating remnants of a second terrace, higher by about fifty feet.

I-8   In passing Gaviota inbound, good views are available of the spectacularly rugged, rocky, massive sandstone front (Oligocene and Eocene) of Santa Ynez Mountains on the left at 9-11 o'clock. San Miguel Island is visible in clear weather at 3 o'clock, with Santa Rosa at 2 o'clock (Photo G-8). Just beyond 43^{00}, three terrace levels are seen, one about twenty-five feet and another fifty feet above the highway terrace. The coverhead on the highway terrace, as exposed in highway and railroad cuts, is boulder-rich. Beyond, as the highway terrace narrows, we catch occasional glimpses of the sea cliff in white Monterey shale. An offshore drilling platform is in view at 3 o'clock not far out, and views up side canyons to the left, particularly about 0.2 mile beyond 42^{00}, show impressive dip slopes on sandstones making up the high Santa Ynez Mountains front. Kelp beds are conspicuous a short distance offshore. Beyond "Santa Barbara 25, Ventura 53, Los Angeles 121," the highway terrace is a little wider, and two higher terrace levels are visible inland, one about seventy and one about one hundred feet above highway level. Approaching Refugio Beach, as indicated by the signs, we rise to cross a bedrock spur in a double-walled roadcut in shale (Monterey) before descending to Refugio Creek.

I-7   For inbound travelers, Refugio Creek is crossed a little beyond "Refugio Road, Next Right." Refugio Cove and Beach are in good view on the right before turnoff into the park. Beyond Refugio Canyon, the highway terrace is accompanied by a narrower terrace remnant about thirty feet higher on the left. In less than a mile, you catch a pretty good view of the sea cliff ahead cut into steeply dipping, light-colored shale beds (Monterey) and sporting an occasional little cove beach at its base. Coverhead is seen in railroad cuts to the right. Beyond an unusually large canyon (Cañada del Corral) is El Capitan oil field, largely on the left, and then glimpses of El Capitan Beach and Point (Photo H-4) are seen ahead at about 12:45 o'clock.

I-6   Eastbound travelers looking ahead from the exit into El Capitan State Beach see railroad cuts exposing unusually well-sorted gravel containing large, well-rounded boulders composing part of the coverhead on the highway terrace. Similar exposures extend beyond Cañada del Capitan. Just beyond that crossing, at about 12:30 o'clock, a long, straight sea cliff cut into steeply dipping, light-colored shale beds (Monterey) is in view. The beach at its foot and the terrace extending inland are both exceptionally narrow. Beyond El Capitan Ranch Road exit, the front of Santa Ynez Mountains with massive sandstones is again in good view, and the highway terrace is widening. Lemon and avocado orchards become more abundant approaching Dos Pueblos Ranch.

I-5   Coming from the west, travelers see the red tile roofs of Dos Pueblos Rancho on the right at 2-3 o'clock beyond marker 31^{00}, a little before descending into Dos Pueblos Canyon with its large oak and sycamore trees. The turnoff onto Dos Pueblos Canyon Road is nearly a mile beyond the first sighting of the ranch. A little beyond "Hollister Avenue-Winchester Canyon Road Exit, 1 Mile," you may be able to catch glimpses to the right, through eucalyptus and cypress trees, of piers with oil derricks, part of the Ellwood field. This was one of the early ocean floor oil operations along this section of coast.

I-4   Travelers headed toward Santa Barbara easily sense the change in terrain as the highway drops off the terrace just a little west of Winchester Canyon Road-Hollister Avenue intersection. The Ellwood oil field, Coal Oil Point (Photo H-1) and La Goleta gas field are in the same locations as indicated for outbound travelers. Coming up on Glen Annie Road, views of Goleta Plain are good. Beyond that intersection, the high, rugged face of Santa Ynez Mountains behind Santa Barbara in the area of La Cumbre Peak at about 11:45 o'clock is striking.

I-3   Approaching Fairview and Patterson avenues from the west, inbound motorists can appreciate the flatness of Goleta Plain. Hills south of the freeway, bounded by More Ranch fault, are visible approaching and beyond Turnpike Road. Beyond Turnpike, the freeway abandons Goleta Plain ascending into a somewhat hilly area. Cuts on both sides beyond "Business District, Next Right" (center-divider) show these hills to be made up of Santa Barbara Formation overlain by bouldery fanglomerate (Quaternary). Hope Ranch lies south of La Cumbre Road exit. Just beyond Las Positas overpass, to the right is more Quaternary gravel on Santa Barbara beds.

I-2   Inbound travelers get a reasonable view down the Santa Barbara graben with The Mesa on the right and Mission Ridge on the left from vicinity of Las Positas Road coming into the city on Highway 101. The face of The Mesa is seen at 12:30 to 3:00 o'clock beyond "Carrillo Street Exit, 1 Mile."

The harbor area can be visited by turning off on Castillo Street at "Beaches and Stoplight Ahead," turn right on Castillo and continue straight ahead, southwest, to the shore, then turn right on Shoreline Drive. The fossiliferous bluffs are one hundred yards along Shoreline. Park in the area across the street.

I-1   This segment ends at State Street (stoplight) in Santa Barbara.

Segment I

Santa Barbara to Los Olivos, 36 Miles

O-1 This segment separates northbound from Highway 101 near the west edge of Santa Barbara and provides an alternate, back-country, shorter trip upcoast than Segment H. Outbound motorists electing it take the Highway 154-State Street off ramp. They follow 154 to San Marcos Pass (2,224 ft.), cross Santa Ynez Mountains, descend Santa Ynez River, pass Lake Cachuma, and cross Santa Ynez Valley to Los Olivos before rejoining Highway 101, 2.5 miles beyond.

This route is the northwesterly hypotenuse of a right triangle, the other sides being made by Highway 101 through Gaviota Pass (Segment H). Travelers interested in urban developments can divert to the Danish tourist center of Solvang by way of Highway 246 in Santa Ynez Valley. They rejoin Highway 101 at Buellton, where the streets are awash with green split-pea soup. Geology comes in concentrated gobs along this route, so motorists will do well to proceed leisurely and to stop in turnouts to read ahead. Record an odometer reading at the start.

(Inbound travelers see p. 141.)

O-2 Upon clearing the offramp mess, outbound travelers on 154 are headed north toward the steep face of Santa Ynez Mountains. The high, rugged, rocky skyline at 2:00-2:30 o'clock features Cathedral (3,333 ft.) and La Cumbre (3,985 ft.) peaks, underlain by massive sandstone beds (Eocene, Matilija) dipping steeply south. In 3/4 mile, the route passes over Highway 192 (Foothill-Cathedral Oaks roads) and ascends gradually through forelying foothills of Santa Ynez Mountains. The first few roadcuts north of 192, in secondarily-derived rock detritus, won't excite you. Formerly a relatively smooth piedmont surface, capped by coarse, bouldery fanglomerate, sloped gently outward from the foot of the mountains here. Stream dissection of this surface has created the present foothill terrain. Scattered boulders from the fanglomerate capping are seen in a few of the first roadcuts and in side gullies.

O-3 Highway 154 soon narrows to two lanes and descends through a double-walled cut in coarse fanglomerate approaching San Antonio Creek. In crossing the bridge, see if you can spot its mileage mark of 30^{25}. Reference to mileage marks and markers along this route aids location and navigation. In the deep, double-walled roadcut just beyond San Antonio Canyon, beds of red sandstone and mudstone (Oligocene, Sespe) are exposed. We now travel more than two miles through similar strata. The beds first seen beyond San Antonio Creek look horizontal, although they ac-

133

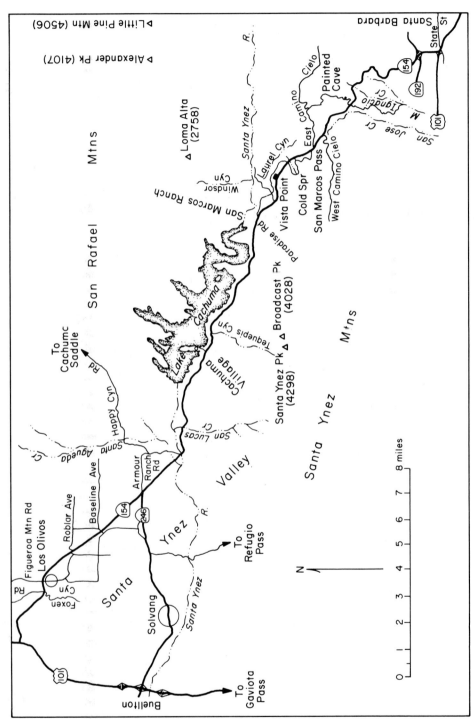

Figure I-1. Segment I, Santa Barbara to Los Olivos.

tually dip south at 15°-20°. They are cut by the road parallel to the strike, thus giving an impression of horizontality. In California, strata as old as these (26-37 million years) that seem horizontal should arouse your suspicions. Most California rocks more than a few tens of thousands years old are too much deformed to allow for much horizontal bedding.

For more than a mile beyond San Antonio Creek, roadcuts expose a sequence of land-laid red, green, gray, and brown sandstone, siltstone, and mudstone beds (Sespe), all dipping south at modest inclinations of 20°-30°. Apparent differences in dip are a function of changes in roadcut orientation as the highway negotiates a passage across a wide canyon (east fork of Maria Ygnacio Creek). About 0.2 mile beyond the big power line, a deep, double-walled roadcut exposes massive red sandstone, and almost immediately thereafter the beds become partly conglomeratic. These conglomerates characterize the lower part of the red-bed sequence, and turnouts afford opportunity for a closer look by people interested in details. The lithology of the generally well-rounded pebbles, cobbles, and boulders in the conglomerates is varied and rather exotic, featuring mostly resistant crystalline igneous and metamorphic rocks, some of known and some of unknown source. From these turnouts, Santa Barbara Channel and the four Channel Islands (Anacapa, Santa Cruz, Santa Rosa, and San Miguel [Photo G-8], east to west) may be visible. The coastal foreland below displays a pattern of extensive urban development.

Just over two miles from San Antonio Creek, the highway curves north into a large canyon (main branch of Maria Ygnacio Creek), and there an unusually deep, two-walled roadcut exposes red conglomerate, sandstone, and mudstone, but the next roadcut (also double-walled but smaller) is all in brown sandstone. This sandstone belongs to an older, largely marine formation (upper Eocene, Coldwater). Mileage marker 28⁰⁰ is at the far (north) end of the brown sandstone cut, and mountain slopes ahead and above display massive dip-slope exposures of this same sandstone. The cluster of houses near top of the mountains is the settlement at Painted Cave.

O-4   Our route remains principally in the brown Eocene sandstone, with intercalations of shale, all the way to the crest of San Marcos grade, about 3.5 miles ahead. Shale partings between massive sandstone layers have facilitated sliding where dip of the strata and direction of slope coincide. Some roadcuts are wholly in this slide-broken rock debris.

The sandstone strata are folded into an anticline and a syncline in vicinity of San Marcos Pass. However, you can experience considerable frustration trying to recognize these structures from the highway traveling at speeds required by the traffic on this mostly two-lane road. The first exposures of brown sandstone seen dip south, but in the roadcut just beyond marker 27⁰⁰ bedding dips north, suggesting that we have crossed to the north limb of the anticline. About 0.3 mile farther, at Painted Cave Road junction, the beds dip south, and we have crossed back a little way onto the south limb of the fold. South dips are also seen about 0.3 mile beyond this junction. Shortly, the highway turns north for a good half-mile before taking up a west-north-westerly course along the north side of San Jose Creek, the canyon with many oaks and a scattering of houses. Looking ahead along the wall of San Jose Creek, cliffy outcrops are made by north-dipping beds. To the left, beds making bluffs on the far wall of the creek dip gently south. The axis of the fold (Bush Mountain anticline) here runs along the course of the creek. Approaching the wide intersection at San Marcos Pass crest, massive sandstone beds in roadcuts display a variety of sedimentary structures such as;

cross-bedding, concretions and included shale fragments. They also exhibit considerable brown staining by iron oxide.

At top of the grade adventuresome travelers can turn right onto East Camino Cielo, a road that traverses the crestal ridge of Santa Ynez Mountains for about nine miles, with spectacular views to both sides. A shorter option is to the left at "Kinevan Road" and then immediately right onto Stagecoach Road to follow its winding course two miles into the cool sylvan glade of Cold Spring Canyon. Stagecoach Road is the old San Marcos Grade highway. Big leaf maple and California bay trees contribute much to the green lushness of this locality. A branch of Stagecoach Road enters from the right part way down—just keep on ahead. Before getting to Cold Spring Inn at the canyon bottom, the sandstone (Eocene, Coldwater) gives way to an underlying brown, nodular shale (Eocene, Cozy Dell). Good exposures of the shale are seen in roadcuts just beyond Cold Spring Inn. As you have climbed upward into Santa Ynez Mountains, the rocks have become progressively older, and this continues to a crossing of Santa Ynez fault, before getting to Lake Cachuma. By continuing 0.5 mile beyond the inn, you get a striking view of the high arch bridge for Highway 154 across Cold Spring Canyon.

Since anticlines and synclines tend to come in pairs, it is not surprising that Bush Mountain anticline has a girlfriend, Laurel Canyon syncline, which extends along the course of Laurel Canyon to which Cold Spring Canyon is tributary. From beneath Cold Spring Arch bridge, south-dipping beds of brown sandstone are seen on the far wall of Laurel Canyon and north-dipping beds make up the walls of Cold Spring Canyon. These attitudes define the Laurel Canyon syncline. (How does it happen we don't name more of our daughters Laurel? It's a nice name for a girl.) Now retrace your route to the Kinevan Road turnoff at the summit of San Marcos Pass. A glimpse of the high arch bridge is seen climbing out of Cold Spring Canyon, and north-dipping beds on the south limb of the syncline are exposed on the west wall of Cold Springs Canyon.

O-5   Outbound travelers remaining on or returning to Highway 154 have a great view north into Santa Ynez River country and to rugged San Rafael Mountains starting down from San Marcos Pass. A synclinal axis runs up Laurel Canyon on the right. North-dipping beds of sandstone on the south limb of the syncline or the north limb of Bush Mountain anticline (they share a limb) are seen in roadcuts and in the little knob on the right just before crossing under the large power line ahead. Just beyond, a branch of Stagecoach Road affords a second access into Cold Spring Canyon for those who passed up the Kinevan Road turnoff. We cross the huge Cold Springs Arch bridge (mileage 9[19]) and just about two miles below San Marcos Pass come to a vista point turnout and parking area. This is a stop worth making for scenic and geological views into Santa Ynez River country (Photo I-1) and to San Rafael Mountains.

Looking north from the diorama board at the vista-point parking area, the isolated mountain on the near skyline is Loma Alta (2,758 ft.). For purposes of reference, its position is designated as 12 o'clock. An oak tree-dotted grainfield on the surface of a low terrace across Santa Ynez River below at 11 o'clock should catch your eye. In spring, when green, it's a most attractive scene. Behind the field, partly bare bluffs expose beds dipping gently northward (Plio-Pleistocene, Paso Robles Formation). The south slope of Loma Alta is relatively smooth and largely brush- and grass-covered, with scattered oaks only near the base. The lower area west and southwest of Loma Alta is rougher and has more brush, trees, and bare bluffs. This difference might lead you to infer that different rock materials

Belt of Franciscan Rx.   Loma Alta   Alexander Pk.   Franciscan Rx.

Santa Ynez R.   San Rafael Mtns.   Old Man Mtn.   Little Pine Mtn.   Santa Ynez R.

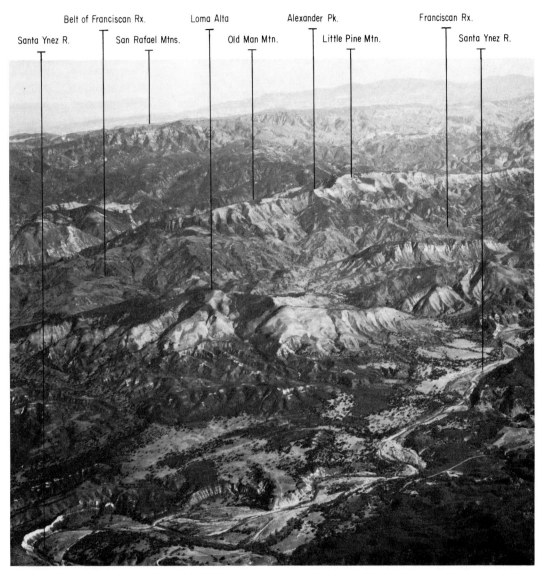

Photo I-1. Looking north across Santa Ynez River to San Rafael Mountains of interior Santa Barbara County (Fairchild air photo 0-5016, 11/3/36).

underlie the two areas, and you would be right. Loma Alta is largely shale (**upper** Monterey), and the lower area is largely sand and gravel (Paso Robles). Normally, these two sequences of strata are not in contact, as several Pliocene and Pleistocene formations should come between. They are

brought together here by a north- and northeast-dipping thrust fault which passes along the west side and southwest base of Loma Alta. This Loma Alta fault is a branch of a larger, more continuous structure, Little Pine fault, which passes behind Loma Alta and extends for many miles to the northwest and southeast. By close inspection you may be able to make out a complex of north- and south-dipping beds within the lower area west of Loma Alta. These beds are folded into at least seven anticlines and synclines.

At 1:30 o'clock on the northeast skyline is Little Pine Mountain (4,506 ft.) with a cluster of coniferous trees. The bare peak a little to the west is Alexander Peak (4,107 ft.), and the long ridge extending still farther west is Old Man Mountain. Rocks composing the bluff on the south face of that ridge look horizontal, but they actually dip north into a syncline. They are largely upper Monterey shales, the same unit that makes up Loma Alta.

Now take the 100-yard trail from the west end of the parking area to a viewing point and a second diorama. You pass by dense chaparral composed of holly leaf cherry, ceanothus, chamise, buck brush, sumac, scrub oak, manzanita, California bay, black sage, toyon, bush poppy, coyote bush, and a number of other bushes and plants. From here the view to the far skyline of the San Rafael Mountains, including San Rafael Mountain (6,593 ft.) and McKinley Mountain (6,182 ft.) (identified on the diorama) is particularly good. The skyline ridge and the country for a considerable distance toward us are underlain by upper Cretaceous (70-100 million years) beds, largely sandstone. However, there is a strip of lower country lying between Loma Alta and the high San Rafael ridges. With good light you can see dark-colored rocks and a curious knobby terrain within this strip where it appears to the left of Loma Alta. To the right of Loma Alta, similar terrain exposes bluish gray rocks. This strip is underlain by a slice of Franciscan Formation, one of the more unusual units to grace the California geological scene. It is named from the San Francisco area and is more widely exposed and distributed in central California than in the southern part of the state. The Franciscan consists of a remarkable array of sedimentary, metamorphic, and altered igneous rocks, including cherts, dirty-gray sandstones, blue schists, green schists, serpentine, and less altered basic igneous rocks. In places, these are all mixed together in hopeless confusion as though shoved by a gigantic bulldozer. The full story and character of the Franciscan is too long and complex to recount here. The strip behind Loma Alta is one of the more southerly exposures of this unit. It exists as a slice between Little Pine fault on the south and Camuesa fault on the north.

O-6   Closer at hand is the floor of Santa Ynez River and downvalley at 9 o'clock is Lake Cachuma reservoir. Light colored bluffs north of the river and the lake are composed of Miocene shales (Monterey) and Pliocene sandstones (Tequepis and Careaga). North of the bluffs at 9:30 o'clock is a large area of beds (Paso Robles) within which you can see strata dipping gently to the north and south, forming an open syncline. On the far side of the river, at 10:15 and at 12:00 o'clock, are wide, flat, largely cultivated benches up to two hundred feet above the stream. These are terraces representing old Santa Ynez valley floors, now partly destroyed by dissection. We stand on Eocene rocks, but rocks just across the river are all Pliocene and Miocene—how come? Those younger formations have been brought down along Santa Ynez fault which runs along the bed of the river below.

Shales and sandstones exposed in the first roadcut just to the west of the vista point are near the base of the Coldwater (Eocene). The abundance of shale suggests that a gradual transition into the underlying Cozy Dell is underway.

At marker 22⁰⁰, the highway crosses a bridge over a deep canyon, and in the succeeding double-walled roadcut, at blue/ white "Phone, ¼ Mile," is good Cozy Dell Shale (Eocene). Actually, we entered the

Cozy Dell just before crossing the bridge. This formation is not all shale in spite of its name, as demonstrated by massive sandstone interbeds in the next roadcut, a little beyond the turnoff of Paradise Road.

Just beyond is still another junction with Stagecoach Road. Shale beds (Miocene, Monterey) in a cliff at 3 o'clock across Santa Ynez River look like they compose an open syncline. This is an illusion created by the concave geometrical configuration of the bluff. The beds actually dip consistently northward (35°-55°). Lighter colored bluffs downstream at 1 o'clock are largely sandstone (Mio-Pliocene, Tequepis), with a thin band of nearly white sandstone (Pliocene, Careaga) at the top.

O-7   Half a mile west of this last Stagecoach Road junction is the sign identifying San Marcos Ranch (paved road to right). Here the highway starts rising to cross a projecting spur. It ascends first onto a small terrace remnant, beyond marker 21[00], before attaining the spur. Successive roadcuts in the spur show near-horizontal beds of old alluvial deposits resting on shale beds of various colors from gray to reddish (presumably Cozy Dell). A glimpse of upper Lake Cachuma is seen ahead on the right descending from the spur. Beyond is an attractive, neatly fenced, tree-dotted terrace on which the red-roofed buildings of San Marcos Ranch are 3/8 mile to the right. The large ranch residence nestles against the foot of the hills to the left.

At the far edge of this flat terrace, as you rise from San Marcos Ranch terrace and begin to curve right, the first roadcuts, at "55 Maximum Speed," expose bluish-gray shale, locally weathered tan. This is the oldest bedrock seen on this trip. It is part of the Jalama Formation (late Cretaceous, eighty million years). About 0.3 mile farther, 0.1 mile short of marker 18[00], a large roadcut on the right exposes a steeply inclined, sharp contact between the gray shales and tan-colored, fine, sandy, silty,

shaly Miocene beds. This is Santa Ynez fault, crossed at a very oblique angle by the highway. Local accumulations of rounded sandstone boulders in some cuts here are derived from Quaternary terrace gravels. In straightening out on a course that brings us close to lakeshore, the highway traverses tan colored Miocene rocks. Coarse, gritty sands with oyster shell fragments exposed just before the turn near the lake's edge are probably lower Miocene (Vaqueros).

O-8   Outbound travelers approaching the edge of Lake Cachuma, about 0.2 mile after crossing the fault, see a stream terrace, seventy feet above water level, across the lake at 12:30 o'clock. Succeeding highway cuts are mostly in light-colored sandstones, siltstones, and shales, probably all part of the lower Monterey (middle Miocene). Within half a mile, the rocks become typical, thinly bedded, whitish upper Monterey Shale beds (upper Miocene) with variable and steeply inclined dips.

Just beyond marker 17[00] is the turnoff (left) into Rancho San Francisco de los Robles. Immediately thereafter we cross a canyon and start upgrade. Within 0.2 mile, roadcuts expose nearly horizontal layers of coarse, bouldery fanglomerate capping a surface sloping gently north. The rounded boulders are fragments of sandstone (Eocene) derived from the steep north face of Santa Ynez Mountains. These fanglomerates continue for 0.3 mile before white, massive, fine-grained sandstones are seen in a large cut on the left. These are probably late Pliocene marine deposits (Careaga). In another 0.3 mile, fanglomerates reappear and continue for nearly 0.4 mile before the highway dips toward the turnoff (left) of Tequepis Canyon Road.

O-9   Beyond Tequepis Canyon Road, westbound, roadcuts alternately expose white shale and brown, bouldery fanglomerate. All along, one gets glimpses of Lake Cachuma and of the white bluffs on its north side, locally topped by flat terrace remnants. Approaching Cachuma Village, the high Santa Ynez crest, including Broadcast Peak (4,028 ft.) with radio towers, is in view at 9 o'clock. About 1.2 miles beyond Cachuma Village is a vista-point turnoff (right). This point affords a look at Bradbury Dam, constructed in 1953, and provides picnic facilities with restrooms and shaded tables.

O-10   Just west of the vista-point turnoff, the highway drops to a lower surface from the fanglomerate-mantled bench. Oak trees here sport long festoons of Spanish moss. Terraces are visible on both sides of Santa Ynez River once we clear the trees. Our route continues across low terrace surfaces and alluvial flats before crossing through a narrow ridge of upper Monterey Shale just short of San Lucas Creek. Santa Ynez River is approached over the smooth surface of a low terrace and crossed about three miles from the vista point. Armour Ranch Road takes off right (north) just beyond Santa Ynez River, but before the crossing of San Agueda Creek. Highway 154 then turns northwest and ascends to a higher level in two steps, each step representing the remnant of a Santa Ynez River terrace. Steeply dipping Miocene (upper Monterey) beds are exposed in roadcuts a half mile beyond the Santa Ynez crossing, and coarse fluvial gravels are seen ascending to the higher terrace. When the upper flatland is attained at marker 9⁰⁰, Figueroa Mountain (4,528 ft.), a tree-covered ridge in the San Rafael Mountains, is on the far skyline at 3 o'clock. The sharp, conical mountain at about 2:15 o'clock is Zaca Peak. Access to Figueroa Mountain and some of the San Rafael Mountain back country north of Cachuma Saddle can be attained by turning onto Armour Ranch Road at its second junction ahead (or at the first junction) and ascending Happy Canyon. About two miles west of Santa Ynez River, Highway 246 separates, leading to Santa Ynez, Solvang, and Buellton, for those wishing to elect that diversion.

O-11   Beyond the 246 intersection, westbound, Highway 154 traverses a shallowly dissected, gently rolling terrain. Roadcuts expose alluvium derived largely from the Paso Robles Formation, a sandy gravel rich in fragments of white shale derived from upper Monterey beds. Low foothills of Paso Robles beds lie in front of the San Rafael Mountains. The mid-slopes on the south face of Figueroa Mountain ridge, at 3 o'clock from the Edison Street-Baseline Avenue intersection, expose brown to blue-gray Franciscan rock. Figueroa Mountain itself consists of much younger Miocene beds dropped into contact with the Franciscan by faulting.

O-12   Continuing west toward Los Olivos, the terrain becomes a little more dissected and rolling. Alfalfa and grain fields, as well as walnut orchards, vineyards, houses, and the estates of gentlemen or gentlewomen ranchers grace the landscape. Alluvial material in roadcuts continues to look like debris derived from the Paso Robles Formation, but cuts in the hillier terrain a mile beyond Roblar Avenue, near Los Olivos city sign, supposedly expose Paso Robles beds themselves. At Los Olivos, Figueroa Mountain Road going north provides access to San Rafael Mountains, and a half-mile beyond, Foxen Canyon Road provides a back-country route to the Santa Maria area. Beyond Los Olivos and the famed eating spot, Mattie's Tavern, higher hills lie ahead on both sides. Old and new roadcuts, as well as stream bank exposures, show nearly horizontal layers of poorly consolidated, fine-grained to gravelly materials containing fragments of whitish shale. This is the Plio-Pleistocene Paso Robles Formation, a land-laid deposit. Somewhat more than two miles beyond Los Olivos is intersection with Highway 101 and the end of this segment. The last roadcut before the intersection is in uniform, white, coarse-grained, poorly consolidated Upper Pliocene marine sands (Careaga).

Segment I—
Inbound Descriptions

(The corresponding outbound material should be read first.)

I-13 Motorists traveling downcoast on Highway 101 can elect this segment inbound by taking Highway 154 at the well-marked junction (no buildings) 8.3 miles southeast of Los Alamos. Record odometer reading here.

I-12 The intersection of highways 101 and 154 occurs in the vicinity of the near quadruple-point junction of four Miocene to Pleistocene sedimentary formations (Monterey, Sisquoc, Careaga, and Paso Robles). The first three are marine and the last is land-laid in this area. After turning from Highway 101 onto Highway 154, the first roadcut on the right is in white, coarse-grained, unconsolidated sandstone (late Pliocene, Careaga), but after that, the inbound traveler sees only the near-horizontal, poorly defined layers of relatively unconsolidated sands and gravels containing smoothly worn, rounded fragments of white Miocene shale that characterize the Paso Robles (Plio-Pleistocene) in this region. The terrain consists of rolling hills with smooth slopes and rounded crests, largely grass-covered and dotted with both deciduous and live oaks. Roadside mileage markers start with zero at the 101-154 intersection, and marker 1^{00} is seen within the hills. Get in the habit of checking these markers as we need to use them on this trip. In about two miles, Highway 154 emerges onto the wide floor of Santa Ynez Valley. Foxen Canyon Road shortly takes off north, Alamo Pintado Creek is crossed on a concrete bridge, Figueroa Mountain Road separates

northward opposite Grand Avenue, the crest of San Rafael Mountains, dotted with coniferous trees, makes up the north skyline from 9 to 12 o'clock, and the Santa Ynez Mountains compose the southeast skyline.

Beyond Los Olivos, the course is southeasterly through gently rolling terrain in which roadcuts expose material generally regarded as Paso Robles. Soon the relief becomes gentler, and a little beyond "Cachuma Lake 11, Santa Barbara 29" we come out onto the flat, alluviated floor of Santa Ynez Valley. Beyond Roblar Avenue, the country is even flatter and smoother. At marker 5^{00} and beyond, the foothills of San Rafael Mountains on the left are carved in Paso Robles beds. The steeper, grassy, partly wooded, knobby slopes behind, rising more steeply toward the upper part of the Figueroa Mountain ridge at 8:50 o'clock, are underlain by diverse rocks (brown and gray-green) of the Franciscan Formation. At the Edison Street-Baseline Avenue crossing, McKinley Mountain (6,182 ft.) and San Rafael Mountain (6,593 ft.) are prominent on the skyline at 9:30 and 10:00 o'clock, respectively. Approaching junction with Highway 246, the country becomes more dissected and gently rolling. Roadcuts here expose materials looking much like Paso Robles but which are actually regarded as alluvium derived largely from that formation. Beyond Highway 246, the dissection sharpens, heralding approach to Santa Ynez River.

I-11 Travelers coming to the 154-246 junction from the northwest can see these features at the indicated localities. They get a good view of the north side of Santa Ynez Mountains, but they can't see its geology through the heavy vegetation cover.

I-10 Going east from Highway 246, motorists will note the addition of smoothly worn, rounded cobbles, derived from stream gravels in materials exposed in roadcuts, as Santa Ynez River is approached. As the highway descends to river level, nearly a mile beyond marker 9[00], the last cut on the left exposes whitish shales (upper Miocene). Approaching the eastern junction with Armour Ranch Road, Broadcast Peak with radio towers may be visible on the Santa Ynez Mountains skyline at 12:10 o'clock. Santa Ynez Peak lies a little to the west. After crossing Santa Ynez River, the highway ascends the open canyon of Santa Ynez River on a more easterly course. Gently dipping, brownish shale (Monterey) is visible in bare bluffs along the far side, and as we round the curve at marker 11[00], a nice stream terrace, 50-60 feet above the river, is seen across the valley at 10 o'clock. Most of the flat surfaces, some planted to grain, traversed by our highway are part of a lower terrace level. Just beyond San Lucas Ranch and San Lucas Creek (mileage 11[51]), the highway cuts through a narrow ridge of Miocene shale to emerge into fields of alfalfa and grain. The 50-foot stream terrace is again in good view across the river at 9 o'clock. At marker 12[00], the highway ascends into hills underlain by light-colored shales. Trees obscure views, but occasional glimpses of Bradbury Dam can be seen ahead to the left.

I-9   Inbound travelers first come to fanglomerates beyond marker 13[00], a little before the vista-point turnoff to Bradbury Dam. Good, almost spectacular, exposures of fanglomerate continue in roadcut after roadcut for more than a mile beyond the vista point. Lake Cachuma facilities and county park are passed, glimpses of the lake are seen, and a lot of thinly bedded, variously inclined Miocene shale beds and more fanglomerate layers are seen as the journey continues east.

I-8   Eastbound from Tequepis Canyon Road, travelers rise toward a bench and begin seeing layers of coarse fanglomerate in cuts on both sides within 0.3 mile. An exposure of massive, white, uniform, fine-grained sandstone (Careaga) interrupts the fanglomerate on the right about a mile beyond Tequepis Canyon Road. It is succeeded by more fanglomerate before the descent to the turnoff for Rancho San Francisco de los Robles. Beyond that point, and beyond marker 17[00], are more white Miocene (upper Monterey) shales which are eventually succeeded by beds richer in sand (lower Monterey, middle Miocene).

I-7   About a mile east of the rightside turn-in to Rancho San Francisco de los Robles, for inbound travelers, the highway swings away from Lake Cachuma and approaches Santa Ynez fault through tan-colored Miocene beds. Watch for marker 18[00]; just beyond it the fault is seen as a contact between light and dark beds in the large roadcut on the left. A small macadamized turnoff to the right provides parking for inbound travelers wishing to make a more leisurely inspection. Dark shale beds (late Cretaceous, Jalama) are exposed in roadcuts beyond the fault during the curving descent to the wide terrace flat at San Marcos Ranch. In crossing this flat, inbound travelers see a terrace nearly one hundred feet above stream level ahead at 11-12 o'clock.

I-6   Inbound, the false syncline in shale beds is seen across the river at 9:15 o'clock approaching the Los Padres National Forest sign and Stagecoach Road. Roadcuts beyond expose horizontal, well-layered, dark-brown Quaternary stream gravels, which give way to brown shale (Cozy Dell) with local massive sandstone interbeds. More typical Cozy Dell shales are seen in the big, double-walled roadcut beyond Paradise Road turnoff (left). At that turnoff, stream terraces are prominent on both sides of Santa Ynez River. The bridge, with marker 22[00] near its midpoint, is soon crossed, and in the roadcut beyond, not far from blue/white "Vista Point, ¼ Mile," is the contact between Cozy Dell and the overlying Coldwater Sandstone, a formation that will dominate the next few miles of our journey.

I-5 A stop at the vista point is also recommended for inbound travelers. Ascending toward San Marcos Pass from the vista point, the huge Cold Spring Arch bridge is crossed, affording a good view to the right into Cold Spring Canyon. Beyond, Laurel Canyon and the syncline of that name are on the left. North dips in massive Coldwater Sandstone beds on its south limb can be seen approaching San Marcos Pass summit. Opportunity to divert into Cold Spring Canyon is afforded by a branch of Stagecoach Road taking off to the right a little beyond Cold Spring Arch bridge.

I-4 Travelers coming to San Marcos Pass from the north have the same options of side-road diversons. Descending from the pass, views into Santa Barbara Channel and to the Channel Islands (Photo G-8) can be spectacular. Although the first two miles of descent are along the north side of San Jose Creek with the axis of Bush Mountain anticline along its floor, this structure is hard to recognize. Occasionally north-dipping beds can be spotted along the highway and south dips may be discerned in bluffs along the far wall of San Jose Creek.

I-3 Descending from San Marcos Pass, motorists see a lot of the massive brown sandstone (Coldwater) and should have little trouble recognizing the change to reddish strata (Sespe), beyond marker 28^{00}, about 3.5 miles from the pass. Conglomerates and sandstones in the basal part of the Sespe are seen first, followed by sandstone and mudstone strata, partly red but also buff, gray, and even occasionally green, downgrade for two miles to San Antonio Creek bridge.

I-2 After crossing San Antonio Creek bridge, the inbound route curves into a more southerly course and descends through the dissected, piedmont-bench remnants. Exposures of bouldery fanglomerate are seen in the first narrow, double-walled roadcuts beyond the bridge. The view southward is directly into the rolling, oak tree-covered hills of Hope Ranch, one of the more fashionable residential settlements of the region. The north face of these hills is determined by More Ranch fault. To the right is Goleta (Photo H-1), where tall buildings of the University of California, Santa Barbara, occupy Goleta Point at about 2 o'clock. To the left is The Mesa (Photo H-2), a higher-standing, fault-bounded feature described in Segment H.

I-1 This segment ends at the junction with Highway 101.

Segment J

From Highway 154 to San Luis Obispo, 59 Miles

O-1   This segment proceeds northwesterly on Highway 101 from its northern intersection with Highway 154 in central Santa Barbara County, 5.4 miles north of Buellton. It passes through low hills of the California Coast Ranges, crosses Santa Maria basin, traverses the Pismo coast, and eventually turns inland to San Luis Obispo. It is a particularly lovely drive in spring. Young Cenozoic marine and land-laid sedimentary rocks, layers of altered volcanic pyroclastics, mid-Cenozoic igneous intrusive bodies, "fossil" Pleistocene sand-dune sheets, and exposures of the famed Franciscan Formation are seen in addition to coastal scenery. A record of your odometer reading at the start should prove useful.

(Inbound travelers see p. 153.)

O-2   At the beginning, Highway 101 continues a short way up Zaca Creek, but it soon curves to a more northwesterly course and ascends a tributary. Upon leaving the alluviated floor of Zaca Creek beyond the Zaca Station Road separation, the highway passes onto the Paso Robles Formation (Plio-Pleistocene), a sequence of weakly consolidated, land-laid, silty, sandy, and gravelly beds that erode to a smooth, modestly rolling landscape. Grassy slopes prevail, dotted with oak trees, both live and deciduous. Rock outcrops on slopes are lacking, but exposures occur in gully banks, as on the right beyond marker 64^{00}. The high crest of San Rafael Mountains composes the far skyline at 2-3 o'clock.

About 2.5 miles from the start, a broad summit is approached where a bare bluff, one hundred and fifty feet to the right, shows near-horizontal Paso Robles beds. The summit is attained at marker 65^{00}, from which the highway descends along San Antonio Creek to the wide, alluviated floor of Los Alamos Valley. Oak trees on slopes to the right of marker 66^{00} show perceptible eastward tilt, an effect of the prevailing westerly winds.

The axis of a major syncline parallels the floor of Los Alamos Valley, but dips confirming that fact are hard to see in the weak, poorly exposed Paso Robles beds. Mapping by geologists shows the syncline to be strongly asymmetrical, with gentler dips on its northeast limb and steep-to-overturned beds on its southwest flank (Figure J-2). Approaching marker 68^{00}, exposures of Paso Robles beds are seen in a gully bank one hundred and fifty yards to the right with modestly steep dip to the northeast, indicating that the synclinal axis is off in that direction. Somewhat over a mile farther, Alisos Canyon Road separates right. Here grassy, rolling, oak tree-dotted slopes on the right contrast strongly with the higher,

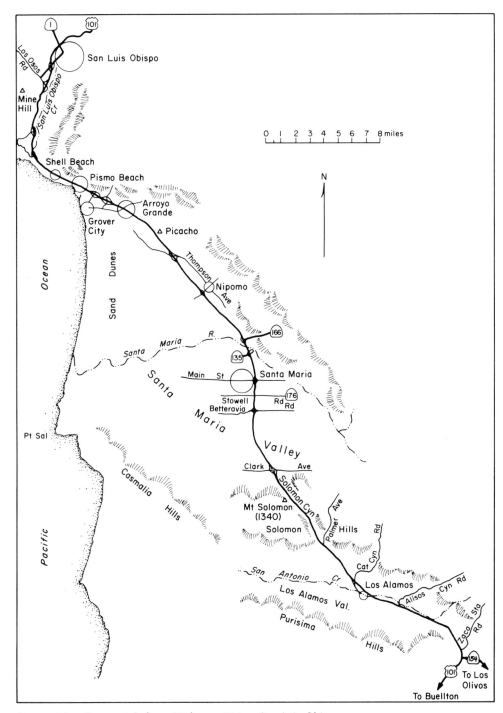

Figure J-1.   Segment J, from Highway 154 to San Luis Obispo.

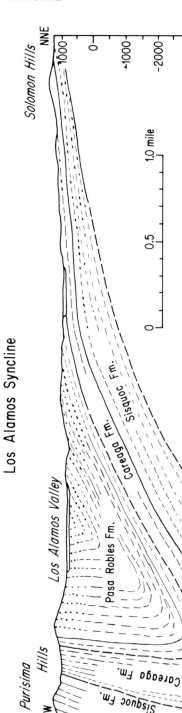

Figure J-2.   Cross section of Los Alamos syncline (after Woodring and Eramlette, 1950).

steeper, more rugged, and more heavily brush- and tree-covered Purisima Hills to the left. If Purisima Hills appear to you as being underlain by rocks different than the Paso Robles Formation, your perceptions are good. The part of Purisima Hills seen from Highway 101 approaching Los Alamos is made up of the Careaga (upper Pliocene) and Sisquoc (Mio-Pliocene) formations, largely marine sandstones and shales. Besides being lithologically different, the Careaga and Sisquoc beds dip very steeply, compared to the gentle inclination of Paso Robles beds northeast of Los Alamos Valley. Beyond "Los Alamos-Vandenburg AFB Exit, 1 Mile," at 1 o'clock, about 1/4 mile away, a low, stream-cut bluff shows Paso Robles beds dipping gently toward the highway, indicating that the synclinal axis is now beneath the alluvial fill of the valley floor. Shortly, comes the settlement of Los Alamos.

O-3 Beyond Los Alamos, the highway leaves the alluviated valley floor and climbs into hills, crossing a succession of small canyons, on a more northwesterly course. Areas between these canyons are benched and veneered by Quaternary materials resting on tilted Paso Robles beds. We don't see that contact, but we do see essentially horizontal bedding in Quaternary deposits approaching "Cat Canyon Road." A little beyond "Santa Maria 16, San Luis Obispo 48," the highway curves northward, and within half a mile horizontal bedding is seen to the left in deposits, presumed to be Quaternary. Beyond Palmer Road turnoff, the route ascends the upper part of a canyon (Las Flores) where hillslopes on both sides are underlain by Paso Robles Formation. In another two miles, a little beyond marker 78⁰⁰, is a broad summit marked "Exit" (an exit to nowhere except off the highway). This is the high point on the crossing of Solomon Hills.

O-4 On the skyline at 11:30 o'clock from Solomon Summit, communication towers on Mt. Solomon are visible. Going north, the highway follows Solomon Canyon which is unusually straight because it is aligned along a fault. Initially, hillslopes on both sides appear similar reflecting the fact that they are underlain by Paso Robles beds, but within a mile, higher, rougher slopes with heavier brush cover make up the left skyline suggesting a different rock type, the Careaga Sandstone (upper Pliocene). Careaga beds come to the surface along the core of Mt. Solomon anticline which parallels Solomon Canyon on a course about 0.5 mile southwest. This anticline is asymmetrical with a steeper north limb. Watch the left skyline as seen up side canyons, and before getting to marker 80⁰⁰ you should get a good view at 9 o'clock of flat-topped Mt. Solomon (1,340 ft.). You may be able to see that the strata composing it are nearly horizontal. They lie almost on the axis (or crest) of the anticline. In lower Solomon Canyon near "Santa Maria, 8 Miles," slopes on both sides become bushy, suggesting that we are entering a new kind of material, the Orcutt Sand, a gently deformed, relatively unconsolidated, Quaternary, stream-laid sand and gravel.

O-5 Approaching Orcutt-Clark Avenue junction from the south, vistas open as we enter wide, flat Santa Maria Valley. Views are particularly expansive to the left at 10 o'clock. The higher terrain, usually visible on the far skyline at about 11 o'clock, is Casmalia Hills, close to the coast. As we rise from beneath Orcutt-Clark Avenue overpass, oil wells are at 12:45 o'clock. The Santa Maria area encompasses a number of producing oil fields, and we will see more wells and pumps farther along. Terrain alongside the highway has a gently rolling, hummocky character. We are crossing the surface of a sheet of old, vegetated, stabilized dunes composed of sand blown inland from the beach sixteen miles west-northwest. The low, gentle, but irregular relief, including closed depressions, represents a dune topography subdued and modified by erosion and redistribution of materials. Occasional highway cuts expose brownish, homogeneous, windblown sand, and once in a while a bare spot exposes such sand. We will see more of this type of terrain north of Santa Maria River. The dune topography is especially good in vicinity of "Santa Maria, Next 5 Exits."

A little beyond the first turnoff into Santa Maria, the highway curves to a northerly course to bypass the city along its eastern side. Just beyond "Betteravia Road-Sisquoc Exit, 1 Mile," the highway leaves the dune sheet and a little farther at "Stowell Road Exit, 1 Mile" descends an escarpment, 10-15 feet high, onto a smooth, flat, alluvial surface. The escarpment is seen by looking back. Ahead at 12:30 o'clock are the many pumps of another oil field. Beyond Betteravia Road, extensive truck gardening of the Santa Maria alluvial flat is evident in proper season. Beyond "Broadway Exit, 1 Mile," bluffs about fifty feet high on the far side of Santa Maria River should be in view at 12:00-12:30 o'clock. Behind the bluffs is a gently sloping bench or series of benches rising to higher skyline hills composed of much older, sedimentary, volcanic, and metamorphic rocks ranging from Cretaceous (Franciscan) to Miocene in age.

The river bluffs become intriguing as we get increasingly better views approaching and crossing the wide Santa Maria River. The uppermost 10-15 feet of the bluffs expose a dark-brown, homogeneous deposit which rests upon lighter-colored, near-horizontal layers of fine, poorly consolidated, deeply rilled materials, the Orcott Sand (Quaternary). A small slide block, with tilted bedding, lies on the face of the second large bluff upstream from the bridge. San Luis Obispo County is entered at the south portal of the bridge, and just beyond its north end Highway 166 East separates.

O-6   Just north of Santa Maria River is a wide, smooth terrace, 50-60 feet high. The highway travels at this level for several miles after climbing from the crossing of Nipomo Creek at mileage 1³⁷, meaning 1.37 miles north of San Luis Obispo County line. Within a mile beyond the power line and the large electrical interchange, the terrain left of the highway becomes perceptibly rolling, about where groves and windbreaks of eucalyptus trees, with a sprinkling of cypress, begin. Relief within this gently rolling terrain increases northwestward. By the time Nipomo is reached, you should realize that the highway is following a lobate contact between flat and rolling terrains. Keep your eyes peeled for bare spots on the left, and you will see that the bumpy area is underlain by homogeneous, brownish sand. This is another old stabilized sand-dune sheet, much like the one earlier traversed at the south edge of Santa Maria Valley. To the west, these old, vegetated dunes give way to younger, fresh, largely unvegetated sheets of white dune sand (Photo J-1) recently blown inland from the wide, sandy beaches south of Pismo. This arrangement largely reflects changes in sea level which alternately increased and decreased the amount of sand available to prevailing westerly winds blowing inland. At least three separate episodes of dune-sheet development has been distinguished in this region, one of the most spectacular areas of shoreline dunes along the North American Pacific coast (Photo J-2).

At "Arroyo Grande 7, Paso Robles 52," an isolated conical peak begins to loom on the skyline a few miles ahead at 12:05 o'clock. That is Picacho, a geologically interesting feature which remains in view for several miles. We pass along its southwest flank.

At "Los Berros Road-Thompson Avenue Exit, 1 Mile" we are still traversing flatland just outside the dune sheet on the left, but in less than a mile the country

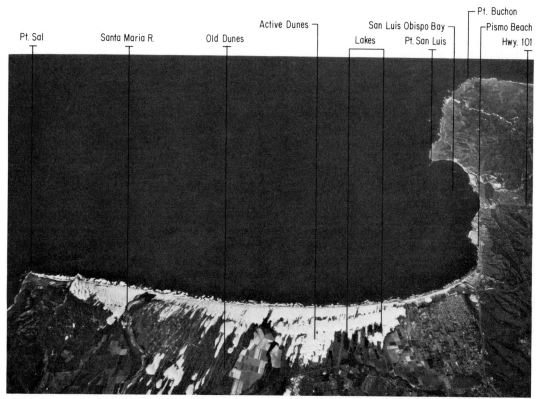

Pt. Sal   Santa Maria R.   Old Dunes   Active Dunes   Lakes   San Luis Obispo Bay   Pt. San Luis   Pt. Buchon   Pismo Beach   Hwy. 101

Photo J-1. High-altitude oblique view of San Luis Obispo County coast from Point Sal to Point Buchon. (U.S. Air Force photo taken for U.S. Geological Survey, 041-R-065).

on both sides of the highway becomes irregularly knobby. This difference suggests a change in geological materials, and a little beyond "Oceano, Next Right," hillsides and roadcuts confirm this inference by showing white fragmental material indicative of the Paso Robles Formation. Soon we drop steeply to cross Los Berros Creek near blue/white "Truck Parking Area, 1/4 Mile." Upon climbing out of the canyon, Picacho is prominent at 12:15 o'clock. A deep, double-walled roadcut about 3/4 mile beyond Los Berros Creek exposes near-horizontal, poorly layered, typical Paso Robles materials.

Watch for the big blue "Visit Morro Bay" billboard on the right. Just beyond is the first of several rounded, elongate, whaleback-like exposures of tough, altered, and silicified volcanic material (Obispo Formation, early mid-Miocene). This is the stuff of which Picacho is made and explains why it stands up so prominently. The succeeding big McDonald's billboard sits between two of the volcanic whalebacks. As exposed in roadcuts, these volcanics are distinguished by brownish color and sharp, angular fragments and joint-determined faces. A closer inspection would show the rock to be primarily twisted, banded, punky, and highly altered volcanic pyroclastics, largely tuff.

O-7   On hillsides just east of the high-

Photo J-2.   View west to the Callender dune complex south of Oceano. Lakes largely enclosed by older, vegetated dune lobes. Note lobe of old dune sand extending east of railroad and highway just left of center. (Fairchild air photo 0-5112, 3/3/37).

way beyond Picacho are more outcrops of resistant volcanics. We pass Arroyo Grande, cross Arroyo Grande Creek, and reenter the Paso Robles Formation as the descent toward the coast begins. At "Grover City-Oak Park Exit," not far to the right at 12:30 o'clock, is an exposure of light-colored, tilted, fine sandstone in the Pismo Formation (Mio-Pliocene), which makes up part of the high ridge behind the settlements of Pismo and Shell beaches. Beyond "Five Cities Drive Exit" and at "Pismo Beach Exit, 1 Mile," exposures in cuts and gully walls are also Pismo Formation. Beyond the high overpass crossing the railroad, the ocean comes into view and the smooth terrace at Pismo Beach (city) becomes evident. An intrenched freeway course and roadside vegetation obstruct views of the scenic Shell Beach coastline (Photo J-3). At Wadsworth exit, the steep hills behind Pismo are composed of the Obispo and Monterey formations (early to middle Miocene).

Beyond "Shell Beach, Right Lane" (center-divider), an angular pyramidal knob of rock sits within the strip between opposing freeway lanes. On closer approach it will be seen to consist of tilted, well-layered rocks of brownish color, angular fracture, and ratty appearance. This is another sample of the altered volcanic pyroclastics seen near Picacho.

At Shell Beach turnoff, the steep hill face immediately on the right consists of Monterey beds, and the marine terrace on the left has become narrow. About 0.5 mile farther comes our only good look at the highly scenic shoreline. We see the terrace, a sea cliff, and some offshore rocks (stacks) rising from deep blue water. Beyond "San Luis Obispo 10, Salinas 130," the terrace is wider. At Spyglass Drive exit, the highway starts a gradual curve inland to ascend San Luis Obispo Creek.

O-8   Northbound between "Avila Beach Exit, 1 Mile" and "Avila Beach, Next Right"

Photo J-3. Shell Beach (west of Pismo) as it looked in 1931, viewed northeasterly. Offshore stacks, sea caves, sea cliff, terrace and steep hill face of Miocene rocks all shown. Banding on tree-dotted slopes made by north-dipping beds in Mio-Pliocene Pismo Formation on south limb of Pismo syncline. (Fairchild air photo 0-2693, 12/17/31).

the view upcoast is into San Luis Obispo Bay and to Point San Luis on its north side (Photo J-1). The ships, pier, tanks, and other installations are part of Port San Luis and Avila Beach. Beyond "Avila Beach, Right Lane" (center-divider), the highway enters a huge roadcut through a *cuesta* of sandstone and shale beds within the Pismo Formation (Mio-Pliocene). Beds dip north because they are on the south limb of the large Pismo syncline. The color of these rocks changes from white and brown at the top to gray in the core of the cut as it penetrates unweathered material. Avila Beach turnoff is within this cut, and a little beyond is a second, deep, double-walled cut in massive, fine, whitish Pismo sandstone

with beds still dipping gently northward. A little farther, a bridge crosses San Luis Obispo Creek, and the highway emerges onto a wide, flat, alluvial valley floor.

O-9   After a half mile or so of flat, alluvial floor, the valley begins to narrow and to the left *south-dipping beds* on the north limb of the syncline can be seen. The synclinal axis lies behind us under the alluvial flat, about 0.4 mile north of the concrete bridge. The canyon narrows northward, and reef-like ribs on its walls are made by resistant sandstone beds with southward dips. At "Higuera Street, 1 Mile," south-dipping Pismo beds are exposed in cuts on the left.

The valley opens again in vicinity of "Business District," and beginning at "Higuera Street Exit" a profound change in rocks occurs. On the left, roadcuts expose greenish-gray, fractured, harder rocks, and ahead on the left is a deep roadcut with a spectacular green strip extending from top to bottom. Adjoining hillslopes become stonier, more rugged, and bedrock outcrops more abundant. We have entered the late Mesozoic (largely Cretaceous) Franciscan Formation. Wide strips of these rocks extend to well north of San Francisco Bay. They constitute one of the principal and more unusual formations of the central and northern California coastal ranges. Many different lithologies are represented and in places, as along the San Simeon Coast, are mixed in near-hopeless confusion, a sort of geological mulligan stew. Many Franciscan rocks have been metamorphosed, usually under very high pressure and relatively low temperature, to produce an unusual assemblage of minerals. The green-rock strip ahead is serpentine, formed by alteration of highly basic (iron- and magnesium rich) igneous rocks. Serpentine is a major component of the Franciscan mélange, and one of the easiest means of identifying oc-

currences of the formation. Not all serpentines in California are Franciscan, however. Opposite "Los Osos-Baywood Park Exit, 3/4 Mile" is the green-serpentine strip.

Beyond that exit, on the skyline at 12 o'clock is a prominent peak—Mine Hill. It is one of a line (Photo J-4) of earliest Miocene igneous, intrusive plugs extending from several miles southeast of San Luis Obispo northwestward to Morro Bay. Morro Rock (Photo J-5) is the most northwesterly of these intrusive plugs, numbering about a dozen. The igneous rock composing them is more resistant than the Franciscan Formation which it intrudes, so the plugs have been etched into features of positive topographic relief by weathering and erosion. Shortly the highway curves, goes under an overpass and beyond, to the left, are four of the plugs (knobs) in a line extending northwestward. Rocky hillslopes along the highway continue to expose Franciscan rocks for the next mile or so, especially well beyond "Madonna Road Exit, 1/2 Mile" and at "San Luis Obispo, Next 8 Exits." Madonna Inn is in view on the left just beyond the overpass for Madonna Road. At the brown/tan "Mission San Luis Obispo," Mine Hill knob is 1/4 mile to the

Photo J-4.   View southwest to Morro Bay, Morro Rock at right. Line of intrusive plugs indicated by knobs this side of Morro Bay. (Photo by John S. Shelton, 4378 cr).

Photo J-5. Morro Rock, the northwesternmost member in a line of mid-Tertiary intrusive plugs of the San Luis Obispo area. Mine Hill near Highway 101 is one of these plugs. (Fairchild air photo 0-3522, 12/17/31).

left. This segment terminates ahead at intersection of highways 101 and 1 on the west edge of San Luis Obispo. If you are continuing on either route, keep the eyes open—there's lots of good geology to be seen. Maybe someday someone will do a guide for travelers along those routes.

Segment J— Inbound Descriptions

(The corresponding outbound material should be read first.)

I-10 Travelers headed south on Highway 101 from San Luis Obispo start this segment at intersection with Highway 1 on the western edge of that city. Record your odometer reading at this point.

I-9 After clearing the first overpass south from the highways 1 and 101 intersection, Mine Hill (intrusive knob) is in view on the skyline at 12:30-2:00 o'clock. Approaching Marsh Street, roadcuts expose greenish-gray Franciscan rock, and beyond Marsh Street the near skyline on the right is a stony ridge of Franciscan. Madonna

Inn sits against the base of this ridge, fronted by an attractively fenced pasture, often populated by happy cows. To the left is another ridge of Franciscan rock. Beyond Madonna Road exit is a wide, open, flat, alluvial valley floor bounded by prominent ridges to right and left. The nearer ridge on the right consists of Franciscan rock, but the farther ridge on the left is underlain by Pismo Formation (Mio-Pliocene) on the north limb of Pismo syncline. At "Los Osos Exit, 1 Mile," the highway is well onto the flat, alluviated floor of San Luis Obispo Creek. After passing Los Osos exit and going under an overpass, the highway curves left around a knob of Franciscan rock, atop which sits Breakers Restaurant. After rounding this knob, the big cut with the green serpentine strip is in view.

Just a few hundred yards beyond Higuera Street exit, the route passes from the Franciscan into Cenozoic volcanic and sedimentary rocks. In less than half a mile, the canyon narrows and massive sandstone beds ranging from early Miocene (Vaqueros) to early Pliocene (Pismo) age succeed each other southward. The consistent southward dip of these beds, as seen in roadcuts and on hillsides, shows they are on the north limb of the Pismo syncline. South dips continue on the walls of this narrow part of the canyon until it opens beyond the large power line. The synclinal axis is judged to lie about midway between San Luis Bay Drive overpass and the concrete bridge across San Luis Obispo Creek. After traversing more flat valley floor, we approach "Pismo Beach 5, Santa Maria 26," where *northward* dips on the south limb of the syncline can be seen in Pismo beds composing the valley walls.

I-8   After southbound travelers cross San Luis Obispo Creek bridge, they enter the deep, double-walled roadcut exposing massive Pismo sandstones in vicinity of the Avila Beach exit. Beyond the overpass across Avila Beach Road, the highway crosses north-dipping beds of shale and sandstone in the huge cut across the cuesta.

I-7   Southbound travelers approaching the coast get a good ocean view, with an offshore rock, at the crest of the rise near "Pismo Beach City Limit." A terrace lies a little below highway level and remains in view to "Spyglass Drive, Next Right." Hills immediately to the left are composed of Pismo Formation, which shortly gives way to harder, thinner-bedded Monterey rocks, and eventually to altered volcanic pyroclastics of the Obispo Formation. Their steepness is partly the result of cutting that formed the terrace on which Shell (Photo J-3) and Pismo beaches are built. At Shell Beach exit, the terrace becomes narrower and densely house-covered. About three hundred yards beyond "Price Street Exit, 1/2 Mile," roadcuts to the left expose brownish, highly deformed, altered volcanics, and approaching Price Street turnoff, inbounders get a glimpse of the sea cliff and offshore stacks by looking back to the right at 3-5 o'clock. About one hundred and

fifty yards beyond "Pismo Beach, Right Lane" on the left is the pyramidal knob of volcanics in the center-divider strip.

Beyond "Pismo Beach-Highway 1 South Exit," occasional rises on the freeway provide glimpses at 1:30-2:00 o'clock of the broad, sandy, pismo-clam beach of this area. The beach view is best approaching Hinds Avenue. Roadcuts on the left beyond "Five Cities Drive-Price" expose massive, soft, white, fine Pismo sandstones. Beyond "Arroyo Grande 3, Santa Barbara 74," the hilly countryside is composed largely of similar sandstones. Before getting to Arroyo Grande, cuts will expose essentially horizontal Paso Robles beds.

I-6   Almost directly ahead at "Fair Oaks Avenue Exit," we see Picacho on the skyline, and it stays prominently in view for the next two miles until passed. Roadcuts along southbound highway lanes do not expose volcanic rock very well, but the whaleback ridges southeast of Picacho, just across the northbound highway lanes, are easily visible. Roadcuts approaching and beyond Picacho are principally in white fragmental Paso Robles materials, and the exposure in the double-walled cut just beyond the whalebacks is particularly representative. Paso Robles deposits continue nearly a mile beyond the crossing of deep Los Berros Canyon. Approximately at marker 7^{00}, and more certainly at "Santa Maria 9, Santa Barbara 85, etc." the old dune sheet begins on the right and continues for better than four miles. At "Nipomo Exit, 1 Mile," a very sandy, cultivated field on the right indicates the nature of material composing the dune deposits. Relief within the dune sheet becomes gentler southeastward, and at the big electrical interchange knobby dune terrain has given way to a smooth terrace surface.

I-5   For southbound travelers, best views of the deeply rilled bluffs of light-colored Orcutt Sand are to the left at and crossing

Santa Maria River bridge. Views continue beyond the bridge over the left shoulder at 8 o'clock. The high skyline hills of older rock are usually visible at 9 o'clock approaching Santa Maria, particularly near "Santa Maria-Guadalupe Exit, 1 Mile." In bypassing Santa Maria on the east, views of the alluvial flat with truck-garden operations (in season) are good. Beyond "Vandenburg AFB-Lompoc, Next Right," the highway approaches the sharp little (fifteen ft.) escarpment. The Betteravia-Sisquoc Exit is at the escarpment. Upon rising above the escarpment, pumping oil wells are abundant, particularly on the left, and we traverse a flattish, extensively cultivated terrace surface on Orcutt Sand. About 0.5 mile ahead, the edge of the gently rolling, bumpy terrain of the old stabilized dune sheet is visible. After ascending onto the dune sheet, we cross its surface for several miles. As the highway curves into a more southeasterly course, Solomon Hills come into view on the south skyline. Beyond "Los Alamos, 13 Miles" bare patches of brownish, homogeneous, dune sand are seen. At "Orcutt-Clark Avenue Exit, 1 Mile," the highway runs straight, and on the skyline at 12:30 o'clock is Mt. Solomon (1,340 ft.) with communication towers. This is about the best view you will get, southbound, of this hill situated on the crest of Mt. Solomon anticline. Orcutt-Clark Avenue overpass is close to the southern limit of the dune sheet, and the flatter terrain and gentle hills beyond are underlain by the fluvial Orcutt Sand.

I-4 We leave Santa Maria plain and start up Solomon Canyon about a mile beyond Orcutt-Clark Avenue exit. The first hills, brush-covered, are underlain by Orcutt Sand, but it gives way to Paso Robles Formation about opposite "Los Alamos 9, Santa Barbara 67." There the slopes become grassy and tree-dotted, particularly on the left. At "Los Alamos, 9 Miles," we are well into Solomon Canyon and traversing its alluviated floor. No rock outcrops are visible on either side, but the linearity (fault-controlled) of the canyon is obvious by now. Mt. Solomon is not easily seen going southeast, but exposures of Careaga Sandstone along the crest of Mt. Solomon anticline are indicated by the higher, rougher, brush-covered slopes to the right, as glimpsed up side canyons. Solomon summit on the highway is attained just beyond "Exit" at the head of Solomon Canyon.

I-3 From Solomon Summit southbound travelers descend Las Flores Canyon. The skyline ahead is made by Purisima Hills. About 0.5 mile beyond marker 77^{00}, the highway curves a bit east to climb out of Las Flores Canyon, and shortly Palmer Road exits. The rougher country seen a mile or two to the north (left) may be underlain by Careaga sandstones coming to the surface from beneath Paso Robles beds which are dipping southwest. About one hundred yards beyond "Los Alamos Exit, 3/4 Mile," the highway starts a descent toward the cultivated alluvial floor of Los Alamos Valley. On its far side are Purisima Hills—rough, tree-covered, and about five hundred feet high. Beyond Cat Canyon Road, horizontally bedded, soft, brownish beds exposed in roadcuts are probably part of a Quaternary veneer on the Paso Robles Formation. Shortly thereafter, we reach the floor of Los Alamos Valley.

I-2 Southbound from Los Alamos overpass, the highway ascends the wide, gently sloping, alluviated floor of Los Alamos Valley. In the far distance, at 10 to 11 o'clock, is the crestal ridge of San Rafael Mountains with sharp, pyramidal Zaca Peak at 11 o'clock and Figueroa Mountain ridge to the right. Purisima Hills, with a heavy vegetative cover, make the southwest side of the valley. Bluffs along a stream bank, paralleling the highway 1/4 mile to 3/8 mile to the left, expose soft, light-brown Paso Robles materials, but bedding is not strongly expressed and dips confirming the Los Alamos syncline are hard to make out.

Beyond Alisos Canyon Road, the valley narrows, ascent steepens, and Purisima Hills press in closer on the right. About 0.7 mile beyond Alisos Canyon Road, a reef-like ridge within Purisima Hills can be glimpsed by looking up side canyons. In good light, you can see that the resistant beds holding up that ridge are inclined steeply northeastward, toward the highway, which is proper for beds on the southwest limb of Los Alamos syncline. Opposite marker 68^{00}, in the bluff one hundred and fifty yards north, indistinct layering of Paso Robles beds is inclined northeast, so they too must be on the southwest limb of the syncline. Near top of the climb out of San Antonio Creek, to the left opposite "Buellton, 8 Miles," near-horizontal bedding in poorly consolidated Paso Robles Formation materials is seen. These beds are near the axis of the syncline. Descending, beyond marker 65^{00} at the summit, the highway curves to a more southeasterly course, and the far skyline at 12 o'clock is made by the crest of Santa Ynez Mountains. Slopes on both sides going downhill are underlain by Paso Robles beds. At Zaca Station Road, we are onto the alluviated floor of Zaca Creek and turn into a southerly course for junction with Highway 154 (Segment I). Segment H completes the trip to Santa Barbara via Highway 101, and Segment I does the same job by way of Highway 154.

I-1   This segment ends at junction of Highways 101 and 154, 8.3 miles southeast of Los Alamos.

Segment K

El Toro to Oceanside, 43 Miles

O-1   Start this segment outbound at San Diego (I-405) and Santa Ana (I-5) freeways junction in south-central Orange County (Photo K-1). The course is southeasterly and, after the first eighteen miles, closely parallels the shoreline. Sedimentary rocks, mostly marine, and marine terraces are the features of principal geological interest.

The starting point can be approached on either freeway. Each passes from the low relief of Los Angeles Basin into a smooth-floored indentation of its southeastern margin, the Tustin Plain. This is a synclinal downwarp filled with alluvium. Travelers on San Diego Freeway pass near knobs and spurs of massive sandstone (lower Miocene, Vaqueros Formation) projecting from the north edge of the San Joaquin Hills a mile before junction with I-5, but motorists on I-5 see only the flat alluvial surface of Tustin Plain, albeit fertile and cultivated. However, from both routes, rugged, relatively lofty (higher than 5,000 ft.) Santa Ana Mountains (north) and lower, more subdued San Joaquin Hills (south) are visible in clear weather.

The higher parts of the Santa Anas, at about 11 o'clock, are underlain by relatively old (Jurassic) Santiago Peak Volcanics and Bedford Canyon Formation metamorphic rocks. Coarse-grained intrusive rocks of the southern California batholithic complex are also widely exposed in the higher Santa Anas. In proper lighting, parallel ridges can be distinguished on the south flank of the Santa Anas, intermediate in height and position. They are composed of Cretaceous to Eocene sedimentary beds, aggregating a thickness of many thousand feet. Still lower hilly country farther south is underlain by Oligocene to Pliocene mostly sedimentary rocks. San Joaquin Hills, south of the freeways, are made up principally of Miocene sedimentary rocks, including volcanics, a little Oligocene, and some Pliocene, with a veneer of Pleistocene terrace deposits on the south side. Rock units older than Pleistocene are strongly deformed by folding and faulting. Record odometer reading where the two freeways become one.

(Inbound travelers see p. 165.)

O-2   First roadcuts southeast of the 5 and 405 junction show deeply rilled, horizontal, poorly bedded, soft, muddy-looking, nondescript materials characterized in U.S. Geological Survey parlance as Quaternary terrace deposits, even where such deposits may have nothing to do with terraces. Let us just refer to them as Quaternary alluvium, meaning that they are land-laid and

157

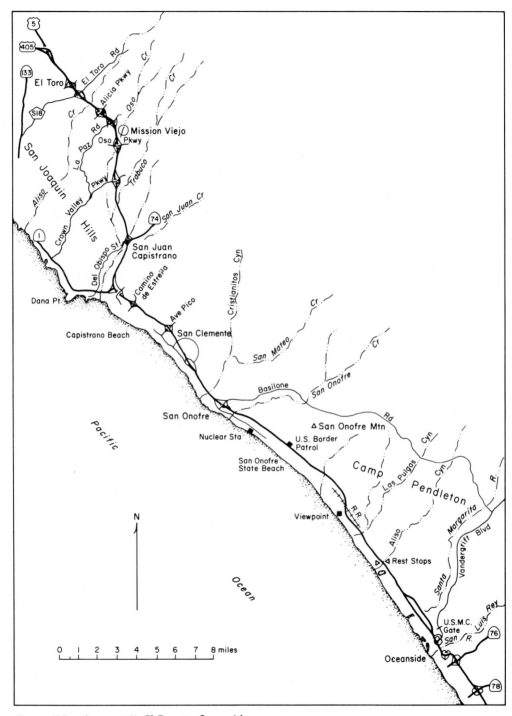

Figure K-1. Segment K, El Toro to Oceanside.

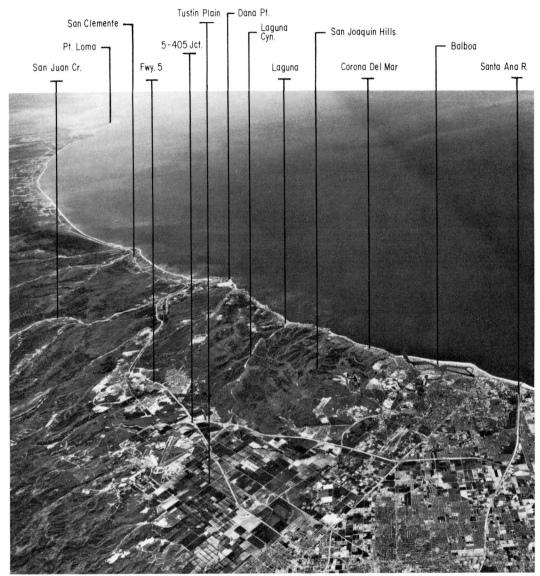

San Juan Cr.   Pt. Loma   San Clemente   Fwy. 5   5-405 Jct.   Tustin Plain   Dana Pt.   Laguna Cyn.   Laguna   San Joaquin Hills   Corona Del Mar   Balboa   Santa Ana R.

Photo K-1. High-altitude oblique view to southwest of southern California's south coast, Newport to San Diego. (U.S. Air Force photo taken for U.S. Geological Survey, 041-R-097).

a little older than the recent alluvium flooring modern valleys. In 1.5 miles, as signs indicate an approach to El Toro Road, more intense dissection has produced a rolling terrain with 20-30 feet of relief, and the freeway exercises a few gentle ups and downs. Just before El Toro Road turnoff, a long cut exposes deformed, light-colored, massive sandstone beds. This is a small outlier of Miocene rock (Monterey Formation) projecting through the Quaternary alluvium. The material is more coherent, bedding is better defined, and color is lighter than the alluvium.

O-3   Southeast of El Toro Road, a narrowing of Tustin Plain presages its transition into a wide valley extending to San Juan Capistrano. The first cuts beyond El Toro Road expose more Quaternary alluvium. Aliso Creek is crossed on a concrete bridge just before Alicia Parkway turnoff. Aliso Creek drains from the foothills of the Santa Ana Mountains, flows south-south-westward across the plain, and crosses San Joaquin Hills to the ocean. It appears that Aliso Creek was powerful enough to maintain its course across San Joaquin Hills as they were uplifted athwart its path. Other similar streams to the southeast (Oso, Trabuco, Horno, and San Juan) detour around the end of the hills. This valorous performance was fortunate because Aliso Creek carries sand to the ocean where waves use it to maintain the sandy strand at Aliso Beach in South Laguna.

Beyond Alicia Parkway overpass, left-side roadcuts expose homogeneous, soft, finer-grained, better-layered, and lighter-colored sedimentary materials, which do not look like Quaternary alluvium. They are part of Niguel Formation (Pliocene), a sequence of light-brown to grayish, marine, siltstone, sandy siltstone, and locally conglomeratic beds, exposures of which extend southeastward to vicinity of Oso Creek crossing. A good sample is seen in a double-walled, strongly rilled, high roadcut approaching La Paz Road exit. Bedding is essentially horizontal except for areas of local deformation, which you may spot.

O-4   Just beyond La Paz Road, the freeway curves to head nearly due south, we cross above railroad tracks, and there we can look to the right directly down the narrowing stream valley along which the freeway travels. At Oso Creek crossing, about 0.5 miles beyond Oso Parkway overpass and just before "Crown Valley Parkway, 1 Mile," we enter a somewhat older

sequence of marine beds belonging to the Capistrano Formation (Mio-Pliocene). Much of the Capistrano is brownish gray, muddy-looking siltstone and sandstone.

O-5   In addition to roadcuts in brownish Capistrano siltstone beyond Oso Creek, pay some attention to the contrast in terrain on opposite sides of the freeway. To the west (we are now headed south), the hills are mostly smoothly sloped with rounded divides and summits. To the east, the break between smooth upland flats and steep hillsides is sharp. This contrast is due to the fact that upland areas to the east have cappings of Quaternary alluvium, or of near-horizontal Niguel beds. Such near-horizontal strata are lacking in the hills to the west. As we continue southward the valley becomes deeper, but not much narrower. Scattered benches on both sides, as much as one hundred feet above stream level, are stream-terrace remnants.

O-6   Roadcut exposures, mostly nondescript and obscure, continue in the Capistrano Formation to Crown Valley Parkway. After that, to and beyond Trabuco Creek, crossed at "Junipero Serra Road Exit," unconsolidated Quaternary sands and gravels compose the roadcuts. These deposits represent materials carried down from the Santa Ana foothills by streams like Trabuco Creek.

Approaching San Juan Capistrano, the valley opens considerably, and the hills to the east begin to look more like those to the west. High, double-walled roadcuts, with benches, just before Highway 74 turn-off, again expose brownish siltstones and mudstones of the Capistrano Formation. Highway 74 (Ortega Highway) follows a northeasterly course across the Santa Ana Mountains, as described in Segment O.

O-7   Beyond Highway 74, hillslopes east of the now wider valley have a jumbled, irregular appearance produced by nearly overlapping landslides, some of considerable size and at least 17,000 years old. In professional eyes, this is one of the major areas of large landslide development in southern California. During the last ice age, lowering of sea level presumably allowed San Juan Creek to incise its floor, thus steepening the valley walls. The combination of steeper slopes and the weak, incoherent Capistrano siltstones composing them, led to the formation of an unusual number of large slides here. As sea level rose, following the ice age, alluvial filling on the floor of the valley has buttressed the toes of some of the larger slides making their lower parts, at least, quasi-stable.

As the highway curves into a course directly down San Juan Creek which is crossed just before the San Juan Creek Road exit, look ahead to where the freeway approaches the base of the hills. The rounded, projecting lobe there is the toe of the huge Forster landslide involving most of the hillslope almost to the skyline. The toe of this slide is reached at the San Juan Creek Road exit, a mile beyond the Highway 74 intersection. Other large slides of similar size scar the hillslopes east of San Juan Creek downstream to the shoreline.

O-8   About 2.5 miles beyond San Juan Capistrano, the freeway rises and curves eastward around a steep hill face. Shortly, we break out to a view of the ocean and, particularly, of Dana Cove and Harbor at 2 o'clock. The sandy strand at Doheny State Beach ahead is provided largely through the courtesy of San Juan Creek, which delivers to the ocean waves and currents the material they need to build such a strand.

O-9   As the freeway curves into a course southeastward down the coast, a high roadcut on the left exposes light-colored sand filling an old submarine channel cut into brown, muddy Capistrano siltstones. See Dana Harbor descriptions in Segment L for more detail on this type of feature. Beyond Camino de Estrella the freeway emerges onto a smooth, gently sloping surface composed of a succession of terraces mantled by fine-grained coverhead, exposures of which are seen in roadcuts just beyond Camino de Estrella. Our course for the next several miles is along the inner edge of this smooth surface, close to the base of the hills. You can't see it from the freeway, but at the shoreline is a high sea cliff, and streams flowing from the mountains across the smooth surface have cut down through the cliff to get to the sea. Otherwise, each of them would be pouring into the ocean in a waterfall whenever the stream carried water (Photo L-11). This dissection has created the deep arroyos crossed in our journey toward San Clemente. Since the Capistrano Formation is widely exposed in the Capistrano Beach-northwest San Clemente area, you might ask whether landslides have occurred here. The answer is a firm "yes," landsliding is a major problem in much of this area.

The ride to San Clemente (city) does not show much geology. Roadcuts going down into gullies occasionally expose brown, muddy, Capistrano siltstone layers, locally capped by fine-grained coverhead. Extended views of the wide, terraced surface occur from time to time to the right. Hillslopes inland are mostly smooth, grassy, and locally contoured by terracettes (Photo 1-4) formed by slumps and accentuated by animals. Occasionally, larger slumps and earthflows of recent date scar these slopes. Southeast of the center of San Clemente (city) a lower terrace, the site of Casa Nixon, becomes prominent. It is seen nicely from the elevated position of the freeway on the hill face a little beyond El Camino Real turnoff. We descend to this level at "Ave Calafia Exit." Hills directly behind downtown San Clemente are higher and more rugged because they are made up in part of older, tougher rocks, principally sandstone of Eocene age.

O-10   Through southeastern San Clemente, the freeway is depressed and views are restricted. As it rises to the surface at San Diego County line ("Basilone Road-San Onofre Exit, 1 Mile"), a quick look right to about 5:30 o'clock may give you a glimpse of one of the gates to the Casa Nixon area. Just beyond, on the right, is the fenced flat adjoining a Coast Guard station (communication towers). In another quarter-mile is a bridge over the wide, flat-floored valley of San Mateo Creek, a fertile area of extensive truck farming (left). A little beyond is Basilone Road-San Onofre exit. Anyone wishing to visit San Onofre Beach State Park or the San Onofre nuclear power plant should exit here.

Geologists will react to the word "San Onofre" by thinking of a classical and famous formation, the San Onofre Breccia, extensively exposed in sea cliffs in the Laguna area (see Segment L). Others interested in power generation or environmental problems will think of the San Onofre nuclear plant. It is just ahead, and we catch views of the installations at 12:15 o'clock, a little beyond the Basilone-San Onofre overpass. This is currently (1977) the largest and oldest commercial nuclear power plant in southern California, and the facility is being expanded. Environmental concerns have involved discharge of warm water into the ocean, which adversely affects growth of kelp, and the ever-present worry concerning what earthquakes may do to nuclear plants. Southern California Edison Company has expended considerable effort to ameliorate the warm-water problem, with encouraging results. The Cristianitos fault goes out to sea on a southeast trend a mile or so beyond the power station. The Cristianitos is a modest fault (for southern California); nevertheless it was thoroughly studied by geologists prior to power plant construction. Based upon undisturbed youthful surface deposits which blanket the fault trace, and an apparent lack of even minor seismic activity at depth, the Cristianitos is presently believed to be an inactive fault. It does not compare in seis-

mic importance to the larger San Andreas, San Jacinto, or Newport-Inglewood faults, all of which have been historically active.

In crossing the valley of San Onofre Creek the freeway drops to floodplain level. To the right is a nice beach at the stream's mouth. Upon ascending the southeast bank, domes of the nuclear reactor are directly ahead. Steep rugged hillsides are relatively close on the left, and the high peak at about 10:30 o'clock is San Onofre Mountain. The dark-brown, locally bluish gray, rocks exposed on its slopes and on hillsides for a few miles southeast are the San Onofre Breccia, but we do not get close enough to see the unusual nature of this deposit (see Segment L).

O-11   In the next three or four miles, a sequence of marine terraces is well displayed (Photo K-2). About a mile beyond the nuclear plant, near "All Trucks," we ascend to a terrace upon which the highway travels for several miles. This surface, roughly one hundred feet above sea level, becomes broader and somewhat lower southeastward toward Oceanside. The basal steepening of the hillside a few hundred yards inland represents its old sea cliff. Most marine terraces should have a sea cliff at the inner edge, although in many instances it is greatly modified by weathering and erosion or completely buried by coverhead (Figure 1-7). Within another mile narrow remnants of another terrace, higher by about forty feet, begin to appear in the form of benches on the hill face inland at 11 o'clock. Keep watching this hill face, and at blue/white "Vista Point, 2 Miles—Rest Area, 5 Miles," you should be able to recognize remnants of at least two terrace levels above the highway surface. Within the next mile, especially where the highway curves to rise on an overpass across the railroad, a still higher terrace, about one hundred and fifty feet above highway level, can be distinguished, making a total of four levels visible here.

Photo K-2. Looking downcoast from south of San Onofre Mountain toward Oceanside. Roads and railroad on wide, lower terrace. Higher terraces make benches on hills to left at three easily recognized levels. (Photo by John S. Shelton, Kc 5026).

O-12 Beyond the vista point, the highway terrace maintains its width but becomes progressively lower, suggesting southeastward tectonic tilting or a gradual transition to a lower terrace. It is also dissected by broad, flat-floored arroyos causing downs and ups in the highway. Steep arroyo banks and occasional railroad or highway cuts expose fine-grained, unconsolidated, horizontally bedded Pleistocene deposits. Arroyo floors are close to sea level, and the height of their walls lacks only five or ten feet of indicating terrace elevation above the sea. Las Pulgas arroyo, just beyond Las Pulgas Road, is a representative example. The wide, smooth arroyo floors are the product of alluvial accumulation behind the prominent beach ridge at their mouth.

You have probably realized that the area on both sides for the past several miles is part of the Camp Pendleton reserve of the U.S. Marine Corps. Roads, tracks, and other signs of vehicular traffic beyond the freeway fence are largely the product of training exercises. The main entrance is ahead near the northwest corner of Oceanside. Regulations have been relaxed so it is easy for civilian motorists to tour the area. You can make an interesting inland loop-drive, starting from the Oceanside entrance and coming out at the Basilone Road entrance, or vice versa. Just follow signs on the outskirts of Oceanside directing you into Camp Pendleton.

The highway terrace remains wide but becomes progressively lower southeastward. At San Onofre its height was nearly one hundred feet, but approaching Oceanside it is barely twenty-five feet. Our route ultimately descends to an even lower alluvial level. About five miles beyond Aliso Creek rest stop, the broad flats of Santa Margarita River are crossed partly on a concrete bridge. All streams along this section of coast have been drowned, including the flat-floored arroyos just seen. By this, we mean that after valleys were created by stream erosion, a rise of sea level (or a

sinking of the land) caused their lower reach to be flooded by the sea, forming an estuary. In most instances, waves have built beach ridges cutting off such estuaries from the ocean, and subsequently some of the estuaries have been completely filled by alluvium. The estuary of Santa Margarita River has been reduced to a narrow ribbon of water flanked by broad mud flats by such filling.

O-13   Beyond Santa Margarita River, the highway climbs about twenty feet onto a smooth surface. It would have to drop again in less than two miles to cross the narrower floor of San Luis Rey River (Photo K-3) were it not for the concrete bridge at

Photo K-3.   View southeast across Oceanside area, Buena Vista Lagoon in mid-distance. (Spence air photo E-6623, 2/28/36).

"Oceanside City Limit." This river has only a small remnant estuary at its mouth, owing to extensive alluvial filling of its lower valley.

For the next three miles the freeway skirts the inland edge of Oceanside in a largely depressed course, showing little scenery and even less geology. Oceanside sits atop a marine terrace (Photo K-3), or a succession of terraces dissected by arroyos. Like the larger rivers, smaller streams cutting these arroyos were drowned; hence the wide, flat, alluviated floors or, in some instances, water-filled estuaries. Arroyo walls provide occasional glimpses of near-horizontal, soft, sedimentary beds, strongly rilled or deeply dissected into miniature badlands. The most easily seen badland area is on the left opposite "Mission Avenue, Downtown 76." It lies on the south wall of the first arroyo beyond San Luis Rey River, a distance of roughly 0.5 mile. Another is seen on the left in the south wall of a flat-floored arroyo, packed with closely spaced trailers and mobile homes, just beyond Oceanside Boulevard exit. Materials exposed in these badlands are part of a sequence of marine Eocene beds that mantle the coastal foreland from here to San Diego.

In another mile comes junction with Highway 78 to Vista and Escondido, the end of this segment. Segment P continues southeast to San Diego. People wishing to return to the Los Angeles region by a different route can take Highway 78 east seventeen miles to Escondido and there pick up Segment M, which describes the route inbound to Riverside via Freeway 15.

Segment K—
Inbound Descriptions

(The corresponding outbound material should be read first.)

I-14   Travelers bound northwest up the coast start this segment at the junction of Freeway 5 with Highway 78 at the south edge of Oceanside, or at any intermediate point of their choice. Note odometer reading at the start.

I-13   Travelers headed northwest on Freeway 5 see a little badland exposure of grayish Eocene beds, 100-200 yards to the right in the first deep gully about 0.3 mile north of the Highway 76-Mission Avenue exit. The turnoff into Camp Pendleton, for anyone wishing to travel through the base, is clearly marked a little after crossing San Luis Rey River bridge. From that bridge, one gets a distant view to the left of the beach and surf extending along shore. The vertical bank just to the right on the north side of the Santa Margarita River bridge, identified by mileage 56[42], exposes horizontal beds of soft, fine, Pleistocene sedimentary materials.

I-12   Navigational points, such as Santa Margarita River bridge, with mileage 56[42], the Aliso Creek rest stop, Las Pulgas Canyon, and the vista point, are easily identified so inbound travelers should not experience much difficulty in locating features or relationships described in O-12. San Onofre Mountain looms on the far skyline at 12:15 o'clock at "Rest Stop, 1 Mile," and continues in view. Opposite "Las Pulgas Road Exit, 1 Mile," northbound tourists see remnants of a high terrace extending along the hill front this side of San Onofre Mountain. This is the highest of the four terrace levels mentioned in O-11. The seaward flank of San Onofre Mountain also displays faint suggestions of a considerably higher fifth terrace, as seen from this angle.

I-11   Approaching the railroad overpass, the large peak ahead on the skyline is San Onofre Mountain. The hill front inland here displays narrow remnants of an intermediate terrace, about thirty feet above the wide highway terrace, and wider benches of another terrace fully seventy feet higher (Photo K-2). Descending from the overpass, remnants of terraces at three levels are well displayed directly ahead on the hill face. Northwestward, benches of the higher terrace gradually become less easily distinguished, and opposite the Immigration Service checkpoint, they are difficult to make out. The highway terrace continues northwestward, but with reduced width.

I-10   Inbound travelers should have little trouble spotting the atomic reactor on the left at 11:30 o'clock opposite marker 69^{00}, a little more than a mile beyond the Immigration Service checkpoint. San Onofre Creek is crossed at marker 71^{00}, just before the Basilone turnoff. Anyone wishing to visit either the nuclear power plant or San Onofre Beach should exit at Basilone Road, cross over the freeway, and follow signs to the preferred destination. The floor of San Mateo Creek is opposite "San Clemente State Park, Next Right." The Casa Nixon area is ahead on the left about 0.1 mile beyond El Camino Real turnoff, near "Avenida Magdalena, 1¼ Mile."

I-9   For travelers headed upcoast, the bluffs of Eocene rock are visible behind the first "Ave Presidio." In crossing the deep arroyo at the Avenue Pico turnoff, two marine terrace levels can be seen in profile downstream at about 10 o'clock on the far side. As the highway curves into the valley of San Juan Creek, the deep roadcut on the right exposes the filling of white sand in an old submarine channel cut into brown Capistrano siltstone.

I-8   Dana Point and Dana Cove are visible at 11 o'clock approaching turnoff to Pacific Coast Highway (Highway 1). The geology of Dana Harbor area is described in Segment L. Anyone wishing to follow that segment inbound up the Laguna coast should turn onto Highway 1 at the Las Ramblas exit and subsequently on Del Obispo Street in the town of Dana Point.

I-7   Unfortunately, inbound travelers get less satisfactory views of slide-disrupted hillslopes east of San Juan Creek, but by watching over their right shoulder they can gain some impression of the situation. They are partly compensated by views of Santa Ana Mountains directly ahead.

I-6   Motorists headed north from San Juan Capistrano get a better look at the sandy Quaternary gravels in roadcuts on their side of the freeway.

I-5   This terrain contrast is seen shortly after leaving San Juan Capistrano, and it continues for several miles.

I-4   The roadcuts and adjoining hillsides, particularly to the west, as far as Oso Creek crossing, have been composed principally of Capistrano Formation beds since leaving San Clemente.

I-3   The Niguel Formation is seen best in roadcuts beyond Oso Parkway, especially on the right approaching La Paz Road. Right-side cuts beyond La Paz Road exit expose some of the conglomeratic layers. Fine, well-stratified Niguel beds are also exposed just beyond Alicia Parkway overpass.

I-2   Miocene beds are seen in roadcuts just beyond El Toro crossing. Then come exposures of Quaternary alluvium the rest of the way to separation of San Diego and Santa Ana freeways.

I-1   This segment ends at the separation of the San Diego (I-405) and Santa Ana (I-5) freeways.

Segment L

Corona del Mar to Dana Point, 15 Miles

O-1   Travelers bound southeast on Highway 1 (Pacific Coast Highway) start this segment near the southeast edge of Corona del Mar at Cameo Shores Road (stoplight). Direction of travel is southeast and always within 0.5 mile of the ocean (Photo L-1). This segment is a spur attached to the San Diego Freeway route (Segment K) because of its scenic beauty and some striking geology. Note your odometer reading leaving the starting point.

(Inbound travelers see p. 178.)

O-2   One-tenth of a mile southeast of Cameo Shores Road, we break into the open on the surface of a wide, smooth marine terrace (Photo L-1). A 40-50 foot sea cliff at the shore shows this terrace to be mantled by fine-grained coverhead, 10-15 feet thick, resting upon gently dipping, locally contorted, white, thin-bedded shales (middle to late Miocene, Monterey Formation). The cliff is based by a sandy beach, intermittently interrupted by rocky reefs. All this you can't see unless you choose to go to the shore at the first officially designated beach parking area just ahead (Treasure Cove), beyond mileage marker 14^{56}. Immediately north of the highway are low, rounded, smooth, and mostly gently sloping forehills of San Joaquin Hills,

also underlain by the Miocene shaly beds (Monterey).

O-3   In less than a mile, between markers 14^{29} and 14^{02}, which in 1977 bracketed some horse corrals, hillsides to the left display remnants of two terraces above the one on which we travel. Narrow remnants of an intermediate surface lie 15-20 feet above the highway and more prominent, wider remnants lie another 40-50 feet higher. The highway then curves before descending into Los Trancos Canyon, and at 11 o'clock on the far side of Los Trancos Canyon the highest terrace appears nicely in profile. On the near side, the intermediate terrace is also relatively prominent.

O-4   In descending toward the bottom of Los Trancos Canyon, the first roadcuts expose fine-grained to cobbly coverhead which rests upon the brown, shaly Miocene beds exposed in succeeding roadcuts. The same succession is seen rising out of the canyon on the southeast side. Just before topping out onto the terrace, the long double-walled roadcut displays an excellent example of horizontally bedded, chocolate-brown, fine-to-pebbly coverhead.

O-5   Directly ahead on the skyline, as we regain the terrace, is a prominent topo-

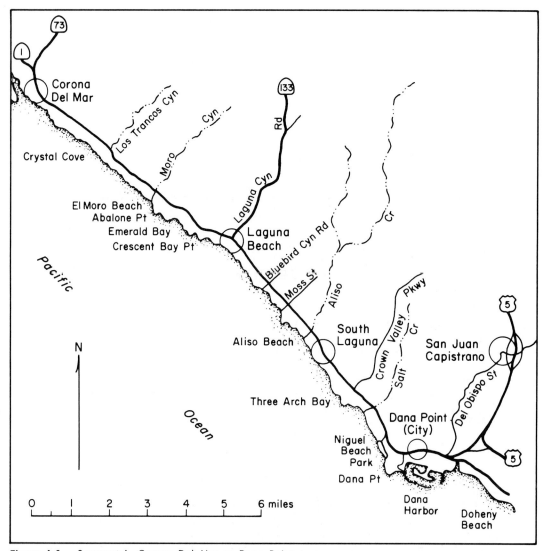

Figure L-1. Segment L, Corona Del Mar to Dana Point.

graphic knob. It is an erosional feature formed on a local mass of relatively hard, coherent, igneous rock, part of a near-surface intrusive body related to lavas and other extrusive volcanic materials widely distributed in San Joaquin Hills. Experts will be interested to know that it is classed as an andesite, and the age is thought to be roughly late Miocene (around ten million years). Within 0.2-0.3 mile, a nice sandy

beach (El Moro) fronting a group of mobile homes and trailers comes into view. The sheer dark cliffs inclosing the east side of El Moro Beach and extending to the cliffed headland of Abalone Point beyond are made of the same igneous rock. The regular, closely spaced jointing (columnar) in the rock near the far end of El Moro cliff is rather characteristic of shallow intrusive bodies of this type. In

Laguna Cyn.   Aliso Cr.   Los Trancos Cr.   Downtown Laguna   Terrace   El Moro Beach   Emerald Bay   Andesite Knob   Aliso Beach   Abalone Pt.   Three Arch Bay   Dana Pt.

Photo L-1.   Looking down the Laguna coast from a little south of Corona Del Mar. (Photo by Robert C. Frampton and John S. Shelton, 4-1808B).

approaching El Moro Beach, we pass the entrance to Scotsman Cove beach parking (just beyond marker 12⁵⁹), temporarily drop into a small gully with roadcuts showing coverhead resting on shaly Miocene bedrock, pass El Moro school (on the left) and descend to El Moro Beach where the features above described are laid out before us. This beach is sometimes beautifully cusped.

The view ahead is so engrossing that it's easy to miss relationships in roadcuts on the left (descending) which show a marine abrasion platform, opposite marker 12⁰⁷, truncating tilted shale beds and capped by coverhead. The shale (Mio-Pliocene, Capitrano Formation) contains spherical concretions, up to two feet in diameter, exposed on the left beyond marker 12⁰⁷. Concretions have been reworked from the shale and distributed along the abrasion platform by waves of the ancient sea. A high roadcut to the left of the mobile homes at El Moro Beach, just where the upgrade starts, provides another good look at the concretion-bearing shales, here somewhat fractured and distorted. Uphill from El Moro Beach, the andesite cliff and its jointing are well displayed to the right.

O-6 Back up on the terrace, southbound, the andesite knob is passed almost immediately, and "Laguna City Limit" appears shortly on the right. Subsequent roadcuts expose modestly coarse coverhead as befits the proximity of steeper and higher hillsides to the north.

In less than half a mile, "Irvine Cove" is passed and shortly Emerald Bay lies to the right. Unfortunately this lovely stretch of rugged rocky coast is out of sight except for those influential enough to have entry. Cliffs backing the irregular shore of Irvine Cove and the peninsula-like point inclosing Emerald Bay on the northwest are composed of resistant andesite.

Just beyond the guard house and main entrance to Emerald Bay (on the left), roadcuts expose massive sandstone beds (Topanga Formation, middle Miocene). We

have just crossed a complex fault zone (Pelican Hill fault) separating these older beds from the softer, more fissile shale (Monterey and Capistrano) seen earlier. The narrowing of the terrace, and the greater height and steepness of the hillslopes reflect this difference in lithology.

Watch for a blue/white vista point sign on the right side of the highway about 0.7 mile beyond the main entrance to Emerald Bay. If you would like a look at the shore and coast at Crescent Bay Point, turn right on Crescent Bay Drive just beyond the sign. Parking may be difficult in summer as this is a beach-access area. You should be warned that opposing side streets in Laguna may have different names on opposite sides of Highway 1.

From Crescent Bay Point you get a good view of an active sea cliff (Photo L-2), an offshore rock (or stack), a bouldery beach upcoast and a sandy beach downcoast. The cliff has something of an undercut nip, and at low tide a storm-wave platform is ex-

Photo L-2. Looking upcoast from Two Rock Point off Crescent Bay Drive, Laguna. Foreground shows sea cliff with indenting nip at base, fronted by abraded joint blocks of Miocene andesite. Level storm-wave platform exposed by low tide fronts sea cliff in background.

posed. Smoothly worn, large joint blocks of andesite on the beach just upcoast from the point testify to the power of wave action (Photo L-2). The point is well worth a visit, time permitting.

O-7   About 0.4 mile southeast of the stoplight at Cliff Drive 700 is a high, dark cliff at the left edge of the highway with buildings perched on its brink. This is another exposure of andesite, like that seen at Abalone Point. It too displays crude columnar jointing.

O-8   Soon southeast-bound travelers start a gradual descent to beach level and the central city area of Laguna Beach. Laguna Canyon Road takes off left at the stoplight (also marked as Broadway) and provides an interesting drive across the San Joaquin Hills to the San Diego Freeway. En route one sees a good many massive sandstone bluffs (middle and lower Miocene, Topanga and Vaqueros formations) as well as some red sandstones (Oligocene, non-marine Sespe Formation).

O-9   After two or three curves and several stoplights, outbound travelers climb back to the terrace level at Legion Street (stoplight). Hereafter, the terrace is narrow and rather irregular with ups and downs owing to dissection by gullies and burial by coarse coverhead. Roadcut exposures for some distance now are all in deposits of chocolate-brown coverhead. Watch for the stoplight at Bluebird Canyon Road, something over a mile southeast of Laguna city center. Behind and beyond the Denny's restaurant on the southeast corner is a good exposure of thick coverhead in a freshly excavated face.

In another quarter mile, Diamond Street stoplight is passed, in another 0.15 mile is Moss Street (on right), and in another 0.3 mile is Victoria Drive. Moss and Victoria are mentioned because they lead to paths of public access to the beach at the foot of the Laguna sea cliffs. You are urged to stop at Aliso Beach ahead to in-

spect the unusual formation (San Onofre Breccia) in these cliffs. Devotees of the San Onofre Breccia may want to study it in several places, and exposures at Moss Point and along Victoria Beach are well worth their attention. Beyond Diamond Street, exposures of brown sandstone and occasionally of San Onofre Breccia, as behind Duke's Hamburger establishment, are interspersed with cuts in coverhead deposits.

O-10   Be alert to spot Wesley Drive. It's marked by a prominent sign and stoplight. Beyond Wesley the highway starts a descent into Aliso Canyon, goes under a pedestrian overpass, and shortly comes to the turn-in for parking at Aliso Beach (Photo L-5). In winter, parking is free and amply available. In summer, it costs $1 and may not be available at any price. This is one of the nicer cove beaches of the Laguna area.

If you choose to stop, walk southeast along the beach from the parking area at least as far as the first projecting rocky point, about two hundred yards beyond the pier. Look carefully at the rock exposed in the cliff; this is the San Onofre Breccia (Photo L-3), one of the most spectacular sedimentary deposits in southern California. It is world famous, having been the subject of a classical study by Professor A. O. Woodford of Pomona College. You will find that the breccia consists of tabular, angular fragments, up to several feet in diameter, of a wide variety of metamorphic rocks, mostly greenish to black in color with a wide range of textures and compositions. Look carefully and you may find occasional fragments of a fine-grained rock of bluish lavender hue; it's known as glaucophane schist and is especially diagnostic of this accumulation and the source from which it came. The nearest exposures of bedrock like the fragments in this breccia are on Catalina Island and in a small patch in Palos Verdes Hills. The large, angular blocks (Photo L-4) in the sedimentary brec-

Photo L-3. San Onofre Breccia in sea cliff at Aliso Point just southeast of Aliso Beach. Angular fragments are metamorphic rocks of Franciscan Formation lithology.

Photo L-4. Unusually coarse layer in San Onofre Breccia behind Coast Royale Beach just southeast of Aliso Point.

cias at Laguna had to come from a source much closer than those places.

Sedimentary structures and variations in size of fragments within the breccia, indicate a source nearby to the south and southwest where at present there is only open ocean. This leads geologists to the conclusion that in middle Miocene time, when this deposit was laid down, a high, rugged landmass stood just off the present coastline in that direction and shed very coarse debris into a shallow sea covering what is now the Laguna area. This interpretation is consistent with the near-offshore location of the Newport-Inglewood fault, which probably caused the 1933 Long Beach earthquake. A steep, rising fault scarp is just the sort of feature that could provide, by means of rock slides, debris avalanches and debris flows, the type of material seen in San Onofre Breccia. During quieter periods between these catastrophic events, beds of sand were laid down, as you will see in places. These associated sandstones locally contain fragments of fossil shells showing that the deposit is largely marine, although in some areas land-laid alluvial fan materials may make up part of the formation. Small faults and coarse calcite veinlets cutting through the breccia are of additional interest. In central and northern California, rocks of the type composing the fragments in the San Onofre Breccia compose the Franciscan Formation, a famous and much-studied rock unit. It is a marvelously complex, mixed-up bunch of rocks with a remarkable geological story to tell, and geologists are just now beginning to read that story more clearly in light of modern theories of sea floor spreading and plate tectonics, which involve the movement of large crustal plates across the face of our globe.

After deposition, about 15-20 million years ago, the beds of San Onofre Breccia were tilted into their present inclination, the offshore source was removed (probably both by erosion and faulting) and the present sea cliff was cut into the edge of a landmass formed by uplift of the San Joaquin Hills. Coupled with the scenic beach, coast, and surf, this makes a thoroughly delightful little geological hike at Aliso Beach, well worth the $1 parking fee, if you have to pay it. You will seldom see such unusual rocks so well exposed as in these sea cliffs and in the little storm-wave benches or platforms across which you can walk at low tide.

O-11 As the highway rises out of Aliso Canyon, the San Onofre Breccia is exposed in bluffs to the left. Access to beaches immediately south of Aliso can be gained by little public walkways among the houses near the top of the rise, but the walkways are hard to spot and parking is difficult. About 0.4 mile beyond Aliso Beach is a large apartment building, Laguna Royale, and 0.1 mile beyond it, near a vacant lot just short of Bluff Drive (and West Street), are some public steps leading one hundred feet down to a sandy beach. If tides are not too high and surf not too heavy, it's an easy walk back to the San Onofre exposures just south of Aliso Beach. Cliffs backing the beaches along the walk afford good exposures of other aspects of the San Onofre, including a layer of huge rock fragments, all several feet in diameter (Photo L-4).

O-12 Beyond the stoplight at the South Coast Community Hospital (7th Street), a mile southeast of Aliso Beach, north-side roadcuts expose more coverhead, much of it fairly coarse-grained, as befits the location close to the base of the hillslope. Watch on the left, about 0.4 mile beyond the hospital, for a brown knob of San Onofre Breccia projecting up into the coverhead as exposed in cross section by a highway cut. Lower beds within the coverhead abut against flanks of this knob, demonstrating that the knob was there before the coverhead was laid down.

O-13 Beginning at Three Arch Bay (Photo L-5), hills to the north become more gentle, smoother in slope and contour, and

recede from the shore with a consequent widening of the terrace (Photo L-6). This reflects a change in nature of the bedrock from massive, hard sandstones and San Onofre Breccia, to softer, finer shales and sandstones of the Monterey and Capistrano formations. This change in lithology is expressed by the wide and open nature of Salt Creek valley ahead.

O-14 Southeast from Crown Valley Parkway and Monarch Bay Plaza, the highway descends into the valley of Salt Creek, marked by an open, barren, partly graded area on the left. This area is currently a subject of dispute between Avco Corporation and the California Coastal Commission. Dark boulders in roadcuts on the right are derived from the San Onofre Breccia. Near bottom of the descent, thinly bedded, light-colored shales of Monterey type are seen in the roadcut on the north. Immediately after regaining the terrace level beyond Salt Creek is the right-side turnoff into Niguel Beach Park. This facility provides a large parking area, free in winter with $1 charge in summer, and access to a wide, gently sloping sandy beach (Photo L-7). The offshore waters are shallow and wave refraction patterns often provide the large, obliquely breaking swells so prized by surfers. Just walking to the edge of the cliff to observe the scene is rewarding, and for those who don't mind a quarter-mile jaunt, the trip down to the beach is worthwhile. The downshore sea cliff exposes rather severely deformed light-colored shale and sandstone beds (Monterey), especially near the rocky point south of the beach.

O-15 On Highway 1 southbound, Selva Road (stoplight) is crossed in about 0.5 mile and ahead on the near skyline is a ridge rising fifty feet above terrace level. This is a bedrock feature extending southwest to Dana Point (Photo L-7). The highway curves left to ascend the ridge, and left-side roadcuts at the crest expose irregu-

Aliso Cr. ¬   ┌ Three Arches Coves
Coast Royale Beach   Tenth Ave Beach ¬   ┌ Whale Rock   Pescadero Pt.
Aliso Beach   ┌ Table Rock   Tortuga Beach   Mussel Cove   Terrace

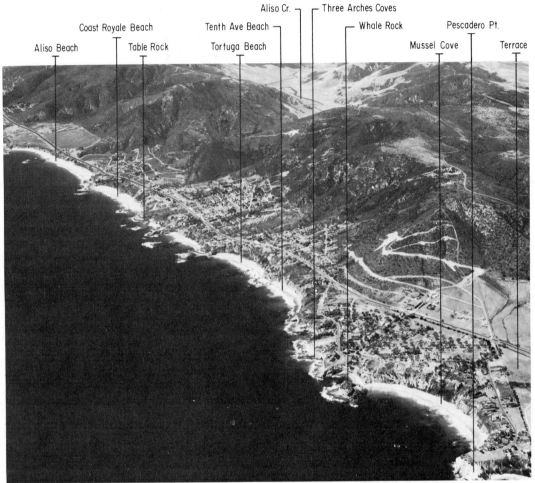

Photo L-5.   View north up South Laguna coast from Mussel Cove (lower right) to Aliso Beach. (Fairchild air photo 0-9854, 5/8/47).

larly bedded sandstone with intercalations of shale (Mio-Pliocene, Capistrano Formation). Immediately beyond the crest, a large, right-side, white/green sign indicates Dana Harbor ahead and a lookout point. Our route goes to the lookout, so we turn onto Blue Lantern Street a block beyond the sign. Drive a block and a half south to the end of Blue Lantern and park in the designated area. In good weather, views of Dana Harbor (Photo L-8) and a downcoast vista are well worth the time.

There's some geology here, too. The high cliff behind Dana Harbor is composed of Capistrano Formation, a marine deposit containing much light-colored sandstone and white-to-dark shales. Within these beds are some spectacular breccia layers and lenses, seen better while traveling along the cliff base a little later. Just right of the lookout is a small gully, and on the far side are reddish conglomeratic beds, part of the San Onofre Breccia. A fault, steeply inclined inland, runs up the gully

Photo L-6. Looking northwest to Mussel Cove. Dipping beds of San Onofre Breccia make near point, terrace well shown. (Fairchild air photo 0-2896, 2/22/32).

Photo L-7. View north at Dana Point (left) and Dana Cove. Inclined beds in cliff extending to Dana Point are San Onofre Breccia. White beds in cliff to right of pier at Dana Harbor are Capistrano Formation. Open country inland is valley of Salt Creek. (Fairchild air photo 0-9848, 5/8/47).

separating the San Onofre and Capistrano formations. Farther to the right is the south edge of Dana Point (Photo L-7) composed of coarse San Onofre Breccia.

O-16   To get a closer look at Dana Harbor cliffs, backtrack from the parking area a half block to Santa Clara Avenue, turn left one block to Green Lantern Street,

Photo L-8. View of Dana Cove and harbor east from out-look point as of early 1977. Cliffs are composed of Capistrano Formation (Mio-Pliocene), capped by a few feet of Pleistocene coverhead on a marine terrace.

and go left on it to Cove Road, thence left steeply downhill on Cove. Descending toward the first curve, reddish conglomerate and breccia of the San Onofre are exposed on the left and gently dipping San Onofre sandstone beds are on the right at the curve. Just beyond "Stop Ahead," we cross the fault, seen from the lookout, between the San Onofre and the Capistrano formations. At the stop sign, the option is available to turn right, park in one of the two areas on opposite sides of Del Obispo Street, and take a walk to Dana Point. It is a short, easy stroll and gives an opportunity to look upcoast past the high Dana Point cliff, to inspect the coarse San Onofre Breccia deposits with an overlying cap of finer Miocene strata, and to walk out on the breakwater for a closer look at the sea and a view back to land. On return, Dana Point visitors then cruise the base of the Dana Harbor cliffs by driving east along Del Obispo, as those not electing the Dana Point diversion will do directly.

O-17 In about 0.2 mile eastbound on Del Obispo, travelers come to nice picnic

facilities with restrooms, tables, water, grass and good views of the cliffs. In the cliffs opposite these facilities are layers, lenses, and irregular masses of coarse, angular breccia (Photo L-9), interbedded with the more usual sandstones and shales of the Capistrano Formation. These breccia bodies (Photo L-10) are interpreted as

Photo L-9. Layers of channel-fill breccia in Capistrano Formation north of picnic area, Dana Cove; interpreted as mass-flow deposits within a channel on a submarine fan.

Photo L-10. Blocks of largely Miocene rocks within breccia of submarine channel filling (Capistrano Formation) picnic area Dana Cove. Pocket watch in center gives scale.

channel fillings on a submarine depositional fan built outward from a submarine fault scarp to the south. The breccias were emplaced in the form of flows of debris that moved down channels in the fan. Some breccia bodies may look like inclined dikes because they merely line the steep walls of wide, sand-filled channels. Cliffs in massive sandstone beds here display nice cavernous weathering.

The waterfall over the cliff, shown in Photo L-11, is an ephemeral feature which you probably won't capture unless you arrive during or just after a heavy rain. However, rain or shine, you should be able to see the ten feet of Pleistocene coverhead at the top of the cliff lying with angular discordance on the tilted Capistrano beds. Just a little beyond the picnic grounds, Island Way turns off right to Dana Island, and the breccia layers pinch out about two hundred feet farther east. Casitas Place turns off right a little farther along, where the cliffs are predominantly massive white

sandstone. Then a bit farther comes Prado Road, leading right to Mariners' Village. A large parking area is available on the southwest corner of this intersection for anyone wishing to stop in order to take to the sidewalk for a closer look at the cliff ahead. Between Prado Road and the next intersection 0.2 mile east (Embarcadero), the cliff displays a wide, near-vertical, walled channel filled with light-colored sand which abuts against darker shale beds in the west channel wall (Photo L-12). This feature, known as Doheny Channel and much studied by geologists, is regarded as a classic example of a subaqueous sand flow filling a submarine fan channel.

Photo L-12. White sand filling steep-walled submarine channel cut in dark mudstone (left). Only the left wall of this feature, the Doheny Channel, is shown. All in Capistrano Formation as exposed in bluff at Dana Cove, between Prado Road and Embarcadero Place.

O-18   The bluff in Capistrano Formation continues on the left for outbound travelers as Del Obispo curves into a northerly course toward intersection with Highway 1. Entrance to Doheny State Park is passed on the right, and across the street bouldery gravels at the base of the bluff are regarded as Pleistocene stream deposits. At intersection with Highway 1, the option

Photo L-11. Temporary waterfall over cliff face north of picnic area, Dana Cove, resulting from short-lived heavy winter rain.

is available to turn right for about 1 mile to the San Diego Freeway where Segment K can be picked up and followed in either direction.

Segment L—
Inbound Descriptions

(The corresponding outbound material should be read first.)

I-19   Motorists headed northwest up the coast can follow this segment in reverse direction by turning south off Highway 1 onto Del Obispo Street at the eastern edge of the settlement of Dana Point. Note odometer reading there.

I-18   After starting south on Del Obispo street from Highway 1, inbound travelers see well-rounded stones from Pleistocene stream gravels in the first roadcuts on the right. Beyond the entrance to Doheny State Beach is the Capistrano Formation bluff and the features described in O-18.

I-17   Inbound travelers see Doheny Channel (Photo L-12) 0.25 mile west of the entrance to Doheny State Beach, or a scant 0.15 mile west of Puerto Place, just beyond the Embarcadero Place sign. Their view of the breccia masses (Photos L-10 and 11) farther west is just as good as for eastbound travelers, and they see the fault separating San Onofre Breccia (reddish) from the light-colored Capistrano beds at Cove Road clearly as they drive west past the picnic area. A pipe descends the face of the cliff not far from the trace of the fault. Outbound travelers get this view of the fault only by stopping at the picnic grounds—it is directly behind them as they drive east.

I-16   The walk to Dana Point can be made by continuing west on Del Obispo beyond Cove Road, and then returning later to ascend Cove Road to the top of the bluff.

I-15   The lookout point is reached by ascending Cove Road from the beach level at Dana Harbor, turning right at the top on Green Lantern Street, right again on Santa Clara Street, and then right on Blue Lantern Street to the parking spot.

I-14   The Niguel Beach parking area is seen before coming to its entrance a little less than 0.5 mile north of Selva Road stoplight. The roadcut in light-colored, thin-bedded shales (Monterey) is easily seen on the right climbing out of Salt Creek ahead.

I-13   Inbound motorists see this transition in reverse in traveling from the open, largely unbuilt area of Salt Creek past Crown Valley Parkway toward Three Arch Bay.

I-12   This cross-section exposure of a buried San Onofre knob is on the right at the curve about 0.2 mile north of the stoplight at the entrance to Three Arch Bay, but it's harder to see being so close at hand on the right.

I-11   People traveling northwest can locate these steps opposite West Street, about 0.5 mile beyond the stoplight at the South Coast Community Hospital. The bluffs and cuts exposing San Onofre Breccia north of the highway are seen on the right descending toward the Aliso Beach entry gate.

I-10   Aliso Beach is one mile beyond the 7th Street stoplight at the South Coast Community Hospital. Aliso Beach turn-in is well marked, and lies at the bottom of the only major descent along this stretch of highway.

I-9   Traveling northwest one can begin watching for Victoria Drive and Moss Street after passing "Laguna City Limit" and crossing Nyes Place (stoplight). It's roughly a quarter mile to Victoria, and 0.55 mile to Moss from Nyes. Remember that a cross street may have different names on opposite sides of Highway 1. The exposure behind Denny's is a block or so beyond Pearl Street.

I-8 Laguna Canyon Road comes after descending from the terrace and negotiating several curves and stoplights in central Laguna.

I-7 Watch for the stoplight at Myrtle Street, and then find this andesite cliff about 0.15 miles ahead close on the right.

I-6 Anyone wishing to make the Crescent Bay Point stop, 0.4 mile ahead, should watch for the two closely spaced stoplights at Cliff Drive 1300. A blue/white vista point sign (on the right) announces the turnoff, but drivers are well-advised to be in the left lane even before seeing it. Crescent Bay Drive is a little beyond the stoplight at Cliff Drive 700. Roadcuts in brown Topanga Sandstone are seen on the right approaching the main Emerald Bay entrance (on the right).

I-5 Travelers headed northwest see the Abalone Point andesite knob beyond "Irvine Cove," about opposite "Newport Beach 4, Long Beach 28," but they have to look back sharply left to 7 o'clock descending to El Moro Beach to see the jointed rock in the sea cliff. They are some-

what compensated by better views of the concretionary shales in roadcuts on the right. The marine abrasion platform with its overlying coverhead is seen both descending to and ascending from El Moro Beach, particularly on the ascent at marker 12^{07} where reworked concretions are concentrated along the buried abrasion platform.

I-4 This good example of coverhead is seen starting the descent, at marker 13^{02}, into Los Trancos Canyon, the first major gully northwest of El Moro Beach. Travelers will be less impressed with the poorer exposures going up the other side.

I-3 Going northwest corresponding terrace remnants are seen to the right and in profile ahead beyond Los Trancos Canyon, starting at marker 13^{66} and extending beyond 14^{22}.

I-2 Persons traveling upcoast can see the terrace remnants on the hill front approaching Corona del Mar and can make the diversion left to the sea cliff, if they so choose, at Treasure Cove beach parking beyond mileage marker 14^{35}.

I-1 This segment ends at the south edge of Corona del Mar.

Segment **M**

Riverside to Escondido, 68 Miles

O-1   Begin this trip, outbound, near the northeast corner of Riverside at the interchange of Riverside (Highway 91), Pomona (Highway 60), and Escondido (15E) freeways. Watch the signs and with luck and native intuition you should end up headed southeast out of this maze on 15E-60 toward San Diego and Indio.

The route to Escondido is mostly southward through interior Riverside and San Diego counties across the Peninsular Ranges, a group of northwesterly-bearing mountainous ridges separated by wide valleys. For details concerning the Peninsular Ranges, see pages 16-19 in the earlier southern California guidebook. Note odometer reading at the interchange.

(Inbound travelers see p. 188.)

O-2   Upon clearing the massive Riverside interchange, to the left at 10-11 o'clock are the Box Springs Mountains. At 9 o'clock on the far skyline is the crest of San Bernardino Mountains, and at about 10:30 o'clock, through a gap, the western part of San Jacinto Mountain ridge may be visible on the far skyline. On the far south skyline at 3 o'clock is the northeast face of Santa Ana Mountains. As the freeway curves to a more southeasterly course, Box Springs Mountains are replaced on the near skyline ahead, by the even surface of the Perris Upland

(Photo M-1) to which we shortly ascend. The geological significance of this recitation is that all of these features are composed predominantly of older igneous or metamorphic rocks.

O-3   After 1.5 miles outbound, the freeway rises over an underpass for University Avenue giving a good view a mile away at 9 o'clock of hillslopes littered with residual wool-sack boulders, so typical of the weathering behavior of homogeneous, coarse-grained igneous rocks in semi-arid environments. Many of these surface boulders originated as subsurface core stones (Photo M-2). At Pennsylvania Avenue most of the campus of the University of California, Riverside, has been passed on the left. A little beyond, ascent of Box Springs grade begins, and within half a mile exposures of coarse-grained igneous rock appear on hillsides and in roadcuts. Beyond El Cerrito Drive, wool-sack boulders again dot the hillslopes three hundred yards north. Near Central Avenue the steep, abrupt southwest face of Box Springs Mountains is in view on the left. At top of the grade, we emerge onto the smooth surface of Perris Upland. There the abrupt junction between the steep face of Box Springs Mountains and the flat upland surface is striking. This is seen best at 9:00-

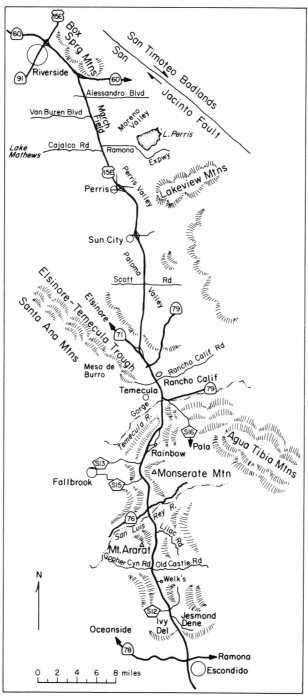

Figure M-1.   Segment M, Riverside to Escondido.

Photo M-1. View northeastward across the Perris Upland southeast of Lake Mathews. Igneous rocks on flank of Gavilan Peak in foreground. (Photo by John S. Shelton, 6419).

10:30 o'clock beyond the Box Springs exit. Although the abruptness and linearity of the mountain face are attributed to displacement along Box Springs fault, the geometry of the junction between mountain face and forelying flat is typical of areas underlain by homogeneous, coarse-grained, igneous rocks in arid and semi-arid regions. It reflects the weathering behavior of such rocks which produces fragments of two very different sizes, large wool-sack boulders on slopes, and finer, disintegrated granitic grus on flats. A gently sloping erosion surface at the foot of a steep mountain face is a pediment. Pediments abound in southern California desert areas, and we see one here at the base of Box Springs Mountains. Ahead is the separation of highways 60 (to Indio) and 15E (to San Diego and Escondido).

O-4   This journey traverses an extensive area underlain largely by a family of coarse-grained, intrusive, igneous rocks, differing considerably in composition but only slightly in age, all being mid-late Creta-

Photo M-2. Core stones within deeply weathered igneous rock of Southern California batholith, San Diego County.

ceous (around 80-90 million years). These rocks comprise the Southern California batholith. Much of the country between Salton Depression and the ocean is underlain by rocks of this group. They also extend far south into Baja California. In composition the rocks range from olivine gabbro to granite, that is, from basic rocks relatively low in silica and rich in iron, magnesium, and aluminum to acidic rocks much richer in silica and alkali elements like potassium and sodium, and poorer in iron and magnesium. Three of the most widespread units are: San Marcos Gabbro, Bonsall Tonalite, and Woodson Mountain Granodiorite, a rock displaying characteristics of both granite (grano) and diorite. A tonalite is simply a quartz-rich diorite. You have already seen exposures of Bonsall Tonalite coming up Box Springs grade. These and a half-dozen other rock types comprise a complex of interrelated intrusive bodies. Younger units intrude older members of the batholithic group, and they all intrude

still older, largely Jurassic, metamorphic country rock.

Be alert for separation to the right of 15E which we take to Escondido and San Diego. Anyone continuing straight ahead will end up on Highway 60 bound for Beaumont, Banning, and Palm Springs, worthy destinations treated in the second edition of the earlier guidebook.

As we curve through the interchange to get headed south-southeast on a straight 12-mile run toward Perris, San Jacinto Peak, (10,804 ft.) is on the left skyline at about 11 o'clock. The flat surface traversed is the floor of the northern end of Perris Valley. It is but one of several low-relief surfaces at different levels composing the Perris Upland (Photo M-1). Low hills rise slightly above Perris Valley, a little to the west, and higher, rugged peaks and ridges surmount it in several other directions. The evolutionary history of the Perris Upland is complex and involves extended erosion of the crystalline rocks, reducing them to extensive areas of low relief about nine million years ago. Lava eight million years old (seen later) was subsequently extruded onto parts of this surface, then stream rejuvenation (presumably by uplift) caused deep dissection and creation of a rugged topography which was later buried in a flood of alluvium to levels higher than the present floor of Perris and other valleys. The present flat floors of these valleys have been developed by later stream erosion. The even skyline of the low hills 0.5 to one mile away. at 3 o'clock, entering and beyond Edgemont, is a remnant of the nine million year-old surface truncating crystalline rock.

O-5   Since separating from Highway 60, depending upon time of day, wind direction, and flight schedules, you have probably been made aware of operations at March Field Air Force Base (coming up ahead) by the thunder of large bombers and other planes climbing skyward almost directly overhead. After passing the main part of March Field, keep your eyes peeled to catch a glimpse of some black, lanky, droopy-winged, U-2 scouting planes with unusually high, pointed tails parked in the southernmost part of the airbase. These are the planes that so irritated the Russians a few years back by flying at lofty (70,000 ft.) altitudes over their country on photographic missions. This is now a dead issue as satellites have taken over the task of surveillance for both sides. About six or seven miles east of March Field are rugged ridges and peaks of Bonsall Tonalite. San Jacinto Peak is now at 9:45 o'clock, and if weather is good, Mt. San Gorgonio (11,502 ft.) may be visible at 8:45 o'clock.

O-6   Beyond March Field, mountains on the far skyline at 11:30-11:45 o'clock are part of the Peninsular Ranges. Depending upon lighting and time of day, they may look like profiles cut out of cardboard. At Ramona Expressway (stoplight), Bernasconi Hills lie a short three miles east. Within them is Lake Perris, the reservoir at the south end of the east branch of the Central Valley Aqueduct which brings water from Feather River in northern California. About six miles west is much larger and older Lake Mathews, which stores Colorado River water brought by Metropolitan Aqueduct. If you wish to visit Lake Mathews, continue south another 0.7 mile and turn right on Cajalco Road.

Metropolitan Aqueduct crosses our route underground just south of Cajalco Road, and about a mile west are piles of waste rock from the aqueduct tunnel. If you would like to know what fresh Bonsall Tonalite looks like, that's a good place to visit. Take Cajalco Road and turn off south in about a mile on a dirt road leading to the rock piles. Besides going to Lake Mathews, Cajalco Road takes you near the site of the old Cajalco mine, a little west of Lake Mathews dam. This was the only tin mine of any significance in California, and indeed in the United States, but even

so, it didn't produce much. For more on Cajalco mine, see Segment N. Beyond Cajalco Road, in vicinity of Water and Orange avenues, low rocky hills to the west display nice wool-sack boulders derived from Bonsall Tonalite.

O-7   As the highway curves east to bypass Perris, the smoothness of the valley floor reflects complete burial of the crystalline bedrock by alluvium. The rugged, rocky Lakeview Mountains a few miles east ahead are composed largely of Lakeview Mountain Tonalite. Since these mountains were named long before either lakes Perris or Mathews existed, one wonders what lake was viewed. It was Lake Moreno (or Brown's Lake), a shallow water body, since drained. Beyond Perris, approaching Highway 74 to Hemet, compare the dark smooth slopes of the ridge three miles west with the wool-sack boulders on slopes in the Lakeview Mountain to the east. This contrast reflects the difference in bedrock, Bedford Canyon metamorphics (middle Jurassic, 175 million years) to the west, tonalite to the east.

About ten miles beyond Perris, the highway zigs east to go around the retirement community of Sun City. Just beyond the central part of the settlement is a deep, double-walled roadcut through a ridge exposing dark-gray, well-jointed rock. The cut on the east side is mostly in San Marcos Gabbro, that on the west is largely in Bedford Canyon Formation metamorphic rocks, a unit of considerable areal exposure in Santa Ana Mountains. Other hills in vicinity of Sun City are also composed largely of these metamorphic rocks. A stop is inadvisable because parking is difficult and traffic is dangerous. Beyond the roadcut, hills on the mid-skyline at 1 to 3 o'clock mark the southern edge of the Perris block as it drops to the Elsinore-Temecula trough.

O-8   Within the first mile or two beyond Sun City, the mountainous terrain of the Peninsular Ranges is prominent on the east

Photo M-3. Overview of Peninsular Ranges country from vicinity of Palomar Mountain, looking northeast. Dome of 200-inch telescope, lower right. San Jacinto and Santa Rosa mountains on far skyline. Intervening area is Anza Upland. (Spence air photo E-10057, 10/10/39).

and southeast skyline. The large mass at 11:15-11:45 o'clock is Agua Tibia Mountains, 5,000-6,000 ft. elevation, where Palomar Mountain and the famed 200-inch telescope (Photo M-3) are located. In another mile, Santiago Peak in the Santa Ana Mountains is prominent at about 3 o'clock. We are now in Menifee Valley, and beyond Quail Valley-Canyon Lake Road we will pass into Paloma Valley. Both, like Perris Valley, are heavily alluviated areas, although locally low-bedrock hillocks poke through the alluvium (Photo M-1). Approaching the southern rim of the Perris block, these bedrock hillocks become more numerous as the terrain rises gently. Soils here are darker brown because the neighboring hills contain considerable San Marcos Gabbro, a rock relatively rich in iron, and, as you know only too well, iron rusts to brown hydrated oxide.

About five miles south of Sun City is Scott Road, and in less than a mile farther south the highway rises into bedrock hills covered by dense chaparral, largely chamise brush. The principal rock is San Marcos Gabbro, but local masses of younger Woodson Mountain Granodiorite intrusive into the San Marcos are indicated by light-colored hillside boulders. These are best seen at marker 14^{00} and beyond.

To the west, Woodson Mountain Granodiorite composes a thick dike forming a crude ellipse nearly nine miles long west-northwesterly. Not surprisingly, geologists call such structures ring dikes. Features of this type have been studied within the igneous rock complexes of Scotland, Norway, and New England. In classical view, ring dikes are developed at centers of igneous activity where strong vertical forces produce fractures that define cone-shaped blocks of country rock which subside a little, thus admitting thin sheets of intrusive material. Unfortunately, along Highway 15E exposures do not tell much of the story. Interested geologists can get more of the ring-dike story by taking Scott Road west and descending Bundy Canyon via Bundy Canyon Road, but even so, limited roadside exposures give only part of the picture.

O-9   After crossing the summit of bedrock hills and starting downgrade, note the smooth, even skyline to the south on the crest of Santa Ana Mountains. That is Mesa de Burro, and it is capped by basaltic lava flows, now known to be eight million years old (uppermost Miocene), but formerly thought to be considerably younger (Pleistocene). A still larger lava-capped surface, Mesa de Colorado, lies farther back, and smaller outlying remnants of this lava also cap ridges and peaks (The Hogbacks) a little to the east within the hills just crossed.

Upon clearing the bedrock hills, southbound travelers continue a gradual descent into Elsinore-Temecula trough. The country is gently rolling owing to shallow dissection, and the smoothness and gentleness of slopes, lack of boulders, and no rock exposure in roadcuts, suggests we have passed onto fine-grained, softer materials. Eventually roadcuts, particularly in vicinity of large interchanges ahead, will reveal that this material is unconsolidated, disintegrated, granitic debris (grus). Late Pleistocene deposits of this character, several hundred feet thick, overlie a still greater thickness (2,500 feet) of similar but more firmly consolidated deposits, the Temecula Arkose (early Pleistocene). We don't see the Temecula Arkose along this highway, but it is not much different from the late Pleistocene grus we do see.

Highway cuts at and beyond Murrieta Hot Springs turnoff expose the rather dirty-looking, poorly layered, relatively unconsolidated Pleistocene grus, over which we have been traveling for several miles. Similar exposures continue for another 0.7 mile to the interchange with Highway 71. Segment N describes geological features along that highway as it traverses the Elsinore-Temecula trough to Corona. Beyond junction with Highway 79 (North, Winchester),

the abrupt, linear, faulted face of the Santa Ana Mountains is closer and clearer. The northwest end of the Agua Tibia Mountains looms at 11 o'clock, and San Jacinto Peak may be visible at about 8:50 o'clock.

Approaching Rancho California and Temecula, the homogeneous appearance and lack of visible outcrops or residual boulders on the Santa Ana Mountains face to the right contrasts with its bouldery appearance straight ahead. The smooth slopes are underlain by metamorphosed sedimentary rocks of the Bedford Canyon Formation, now largely slates, phyllites, quartzite, and locally marble. The face directly ahead is underlain by coarse-grained igneous rock, as we shall see shortly after passing Rancho California and Temecula.

O-10   At separation of Highway 79S to Indio, look to the mountain face at 12:45-1:00 o'clock to see the slot made by the gorge of Temecula River as it cuts through the Santa Anas to join Santa Margarita River which reaches the ocean just northwest of Oceanside. The head of the gorge is seen more closely at 2:30-3:00 o'clock approaching Temecula River bridge. This is a puzzling arrangement. A river flows out of a lowland area by means of a deep, steep-walled gorge transecting a major mountain barrier across its path. How did the river develop such a course? Several explanations are possible, but the most likely one is that Temecula River was here before the mountains were raised across its path. Uplift of the mountains was slow enough and the cutting power of the river great enough, so it was not blocked and shunted aside. As the mountains rose, the stream kept cutting deeper and deeper producing the gorge. Since the river anteceded (came before) the mountains, it is called an *antecedent stream*. In the late 1880s, Santa Fe Company built a railroad down this canyon as part of its Los Angeles to San Diego route. Repeated flood washouts forced abandonment of the tracks in favor of the present coastal route.

Immediately beyond "Thank you for visiting Rancho California," just before Temecula River bridge is crossed, Pauba Valley from which Temecula River drains is in view to the left at 9:00-10:30 o'clock. The gap in the mountain front at about 11:00 o'clock marks the head of Pala Creek. Temecula River is now a principal tributary of Santa Margarita River, but possibly not for long. If Pala Creek, a tributary of San Luis Rey River, continues to work headward, as it has in the past, it is going to cut through the divide and capture Temecula River converting it to a tributary of San Luis Rey. That will be bad news for Santa Margarita River which is powerless to do anything to prevent the capture. This sort of piracy occurs with modest frequency among rivers competing for the drainage of adjoining areas.

Directly ahead, after crossing Temecula River, the mountain front consists largely of massive Woodson Mountain Granodiorite. The light color, outcrop expression, and boulder-littered slopes of the Woodson contrast with the smooth slopes underlain by Bedford Canyon Formation to the right. Going upgrade, deep weathering and disintegration in Woodson Mountain Granodiorite are apparent in the huge roadcuts, especially toward top of the grade. Compare this condition with the large, solid, whitish boulders on hillsides. Boulders on the surface dry off rapidly after a rain; hence they weather much more slowly than rock beneath the ground which stays wet much of the year and is thus subjected to greater chemical alteration. Dark material exposed in the cut near top of the grade, just before the beginning of the two-lane highway, is probably a small chunk of Bedford Canyon Formation which the Woodson Mountain intrudes.

O-11   Beyond top of the grade, southbound travelers descend gently on a two-lane highway through a pleasant little canyon filled with oaks, sycamores, and some California bay trees, leading into alluvium-floored Rainbow Valley. A significant atmospheric change, especially in warm weather, usually occurs here because this is the seaward side of the mountains, and the cooling influence of the ocean is felt. Adjacent hillslopes are spectacularly littered with white residual boulders of Woodson Mountain Granodiorite.

For a number of miles after crossing the San Diego County line, this route traverses typical Southern California batholith terrain. The coarse-grained, relatively homogeneous, batholithic rocks produce a landscape without strong structural grain, featuring knoblike hills and short ridges separated by little valleys and vales. Approaching Mission Road turnoff to Fallbrook (County Highway S-13), these vales, valleys, and hillslopes are heavily planted to avocado and citrus orchards. White boulders have disappeared, and hillside cuts and excavations expose reddish soils. We have moved from the Woodson Granodiorite into San Marcos Gabbro. Roadcuts show the San Marcos to be a grayer rock, which, upon weathering, yields red soils and nearly boulder-free slopes. Roadcuts along Highway 15 between S-13 and S-15 (Reche Road going to Live Oak Park and Fallbrook) show that the San Marcos disintegrates rather easily and uniformly without formation of many core stones. This makes areas of San Marcos Gabbro easier to cultivate; hence, the abundance of orchards.

O-12   After several more miles of typical batholithic terrain and many roadcut exposures of San Marcos Gabbro, Bonsall Tonalite, and dark Bedford Canyon Formation rocks, we descend toward a flat, alluviated floor which leads us into the valley of San Luis Rey River. Ahead on the left, is a ridge of light-colored rock yielding large residual white boulders. Although this rock looks like Woodson Mountain, it is actually a different unit, described shortly. The contact between this rock and the darker, smoother, essentially boulder-free San Marcos Gabbro slopes can be glimpsed at intervals across the valley to the left, beyond Pala Mesa Resort and about opposite marker 47[00]. Shortly comes the stoplight at Highway 76, right to Oceanside and left to Pauma Valley. In another 0.7 mile a large bridge spans San Luis Rey River. Many of the neighboring hillslopes, especially to the east, are underlain by an unusually light-colored rock forming massive outcrops and abundant whitish boulders on slopes. Although it looks like Woodson Mountain Granodiorite, this is the Indian Mountain *leucogranodiorite,* which sounds like some incurable disease. *Leuco* simply means light-colored, so let's just say that. Freeway construction locally underway (mid-1977) will alter the route somewhat after this book is published, but not fatally.

O-13   Going upgrade beyond San Luis Rey River, first roadcuts are in the leucocraticgranodiorite, but within a mile or two we will be back in Bonsall Tonalite. At top of the grade, near West Lilac Road, a glimpse is caught, at 3 o'clock, of the country sloping down to the coast. Going downgrade, the rocks are Bonsall Tonalite, but ahead are ridges and slopes underlain by Woodson Mountain Granodiorite. The high ridge behind Lawrence Welk's establishment at Champagne Boulevard is typical of Woodson Mountain Granodiorite. Continuing toward Escondido, the route is flanked on both sides by ridges of Woodson Mountain Granodiorite, although for much of the next five miles the highway runs along a narrow band of fine-grained, dark-colored rocks regarded as near-surface intrusives related to Santiago Peak Volcanics (late Jurassic) and, therefore, older than the Woodson Mountain Granodiorite (late Cretaceous). These rocks form a septum or divider within the body of Woodson Mountain rock.

Approaching Escondido the country adjoining the highway opens up, valleys are wider, more extensively alluviated, and hills are lower and farther apart. This aspect develops gradually over the last three or four miles of the journey and is related to the less resistant nature of the Green Valley Tonalite surrounding Escondido. This segment ends at the north edge of Escondido, about two miles south of "City Limit," where Highway 78 takes off to Oceanside (right) and Ramona (left).

Segment M— Inbound Descriptions

(The corresponding outbound material should be read first.)

I-14   Travelers bound for Riverside from Escondido pick up Freeway 15 at intersection with Highway 78 near the northwest corner of Escondido and head north. Record odometer reading at this intersection.

I-13   As inbound travelers head north on Interstate 15 from Highway 78 near the northwest corner of Escondido, the contrast of high, bouldery, mountainous ridges ahead with the broad, open valley and more subdued, low, rounded hills near Escondido is striking. A considerable mantle and filling of alluvium on the flat valley floor surrounding Escondido is part of the reason, but a difference in nature of the bedrock is also a factor. In the Escondido area the bedrock is principally Green Valley Tonalite, a rock which weathers and disintegrates readily. This results in a terrain of wide valleys, relatively smooth slopes, and knobs and ridges of modest size and gentle contour. The country ahead is underlain, in good part, by Woodson Mountain Granodiorite, as indicated by the abundance of large, white boulders on slopes and the higher, more rugged configuration of the mountains. Some of the dark rocks exposed in the first roadcuts going north are probably Bedford Canyon Formation (middle Jurassic, 160-170 million years). However, in about 2.5 miles our route enters the Woodson Mountain terrane, and slopes on either side of the highway are mantled by the large white boulders so typical of that unit. At Ivy Del Lane, we are well into the granodiorite. However, much of the rock exposed in cuts along the freeway beyond Ivy Del Lane will be dark-colored, for the highway runs directly up a vale underlain by a narrow septum of dark-colored, shallow, intrusive rocks related to the Santiago Peak Volcanics. This septum extends for roughly 5.5 miles, nearly to Champagne Road and Lawrence Welk's establishment. In this stretch, we pass Jesmond Dene Road and County Highway S-12 (Deer Spring Road-Mountain Meadow Road) to San Marcos and Vista, rise over a low summit at the Travel-In Motel, and then descend a narrower canyon with ridges of Woodson Mountain Granodiorite pressing in more closely on both sides. Farther down, this canyon, Moosa by name, opens into a smooth alluviated valley floor on which the Welk facilities are sited.

The high ridge behind Welk's country club is Woodson Mountain Granodiorite, but lower parts of slopes to the left are beginning to look different, partly because of smaller and fewer residual boulders. Roadcuts soon show the rock to be the more even-grained, grayer, Bonsall Tonalite. Soon Bonsall makes up the country on both sides of the highway. Avocado orchards, which are more easily planted and cultivated on Bonsall Tonalite and the San Marcos Gabbro, than on the Woodson Mountain Granodiorite, will soon become more abundant.

After traversing several narrow, alluvial-filled valley floors, crossing a bedrock spur or two (usually of dark rock), and passing side roads leading to such enticing places as Old Castle, Gopher Canyon, San Luis Rey Downs, and Bonsall, the highway starts steeply upgrade beyond marker 41^{50}, still in Bonsall Tonalite. Eventually we come to Lilac Road, separating to the right, and about 0.7 mile farther, attain the summit for a striking view (in good weather) west to the coast.

Going downgrade toward San Luis Rey River from this summit, we pass into a mass of unusually light-colored rock, and similar material composes the ridges and slopes, inland to the east. The cliffy outcrops and large white boulders are suggestive of the Woodson Mountain granodiorite, but this unit is actually the leucogranodiorite described in O-13. The slopes have more rock outcroppings and fewer boulders than typical of the Woodson Mountain. Views of the wide, flat, alluvial floor of San Luis Rey valley, locally planted to row crops, are seen going downgrade, and near the bottom steep hillside slopes ahead and left are heavily planted to avocados.

I-12 Beyond the stoplight at Highway 76, our route proceeds up the alluviated floor of a valley tributary to San Luis Rey River from the north. Ahead at 12:30 o'clock is the south end of Monserate Mountain, composed of San Marcos Gabbro. Beyond "Temecula 12, Riverside 51, San Bernardino 63" at 2:30 o'clock on the mountainside is the contact between light-colored, boulder-mantled slopes of Indian Mountain leucogranodiorite and the darker, smoother, boulder-free slopes of San Marcos Gabbro, locally displaying red soil. This contact remains in view for some distance, even beyond the golf course ahead on the left. Upgrade ahead, dark rocks exposed in roadcuts belong to the Bedford Canyon Formation.

I-11 By the time we get to County Highway S-15 (Reche Road), we are well into the San Marcos Gabbro, as indicated by red soils and abundant avocado orchards on neighboring slopes and by the gray, granular rock exposed in roadcuts. We continue in the San Marcos for at least two miles. Just beyond Mission Road to Fallbrook (S-13) is a roadcut on the left showing white dikes (probably of Woodson Mountain Granodiorite) cutting the San Marcos. A little beyond "Temecula 8, Riverside 47, San Bernardino 59" are some red-brown soils in roadcuts, a typical weathering product of the San Marcos. A little farther, we rise to a low summit and see white boulder-mantled slopes of Woodson Mountain Granodiorite ahead. At Rainbow Canyon Road, the contact of San Marcos and Woodson Mountain is clearly seen on hill-slopes at 11 o'clock. On both sides beyond Rainbow Glen Road are extensive, boulder-mantled slopes of Woodson Mountain Granodiorite. Soon, we traverse the west margin of the alluvial flat in Rainbow Valley, site of an extensive nursery. From here to the summit, a little more than a mile beyond the Riverside County line, Woodson Mountain boulder-clad slopes dominate the scene.

I-10   Downgrade from the summit, in-bound travelers see the Temecula trough below and the projecting peaks and ridges of the Perris Upland (Photo M-1) beyond. If weather is clear, San Jacinto Peak could be impressive on the far skyline at about 3 o'clock when you get far enough down-grade. Just after crossing the bridge over Temecula River, look sharply left at 8:45 o'clock to see the Temecula River gorge through Santa Ana Mountains.

I-9   Going north the smooth, boulder-free face of Santa Ana Mountains is seen to the left after crossing Temecula River bridge, but the boulder-strewn face lies behind, the contact being about at the Temecula River gorge. At the blue/white "Food, Gas, Lodging" and brown "Lake Skinner," one can look at about 11:50 o'clock directly up the floor of the Teme-cula-Elsinore trough. Beyond Rancho Cali-fornia, near "Winchester Road, 79N, 1/2 Mile," we leave the lower part of the trough floor, graded to Temecula River, and climb a little into gently rolling, softly contoured country of grassy slopes and grain fields with a relief of twenty to forty feet. This topography characterizes the granitic grus deposits described in O-9, and something of their nature is revealed in roadcuts in the vincinity of major highway intersections

ahead. Left at 9:00-9:30 o'clock is the smooth, even skyline of lava-capped Mesa de Burro. Peaks and ridges at the south edge of the Perris Upland make the ragged skyline ahead. We soon ascend into that country, reaching the first crystalline rock exposures (San Marcos Gabbro) near marker 11[74].

I-8   Travelers headed north see some of the Woodson Mountain Granodiorite com-posing the ring dike intruded into the San Marcos Gabbro about 3/4 mile northwest of the highway at 10-11 o'clock from vicin-ity of marker 12[35]. The highway then curves left and crosses this rock near marker 13[49].

I-7   Beyond the bedrock hills, one emerges onto the floor of Paloma Valley. Initially this otherwise flat floor is in-terrupted by low rock knobs poking through the alluvium, but they die out be-fore "Sun City 4, Perris 13, Riverside 30." The deep, double-walled cut in San Marcos Gabbro and Bedford Canyon Formation is about 1/4 mile beyond "Sun City Exit, 1 Mile." The phase of San Marcos Gabbro seen on the right is dark and unusually uni-form. Beyond this cut, if the day is clear, the eastern San Gabriel Mountains make the far skyline at 11:30 o'clock and will stay in view for some time. Wool-sack, boulder-mantled slopes to the right and smoother, boulder-free slopes to the left indicate the difference in bedrock in those directions, as discussed in O-7.

I-6   Approaching and beyond Perris, the flat top of the low, crystalline-rock hills west of the highway marks the level of an old (nine million years) erosion surface dis-cussed in O-4. It continues in good view to and beyond Ramona Expressway (stop-light). Wool-sack boulders are abundant on these hillslopes.

I-5   The droopy-winged U-2 planes are visible, on the right, between the large Bell Feed plant, left of the highway, and Na-dina Avenue. Other features noted should be easily spotted—Mt. San Jacinto at about 3:45 o'clock and San Gorgonio near 2:45 o'clock. The distinctive relief of San Timoteo Badlands in the low mid-distance at 2:30-2:45 o'clock may be recognizable. The badlands lie on the far side of San Jacinto fault.

I-4   The flat floor of Paloma Valley south of Sun City corresponds to the floor of Perris Valley seen here. Travelers have already viewed Gavilan Hills to the west, and Lakeview Mountains to the east, rising well above the Paloma and Perris valleys surface. Those hills are topped by remnants of upland erosion surfaces truncating igneous rocks. Although older than the valley floors, these upland surfaces are regarded as younger than the nine million year old surface.

I-3   Inbound, one gets an unusually good direct-on look at the Box Springs Moun-

tains face and the pediment-mountain relationship after passing through Edgemont, especially beyond Eucalyptus Road.

I-2   All these features have already been seen from different angles. Descending Box Springs grade toward Riverside, one gets a good look at the eastern San Gabriel Mountains on the skyline ahead, and eventually of San Bernardino Mountains at 1 o'clock. Both are composed of older crystalline rocks but are considered part of the Transverse Ranges because of their east-west trend. Lower down, the fore-lying Jurupa Mountains behind Riverside become more apparent. They are part of the Peninsular Ranges.

I-1   This segment ends at the large freeway interchange at the northeast corner of Riverside.

Segment **N**

Corona to Temecula, 33.5 Miles

O-1   Begin this trip near the southeast corner of Corona, in Riverside County, where Highway 71 becomes Corona Freeway. This point is reached from Riverside Freeway (Highway 91) by turning southeastward on Highway 71 toward Elsinore, Temecula, and San Diego. Just have faith, be patient, and pay attention to the 71 signs through various turns and jogs; ultimately you will end up on Corona Freeway, currently (late 1977) at Magnolia Avenue.

The general course is southeast down Elsinore-Temecula trough (Photo O-1) between the rugged Santa Ana Mountains block southwest and the lower Perris block northeast. This narrow, linear trough marks the trace of Elsinore fault zone. Elsinore fault is one of a family of major northwestward-trending fracture zones, with significant right-lateral displacement, slicing across southern California; others are Newport-Inglewood fault to the southwest and San Jacinto and San Andreas faults to the northeast. Note odometer reading as the onramp joins that freeway.

(Inbound travelers see p. 198.)

O-2   After starting southeast on Corona Freeway (Highway 71), near "Ontario Avenue, 1 Mile," ridges and slopes of crystalline rock, pocked with small quarries, make up the hills at 9:30-10:30 o'clock and ahead is the high, abrupt face of Santa Ana Mountains, with citrus groves on alluvial fans in the foreground. Within 0.5 mile, well-jointed, crystalline rock appears in the roadcut on the far side of inbound freeway lanes, and in another 0.3 mile is a deep little pocket quarry just off the left side of the freeway, opposite "Business District, Next Right." Both places expose a dark (where fresh), fine-grained, igneous rock.

O-3   Beyond Ontario Avenue exit the freeway curves, and we see more clearly that our course is down a wide trough. A little beyond Ontario Avenue underpass, opposite "El Cerrito Road, Exit 3/4 Mile" on the flank of the skyline ridge at 9 o'clock about 1.5 miles to the northeast, are the scarred walls of large quarries excavated by Minnesota Mining and Metallurgical Company. This operation is reputed to be the largest source of roofing-granule materials on the Pacific Coast. The principal reason for the many quarries in these hills is the nature of the bedrock, the dark Temescal Wash quartz latite porphyry which you have already seen. This is a fine-grained, durable rock of Jurassic (150 million years) age that fractures nicely into angular pieces of a size suitable for roofing granules. Vibrations set up by huge explosions in the

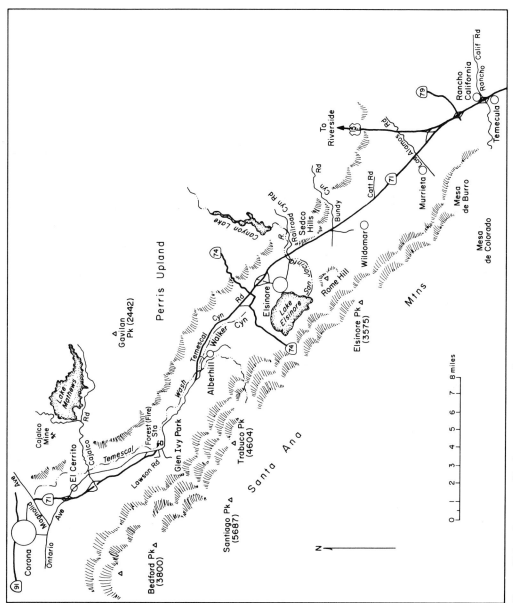

Figure N-1. Segment N, Corona to Temecula.

big quarries have been used by seismologists to calibrate the velocity of earthquake waves in southern California crustal materials. Ahead on the skyline, at 9:00-11:30 o'clock, is the edge of the Perris Upland, a surface of generally low relief on the Perris block. If weather is good, Santiago Peak (5,687 ft.), the highest point in the Santa Anas, should be visible at about 1 o'clock.

O-4   About a mile southeast of El Cerrito Road is Cajalco Road exit. Cajalco is a name that causes knowledgeable geologists to sit up a bit straighter. About five miles eastward up that road are the workings of one of the few productive tin mines ever operated in the United States. Our country is a dependent nation with respect to a number of critical minerals, one of them being tin. Essentially, no significant production of tin has been obtained within the contiguous forty-eight states, and neither Alaska nor Hawaii has been of much help. Although tin production from Cajalco Mine was never great—about one hundred and thirty tons—it was not for lack of effort. Tin-bearing minerals are commonly associated with conditions of high temperature and chemical combinations of rare and volatile elements. Such conditions are represented by areas of black, dense, tourmalinized rock in the Cajalco area.

Just short of Cajalco Road intersection, extensive operations of a Gladding-McBean red-tile plant lie a little northeast of the highway. This and similar plants use local clays. Between "Weirich Road, Right Lane" and Weirich Road exit, fleeting glimpses can be caught of pit walls and waste piles, a few hundred yards left toward 8 o'clock, of a now-abandoned glass-sand operation of Owens-Illinois Corporation. This was one of the few glass-sand plants in California.

Sands suitable for glass-making are rare in southern California because our sands, in geological parlance, are too immature. This means they contain too many mineral particles other than quartz, mostly feldspars and ferromagnesian minerals of several varieties. Good glass sand is composed almost wholly of quartz grains, and it gets that way by having been run through the mill of weathering and transport several times. This eliminates chemically susceptible and physically non-resistant mineral species, leaving just the hard, inert quartz (SiO_2) used to manufacture glass (principally for bottles in this instance). During the Paleocene epoch, some sixty to seventy million years ago, environmental conditions, caused severe chemical weathering of the basement rocks here with the result that quartz was about the only original mineral to survive. These quartz grains were subsequently reworked and concentrated into the Paleocene Silverado Formation which was mined in the deep pit east of the freeway. Unusual environmental conditions preceding and during Silverado time are indicated by low-grade coal (lignite) and deeply weathered clays just ahead near Alberhill. The Owens-Illinois pit and processing plant are well seen from Temescal Canyon Road, which was the main highway before construction of the freeway.

O-5   In another 2.5 miles we approach the current (late 1977) end of Corona Freeway and exit onto Temescal Canyon Road. When the freeway is completed, anyone wishing to follow this guide will have to exit here. Within half a mile on Temescal Canyon Road is a nice fruit stand, and 0.2 miles beyond, Lawson Road turns off right. Anyone interested in recent features of faulting can make an instructive little detour by following Lawson Road southwest 0.2 mile to the first curve where, at the turnout on the left, a recent scarplet faces southwest, based by a sag pond filled with trees and bushes. The paving of Lawson Road is cracked on the line of this scarp, suggesting instability in the underlying materials and possibly some tectonic distortion. In another 0.5 mile northwest on Lawson Road, at intersection with Hunt Road, irregular linear features of the fault zone are seen continuing northwestward across hilly terrain. In retracing our tracks from Hunt Road to Highway 71, the sag pond and southwest-facing scarp are well seen again.

O-6 Back on Temescal Canyon Road headed southeast, the line of green vegetation 0.2 mile southwest marks the trace of the fault seen on Lawson Road. It continues into the Glen Ivy Recreational Vehicle Park and hot spring area, entrance to which is passed shortly ahead. This is one of many parallel fractures within the Elsinore fault zone, appropriately known as North Glen Ivy fault.

In another tenth of a mile is an historical monument for the old Temescal Road, used by Indians, earlier explorers and settlers, and on the right, a little after passing Temescal fire station, are extensive sand and gravel operations. At marker 16[00], about 0.5 mile beyond the narrow concrete subway under the railroad, look at 11:50 o'clock to see the mouth of a narrow gorge cut into a crystalline bedrock spur extending across the course of Temescal Creek. The gorge remains in view until the highway curves to start an ascent around the nose of the spur. Going upgrade, sharp eyes may spot inclined beds (Paleocene, Silverado Formation) in cuts along the railroad just right of the highway. After leveling out at top of the grade, the upper end of the incised gorge comes into view left at 9 o'clock from marker 17[00]. The gorge makes a curious loop joining two relatively straight reaches of Temescal Wash. It looks like the stream could have remained in relatively soft sedimentary materials just by taking a course a little farther southwest. Why did it make this curious loop northeast into a hard, resistant, crystalline rock spur? The answer probably lies in the one word— *superimposition.* In earlier times, sedimentary deposits buried this bedrock spur, and the stream established its course, including the loop, on those deposits without know-

ing of the hard, crystalline rock buried below. Upon cutting down through the soft deposits, the stream found itself trapped on top of the buried spur and had no alternative but to continue the distasteful job of cutting down into the hard rock. Subsequent removal of much of the sedimentary deposits has etched out the hard-rock spur with its curious, superimposed, loop-shaped gorge.

O-7 After traversing about three miles of highway, between Temescal Wash on the left and the railroad on the right, a paved road to Alberhill takes off right. We continue ahead on 71 and shortly start a four-lane section of highway headed uphill. The first deep roadcut on the left, just beyond marker 20[00], exposes gray rocks, locally reddened by oxidation, of the Santiago Peak Volcanics (late Jurassic). Farther upgrade, the extensive clay-product operations at Alberhill come into view on the right. Plant and storage areas occupy the flat, and clay pits and waste piles scar hillsides to west and south. This is the largest commercial clay operation in southern California. It uses residual clays, formed by weathering along the unconformity below the Silverado Formation, and sedimentary clays within the lowermost Silverado reworked from the residual deposits. Most of the clay is of modest grade, so it is used for making heavy red products such as brick, sewer pipe, and tile. Some is suitable for firebricks and flue liners. In the early days, lignite was also mined here, one of the few places in California where coal has been produced. The clay and the coal are indicative of unusual environmental conditions in this area prior to Silverado time. Large waste piles from clay pits are seen high on hillsides to the right beyond the clay-product yards and works.

O-8 A little beyond the second road into Alberhill (right), Highway 71 starts up Walker Canyon, narrow at first and widening headward. Bare, strongly rilled slopes of artificial waste piles are visible on the right skyline at 12:30 o'clock from marker 21⁰⁰ and beyond. Farther up Walker Canyon, moist ground is indicated by willow trees and grassy bottomlands, and stretches of a concrete flume carrying water are seen just right of the highway. Walker Canyon is unusual in that it heads in a broad, relatively featureless meadowland, seen between markers 23⁰⁰ and 24⁰⁰. It is further distinguished by a long linear reach and a position behind a linear ridge within the Elsinore-Temecula trough. Since the upper, linear part of its course is parallel to Elsinore fault zone, the inference is reasonable that faulting, or erosion of ground-up rocks along a fault, have had something to do with this arrangement. The lowermost course of Walker Canyon, where it curves toward Alberhill, may be superimposed, but the evidence is not clear on that point. Walker Canyon is the channel of natural overflow from Lake Elsinore into Temescal Wash.

O-9   Shortly, intersection with State Highway 74 occurs, and here those wishing to follow Segment O via Ortega Highway across Santa Ana Mountains to the coast turn right. Continuing ahead on Highway 71, it is obvious that the floor of this part of Elsinore-Temecula trough has considerable relief caused by intratrough knobs and linear ridges, one of which lies just a half-mile southwest. These ridges and knobs are held up by slices of rock between the numerous, near-parallel, en echelon fractures within Elsinore fault zone. The northeast edge of the trough along which we travel is less sharply defined than the southwest edge at the steep linear base of Santa Ana Mountains, partly because spurs of crystalline bedrock project into the trough from the Perris block. Ahead is such a spur, and we cross it before coming to the turnoff into downtown Elsinore.

O-10   Beyond turnoff to downtown Elsinore, the highway rises and passes through cuts in a weathered, disintegrated, dark gray, modestly coarse-grained, igneous rock (San Marcos Gabbro). Some closely following hillsides display residual core stones. About a mile beyond the end of the divided highway is a double-walled roadcut in disintegrated rock of lighter gray color and more uniform grain (Bonsall Tonalite). Still farther, we emerge into open country affording a view of a flat-floored reach of the trough. On the far side, near the foot of Santa Ana Mountains at about 2:30 o'clock, is a forelying ridge, Rome Hill. Rome Hill is a slice of crystalline rock within the Elsinore zone, with Wildomar fault on this side and Willard fault on the other side. Willard fault determines the base of Santa Ana Mountains in this sector. Before coming to Railroad Canyon Road (stoplight), we cross the bed of San Jacinto River, which was the principal water source for Lake Elsinore before advent of the Metropolitan Aqueduct. As the name suggests, this drainage originates far to the northeast on the slopes of San Jacinto Peak. Within modern times, damming and upstream use of San Jacinto River water had so reduced the flow that Lake Elsinore periodically became little more than a muddy swamp. The lake level is now maintained by addition of Metropolitan Aqueduct water. Lake Elsinore is an aquatic recreational feature. The Elsinore region is also highly regarded by sailplane and glider enthusiasts, as well as hot-air balloonists.

O-11   Southeast of Railroad Canyon Road, Rome Hill remains clearly in view at 3 o'clock. The depth of sedimentary fill within the trough here is estimated at about 8,000 feet, from geophysical data, accounting for the flatness of the floor. If all the sedimentary fill were cleaned out, this would be an impressive bedrock chasm, with Santa Ana Mountains towering nearly 12,000 feet above its floor. Even two-thirds buried, the northeast face of the Santa Anas is impressive. Beyond Lemon Street, about at the end of the divided highway, intratrough hillocks, ridges, and knobs are again seen on the trough floor at 2 to 3 o'clock. They are presumably the product of local faulting.

About 2.5 miles southeast of Railroad Canyon Road, Bundy Canyon Road takes off left. It eventually reaches Highway 15E about 5.5 miles to the east, but before doing so traverses an unusual structure known as a ring dike. The name is self-descriptive— a ring-shaped dike intruded into older rock. The dike consists of Woodson Mountain Granodiorite intruded into San Marcos Gabbro, both rocks belonging to the southern California batholithic group. See Segment M for further notes on this structure, the so-called Paloma Valley ring complex.

O-12   Southeast of Bundy Canyon Road, the hills to the left become more subdued, and within a mile the floor of Elsinore-Temecula trough is again relatively smooth and flat, albeit narrower. However, approaching Baxter Road to Wildomar, near marker 31⁸⁵, in the middle of the valley, at about 2:30 o'clock, is a linear, rounded, intratrough ridge about seventy-five feet high with red-roofed houses on its crest. This is another fault-slice within the Elsinore zone. Beyond Baxter Road, examine the distant skyline at about 12:30 o'clock and note its smooth evenness. You are looking at Mesa de Burro, a gently sloping upland surface thinly capped by lava flows, formerly thought to be of Pleistocene age (one-two million years), but now known from potassium-argon measurements to be a little more than eight million years old (late Miocene). By late Miocene time, much of this region had been reduced by erosion to a surface of low relief onto which basaltic lavas were extruded. Later the area was uplifted and dissected so that now only remnants of the lava-capped surface are left to tell the story of the subdued Miocene landscape.

O-13   Approaching Catt Road, something less than a mile beyond Baxter Road, ter-

rain adjoining the highway becomes gently dissected, and roadcuts expose disintegrated granitic grus. We have entered a sector of Elsinore-Temecula trough deeply filled with such materials. In places, deposits of this type are more than 2,000 feet thick and so characterize the area that they are known as the Temecula Arkose. The material seen in most roadcuts along the highway is a younger overlying arkose (grus), but it is of similar character though less indurated and less darkly stained by oxidation. The rolling dissected terrain characterizing this material extends to the junction with Highway 15E more than five miles ahead. Smooth-topped hills, ridges, and divides within this area mark a former and higher, evenly graded trough floor. Occasionally an anomalous linear ridge or escarpment, parallel to the trend of the trough, and transverse to the normal drainage lines, will be seen. One such escarpment; linear, 20-30 feet high, and locally freshened by erosion, parallels the highway about one hundred and fifty yards to the right between markers 35⁰⁰ and 35¹⁹.

The skyline mountains directly ahead are the western end of the modestly lofty (5,500 ft.) Agua Tibia Mountains, within which are Palomar Mountain and the 200-inch telescope. The dome of the observatory is often visible at 11:50 o'clock beyond the Kalmia Avenue-Antelope Road intersection. Mesa de Burro remains in view on the right skyline moving to a position of 3 o'clock as we travel southeast. After passing the turnoff to Murietta, negotiating the Los Alamos Road overpass, and passing Murietta Hot Springs Road, we come to an interchange with Highway 15E, about three miles northwest of Temecula and Rancho California. Approaching this interchange you may get a good view of San Jacinto Peak (10,804 ft.) on the far skyline at 9:45 o'clock. A capping of winter snow can make it impressive. Here, travelers can elect to go either direction on 15E, following the descriptions of Segment M.

Segment N— Inbound Descriptions

(The corresponding outbound material should be read first.)

I-14 Motorists wishing to travel northwest up the trough, take Highway 71 from Freeway 15 about 3.5 miles northwest of Rancho California Road overpass. This junction, under construction in early 1977, should be completed by the time this volume is published. Note odometer reading leaving Freeway 15.

I-13 After turning onto Highway 71 travelers headed for Elsinore, Corona, or points between will have trouble viewing San Jacinto Peak and the Agua Tibias except in their rear view mirrors. Their views northwest up the Elsinore-Temecula trough and of the face of the Santa Ana Mountains to the south are good. At "Elsinore 12, Corona 33, Riverside 53," the smooth skyline profile of Mesa de Burro lies at 10:30-12:00 o'clock. It has swung to 9 to 10 o'clock by the time Los Alamos Road is reached.

For the next five miles (to Catt Road), the highway passes through the dissected, gently rolling terrain characteristic of the arkosic deposits filling the Temecula end of the trough. Beyond the Kalmia Avenue-Antelope Road intersection, a contact between boulder-free slopes underlain by Bedford Canyon Formation (left) and boulder-dotted slopes underlain by Bonsall Tonalite (right) is intermittently visible at 11 o'clock in the face of the Santa Anas. This contact is seen off and on through openings to the left for the next several miles. Start watching roadside markers beyond Kalmia Avenue. Starting opposite 35^{19}, one hundred and fifty yards southwest of the road, an abrupt, linear escarpment 20-30 feet high cuts through the rolling terrain, discordant to the normal drainage pattern. The escarpment extends, in fresh condition, to at least marker 34^{99} and in modi-fied, subdued form somewhat farther to about 34^{81}. This anomalous topographic feature is probably a fault scarp, representing fairly recent displacement along one of the fractures in the wide Elsinore zone.

Beyond Catt Road, the rolling dissected terrain gives way to a relatively smooth, featureless trough floor. Here, and for the past mile or so, the face of the Perris block to the north is more abrupt, linear, steeper, and better defined than farther northwest near Lake Elsinore.

I-12 Those traveling northwest have already had a good look at Mesa de Burro, the northernmost of two extensive lava-capped, smooth, upland-surface remnants in the southern Santa Ana Mountains. In vicinity of Baxter Road (to Wildomar), between 32^{27} and 32^{08}, toward the middle of the trough at 9:15-10:15 o'clock, is the smooth-sided, subdued, linear intra-trough ridge with red-roofed houses on its crest.

I-11 The Bundy Canyon Road turnoff (right) is easily identified by any northbound travelers wishing to explore the area of the Paloma Valley ring complex. Beyond Bundy Canyon Road, Rome Hill is normally visible at 10:30 o'clock and Lake Elsinore at 11:30 o'clock.

I-10 For travelers headed toward Corona (or Elsinore), the ridgelike form of the Rome Hill fault slice becomes clearer at 9 o'clock beyond "Sedco Hills" and the view of Lake Elsinore also improves as we rise above the trough floor. Intersection with Railroad Canyon Road (stoplight), the crossing of San Jacinto River, and the transection of bedrock spurs beyond, first in Bonsall Tonalite and finally in San Marcos Gabbro, should be easily recognizable.

I-9 Travelers going northwest will probably be impressed with the rough topography created by the intra-trough hills and ridges around Elsinore compared to the flat trough floor farther southeast.

I-8 Heading for Corona one gets a good look at the meadow area from which Walker Canyon drains, to the left beyond El Toro Road between markers 24[19] and 23[63], before the highway curves and starts to descend the canyon at marker 23[21]. Beyond marker 23[00], the concrete flume comes into view just left of the highway. The first clay-pit waste pile is seen on the high left skyline at 11 o'clock at marker 22[46]. Other waste piles come into view farther along; notable is a deeply rilled pile on the skyline at 9:30 o'clock from marker 21[41]. The first paved turnoff into Alberhill is a little beyond marker 20[65].

I-7 Coming downgrade beyond the first Alberhill turnoff, after the highway separates into four lanes, large cuts in gray Santiago Peak Volcanics are passed on the right, and the clay-products operations come into view on the left at 9 o'clock opposite marker 20[22]. Most of the clay pits and waste piles are seen only with some difficulty by looking back sharply to the left. Beyond the roadcut with reddish, oxidized Santiago Peak rocks, at 11 to 12 o'clock are citrus groves on an alluvial fan about seventy-five feet above present stream level.

I-6 After leaving the four-lane section of highway, northbound, and passing the lower road into Alberhill (on left), the highway travels for nearly three miles between and parallel to Temescal Wash on the right and the railroad on the left. The upper end of the entrenched hard-rock gorge is first seen a little beyond marker 17[26] and is in good view crossing the small concrete bridge just short of marker 17[00]. Going downgrade you may be able to spot some of the inclined Silverado beds in railroad cuts to the left. The lower end of the gorge can be seen with some difficulty by looking sharply back to the right toward 5:30 o'clock beyond marker 16[22].

High peaks of the Santa Ana Mountains are in view in good weather at 10 to 1

o'clock after negotiating the narrow concrete subway under the railroad. Sand and gravel operations appear shortly on the left, and Temescal fire station and historical marker come quickly thereafter. The parallel line of green vegetation along North Glen Ivy fault is to the left beyond the entrance to Glen Ivy Recreational Vehicle Park.

I-5 Motorists headed northwest come to Lawson Road a little beyond marker 14[00], 0.5 mile beyond entrance to Glen Ivy Recreational Vehicle Park. The fruit stand is on the right about two hundred yards farther.

I-4 As inbound motorists turn onto Corona Freeway from Temescal Canyon Road, directly ahead on the hillsides are the scars of clay-pit excavations. Just to the right, ascending to the freeway, is a concrete-pipe operation on the floor of Temescal Wash, exploiting the local supply of sand and gravel. At and beyond "Weirich Road, Right Lane," at about 1 to 2 o'clock, waste piles of the glass-sand operation are in view and in rising on the overpass at "Cajalco Road Exit, 1 Mile," the plant facilities become visible at 2 o'clock. The deep pit from which the glass sand was taken comes into view abruptly on the right just beyond "Caljalco Road, Right Lane." It lies this side of the pile of red waste materials. The Gladding-McBean red-tile and sewer pipe operation is on the right just beyond Cajalco Road overpass which bears "El Cerrito Road Exit, 3/4 Mile."

I-3 Motorists headed for Corona see the large quarry scars at 9 o'clock from "Ontario Ave., 1/2 Mile." They will recognize that the Elsinore trough is not as well-defined approaching Corona as it is farther southeast, even though the Santa Ana Mountains front remains high and imposing.

I-2 Travelers approaching Corona from the south see this pocket quarry about 0.5

mile beyond "Corona City Limit," opposite a yellow "Maximum Speed 55." Exposures of dark, fresh rock are seen locally in the quarry and in the succeeding roadcut on the right.

I-1   This segment ends at Magnolia Avenue on the outskirts of Carona.

Segment O

Elsinore to San Juan Capistrano, 33.5 Miles

O-1   This segment starts at intersection of highways 71 and 74, just northwest of Elsinore in Riverside County, separating from Segment N. It follows 74 (Ortega Highway) southwestward across Santa Ana Mountains traversing a varied geological terrain of igneous, metamorphic, and sedimentary rocks and affording some striking views of Elsinore-Temecula trough (Photo O-1). Record odometer reading at the 71-74 intersection.

(Inbound travelers see p. 209.)

O-2   At the Elsinore end, be careful to go right at the first turn of Highway 74 beyond the railroad tracks; don't go obliquely left and end up in downtown Elsinore. Beyond the first boulevard stop, the highway eventually takes a southwestward course toward a gap in the linear ridge to the south. The gap may be part of an old stream course, dismembered by faulting. The ridge consists of mildly metamorphosed rocks of the Bedford Canyon Formation (middle Jurassic, 175 million years), the oldest rock unit in Santa Ana Mountains. Its linear character and unusual setting (in the middle of a valley), indicate that the ridge is a slice between two fractures within the wide Elsinore fault zone, North Elsinore fault on this side and Glen Ivy fault on the south side. Glen Ivy fault

also borders the near side of the Elsinore Lake basin, and the far side is determined by Willard fault, the principal fracture at the base of Santa Ana Mountains. After passing extensive plantings of palm trees, we attain the gap at the intersection with Lash Street and see exposures of Bedford Canyon rocks in roadcuts on the left. Descending, Lake Elsinore is in view ahead to the left.

Originally, the lake was fed largely by San Jacinto River draining from country to the northeast. Now the level is sustained by addition of Colorado River (Metropolitan Aqueduct) water. Good views of the lake continue crossing the floor of Elsinore-Temecula trough.

O-3   Continuing southeast on Riverside Drive, beyond the boulevard-stopped intersection with Lakeshore Drive, the floor of the trough is flat and smooth, indicating a significant alluvial filling. In openings through trees beyond Lake Elsinore State Park, Rome Hill is sighted at the south end of Lake Elsinore, at 9 o'clock from vicinity of mileage marker 12^{88}. Rome Hill is a fault slice bounded on the north by Wildomar fault and on the south by Willard fault.

O-4   Shortly, the highway executes a broad curve left, putting us onto Grand

201

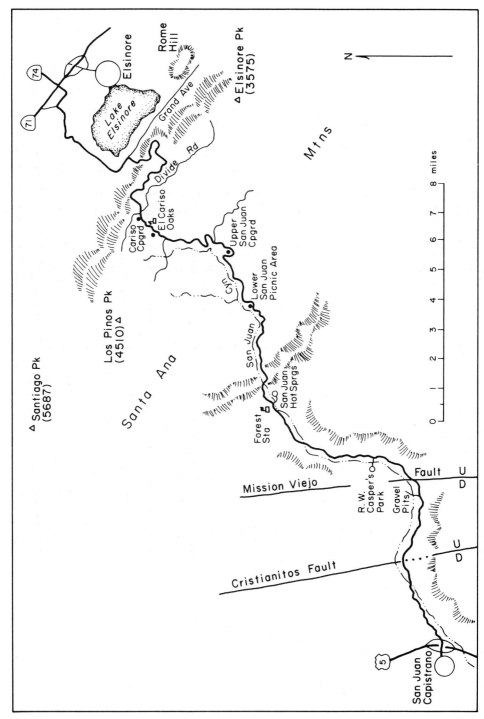

Figure O-1. Segment O, Elsinore to San Juan Capistrano.

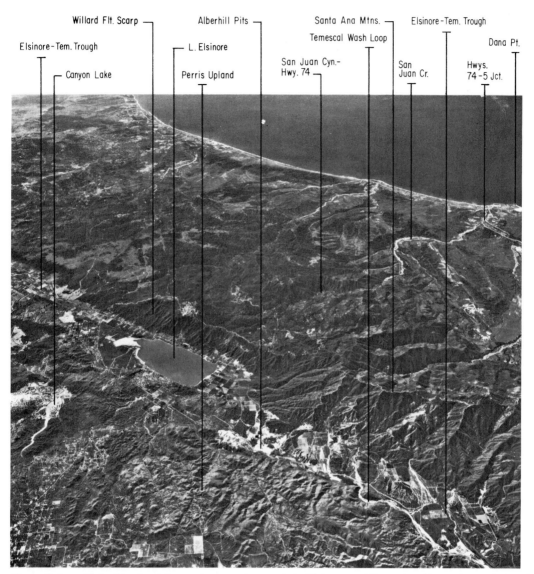

Willard Flt. Scarp

Elsinore-Tem. Trough

Canyon Lake

Alberhill Pits

L. Elsinore

Perris Upland

Santa Ana Mtns.

Temescal Wash Loop

San Juan Cyn.-
Hwy. 74

Elsinore-Tem. Trough

Dana Pt.

San
Juan Cr.

Hwys.
74-5 Jct.

Photo O-1. High-altitude oblique view south over Lake Elsinore and Santa Ana Mountains to the south-coast region. (U.S. Air Force photo taken for U.S. Geological Survey, 041-R-101).

Avenue headed southeastward parallel to the mountain front. In about 0.3 mile we turn southwest on Ortega Highway directly toward the mountains, and the route ascends an apron of disintegrated granitic rock (grus) to a crossing of Willard fault at the mountain base. The mountain front ahead and to the right, displays large boulders of the type typically formed by weathering of coarse-grained igneous rocks in relatively dry environments. Shortly, the highway turns southeast to switch back up the mountain front. Initial roadcuts are in grus. The first bedrock seen is in the double-walled cut through a spur just before mileage marker 10^{84}, and a rather messy assemblage of rocks it is. The principal components are gray Bonsall Tonalite, San Marcos Gabbro, and blocks of finer-grained, older metamorphic rocks (Bedford Canyon Formation). Details concerning the Bonsall, San Marcos, and other igneous-rock units of the Cretaceous Southern California batholith are given in Segment M. Subsequent cuts expose mostly Bonsall Tonalite, but beyond marker 10^{61}, at the hairpin turn where the highway switches back to the northwest, is the somewhat darker, coarser, less homogeneous San Marcos Gabbro. Local oxidation and bleaching by weathering make this anything but a representative exposure. We will see a better sample beyond the top of the grade. By the time marker 10^{26} is reached, the highway is back into Bonsall Tonalite which can be recognized partly by its homogeneity and abundant dark inclusions.

O-5   Continuing upgrade, the route remains in Bonsall Tonalite for the rest of the ascent of the mountain face, but not all phases of the Bonsall look the same. Large, light-colored boulders seen on the slopes to the right across a canyon from marker 9^{98} are derived from a somewhat lighter phase of this unit which is entered on the highway about at marker 8^{78}. Most roadcuts in the Bonsall along this highway are deeply disintegrated, much to the pleasure of highway contractors, but occasionally they display residual core stones (Photo O-2). Some included masses of resistant Bedford Canyon metamorphics also stand out. Approaching the first house on the right, near marker 8^{24}, the Bonsall looks even lighter in color and coarser in grain. It also yields large, white, residual boulders on hillslopes. A little farther along, three viewpoints are passed on the right. The first, at marker 7^{89} with the refreshment stand, is the largest; the second is just past marker 7^{89}; and the third and smallest is just about at the top of the grade at 7^{49}. If weather

Photo O-2.   Core stone in deeply weathered Bonsall Tonalite in roadcut opposite entrance to Lower San Juan picnic area in Santa Ana Mountains.

is at all favorable, a stop at any one or all of these spots is recommended. You see a lot of Peninsular Ranges country from them.

The first and largest turnout affords the best outlook southeast down Elsinore-Temecula trough. The other lookouts give better views up the trough to the northwest. No matter what the direction of view, the trough is clearly an unusual topographic feature which cuts across the country as though a giant had hacked at the earth with a huge cleaver (Photo O-1). It has been formed by displacements on the complex of parallel and en echelon fractures composing the wide Elsinore fault zone. Lake Elsinore (Photo O-3) occupies a basin dropped, relatively, along two of these fractures, and the intra-trough ridges are slices uplifted between other parallel faults. Taking the northwest end of Lake Elsinore as 12 o'clock, the clay-pit workings at Alberhill are visible on the trough floor at 10:30 o'clock. Beyond the trough, to the north and northeast, is the gently rolling Perris

Photo O-3. View north-northeast across Lake Elsinore to Perris Upland, from view point on Ortega Highway on face of Santa Ana Mountains.

Upland (Photo M-1), crossed in Segment M, above which individual peaks and ridges rise a maximum of 1,000 feet. Lakeview Mountains in the mid-distance at 12:15 o'clock are an example of a higher mass. On the far skyline at 1:30 o'clock is San Jacinto Peak (10,804 ft.), likely to be snow-capped in winter and spring, and at 11:50 o'clock, stll farther away, is massive San Gorgonio Mountain (11,502 ft.) in the San Bernardino Mountains, the highest summit in southern California. The San Gabriel Mountains may be visible at 9:30-10:00 o'clock. As one looks northeastward, the rocks underlying the country within view are at least ninety per cent coarse-grained, igneous intrusives of the Southern California batholith.

O-6   After passing the last outlook point, the highway tops out and curves into a more normal southwesterly course. Although it continues to climb gently, the character of the terrain changes from a steep scarp to a gently rolling upland. Most of the rock exposed in roadcuts on the upland is deeply disintegrated and oxidized, making identification difficult. We pass from Bonsall Tonalite into a small exposure of San Marcos Gabbro in a double-walled roadcut, mantled by reddish soil, at marker 6^{97}. This is just short of "Summit, 2,666 ft." The San Marcos exposed here is as good a sample as you will see on this trip. The

Bonsall Tonalite is reentered almost at once and will be with us for a considerable spell.

O-7   Within 0.8 mile after leaving the scarp face, side roads separate, 6S07 to the left and 3S04 to the right leading in five miles to Los Pinos Recreation area and Santiago Peak (5,687 ft.) Just 0.2 mile farther along Highway 74 are El Cariso campground and El Cariso forest station, followed in half a mile by El Cariso village (El Cariso Oaks). Beyond marker 5^{84} we emerge into the open, and slopes of the skyline ridge at 12 to 1 o'clock are covered by white, residual, Woodson Mountain Granodiorite boulders. Then comes El Cariso Potrero (pasture) and, 0.6 mile from the village, the highway descends to a flat with a surprisingly thick mantle of fine-grained alluvium exposed in gully banks between 5^{41} and 5^{01}. Beyond the road to Los Pinos Forestry Camp, at 5^{29}, some outcrops of granitic rock, presumably Woodson Mountain, poke through the alluvium.

Upon leaving the alluvial flat, at marker 4^{96}, the highway descends more steeply and beyond 3^{95} describes a large hairpin curve. At the foot of the descent is a large stone bridge (mileage 3^{50}) followed by a smaller stone bridge (mileage 3^{08}). Sycamore trees and scrub oak have replaced the pines and the dense chamise chaparral of higher elevations. Rocks remain monotonously the same, part of a large, relatively homogeneous Woodson Mountain body, but this changes shortly.

O-8   Southbound, a little beyond the second stone bridge is Ortega Oaks, a store with a private campground, and opposite the store is the San Juan loop trail head. Beyond, roadcuts display much disintegrated igneous rock with occasional good core stones, as in cuts beyond 0^{61} and particularly opposite the entrance to Lower San Juan picnic area (Photo O-2). Woodson Mountain Granodiorite extends beyond Upper San Juan campground, and hillsides are typically boulder-mantled, but we cross into other types of granodiorite before reaching Lower San Juan picnic area. The oaks get larger, and the hillside chaparral is now largely scrub oak. Topographic relief becomes greater, slopes steeper, and the terrain more rugged as we descend into the canyon of San Juan Creek. A little beyond the Orange County line is Lower San Juan picnic area. The roadside mileage marker signs change character at the county line. Riverside County gives mileages frequently and to the hundredth of a mile; Orange County uses a simple sequential numbering system, except for mileage at the whole- or half-mile points. The picnic area turnoff is at Orange County marker 142, for example.

Beyond Lower San Juan picnic area, we enter the transition zone between intrusive igneous rocks of the late Cretaceous Southern California batholith and older metamorphics of the Bedford Canyon Formation (middle Jurassic). Roadcut exposures become darker owing to iron oxide staining. Metamorphic rocks are seen in the roadcut opposite the paved turnout between markers 132 and 131, 0.7 mile beyond the picnic area turn-in, and just beyond marker 130 a double-walled roadcut gives good exposures of Bedford Canyon rocks, here largely dark slaty material and fine quartzite. By inspecting canyon walls to the north, you should be able to trace the contact between white, boulder-littered slopes underlain by granitic igneous rocks, and the more somber, brownish, smoother slopes underlain by Bedford Canyon rocks. The contact extends roughly parallel to the canyon high up on its north wall for some distance. Bedford Canyon rocks fracture easily and yield sharply angular fragments which gather as talus on the slopes. The granitic rocks yield either large, rounded, residual boulders or fine granitic grus and these materials generally do not form talus accumulations.

We travel down the deep, steep-walled canyon of San Juan Creek for more than three miles largely through roadcuts in Bedford Canyon Formation or accumulations of angular debris derived therefrom. Occasionally you see little exposures of disintegrated granitic material representing small intrusions. Bedford Canyon rocks in many of the roadcuts are dark brown because of a liberal coating of iron oxide formed by weathering.

O-9   Descending San Juan Canyon, we eventually cross a large concrete bridge and a tenth of a mile beyond, at marker 98, enter exposures of deeply oxidized, disintegrated granitic rocks, with core stones, which continue beyond marker 89. In rapid succession come "Leaving Cleveland National Forest," the San Juan fire station, and a steel bridge.

O-10   The country now opens out for travelers bound southwest because they are entering a different geological terrane featuring sedimentary rocks, younger and softer than the crystalline complex just traversed. The slopes, a few tenths of a mile beyond the steel bridge, are littered with well-rounded stones, and the accumulations of surface debris exposed in roadcuts are rich in roundstones. These cobbles and boulders are reworked from basal, late Cretaceous fanglomerates and conglomerates (Trabuco Formation), that rest with depositional contact upon the older crystalline rocks. If you stopped to look at the stones, you would find that many were derived from the Santiago Peak Volcanics and the Bedford Canyon Formation. Coarse-grained igneous rocks are more sparsely represented because they yield either huge boulders too large to transport easily, or they disintegrate to grus.

O-11   About 0.4 mile southwest from the steel bridge, at marker 82 and extending to marker 79, the road passes through a double-walled cut in greenish to dark-gray and black nondescript rocks. These are Santiago Peak Volcanics, a formation of considerable extent in the Santa Anas, but not much seen along Ortega Highway. Just one hundred and fifty feet beyond marker 79 and the end of the cut in the volcanics, but just short of marker 78, a bluff on the right exposes large boulders in basal fanglomerates of the Trabuco Formation. Well-rounded stones up to several feet in diameter are intermixed with more angular fragments, all embedded in a poorly sorted matrix. The Trabuco is considered to be a land-laid deposit, although the seashore is judged to have been close by because of marine fossils in the nearby Baker Conglomerate.

O-12   Beyond this Trabuco exposure is a mile-long, straight stretch of road with debris on adjacent slopes displaying abundant Trabuco roundstones. The first bedrock exposures at the southwest end of this reach, where the road curves and descends slightly toward a white-railed wooden bridge across San Juan Creek, just beyond marker 68, are regarded as Trabuco. However, just across the creek, in the double-walled roadcut, are exposures of the marine Baker Conglomerate Member of the upper Cretaceous Ladd Formation. Turnouts at either end of the bridge provide parking for a stop worth making to get a closer look at the Baker Conglomerate. Careful inspection will reveal small fragments of marine shells in some layers, mostly rough-water, thick-shelled critters like oysters. The Baker may be in part a marine equivalent of the land-laid Trabuco.

O-13   Southwest from the Baker Conglomerate exposure, canyon walls recede and become smoother and gentler because they are underlain by fine-grained beds of the Holtz Member of the Ladd Formation. This member is mostly a black shale, here locally oxidized dark brown. Keep watching slopes to the right, beyond marker 67, and you will see shaly material in at least one exposure with beds dipping gently southwestward. Beyond, a huge sandstone

bluff looms on the skyline at about 1 o'clock. It is the Schulz Ranch Member of the Williams Formation, also of late Cretaceous age. This bluff remains on our right as a dominating landscape feature for more than a mile, starting at marker 66.

O-14   The valley of San Juan Creek continues to widen southwestward. The slopes are abundantly sprinkled with well-rounded cobbles and boulders from the Baker and Trabuco conglomerates, reworked into the Pleistocene stream gravels seen in successive double-walled cuts between markers 61 and 58. The first notable bedrock exposure along this stretch of highway, in a left-side roadcut just beyond marker 57, is massive brown sandstone (Pleasants Member of the Williams Formation). Similar exposures follow in subsequent roadcuts, and just beyond marker 50 the sandstone is nicely capped by Pleistocene, fluvial, roundstone gravel. Since the dip of this sandstone is near horizontal, this long traverse through it does not necessarily imply great thickness, although the Pleasants Member is actually about 1,300 feet thick. It forms the top of the Cretaceous sedimentary sequence in Santa Ana Mountains, which has an aggregate thickness of more than 5,000 feet and is one of the more varied Cretaceous sequences in southern California.

O-15   The valley of San Juan Creek continues to widen southwestward, and within half a mile beyond Ronald W. Caspers Recreation Park stream terraces at several levels begin to appear across the valley, for example, opposite marker 40. Geologists identify four terrace levels within the next several miles, intermittently seen through breaks in trees, as at markers 34 and 27. We will recognize at least three of those levels. Each terrace represents a stage in valley development when San Juan Creek became stabilized and used its energy more for widening and smoothing its valley floor than for cutting down. It is now engaged in such a valley-widening phase. For one of several possible reasons, such as tectonic uplift, climatic change, or sea-level lowering, the stream was rejuvenated after each period of stability and cut its floor to a lower level where renewed valley widening was initiated. An episode of valley widening may be so extensive, at least locally, that it destroys the remnants of some or even all earlier episodes of widening. Thus, the terraces remaining may record only a part of the evolutionary history of this valley.

O-16   Between markers 42 and 41, nearly two miles beyond Ronald W. Caspers Park, the Mission Viejo fault is crossed. It separates the Pleasants Member (late Cretaceous) from the Santiago Formation (Eocene), a white, much coarser, somewhat pebbly sandstone exposed in a double-walled roadcut just beyond marker 41. Subsequent roadcuts, to marker 24, provide additional exposures of the near-horizontal, white Santiago sandstone beds. To the right, on the valley floor opposite the Mission Viejo fault site, are the extensive sand and gravel operations of Conrock Corporation.

O-17   About 1.4 miles beyond the paved road going left into the Aeronutronics test site (marker 36), we pass from exposures of typical, coarse, granular, white, massive Santiago sandstones, at marker 24, on one side of a little gully to roadcuts in messy, surficial debris, at marker 23, on the other side. The messy debris is part of a massive landslide which the highway crosses for the next 0.6 mile. If we were on the opposite side of San Juan Creek looking back to the hillside being traversed, we would probably recognize the extent of the landslide by the disheveled appearance of the topography. This slide buries Cristianitos fault, which separates the Eocene Santiago from Miocene rocks. If you look north-northwestward while curving around the toe of the slide, beyond marker 22, you will see an

unusually straight valley (with a narrow, winding road) marking the trace of Cristianitos fault. This scene is also well viewed at 3 o'clock from vicinity of marker 19. The Cristianitos fault has been the subject of attention from geologists and engineers, because to the south beyond San Clemente, it passes not far from the San Onofre nuclear-power plant.

O-18   Travelers headed for San Juan Capistrano shortly pass through a double-walled roadcut, at marker 18, in a mass of dark San Onofre Breccia (middle Miocene). For more information on this unusual rock, see descriptions in Segment L. A little beyond this exposure is a lemon grove on a terrace corresponding to one of the terrace levels seen on the north side of the valley. Then the road drops past La Pata Avenue and traverses the alluvial plain of San Juan Creek to the creek crossing on a concrete bridge.

O-19   Beyond this last crossing of San Juan Creek, Ortega Highway runs west-southwest directly down the north side of the valley, first in Miocene shales (Monterey Formation), as indicated by white fragments near marker 14, and then in the Capistrano Formation (Mio-Pliocene). Both are relatively soft, fine-grained, sedimentary units of marine origin, which accounts for the gentling and softening of valley slopes and widening of its floor.

Hills across the valley to the south, near San Juan Capistrano, as seen from marker 8, are underlain by the incompetent Capistrano Formation which is prone to landsliding. Much of that hillside is disrupted by slides, but they are so old that a relatively experienced eye is required to recognize them.

This trip ends at the stoplight just before the overpass across San Diego Freeway (I-5) on the east edge of San Juan Capistrano. Travelers here have the option of picking up Segment K and following it in either direction on I-5. Or, they can cross the freeway, proceed to Del Obispo Street and follow it to Dana Point where Segment L describes the trip through Laguna Beach to Corona del Mar.

Segment O— Inbound Descriptions

(The corresponding outbound material should be read first.)

I-20 Inbound, this route separates from Segment K (El Toro to Oceanside) at intersection of Highway 74 with San Diego Freeway (I-5), near the northeast corner of San Juan Capistrano, and goes northeastward on 74 toward Elsinore. Record odometer reading at the start.

I-19 The overpass on San Diego Freeway marks the starting point of Segment O for inbound travelers headed for Elsinore (Photo O-1). First roadcuts just beyond the starting point expose Pleistocene gravels of San Juan Creek up which Highway 74 proceeds. Note that some of the white rectangular roadside markers are sequentially numbered, starting with 1 here; only occasionally do they show mileage. This changes at Riverside County line, well ahead, after which many markers show mileage. Nearly two miles out, beyond marker 13, roadside exposures on the left include at least one outcrop of light-colored, thin-bedded Miocene shales (Monterey). Up to this point the hills to the left were underlain by the Capistrano Formation (Mio-Pliocene). Beyond marker 16, San Juan Creek is crossed on a concrete bridge, and beyond La Pata Avenue ascends to the surface of a stream terrace with a lemon orchard.

I-18 You should have little trouble spotting the San Onofre Breccia just beyond the lemon orchard and marker 17.

I-17 Inbound travelers start across the landslide mass beyond the cut in San Ono-

fre Breccia, a little before marker 20 and continue in it to marker 23, beyond which, near marker 24, they enter white Santiago sandstones (Eocene). They see the trace of Cristianitos fault to the north between markers 19 and 21 less easily than outbound travelers but are compensated by good views of stream terraces on the opposite side of San Juan Creek, especially at marker 24 and again between markers 27 and 30. A sequence of at least three terraces is recognizable beyond marker 34.

I-16 The Eocene Santiago sandstones are entered at marker 24 and one should have little trouble seeing that they differ from the brown, finer sandstones of the Pleasants Member. The Mission Viejo fault, separating the two units, is crossed at the mouth of the small gully midway between markers 41 and 42, opposite the cone-shaped piles of sand and gravel on the floor of San Juan Creek to the left.

I-15 Inbound motorists have had the terraces on the opposite side of the valley in view for the last several miles.

I-14 The brown, massive, Pleasants sandstones is entered between markers 41 and 42, a little less than a mile beyond the paved road going left into the Conrock sand-gravel operation and is then seen in subsequent roadcuts to marker 57. Roundstones become abundant on nearby slopes and in surficial debris beyond entrance to Ronald W. Caspers Park (between markers 51 and 52) and increase upvalley. An entry gateway, constructed of roundstones, is on the right just beyond marker 55. Between markers 58 and 61, the highway passes through three successive double-walled roadcuts in Pleistocene stream gravels rich in roundstones reworked from the Cretaceous Baker and Trabuco conglomerates.

I-13 Motorists headed for Elsinore see the Schulz Ranch sandstone bluff directly ahead on the skyline at marker 56, about 0.7 miles northeast of the entrance to Ronald W. Caspers Park, and have it in view on the near left skyline to marker 66. They also see the smoother slopes underlain by the Holz Member of the Ladd Formation beyond marker 66, approaching the white wooden bridge locality.

I-12 You should have no trouble spotting the white wooden San Juan Creek bridge, beyond marker 67. Parking is easiest just beyond the bridge on the right. The first Trabuco conglomerate exposure is a little way up the road beyond marker 68, and roundstones from the Trabuco are abundant on hillslopes and in roadcuts in the subsequent mile-long straight stretch of highway.

I-11 For inbound travelers, this exposure of coarse Trabuco fanglomerate is just beyond marker 78, about 1.2 miles northeast of the white-railed wooden bridge across San Juan Creek. It lies at the northeast end of a lengthy stretch of straight road just where the valley of San Juan Creek begins to narrow. The volcanics are entered at marker 79.

I-10 Roundstones have already been seen in abundance for a good many miles. You can easily compare the lower, more open, sedimentary-rock country with the higher, rugged, crystalline-rock terrain ahead.

I-9 Travelers headed for Elsinore run this gamut of features in reverse order and get a more striking view of the deep canyon of San Juan Creek as they head up into it. The exposure of deeply disintegrated igneous rock is especially good at marker 92, and the metamorphics begin near marker 98.

I-8 The canyon of San Juan Creek is more impressive ascending than descending, with good views of hillside exposures of small bodies of igneous rock intrusive into the metamorphics, as indicated by patches of light-colored residual boulders.

The contact zone of the metamorphics with the main body of igneous rock is entered beyond marker 132, and we are well into the igneous rocks at Lower San Juan picnic area, where good core stones begin to appear in roadcuts (Photo O-2). At Upper San Juan campground Woodson Mountain granodiorite dominates, and the hillsides begin to display the typical mantle of white residual boulders.

I-7 Travelers headed toward Elsinore start ascending through the Woodson Mountain terrane with white boulder-mantled slopes after crossing the larger stone bridge at mileage 3^{50}. A half-mile after completing the hairpin turn, left of the highway at 10-11 o'clock (beyond 4^{28}) are some striking granite obelisks and a small, rock-walled canyon with a dry waterfall. The alluvial flat begins at 4^{96}.

I-6 You come to this small exposure of San Marcos Gabbro, most readily identified by its dark reddish-brown soil, about 1/4 mile beyond El Cariso Campground and El Cariso Forest Station. The double-walled roadcut exposure is one hundred feet beyond marker 6^{86}, which is opposite "Summit, 2,666 ft." The San Marcos exposure is small, and beyond marker 7^{04} we are into good Bonsall Tonalite, which continues with minor interruption to the bottom of the grade ahead.

I-5 You come to the smallest turnout first, where the highway starts to descend the steep northeast face of the Santa Anas. For inbound travelers, this view point is more difficult of access than the succeeding outlooks. Leaving the view points, the lighter, coarser phase of the Bonsall Tonalite predominates at least to 8^{57}, and the darker phase with dark inclusions, occasional core stones, and scattered included blocks of Bedford Canyon metamorphics, is seen downgrade from marker 8^{78} until San Marcos Gabbro is entered briefly on the hairpin turn beyond marker 10^{26}.

I-4   Coming downgrade, with splendid views of Lake Elsinore and Rome Hill, inbound motorists enter the San Marcos Gabbro from Bonsall Tonalite a little beyond marker 10^{26}, see it rounding the hairpin curve, and reenter the Bonsall beyond marker 10^{61}.

I-3   You have seen Rome Hill coming downgrade to better advantage and have had good views of the floor of the trough with its intratrough ridges.

I-2   You should have already enjoyed excellent views of the lake descending the north face of the Santa Anas. The Bedford Canyon exposures in the gap in the fault-slice ridge are south of Lakeshore Drive. For travelers intending to go northwest toward Corona, Highway 71 (Segment N) can be reached more directly by continuing due north at the railroad tracks.

I-1   This segment ends at the intersection of highways 71 and 74 just northwest of Elsinore.

Oceanside to San Diego, 32 Miles

O-1 Start this trip just south of Oceanside (Photo K-3) at junction with Highway 78, and proceed via Freeway 5 to intersection with Freeway 8 south of Mission Bay in San Diego. Eocene and Pleistocene sedimentary formations, marine terraces, coastal estuaries, other shoreline features, as well as Eocene and Pleistocene marine fossils are featured. It is a cool trip for summer, but pleasant any time of year. Record odometer reading at the start.

(Inbound travelers see p. 222.)

O-2 Immediately beyond Highway 78, southbound, is a valley occupied by Buena Vista Lagoon (Photo K-3). Initially formed as an estuary, when the lower reach of Buena Vista Creek was drowned by rising sea level, it is now separated from the ocean by a broad sandbar built by storm waves. Beyond, the highway rises onto a smooth marine terrace, and inland is the edge of a second terrace higher by twenty to thirty feet. In less than a mile, the central part of Carlsbad lies right, occupying a wide, flat terrace a little below highway level. Many residents of south coastal cities may not fully appreciate the role that shoreline processes and changes in relative level of sea and land have played in creating the physical settings of their communities. Beyond "Leucadia 4, Encinitas 7, San Diego 32," hanging from an overpass, is Agua Hedionda Lagoon, similar in origin to Buena Vista Lagoon.

O-3 Beyond Agua Hedionda Lagoon, the country inland is more intimately dissected and rolling in character. On the far east skyline at 9 o'clock, ragged peaks and ridges of crystalline rocks in the Peninsular Ranges are sometimes visible. Approaching Cannon Road, the large San Diego Gas and Electric steam plant is at 3 o'clock. Just beyond Cannon Road underpass comes the first example of a puzzling topographic feature. About 1/4 mile to the right is a low, house-covered ridge rising twenty feet above freeway level. The country inland is also higher than the freeway which therefore lies in a broad, flat-floored, linear vale between the foreridge to the right and higher country inland. The foreridge is actually seated on a marine terrace that continues westward toward the sea, a relationship you can't see from the freeway. Possible origins of the foreridge will be considered at Leucadia, where another and larger example is seen.

In vicinity of Palomar Airport Road-Carlsbad Boulevard exit, at some seasons, the color of large flower fields on the gently rising slopes inland is spectacular. For the next several miles, flower fields and flower

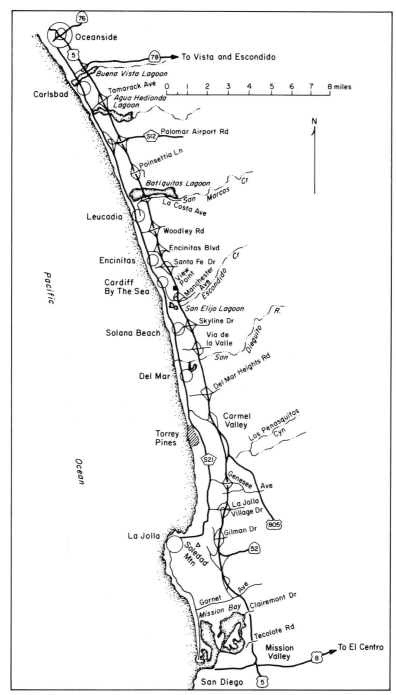

Figure P-1.   Segment P, Oceanside to San Diego.

sheds dominate the near scene. Beyond Palomar Airport Road exit, we emerge onto a slightly higher terrace and traverse it for some distance. Dissection by gullies and arroyos causes occasional dips below the terrace surface. Inland, traces of a still higher terrace can be seen in profile. Between "Poinsettia Lane, Right Lane" (center divider) and Poinsettia Lane exit, three terrace levels are in view; the one traversed by the highway, one above, and one below. A faint suggestion of the foreridge remains on the low terrace.

Beyond "La Costa-Leucadia, Right Lane" (center divider), the highway descends to another lagoon, Batiquitos by name. At 11:30 o'clock, on the far hillside is a large cut in faulted, white, massive, horizontal sandstone (middle Eocene, 45 million years), stained brown by oxidation toward the top. Climbing from Batiquitos Lagoon, more of the same sandstone is seen in cuts along secondary roads on inland hillsides. Shortly we find ourselves traveling in another vale, narrower and deeper than the one seen near Cannon Road and with a higher foreridge to the right. The height of the northern part of this ridge has been emphasized by erosional deepening of the vale, but at the top of the rise near "Leucadia Boulevard, Right Lane" (center divider), we emerge onto the terrace and the ridge remains fully fifty feet high with a steep face toward us. It is clearly more than just an erosional feature. Actually, there are two more ridges to the west (Photo P-1). The first makes a secondary, lower crest on the west flank of the ridge we see, but the other ridge is farther removed, freestanding and similar in size. The vale between the second and third ridges is occupied by downtown Leucadia and traversed by the coastal highway (S-21). Cuts and excavations along secondary roads crossing these ridges show relatively coarse, reasonably well-sorted, clean, heavily oxidized, and surficially cemented sand. The sand in the westernmost ridge, close to the ocean, is less heavily oxidized, less coherent, and looks younger.

To be honest, the origin of these ridges is not really understood, but as a speculation it is suggested that they may be unusually high beach ridges constructed by storm-wave action during pauses in regression of the shoreline across an emerging abrasion platform. The sand grains are angular and lack the high degree of sorting characteristic of wind-blown deposits, so the ridges are probably not solely longshore foredunes, although eolian activity may have contributed to their unusual height. That beach ridges are built along regressive shorelines is a well-recognized phenomenon, although the unusual height of the foreridge at Leucadia Boulevard causes one to be cautious in embracing solely that explanation. At "Encinitas Boulevard, Encinitas Right Lane" (center divider), the foreridge is still with us, but it begins to flatten farther south.

O-4   At "Santa Fe Drive, Encinitas," the Leucadia foreridge has just about disappeared (Photo P-2), and at "Cardiff by the Sea," we traverse a flat terrace surface extending seaward to the right and giving way inland to a gentle rise. Just beyond Birmingham Drive exit is blue/white "View Point, 1/2 Mile." A stop at this point, which has ample parking, is recommended, particularly if you would like to search for fragments of Eocene marine fossils. Approaching the view point, bluffs of iron-stained Eocene sandstone are just above the freeway cuts on the left.

The view point overlooks San Elijo Lagoon, and you can see well the wide sandbar at its mouth. On the lagoon's south side, extending inland from the sea cliff, is a terrace about 3/8 mile wide and thirty feet high which gives way inland to two higher terraces, roughly seventy and one hundred feet above the sea. The face of the roadcut just east of the view point consists of greenish shale and sandstone beds

Youngest Beach Ridge

Intermediate Beach Ridge

Oldest Beach Ridge

Encinitas

Batiquitos Lagoon

Cardiff By The Sea

Leucadia

Photo P-1.   Looking upcoast from over Cardiff-by-the Sea. (Photo by Robert C. Frampton and John S. Shelton, 4-3062A).

Photo P-2. Sea cliff and terraces at Encinitas. (Fairchild air photo 0-2880, 2/28/32).

(middle Eocene, Delmar Formation), overlain in the upper third by normally white, but here brown-stained, massive Torrey Sandstone. Most of the whitish sandstone we have been seeing farther north, and will continue to see going south, is also probably Torrey Sandstone. The large black boulders at the south edge of the parking area have been hauled in. They look like San Marcos Gabbro, a rock widely exposed within the nearby Peninsular Ranges. The unpaved dirt flat south of the parking lot is worth closer inspection. Much of this flat consists of debris from the Delmar Formation derived by cutting and grading for the freeway and view point. The Delmar Formation was deposited in a marine lagoonal environment, and some of its layers are richly fossiliferous. A little searching of the ground surface in bare parts of the dirt flat will reveal fragments of such fossils, mostly shells of clams and oysters, embedded in a green sandy matrix.

O-5   Upon leaving the view point and descending to the level of San Elijo Lagoon beyond Manchester Avenue exit, one can look inland to the skyline peaks and ridges of crystalline rock in the Peninsular Ranges which contrast in ruggedness with the lower, smoother, more subdued terrain underlain by the soft, near-horizontal sedimentary beds (largely Eocene) closer to the coast.

The next major valley, just beyond "San Diego City Limit" features the unusually wide, flat, alluviated floor of San Dieguito River (Photo P-3) providing a site for Del Mar Racetrack and fairgrounds, on the right. The large lagoonal estuary formerly occupying this valley has been completely filled with sediment, presumably because San Dieguito River drains a large area and carries more debris than smaller streams still harboring lagoons in their valleys. Climbing out of this wide valley, the lower gentle slopes without outcrops are underlain by a local marine and continental deposit representing an earlier estuarine filling of the valley (late Pleistocene, approximately 100,000 years, Bay Point For-

mation). The light-colored rock exposures, in higher, bare bluffs and little badland areas on both sides beyond "Del Mar Heights Road, Next Right" (center divider) are Torrey Sandstones (Eocene) and they are capped by a dark-brown coverhead (older Pleistocene, about one million years, Lindavista Formation). Bedding in all three units is essentially horizontal.

After passing Del Mar Heights Road exit and overpass, we descend into Carmel Valley. Anyone wishing to go to Torrey Pines State Reserve (park and beach) can turn off near the bottom on Carmel Valley and Sorrento Valley roads and continue west down Carmel Valley to Highway S-21. If interested in collecting fossil shells from the late Pleistocene Bay Point Formation, exit here and turn east (upvalley) on Carmel Valley Road, pass under the freeway, proceed one block to a dead end at El Camino Real, turn left and park where convenient. East across the street from the Shell station, and across the concrete drainage channel, a low, sandy bluff contains abundant fossil shells (clams and snails, mostly). Don't make a mess and nobody is likely to bother you.

For those electing Torrey Pines beach, a walk south along the high bluff (Photo P-4) beyond the entrance kiosk and beach-

Photo P-3. Looking downcoast past Del Mar to Torrey Pines. Smooth terrace (right) and wide, flat floor (racetrack, parking areas, fairgrounds) of San Dieguito River (far mid-distance). (Spence air photo E-14019, 6/2/51).

Photo P-4. Looking southeast to bluffs and mesa of Torrey Pines State Reserve. Vast expanse of smooth Lindavista terrace in background. Stratified rocks in lower third of bluff are Delmar Formation, overlain by massive Torrey Sandstone (irregular cavernous weathering), topped by Bay Point Formation (upper slope). White exposures among trees, left center, are Torrey Sandstone. (Fairchild air photo 0-2884, 2/28/32).

level parking is fun, scenic, and geologically instructive. The greenish beds in the lower part of this cliff are part of the Delmar Formation. The massive, homogeneous unit displaying cavernous weathering above is Torrey Sandstone stained brown by wash from the overlying dark-brown Pleistocene Bay Point Formation making up the slope at the top of the cliff. Keep close watch at the cliff base, especially in places where resistant sandstone forms an outcropping ledge. There you may find abundant fossil fragments. The Delmar and Torrey formations constitute what is known as a *transgressive* series. They were deposited as the sea level rose slowly and transgressed inland over a gently sloping land surface. Since the sea floor was shallow, an offshore bar formed and inland from it lay a lagoon. This pair of features moved slowly inland as the water level rose, each feature leaving behind a layer of deposits characteristic of its origin and environment—lagoonal sands, silts, and clays, in the instance of the Delmar, and massive, homogeneous offshore-bar sand in the instance of the Torrey. It was like two gigantic concrete spreaders one following the other, and each laying down a layer of different kinds of material. The lagoonal layer underlies the offshore-bar layer because the lagoon preceded the bar in the transgressive march. The off-shore-bar sands are succeeded by muddy shale beds laid down on the sea floor beyond the bar. These deposits, the Ardath Shale, are not exposed here, having been removed by erosion prior to deposition of the Lindavista and Bay Point formations, but they are seen farther south on freeways 5 and 805. There's more to be seen in the Torrey Pines cliff farther down the beach, but space is too limited to do it all justice here.

O-6   Ascending from Carmel Valley, in vicinity of "Junction 805, 1½ Miles" (center divider), to the right at 2:30-3:00 o'clock in bluffs and roadcuts along the highway ascending the east wall of Torrey Pines mesa (Photo P-4), are good exposures of massive Torrey Sandstone (Eocene) horizontally overlain by twenty feet of dark-brown, homogeneous sands of the Lindavista Formation (Pleistocene). As we traverse the east wall of wide Soledad Valley, with a complex of commercial buildings on its floor, signs begin advising of the separation of freeways 5 and 805. This segment continues on 5 toward downtown San Diego, but Segment R follows 805 to intersection with Highway 15 where it joins Segment Q leading to the Mexican border at Tijuana.

O-7   As outbound travelers ascend the southwest wall of Soledad Valley by way of a tributary canyon, after the 805 separation, they see brownish beds (Ardath Shale) in the first roadcuts behind "Miramar Road, NAS Miramar, Next Right." This shale overlies the Torrey Sandstone and represents the offshore bottom deposits that succeeded the offshore bar as the transgressive shoreline moved inland. Farther upgrade, but before emerging onto the flat upland (Lindavista terrace), materials exposed in roadcuts become much sandier and more varied (middle Eocene, Scripps Formation). This change appears abruptly because of small east-west faults, difficult to identify at 55 mph. on the freeway. Because of faulting, you will see brown Ardath Shale again as, for example, at "Miramar Road, NAS Miramar, Right."

As we emerge onto the Lindavista terrace approaching "Gilman Drive, Right Lane," Soledad Mountain (Photo P-5), with large communication towers, rises at 1 o'clock on the right skyline. Very shortly, descent into Rose Canyon begins through some sandstone (Scripps) and at the Gilman Drive exit we are back into underlying brown shales, as shown by roadcuts on the right. At overhanging "San Clemente Canyon, 3/4 Mile," directly ahead at about 12:10 o'clock is Soledad Mountain again, big as life. We are now in Rose Canyon and follow it to Mission Bay, four miles ahead (Photo P-5).

O-8   In less than half a mile beyond the massive interchange with Highway 52, our route slips obliquely into a complex fault zone, heading roughly south-southeast. Rose Canyon fault zone (Photo P-5) is the name usually applied to this complex of near-parallel fractures, the two principal members being the Rose Canyon and Mount Soledad faults. The highway curves into a course down the straight, lower segment of Rose Canyon at "Balboa Avenue-Garnet

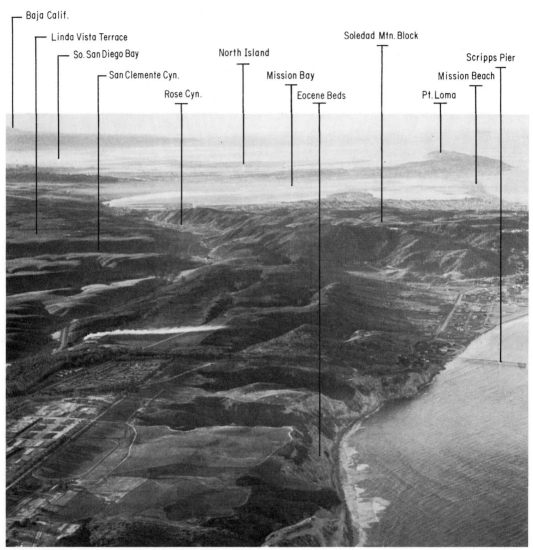

Baja Calif.

Linda Vista Terrace

So. San Diego Bay

San Clemente Cyn.

Rose Cyn.

North Island

Mission Bay

Eocene Beds

Soledad Mtn. Block

Scripps Pier

Mission Beach

Pt. Loma

Photo P-5. View south across La Jolla Bay to Soledad Mountain block and Mission Bay. (Photo by Robert C. Frampton and John S. Shelton, 4-3063A).

Avenue, 1¼ Miles." Hillsides to the right expose some older late Cretaceous strata, mostly sandstone, which we don't see well, and the slopes closer to the highway are underlain by Eocene shale. By looking to exposures of the shales upslope, you may be able to see that their bedding is steeply inclined, a marked departure from the near-horizontal attitude prevailing elsewhere. They are severely deformed within the fault zone. Exposures on the right along Rose Canyon are largely of surficial debris that has crept downslope. The many round-stones come from the conglomeratic part of the Mount Soledad Formation (early Eocene), and some exposures of the conglomerate in that unit are seen in bluffs bordering the highway. Roundstones also weather out of remnants of a Quaternary gravel that at one time partly filled Rose Canyon. At "Mission Bay Drive, Beaches, Next Right," eastward across the canyon in a cut behind the Gestetner building, stony beds of Mount Soledad Formation rest on light-colored, finer materials, possibly of late Cretaceous age. Near the mouth of Rose Canyon, at the Balboa Avenue-Garnet Avenue exit, on the right are well-bedded, brownish layers (Ardath Shale) dipping south. Descending Rose Canyon, the terrain to the west has gradually become lower because the entire Soledad Mountain block is tilted toward Mission Bay (Photo P-5).

After clearing Rose Canyon, the freeway passes under an overpass with a huge, green, steel girder, and we rise within half a mile for a view of Mission Bay at 2 o'clock. The bay represents an area shallowly flooded by the sea because of downwarping of the southern part of the Soledad Mountain block. In passing Mission Bay, don't completely ignore exposures in the bluff to the east across the railroad tracks. Although obscure, you will see low on the bluff occasional exposures of deeply rilled, soft, brown, fine-grained materials (Bay Point Formation). The higher part of the bluff consists of Eocene strata, and the bluff itself marks the southward continuation of the Rose Canyon fault zone.

Beyond the overpass with the sign indicating the upcoming junction with Interstate Highway 8, on the low skyline at 1 o'clock is the profile of the Point Loma Peninsula (Photo P-5), forming the western closure of the north part of San Diego Bay. The peninsula and point are composed primarily of late Cretaceous marine sedimentary formations of the Rosario Group with a thin mantle of Bay Point Formation on the lower flanks and a little capping of Lindavista Formation on the central and northern crest. The peninsula remains in view for a mile or so and is more clearly seen at 12:30-1:30 o'clock from vicinity of "Sea World Drive-Tecolote Road, Right Lane." Shortly we pass into a maze of overpasses, signs, offramps, and whatnots and make junction with Highway 8 to El Centro and points east.

O-9   This segment terminates at Freeway 8, although some travelers will certainly be going on to San Ysidro, Tijuana, and Baja California. Since much of that 17-mile journey is through heavily built areas, and the geological features are not overly visible, a comprehensive description is not attempted. Here are a few items. Just beyond Freeway 8 is a good view east up wide, flat-floored, steep-walled Mission Valley (Photo P-6). Prominent bluffs a little beyond and just to the east are in near-horizontal, brownish sand, silt, and mudstone layers of the largely marine San Diego Formation (late Pliocene). Approaching the radio tower for KSON, one of the high, crystalline-rock peaks of the Peninsular Ranges looms in the background. The drowned, now mud-filled, lower reach of Sweetwater River is crossed just beyond a sign indicating that alphabet-soup streets, E, H, J, and L, are coming up ahead. Low hills across the Mexican border come into view straight ahead at H Street. Approaching Palomar Street, tidal flats with dikes and salt ponds are on the right, and you may catch a glimpse of the salt plant (Western Salt Company) and a large pile of white salt. Otay River is crossed beyond the "Imperial Beach-Palm City, Exit Right." Farther south, the highway curves to a southeasterly course on the floor of wide Tijuana River valley, and at Dairy Mart Road the buildings of Tijuana are plainly in view on the hillslopes at 1 o'clock. The linear north face of those hills across the border is determined largely by faults.

Photo P-6. Looking east up Mission Valley (San Diego River) from over interchange of Freeway 8 (going east) with Highway 163 (from left). Bluffs to right are largely of late Eocene Mission Valley Formation. Peaks and ridges of crystalline rock of Peninsular Ranges province in background. (Spence air photo E-18289, 8/8/62).

Segment P—
Inbound Descriptions

(The corresponding outbound material should be read first.)

I-9   The San Ysidro to San Diego trip is no more exciting northbound than southbound. Inbound travelers get reasonable views of Point Loma peninsula starting at Main Street exit in Chula Vista and continuing into the alphabet soup of E, H, J, and L streets. They pass Palomar Street without seeing the salt operations to better advantage, but they do get some fair views of southern San Diego Harbor (Photo Q-1) and the warships anchored there. The bluffs of Pliocene beds beyond the downtown area of San Diego are closer on the right and easier to see. Mission Bay is on the left ahead approaching Freeway 8, and the view east up Mission Valley (Photo P-6) is good.

I-8   Going north from Freeway 8 on Freeway 5, travelers get views of the downwarped, partly flooded Mission Bay area, and, looking ahead at 11:30 o'clock, they can see the south-tilted, high Soledad Mountain block sloping down to Mission Bay. Approaching Rose Canyon, exposures of near-horizontal, soft, deeply rilled, brownish materials seen low on the face of the bluff to the north are Bay Point Formation. The bluff is along the southward trace of the Rose Canyon fault zone, although the topographic relief is probably more the product of erosion than of fault displacements.

Past the Balboa Avenue-Highway 274 exit, the highway goes under an overpass supported by a huge, green, steel girder.

Just beyond on the left near road level is a good exposure of south-dipping, well-layered shales and fine sands (Ardath Shale) with a local capping of brown Quaternary gravel. Going up Rose Canyon, steep, debris-mantled slopes on the left contain abundant roundstones which come largely from conglomeratic parts of the Mount Soledad Formation (early Eocene). Some of the more coherent, stone-rich bluffs on the left are probably actual exposures of that unit. On the right, a little way up Rose Canyon, behind the Gestetner building on the far side, is an exposure of brownish, conglomeratic Mount Soledad Formation resting on lighter colored, finer materials, possibly of late Cretaceous age. Occasional exposures of light-colored materials underlying conglomeratic deposits in the steep slopes left of the freeway farther along may also be Cretaceous, as rocks of that age are exposed higher on the north slope of Soledad Mountain. At "La Jolla, Next Right," the cross on Soledad Mountain is in view on the high skyline directly ahead at 12:05 o'clock. At "Ardath Road-San Clemente Canyon, Right Lane," the freeway curves right and immediately on the left are steeply dipping Ardath Shale beds. Where seen elsewhere in this region, these beds are usually horizontal. Their steep dip here is a result of deformation within Rose Canyon fault zone. Beyond the exit for West Ardath Road, near the left skyline at 11 o'clock is another exposure of steeply dipping shale beds. Then comes the complex of overpasses marking junction with Highway 52.

I-7   As travelers go north from Highway 52 interchange, directly ahead behind some eucalyptus trees are near-horizontal, brown, shale beds (Ardath Shale, middle Eocene). Their attitude shows we are out of the Rose Canyon fault zone (Photo P-5). Beyond Gilman Drive, we start to climb out of Rose Canyon toward the Lindavista terrace

composing the smooth skyline. Scattered, smoothly rounded stones on some roadcut faces are probably largely reworked from the overlying Lindavista Formation which caps the Lindavista terrace, although locally Eocene formations also contain conglomeratic lenses. Right at the top, a thin layer of very stony Lindavista is seen. Approaching "UC, San Diego, Next Right," the Lindavista terrace surface extends far to the east, but the freeway soon resumes its entrenched course. Torrey Pines State Reserve can be reached by turning off at Genesee Avenue, as well as farther ahead in Carmel Valley. Beyond Sorrento Valley Road exit, the route descends toward Soledad Valley with the complex of commercial buildings, and roadcuts are largely in brown beds (Ardath Shale). Shortly, junction is made with Freeway 805 entering on the left.

I-6   Travelers headed north from the 5-805 freeway junction should look left near "Carmel Valley, 1 Mile" (center divider) to the near skyline at 11:00-11:30 o'clock to see light-brown, massive, homogeneous Torrey Sandstone overlain by dark-brown Lindavista Formation in bluffs and cuts along the edge of Torrey Pines mesa (Photo P-4). In another two miles, a deep double-walled roadcut gives a close-up look at massive Torrey Sandstone, an offshore bar deposit. Upon clearing that cut, directly ahead on the skyline the dark-brown on white sequence of beds (Lindavista on Torrey) can be seen again. At "Carmel Valley Road-Del Mar Exit, 1/2 Mile," mudflats of Carmel Valley are on the left. This former lagoonal estuary is now nearly filled with mud. At the blue/white "Gas, Next Right" coming into Carmel Valley, the brown on white sequence is seen once more in skyline bluffs at 11 o'clock. Coniferous trees on slopes below the bluffs are Torrey pines, relict outliers of what was once a more extensive forest of such trees which flourished here under earlier, more favorable climatic and ecological conditions.

I-5   Northbound travelers can turn off on Carmel Valley Road and proceed east to the fossil locality or west to Torrey Pines beach and park. Climbing out of Carmel Valley toward Del Mar Heights Road, bluffs of light-colored Torrey Sandstone, locally capped by dark reddish-brown Lindavista Formation, are close at hand on the left. Most subsequent roadcut or hillside exposures for about five miles, wherever the rock can be easily recognized, are Eocene sandstones. Del Mar racetrack and fairgrounds are seen ahead on the left descending to the wide, flat floor of San Dieguito River (Photo P-3). Beyond "Lomas Santa Fe Drive, Solana Beach Exit," is a large, red real-estate billboard on the right identifying Santa Fe Hills. There, directly ahead on the skyline across the next valley is a large bluff giving a nice exposure of brown Lindavista Formation on top of light-colored Eocene sandstone. The little water body off left, beyond "Manchester Avenue-Cardiff by the Sea, Right Lane" (center divider) is San Elijo Lagoon.

I-4   Unfortunately, inbound travelers do not have access to the view point unless they over-run it, cross the freeway at the next offramp (Birmingham Drive), and double back. They do see the greenish Delmar beds rather well on the right in roadcuts opposite and beyond the view point which is just about across from "Cardiff by the Sea." About at "Santa Fe Drive, Encinitas, Right Lane" (center divider), the highway emerges onto a smooth terrace (Photo P-2) grading by way of a gentle slope inland to higher terrain. The Leucadia foreridge (Photo P-1) appears about at "Encinitas Boulevard, Right Lane" (center divider). In vicinity of "Leucadia Boulevard, Leucadia, Next Right" (center di-

vider), the foreridge is prominent, and the highway straightens to traverse the swale between it and the higher inland terrain. The highway crests about at the overpass of Leucadia Boulevard.

I-3   Beyond the overpass with "La Costa Avenue, 1¼ Miles," the freeway starts down that part of the vale between the foreridge and higher inland terrain that has been deepened by erosion. Beyond La Costa Avenue exit, Batiquitos Lagoon extends on both sides of the highway and to the left one sees the sandbar blocking its mouth beyond the railroad trestle. The coastal highway travels on the crest of the sandbar which cuts off views of the beach and surf. Beyond "Carlsbad City Limit," vistas are more open. To the left and ahead is an extensive terrace a little below freeway level. Beyond the overpass with "Carlsbad Boulevard-Palomar Airport Road, 1¼ Miles," are remnants of at least three terraces. We travel on one terrace level to the left is a lower surface, and to the right is the profile of a higher terrace. Beyond "San Marcos, Next Right," the interior terrain becomes more rolling owing to greater dissection, and beyond the Carlsbad Boulevard-Palomar Airport Road exit, the highway traverses a flat terrace dissected by gullies. Rising over the underpass for Cannon Road, the large San Diego Gas and Electric steam generating plant with a huge stack is at 11 o'clock, and three terrace levels are still visible. Past the steam plant, rugged ridges in Peninsular Ranges crystalline rocks may be visible on the far eastern skyline. Shortly we descend to Agua Hedionda Lagoon.

I-2   Northbound travelers come to Agua Hedionda Lagoon a little beyond the large San Diego Gas and Electric steam plant. On the left, beyond "Las Flores Drive, 1/2 Mile" is downtown Carlsbad on a wide terrace, and for the next half mile a somewhat higher terrace lies inland. If weather is clear, the far skyline ahead will outline high peaks and ridges in the Camp Pendleton Marine Corps Base, featuring San Onofre Mountain at 11:30 o'clock.

I-1   This segment ends, inbound, at intersection of Freeway 5 with Highway 78 just beyond Buena Vista Lagoon.

Segment Q

Escondido to San Ysidro, 44 Miles

O-1   Southbound travelers begin this trip at the Freeway 15-Highway 78 intersection near the northwest corner of Escondido and follow freeways 15 and 805 to the Mexican border. Construction complicated this route in mid-1977, and segments of two-lane highway and stoplighted streets were included, requiring navigational alertness. Late Mesozoic igneous and metamorphic rocks, Eocene and Pliocene sedimentary sequences, and extensive remnants of a Pleistocene marine terrace are seen. Note odometer at start of journey.

(Inbound travelers see p. 231.)

O-2   We start south in the wide, open, alluvium-floored valley surrounding Escondido which is dotted by isolated rounded knobs and smoothly sloped ridges of crystalline rock. Freeway 15 bypasses Escondido on the west, and the relatively deep cuts along it for the first two or three miles are in surprisingly soft, seemingly homogeneous, structureless material. However, sharp eyes may spot residual core stones in a cut on the left nearly a mile beyond Felicita Road, suggesting that the soft material may actually be a deeply disintegrated igneous rock. That is reasonable because geological maps show this area to be underlain by Green Valley Tonalite, a rock unit known to be easily disintegrated by weathering. Topographic relief around Escondido is relatively subdued because Green Valley Tonalite is the principal rock of the area. This unit extends several miles to the south, and numerous avocado and citrus orchards on hillsides reflect the relative ease of cultivation in this disintegrated material.

Approaching Via Rancho Parkway, slopes mantled with white residual boulders of Woodson Mountain Granodiorite are seen toward the high eastern skyline at 10 to 11 o'clock. Rocks west of the freeway are more mixed and not too well seen traveling south. Beyond Via Rancho Parkway, the high peak to the right is Bernardo Mountain. It is composed of San Marcos Gabbro as are the lower hills on the right descending to a crossing of an arm of Lake Hodges just beyond the center-divider "San Diego City Limit." This arm is often waterless.

O-3   Beyond Highland Valley and Pomerado roads, our route climbs gradually into hilly terrain composed of San Marcos Gabbro. A half-mile to the right of "Rancho Bernardo Road, Exit 1 Mile" at about 2:30 o'clock, a small exposure of Woodson Mountain Granodiorite is indicated by white boulders. It intrudes darker rocks (Bedford Canyon Formation and Santiago Peak Volcanics). On the right at "Rancho

226

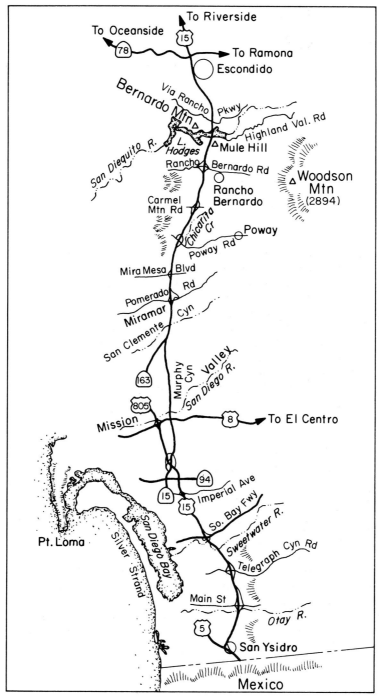

Figure Q-1. Segment Q, Escondido to San Ysidro.

Bernardo Road, Right Lane," disintegrated dark-gray rock mantled by reddish soils exposed in roadcuts is San Marcos Gabbro, which also composes dark bouldery bluffs on hillslopes and the prominent hill on the left (Mule Hill or Battle Mountain). Disintegrated, lighter gray rock seen in roadcuts approaching Rancho Bernardo Road is Green Valley Tonalite.

Beyond Rancho Bernardo Road, on the left, is the retirement community of Rancho Bernardo backed on the far skyline by a high ridge of Woodson Mountain Granodiorite, as indicated by the mantle of white residual boulders. In fact, that ridge is Woodson Mountain, from which the granodiorite gets its name. Within half a mile going upgrade, slopes immediately east of the freeway are unusually smooth, subdued, and grassy. They are underlain by fine, soft, sedimentary beds of late middle Eocene age (Friars Formation), partly marine and partly land-laid. The first hillsides in this terrane on the left show much evidence of mass movements in the form of slips, slumps, and flows. This is characteristic of Eocene beds where they are rich in clay.

Deep roadcuts farther upgrade are largely weed covered, but where scraped clean along the base, they expose soft, gray to greenish, late Eocene beds (Mission Valley Formation). Beyond, the route continues through gently rolling, grassy country underlain by these Eocene deposits. The big roadcut just beyond "Carmel Mountain Road Exit, 1 Mile" is obviously in such material. However, about 0.5 mile south of the above sign, on the left opposite the golf course and the big Rancho Penasquitos billboard, a roadcut exposes dark, angular, blocky, hard Santiago Peak Volcanics forming a knob which projects into the Eocene deposits. The pre-Eocene surface had considerable topographic relief, so that its ridges and knobs, although ultimately partly or fully buried by Eocene deposits, locally project well up into them. Subse-

quent erosion and stripping away of the Eocene beds have exposed the tops of some of these pre-Eocene knobs making them part of the present landscape, as at the above locality.

O-4   South of Carmel Mountain Road, the freeway ascends gradually alongside the alluviated floor of Chicarita Creek. The north part of the ridge to the east is composed of light-colored igneous intrusive rocks, but they soon give way south to Santiago Peak Volcanics. Just before "Poway, Right Lane," a small outlying patch of Eocene beds resting with depositional contact on the volcanics is entered. The basal Eocene beds are conglomeratic, as shown by the abundant roundstones on hillsides and in roadcuts. Before getting to the Poway-Rancho Penasquitos exit, we pass into Santiago Peak Volcanics, as demonstrated by the large roadcut on the left.

At and beyond the Poway-Rancho Penasquitos Boulevard intersection, freeway construction in mid-1977 provided ample exposures of the volcanics, and this should continue to be true after construction is completed. At top of the upgrade ahead, just beyond "Junction Route 8, 13 (miles), Downtown San Diego, 16," huge roadcuts on both sides afford good exposures of dark, angular, well-jointed volcanic rocks (Santiago Peak).

Downgrade from the big cuts, at "Miramar College, Next Right," the broad, flat surface of Lindavista terrace spreads out dramatically at 12 to 3 o'clock. We descend to and travel across this marine abrasion platform for several miles, but it is better seen from above. At Mira Mesa Boulevard, we are onto coverhead (Pleistocene Lindavista Formation) mantling the terrace. Adjacent hills to the east are composed of conglomerates (late Eocene, Poway Group), as indicated by smooth roundstones abundantly seen in roadcuts beyond "U.S. International University" and continuing through low hills to the Pomerado Road-Miramar

Road intersection. Many of the roundstones have been reworked and locally incorporated into the Pleistocene Lindavista Formation. Lithologically, they are about 80 percent silicic volcanic rock, about ten percent quartzite, and the remaining ten percent are other resistant rock types. No local source is known for these rocks, the Santiago Peak Volcanics being much more basic. Sedimentary features and stratigraphic relationships suggest a source to the east, perhaps as far away as Mojave Desert or the Sonora region of Mexico, where suitable bedrock sources possibly exist.

O-5   Continuing south from Pomerado-Miramar overpass, Lindavista terrace can be seen extending a modest distance east of the highway and far to the west. Approaching NAS Miramar exit, the even skyline of low hills one to two miles east may mark the level of the higher Poway terrace. Higher mountains on the skyline at 10:30 o'clock are composed of granitic intrusive rocks. Beyond the Miramar exit, get into the right lane in anticipation of a turn-off onto Highway 15. Much of the surface and shallow cuts bordering the highway, particularly beyond the intersection with Highway 163(S) to downtown San Diego, display roundstones reworked from the late Eocene Poway Group of formations. Shortly, our route starts a steep descent into the head of Murphy Canyon, where on the right is a cut in dark, reddish-brown, Pleistocene Lindavista Formation, with a stone-rich layer at the top. This formation thinly veneers the Lindavista terrace and is normally deeply oxidized by weathering.

Murphy Canyon is abnormally straight because it is aligned along a fault exploited by a headward-working tributary of San Diego River. In descending Murphy Canyon below the level of Lindavista terrace, we penetrate the underlying Stadium Conglomerate (late Eocene), the source of many of the roundstones seen in roadcuts and on hillsides. Here the conglomerate is only about fifty feet thick, and the walls

of Murphy Canyon below are composed of underlying fine sandstone, siltstone, and locally concretionary claystone (middle Eocene, Friars Formation). Locally, this sequence of beds also contains lenses of conglomerate. Beyond Clairemont-Mesa Boulevard turnoff, large excavations high at 2 o'clock show the reddish Lindavista (Pleistocene) resting on white sands (Friars), the Stadium Conglomerate having pinched out. Roadcuts on the left beyond Tierrasanta Boulevard (stoplight) afford good exposures of essentially horizontal beds of sandstone and locally concretionary finer materials (Friars Formation). Many roadcuts here have a surficial veneer of roundstones derived from the overlying Stadium Conglomerate and from local conglomerate layers within the Friars, some of which are seen in exposures along Murphy Canyon. Large excavations in the west wall of Murphy Canyon, behind the sand and gravel operation, are in the Friars. Beyond "Friars Road, Stadium, Right Lane" (center divider) on the left are two deep roadcuts in fine-grained, massive Friars siltstones and mudstones, and high up in the second cut is some Stadium Conglomerate. To the right, upon entering Mission Valley, is San Diego stadium from which the conglomerate takes its name.

O-6   After crossing Interstate Freeway 8, the highway climbs out of Mission Valley by way of a side canyon. Abundant roundstones suggest that the Stadium Conglomerate makes up the base of the bluffs, but we are soon into massive, overlying, gray sandstones (Eocene, Mission Valley Formation), and farther up is an irregular whitish member of that formation. Near the top of the grade, on the left opposite "Adams Avenue, Right Lane" are rilled bluffs about forty feet high in brownish, softer-looking, horizontal beds of finer materials. This is the Pliocene San Diego Formation resting disconformably upon the late Eocene beds. Locally, San Diego Formation contains thin beds of roundstone conglomerate, the roundstones being largely of the Poway type and undoubtedly reworked from that group with additions from local crystalline bedrock sources. The dark-colored, stone-rich deposits right at the top of the grade before breaking out onto the terrace are part of the Lindavista Formation (Pleistocene).

Currently (mid-1977), Highway 15 traverses the terrace surface as a city street (40th Street) through a sequence of stoplights before descending another gully beyond Wightman Street. In descending, we pass from a reddish, 2- to 3-foot layer of very stony Lindavista Formation into interbedded conglomerate and sandstone layers of the San Diego Formation (Pliocene), which is seen in extensive bare exposures to the left. Watch your navigation here so you don't continue on Highway 15, which is the easy thing to do. Keep right to get onto 805 South, headed south-southeast toward San Ysidro and the Mexican border.

O-7   Proceeding on Freeway 805 to San Ysidro we see Pliocene, Pliocene, and more Pliocene beds. In its most typical form, along this traverse, the marine San Diego Formation is mostly fine, brownish, soft sandstone and siltstone that make rilled bluffs and smooth, gentle hillsides. In places, the formation has a distinctive reddish or pinkish cast, and locally it is conglomeratic. Roadcuts are stabilized by heavy plantings or obscured by growths of weeds and grass, and much of the Freeway 805 course is entrenched, so we don't get sweeping views of the country. Beyond "Market Street, 1 Mile," soft, horizontal, fine silty-sandy Pliocene beds occasionally peek through the weeds. Locally, erosion has formed miniature badland bluffs in these deposits, and roadcuts are generally rilled. Conglomerate lenses pretty well disappear from the San Diego beds until we approach San Ysidro.

At "Plaza Boulevard Exit, 3/4 Mile," the freeway emerges from its trench, and at "National City Limit," the surrounding country is in view. To the far east are high peaks of the crystalline-rock Peninsular Ranges, and the nearer, lower hills are underlain by Pliocene rocks. Ahead and to right and left is the smooth, gently sloping terrace surface that we have been seeing in profile for several miles, still the Lindavista level, although a little lower owing to southward tilting. The freeway soon abandons the terrace for another depressed sector with some long cuts in fairly typical Pliocene materials. Approaching the South Bay Freeway exit, we descend into an irregular, dissected area on the north side of wide, flat-floored Sweetwater Valley. Looking downvalley, one may catch a quick view of the southern arm of San Diego Bay and the sandbar (Silver Strand Beach) separating it from the ocean (Photo Q-1). This arm of the bay marks the location of a gentle, synclinal downwarp and a shallow graben trending northwest. Beyond E Street exit, the country opens up somewhat and the terrain immediately to the east is more hilly. Upon completing the climb out of Sweetwater Valley, we regain the Lindavista terrace surface, and in vicinity of "Orange Avenue 1, Otay Valley Road-Main Street, 1½ Miles," southern San Diego Bay and Silver Strand Beach are again seen at 2:30 o'clock and, visibility permitting, also the small offshore rocky island of Coronado.

Ahead on the skyline is the profile of a terrace extending eastward at a height 80-90 feet above our level. This higher terrace is seen to better advantage at about 11:30-11:45 o'clock upon emerging from beneath the overpass bearing "Otay Valley-Main Street Exit, 1/2 Mile." It is regarded by some geologists as an up-faulted part of the Lindavista terrace, but as we drop into the valley of Otay River, it looks as though the Lindavista terrace level extends a long distance east up Otay Valley, suggesting that faulting may not be the correct interpretation. Terraces at two separate levels may exist here. Otay Valley has a modestly wide, flat floor with dike-im-

Photo Q-1. Looking south-southeast to lower San Diego Bay from over Coronado. Silver Strand beach enclosing bay on west side, mountains of Baja California on skyline. Note cusping of beach in lower right corner. (Spence, E-18305, 8/8/62).

pounded, tule-filled ponds to the north. Otay River bridge is identified by "San Diego City Limit." Climbing out of Otay Valley, abundant roundstones are seen on the face of cuts and slopes indicating that the Pliocene beds are again becoming conglomeratic. Upon attaining the terrace surface beyond Otay Valley, Tijuana comes into view on the hillslopes ahead on the far side of Tijuana Valley. This wide valley is at least in part a structural feature, and the "border hills" at Tijuana are uplifted by faulting. Beyond the exit to Highway 117, the freeway again becomes deeply entrenched and passes in quick succession under three overpasses. As of 1977, freeway cuts were fresh and bare, exposing near-horizontal conglomeratic and sandy beds overlain by finer, brown to pinkish layers, all of the San Diego Formation. Upon emerging from beneath the last overpass, Tijuana is directly ahead. You can continue into San Ysidro on 805 Freeway, the last exit in the United States being clearly indicated short of the Mexican border.

Segment Q— Inbound Descriptions

(The corresponding outbound material should be read first.)

I-7   Travelers headed north on 805 Freeway from San Ysidro Boulevard see first horizontal beds of sands and silts (Pliocene) which, within 0.5 mile, give way to conglomeratic layers. Near top of the upgrade, before emerging onto the Lindavista terrace, deeply rilled beds of finer, weakly consolidated materials overlie the conglomerates. Pebbles, cobbles, and small boulders continue to litter roadcut faces and slopes as far as Palm Avenue, just short of Otay Valley floor. Beyond Otay Valley, the freeway rises again to the Lindavista terrace and on the left is a strongly rilled bluff in soft, easily eroded, fine-grained, horizontal Pliocene beds. Rounded higher hills, also underlain by Pliocene beds, are a little to the right and on the far eastern skyline are peaks and ridges of older (Mesozoic) crystalline rocks. At "Gas, Food, Lodging—Next 5 Exits," Point Loma and its peninsula are visible in clear weather at about 10 o'clock. The Point and most of the ridge extending inland from it are composed largely of marine late Cretaceous sedimentary rocks with a local veneer of younger deposits. Point Loma peninsula provides one of the more extensive exposures of Cretaceous sedimentary rocks in the San Diego area. At the L Street-Telegraph Canyon Road turnoff is another view of Point Loma and of San Diego Bay (Photo Q-1). At "National City Limit," we are well down into the wide, ill-defined valley of Sweetwater River. Some modest exposures of fine-grained beds in the San Diego Formation are seen beyond the crossing of that river. Be alert to catch the turnoff onto State Highway 15 (40th Street), or onto 15 Freeway, if it has been completed through to a junction with 805.

I-6   Inbound travelers currently (mid-1977) divert onto State Highway 15 from 805 at 40th Street, but eventually Freeway 15 should be completed through to this junction. After turnoff, a canyon is ascended through conglomeratic Pliocene beds, best seen in a cut-over bare area to the right approaching the top of the grade before emerging onto Lindavista terrace. Descending toward Mission Valley down a side canyon, a 2- to 3-foot layer of very stony reddish Pleistocene Lindavista Formation is seen capping the Pliocene which is somewhat less conglomeratic. Farther down are sandy Eocene beds (Mission Valley) and eventually roundstones from the Stadium Conglomerate appear before getting to the floor of Mission Valley.

I-5   Travelers headed north up Murphy Canyon out of Mission Valley see light-colored, fine sands and silts (Eocene, Friars Formation) in the deep roadcuts on the right and in excavations behind the sand and gravel operation to the left. Good exposures of these beds continue on the right to Tierrasanta Boulevard (stoplight). Beyond Tierrasanta, glimpses are occasionally caught on the left skyline of reddish beds on top of white material. This same contact is seen in the left skyline bluff opposite Clairemont Mesa Road exit, where a 20-foot layer of dark reddish-brown Pleistocene Lindavista Formation is separated from the underlying light-colored Eocene beds by the near-horizontal wave-cut abrasion surface of Lindavista terrace. At the head of Murphy Canyon, we emerge onto the wide, nearly flat Lindavista terrace, or, more properly, onto the top of the Lindavista Formation which caps the terrace, as can be seen in the shallow excavation immediately to the left. We are still on State Highway 15 (as of mid-1977), and shortly effect junction with Freeway 15 headed toward Riverside. We continue to traverse the Lindavista terrace to Pomerado-Miramar intersection, with occasional dips into shallow gullies and arroyos.

I-4   Approaching and beyond the NAS Miramar exit, the low, even-topped skyline, on hills one and two miles to the east, may mark the level of a marine terrace (possibly the Poway) older and higher than the Lindavista which extends east to the base of those hills. North of the Pomerado-Miramar intersection, low hills lie closer on the east, and at and beyond "Mira Mesa Boulevard, 1 Mile," the highway is against their base. The abundant smooth roundstones of all sizes show that the hills are composed largely of conglomerate beds (late Eocene Poway Group). Beyond Mira Mesa Boulevard, the highway leaves Lindavista terrace and starts upgrade toward a deep gap in the high ridge ahead which is composed of Santiago Peak Volcanics (late Jurassic). Going upgrade toward the gap, a good view of Lindavista terrace is seen left at 9 o'clock.

Freeway cuts and excavations beyond show dark, angular, jointed exposures of Santiago Peak Volcanics, the dominant rock on both sides for at least two miles. A little north of the Poway-Rancho Penasquitos Boulevard interchange and beyond "Escondido 12, Temecula 40, Riverside 79," are abundant roundstones derived from basal conglomeratic layers in a little outlier of Eocene deposits that here rest depositionally on the older volcanics. Beyond top of the grade, the highway parallels the open, alluviated floor of Chicarita Creek. Approaching Carmel Mountain Road, the high ridge on the left skyline consists of volcanics and the bedrock ridge to the east exposes some light-colored igneous intrusive rocks. At Carmel Mountain Road we enter the south edge of an extensive sheet of Eocene sedimentary beds.

I-3   For inbound travelers, the pre-Eocene knob of Santiago Peak Volcanics is seen on the right about 0.5 mile north of Carmel Mountain Road, opposite the golf course and the large Rancho Penasquitos billboard. Approaching, you can see weathered-out volcanic fragments on hillslopes, and the volcanic bedrock is well-exposed in the roadcut. A little farther north, we enter an area of smooth, gently rolling, grass-covered terrain underlain by more late Eocene sedimentary beds (Mission Valley Formation). Beyond "Bernardo Center Drive, 1 Mile," near top of the grade, roadcuts, where scraped free of weeds at highway level, show green and white Eocene beds.

After starting downhill and passing Bernardo Center Drive, the open valley of Rancho Bernardo is in view at 12:10-12:30 o'clock. The isolated conical hills rising from the valley floor are knobs of crystalline igneous rock. One of them, Mule Hill (or Battle Mountain) is particularly prominent at 12:15 o'clock. The smooth hills alongside the freeway continue to be underlain by Eocene sedimentary units (Mission Valley, Stadium Conglomerate, and Friars

formations) almost to Rancho Bernardo Road crossing. White boulder-mantled slopes underlain by Woodson Mountain Granodiorite dominate the eastern skyline behind Rancho Bernardo, and Santiago Peak Volcanics continue as the principal rock in the high country to the west.

North of Rancho Bernardo Road, rocks to the west are more mixed. At 9:00-10:30 o'clock, two separate areas of light-colored Woodson Mountain Granodiorite are seen, intruded into older, dark-colored rocks. High Bernardo Mountain on the skyline at 11 o'clock is composed of San Marcos Gabbro. Grayish crystalline rocks exposed in roadcuts as far as "Highland Valley Road-Pomerado Road Exit, 1 Mile" are Green Valley Tonalite, but beyond, the slopes of Mule Hill at 12:15 o'clock on the right are underlain by darker, more resistant San Marcos Gabbro, which locally forms knobby bluffs. Ahead on the far side of the Lake Hodges arm, beyond the Highland Valley-Pomerado roads exit, the rocky ridge at about 11:30 o'clock also displays typical knobby outcrops of San Marcos Gabbro. Bernardo Mountain and Mule Hill stand prominently above the surrounding terrain which is underlain by Green Valley Tonalite, because the San Marcos Gabbro is more resistant to weathering and erosion.

I-2   Motorists headed north approach this arm of Lake Hodges reservoir a little beyond Highland Valley Road exit. Bernardo Mountain is just ahead on the left, with its smooth, dark slopes of San Marcos Gabbro. Beyond Via Rancho Parkway the freeway route curves west a little and ascends gently to bypass Escondido. Deep cuts along this part of the freeway are in thoroughly disintegrated Green Valley Tonalite. A few residual core stones of this rock are seen in a cut on the right one hundred and fifty yards beyond "Felicita Road, 1/4 Mile, 9th Avenue, 1½ Miles."

I-1   This segment ends at intersection with Highway 78 at the northwest edge of Escondido.

Segment **R**

Freeway 805 between Freeway 5 and Highway 15 in San Diego, 14 Miles

O-1   This short segment along Freeway 805 provides a shortcut for travelers headed south to Tijuana and Baja California and forms a link between segments P and Q. It extends from Freeway 5 in Soledad Valley east of La Jolla to Highway 15 just east of Balboa Park. From there, descriptions for the final third of Segment Q (Escondido to San Ysidro) complete the trip to the border. The course on 805 is south by southeast, bypassing downtown San Diego. It won't hurt to note your odometer reading at the 5-805 junction.

(Inbound travelers see p. 236.)

O-2   Just beyond the first overpass on 805, a large canyon, Los Penasquitos, comes from the left, and beyond we ascend parallel to lower Carroll Canyon before crossing it and climbing the east wall. The smooth, rounded cobbles on roadcut faces largely to the left in vicinity of Carroll Canyon Road exit probably come from conglomerate lenses in middle Eocene beds. After leveling out, the freeway is in an entrenched course a little below the level of the Lindavista terrace. Beyond the overpass bearing "Governor Drive Exit, 1¼ Miles," watch the top of roadcut exposures, and in some you will see spectacular scour channels, a few feet deep and ten to twenty feet wide, filled with roundstone conglomerate. These channels and their gravel filling are thought to have been formed when a layer of late Eocene conglomerate (probably the Stadium Conglomerate) was laid down upon the underlying fine, soft siltstone and sandstone (middle Eocene, Scripps Formation).

O-3   South from San Clemente Canyon (Highway 52), just beyond "Clairemont Mesa Boulevard, 3/4 Mile," deep roadcuts expose soft, fine sandstones (Scripps and possibly Friars formations) topped by a thin layer of Stadium Conglomerate (late Eocene) and some roundstone gravels of the Lindavista Formation (Pleistocene). Beyond "Balboa Avenue-Highway 274 Junction, 3/4 Mile," we are again on the Lindavista terrace. Soledad Mountain is back to the right at about 4 o'clock. Coming up ahead, about 3/8 mile to the left, is the west slope of a low ridge rising twenty feet above the terrace surface. A string of commercial buildings occupies its crest, and local excavations expose dark-reddish material. This inconspicuous topographic feature is one of several broad, low, beach ridges built upon the Lindavista marine abrasion platform as the Pleistocene seas withdrew toward the west. Subsequent deep weathering, under presumably warm, moist conditions, produced the red coloring of materials composing the ridge. The ridge

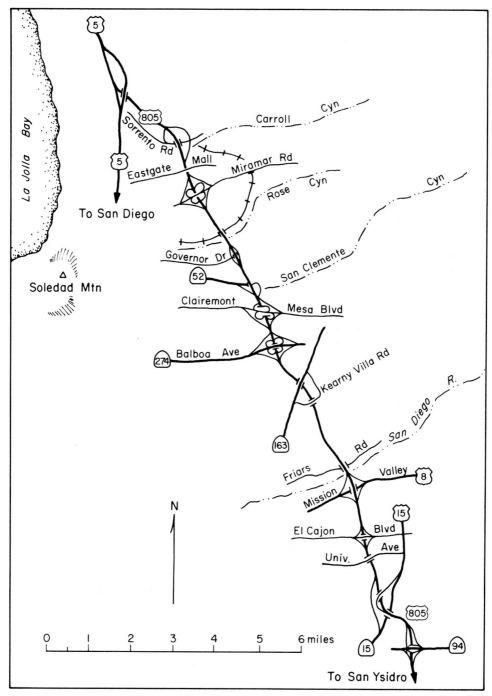

Figure R-1.   Segment R, Freeway 805 Link between Segments P and Q.

is most prominent a quarter-mile to the left approaching Balboa Avenue-Highway 274 exit. Beyond Balboa Avenue exit, the beach ridge is only 200-300 yards away. Approaching the overpass, with "805-163S, Downtown," the freeway rises a bit, curves east, and crosses through the beach ridge. Unfortunately, roadcuts are so heavily vegetated that little is seen of the beach-ridge materials, aside from fleeting glimpses of red-colored debris.

Beyond the Highway 163S exit to downtown San Diego, comes a succession of overpasses, a curve into a more southerly course, deepening roadcuts, and a gentle descent. Soon roundstones, up to small boulder size, become abundant on slopes and roadcut faces. They come primarily from the Stadium Conglomerate (late Eocene) and secondarily from the Lindavista Formation (Pleistocene) which got them from the underlying Eocene beds. Overlying the Stadium Conglomerate, as seen in some cuts, are softer, finer, gray to white, sandy and silty beds (Eocene, Mission Valley Formation).

The freeway continues a gradual descent, crossing a succession of small gullies, and the exit to Murray Ridge Road-Phyllis Place is passed. At the overpass beyond "La Mesa-El Cajon, Use Highway 8E," steep descent into Mission Valley begins. Roadcuts descending the north side of the valley display numerous roundstones, which is appropriate since we are not far from the type locality for the Stadium Conglomerate. The San Diego Stadium can be seen to the left once we are well into Mission Valley. We cross the wide valley and the San Diego River flowing in it, on a high bridge affording good views to right and left. The crystalline-rock peaks of the Peninsular Ranges are visible on the eastern skyline to the left in clear weather.

O-4   Leaving Mission Valley southbound, we ascend a small side canyon with heavy vegetation largely obscuring the geology except for occasional exposures of massive gray sandstones (late Eocene, Mission Valley Formation). Near the top, at overhanging "El Cajon Boulevard, 1/4 Mile," roundstones from gravelly Lindavista Formation and from thin conglomerate beds in the San Diego Formation (late Pliocene) are seen on slopes and in roadcuts. Roadcuts beyond the junction with Highway 15 are too heavily vegetated to be geologically informative.

Segment R— Inbound Descriptions

(The corresponding outbound material should be read first.)

I-4   Travelers headed north from the Mexican border can proceed via this shortcut to Freeway 5 by staying on 805 instead of peeling off on Highway 15 to Escondido via Segment Q. They should use descriptions in the last third of that segment as far as the intersection with Highway 15. As inbound travelers begin this segment northbound on Freeway 805 from the Highway 15 intersection, they won't learn much from the heavily vegetated roadcuts along the depressed freeway course. At the start, some scattered roundstones are seen, probably largely from the San Diego Formation (late Pliocene). Dropping steeply into Mission Valley, some exposures of massive, light-colored sandstone (Eocene, Mission Valley Formation) are passed, mostly on the left. As the highway emerges into Mission Valley, the sand and gravel excavations on the far valley wall, both to east and west, are visible. We never get down to the level of the valley floor, which is well enough, as it's a mess of roads and buildings. The view both east and west from the high bridge is good, and San Diego Stadium is seen half a mile upvalley. The gravel quarries remain in clear view before ascent of the north wall begins, and horizontal layering is sometimes visible in the nearest quarry on the right (upvalley).

I-3   Going upgrade out of Mission Valley, big roadcuts beyond the Murray Ridge Road exit, especially on the right, expose horizontal beds of Stadium Conglomerate overlain by finer gray, white, and tan sandstone and siltstone beds (Mission Valley Formation), best seen on the left at "Mesa College Drive-Kearney Villa Road, 3/4 Mile" (center divider).

Beyond Mesa College Drive-Kearney Villa Road exit, the depressed freeway course is bordered by cuts in fine-grained materials (Mission Valley Formation) displaying near-horizontal bedding, as well as the omnipresent roundstones probably derived both from Pleistocene and Eocene deposits. Beyond the various exits and overpasses of the Highway 163 interchange and the Balboa Avenue-Highway 274 exit, we emerge onto Lindavista terrace, which is better seen to the left than to the right. Immediately to the right is the gentle rise of the west face of the beach ridge described in O-3. It lies at 3 o'clock and continues in view for better than a mile, but at an increasing distance to the east. Commercial buildings clearly favor its elevated crest. Views of the terrace and beach ridge are best beyond the overpass bearing "Clairemont Mesa Boulevard Exit." Beyond that exit, we traverse the flat surface of Lindavista terrace with no roadcut exposures. Beyond "West Highway 52," the highway drops into a small gully with rilled roadcuts in fine, soft materials (possibly Friars Formation, Eocene). Beyond the separation to Highway 52 West, and almost at "Governor Drive, Exit 3/4 Mile," we cross sycamore-tree filled San Clemente Canyon on a high bridge.

I-2   After passing Highway 52 at San Clemente Canyon northbound, roadcuts expose soft, poorly bedded, fine, sandy and silty beds (middle Eocene, Scripps Formation) which are locally indented by the small but spectacular scour channels filled with Eocene gravels. Roundstones on roadcut faces come both from the Lindavista and from these Eocene conglomeratic lenses. At "La Jolla-Miramar Road Exit, 1 Mile," a wide expanse of Lindavista terrace comes into view extending east toward Miramar. Soledad Mountain (Photo P-5), with large communication towers, is several miles away on the left skyline at 9 o'clock. Scour-channel fillings of Eocene gravel continue at the top of roadcuts along the freeway where entrenched below the Lindavista terrace. Beyond "Sorrento Valley Road Exit, 3/4 Mile," the terrain becomes more deeply and fully dissected. At Sorrento Valley Road exit, descent begins into the complex of canyons tributary to Soledad Valley. Soon we make junction with Freeway 5 and pick up descriptions for the trip to Oceanside (Segment P.).

I-1   This segment terminates at the 805-5 intersection.

Appendix A

Geological Time Scale

Era	Period	Epoch	Tentative Absolute Age
CENOZOIC	Quaternary	Holocene	
			11,000 years
		Pleistocene	
			2 million years
	Tertiary	Pliocene	
			8
		Miocene	
			26
		Oligocene	
			37
		Eocene	
			53
		Paleocene	
			70 million years
MESOZOIC	Cretaceous		
			135
	Jurassic		
			190
	Triassic		
			230 million years
PALEOZOIC	Permian		
			280
	Pennsylvanian		
			310
	Mississippian		
			350
	Devonian		
			400
	Silurian		
			430
	Ordovician		
			500
	Cambrian		
			600 million years
PRECAMBRIAN			600-3500 million years

-------------------------Lost Interval-------------------------

Origin of Earth			4600 million years

Appendix B

Partial Listing of Stratigraphic Names and Ages°

Age		San Diego Area		Santa Ana Mtns.	San Joaquin Hills Laguna-Dana Pt.	
CENOZOIC	Pleistocene	Bay Point Fm.		La Habra Fm.		
	Pliocene	San Diego Fm.		Fernando Fm. Repetto Fm.	Niguel Fm.	
	Miocene Lower Middle Upper			Puente Fm. El Modeno Volcanics Vaqueros Fm.	Capistrano Fm. Puente Fm. Monterey Shale / San Onofre Breccia Topanga Fm. Vaqueros Fm.	
	Oligocene			Sespe Fm.	Sespe Fm.	
	Eocene Middle Upper	Poway Group	Pomerado Cg. Mission Va. Fm. Stadium Cg.	Santiago Fm.	Santiago Fm.	
		La Jolla Group	Friars Fm. Scripps Fm. Ardath Sh. Torrey Ss. Delmar Fm. Mount Soledad Fm.			
	Paleocene			Silverado Fm.	Silverado Fm.	
MESOZOIC	Cretaceous	Rosario Group	Cabrillo Fm. Point Loma Fm. Lusardi Fm. Southern California batholithic rocks	Williams Fm. — Pleasants Ss. Mbr. Schulz Ranch Ss. Mbr. Ladd Fm. — Holtz Sh. Mbr. Baker Cyn. Cg. Mbr. Trabuco Fm. Southern California batholithic rocks	°This is not a correlation chart. Parallel listing indicates only approximate similarity in age. Consistency is not fully possible in stratigraphic tabulations. Listing is not complete, focuses primarily on units mentioned in text.	
	Jurassic	Santiago Peak Volcanics		Santiago Peak Volcanics Bedford Canyon Fm.		

Los Angeles Basin	Santa Monica Mtns. Malibu	Ventura County	Santa Barbara Santa Ynez	Santa Maria San Luis Obispo
Palos Verdes Sand San Pedro Fm.		Saugus Fm.　San Pedro Fm.　Santa Barbara Fm.	Casitas Fm.　Pasa Robles Fm.　Santa Barbara Fm.	Orcutt Sand Pasa Robles Fm.
Fernando Fm.　Pico Fm.　Repetto Fm.		Towsley Fm. Pico Fm. Repetto Fm.	"Pico" Fm. Careaga Ss.　Tequepis Fm.　Sisquoc Fm.	Careaga Ss. Foxen Mudstone Pismo Fm.　Sisquoc Fm.
Puente Fm.　Modelo Fm.　Monterey Fm.　Topanga Fm. (Volcanics)　Vaqueros Fm.	Modelo Fm.　Monterey Fm.　Topanga Fm. Conejo Volcanics "Temblor" Fm. Vaqueros Fm.	Santa Margarita Fm.　Monterey Fm. Conejo Volcanics　Rincon Sh. Vaqueros Fm.	Upper Monterey Sh. Lower Monterey Sh. "Temblor" Ss. Rincon Sh. Vaqueros Ss.	Monterey Fm. Point Sal Fm. Obispo Fm.　Rincon Fm.
Sespe Fm.	Sespe Fm.	Sespe Fm.	Sespe Fm.　Alegria Fm.　Gaviota Fm.	Vaqueros Fm. Lospe Fm.
		Coldwater Ss.　Cozy Dell Sh.　Matilija Ss.　Juncal Fm.	Coldwater Ss.　Sacate Fm.　Cozy Dell Sh.　Matilija Ss.	
	Martinez Fm.		Anita Sh. Sierra Blanca Ls.	
Fm.—Formation Mbr.—Member Ss.—Sandstone Sh.—Shale Ls.—Limestone Cg.—Conglomerate	Chico Fm.　Trabuco Fm.	Llajas Fm. Santa Susana Fm.	Jalama Fm.　Espada Fm. Franciscan Fm.	Franciscan Fm.
	Santa Monica Slate			

Appendix C

Glossary

Abrasion platform. A nearly level surface truncating bedrock, a little below water level, created by wave erosion.

Acidic. Used here to describe the composition of igneous rocks relatively rich in silica (silicic).

Agglomerate. A fragmental volcanic rock consisting of somewhat rounded stones in a finer matrix, much like conglomerate in appearance but wholly volcanic in constitution.

Alluvial. *See* alluvium.

Alluvium. Unconsolidated gravel, sand, and finer rock debris deposited principally by running water; adjective-alluvial.

Andesite. Fine-grained, dark, igneous rock, of composition intermediate between rhyolite and basalt.

Angular unconformity. An arrangement in which older deformed stratified rocks have been truncated by erosion and younger layers have been laid down upon them with a different angle of inclination.

Antecedent stream. One which maintained its course in spite of localized uplift across its path; the stream anteceded the uplift.

Anticlinal core. The mass of older rock in the heart of an anticline.

Anticlinal nose. The place where beds at the axis of a plunging anticline pass beneath the ground surface.

Anticline. A fold in stratified rock convex upward. Beds on the flanks are inclined outward.

Apron (alluvial). A broad, gently sloping, alluvial surface at the foot of a mountain range formed by coalescing alluvial fans.

Arch. *See* sea arch.

Arkose. A sedimentary deposit consisting of mechanically disintegrated granitic rock debris, distinguished by a high content of potassium feldspar.

Arroyo. A small, deep, flat-floored, steep-walled, ephemeral stream course, in arid or semi-arid regions.

Ash. *See* volcanic ash.

Asphalt. A dark-brown to black viscous hydrocarbon usually formed by loss of volatiles from petroleum.

Asymmetrical fold. A fold in which the beds on one limb are more steeply inclined than on the other.

Atmospheric inversion. The atmosphere normally becomes cooler with increasing elevation. An inversion occurs when it becomes warmer at greater elevations.

Attitude. A description of the geometrical orientation of a plane surface (usually bedding) in a rock. *See* dip and strike.

Axis. The central line of an elongated geological structure such as an anticline or syncline.

Backwash. The seaward return of water driven up the foreslope of a beach by a breaker.

Badlands. Extremely rough barren terrain with unusually steep slopes and sharp divides, riven by narrow, steep-walled gullies.

Bank (submarine). A flat-topped eminence on the shallow sea floor rising close to water level.

Barranco. A small, steep-walled, flat-floored gully (or arroyo) cut in relatively soft semi-coherent materials by an ephemeral stream.

Basalt. A fine-grained black lava relatively rich in calcium, iron, and magnesium. The extrusive equivalent (in composition) of gabbro.

Base level. The level below which stream erosion cannot continue. Ultimate base level is sea level.

Basement. Old crystalline rocks upon which younger rocks have been deposited.

Basic. Used herein to describe the composition of igneous rocks relatively low in silica and richer in iron and magnesium.

Batholith. A very large igneous body intruded into the earth's crust at considerable depth where it cooled slowly to form coarsely crystalline rock.

Bay. A relatively large, open indentation of the land by waters of the sea or a lake.

Baymouth bar (or barrier). A shoreline bar largely closing off the mouth of a bay.

Beach. A relatively narrow and constantly shifting deposit of sand or stones, between high- and low-tide levels along the shore of a standing body of water.

Beach ridge. A ridge of sand or pebbles built along a shoreline to a level somewhat above the water by high storm waves.

Bedding. The layered structure of sedimentary rocks.

Bedding plane. A planar surface separating successive layers within sedimentary rocks.

Bedrock. Consolidated rock material of any sort.

Bench. A level or gently sloping area interrupting an otherwise steep slope.

Blowhole (marine). Near-vertical hole or fissure in the roof of a sea cave through which water and spray are ejected by waves at high tide.

Bluff. A bold, high bank or cliff with a broad steep face, sometimes rounded at top, overlooking a flat area.

Brea. A viscous asphalt formed around a surface oil seep owing to evaporation of volatiles.

Breakaway-scarp. The steep face at the head of a landslide, slump, or earthflow formed when the moving mass pulled away from unmoved material.

Breaker. A wave in the process of collapsing owing to asymmetrical oversteepening.

Breakwater. An offshore artificial structure designed to protect a harbor, anchorage, or beach by breaking the force of the waves.

Breccia. A rock containing abundant angular fragments of rocks or minerals. There are sedimentary breccias, volcanic breccias, tectonic breccias, landslide breccias, and other types.

Brink. The upper edge of a steep declivity, not necessarily the highest part of the terrain.

Calcareous. Rich in calcite.

Calcite. A common mineral composed of calcium, carbon, and oxygen ($CaCO_3$).

Cañada. A Spanish term used either for a vale between mountains or a narrow valley.

Canyon. A long, deep, relatively narrow, steep-sided valley, often with precipitous walls; cut by either perennial or ephemeral streams.

Carbonate rocks. Those rocks composed of the minerals calcite (calcium carbonate) and dolomite (calcium-magnesium carbonate).

Capture. See stream capture.

Ceanothus. A common bush of the California chaparral community, more generally known as native lilac.

Chaparral. A dense growth of scrubby vegetation, composed of a variety of plants, covering hillsides in areas of limited (12-25 inches) precipitation with strong seasonal distribution.

Clastic dike. A tabular body of fragmental material transecting the country rock, usually sedimentary.

Clay. A group of minerals, usually formed by alteration of other minerals, with a strongly layered internal structure. The term is also used for any mineral fragment of less than 1/256 mm diameter.

Claystone. A fine-grained, massive, homogeneous, sedimentary rock composed largely of clay.

Climbing dune. An accumulation of wind-blown sand of dune proportions being driven upslope before the wind.

Clinker rock. A partly fused, usually highly colored rock mass produced by natural burning of combustible materials (hydrocarbons) within the rock.

Closed depression. A depression in the ground surface with a rim everywhere higher than the bottom.

Coast (coastal zone). A land strip of indefinite width extending inland from the shore and displaying landforms or characteristics related to near-shore processes and environments.

Coastline. The line defined by the base of a sea cliff or the landward edge of a beach.

Colluvium. Unconsolidated, usually ill-sorted, rock debris deposited chiefly by gravity at the base or on the lower reach of a slope.

Columnar jointing. A variety of jointing that breaks rocks into polygonal columns.

Competent. A strong rock that resists bending.

Concretion. A nodular mass within a sedimentary rock distinguished by unusual cementation or secondarily deposited mineral material.

Concretionary. Containing concretions.

Conglomerate. A sedimentary rock consisting of larger rounded rock and mineral fragments embedded in a finer, usually sandy matrix; all cemented together.

Continental. Sedimentary materials deposited on the land as contrasted to the sea.

Core stone. The roughly spheroidal or ellipsoidal core of sound rock within a partly disintegrated subsurface joint block. (*See* Photo O-2.)

Country rock. The prevailing bedrock of a region, into which younger igneous rocks are intruded or in which an ore deposit has been formed.

Cove. A relatively small indentation of a coastline created by marine erosion.

Coverhead. An accumulation of alluvial and colluvial material formed on a terrace surface after terrace-making ceased.

Creep. Slow, continuous, downhill movement of a mantle of loose weathered rock debris under gravity. (Has other meanings in terms of solid-state deformation.)

Crop out. The act of forming an exposure (outcrop) of bedrock on the surface.

Cross bedding (or lamination). Internal bedding within a sedimentary layer forming a distinct angle to the upper and lower bedding planes of that layer.

Crust (of the earth). The outermost solid layer of the earth.

Crustal block. A coherent block of the earth's crust of regional extent.

Crystalline. Substances having fixed internal atomic arrangements.

Crystalline rocks. A term commonly applied to mixed igneous and metamorphic rocks, or to either separately.

Cuesta. A distinctly asymmetrical ridge (steep face, gentle back slope) created by erosion of gently dipping beds of differing resistance.

Cusp (on a beach). A crescent-shaped indentation on the foreslope of a beach created by wave erosion.

Debris. *See* rock debris.

Debris avalanche. A mass of broken rock that slides at high speed down a steep slope, often along a chute.

Debris cone. A cone-shaped accumulation of rock debris at the mouth of a gully or small canyon, usually smaller, steeper, and often rougher than an alluvial fan.

Debris flow. A flow of usually wet, muddy rock debris of mixed sizes, much like a slurry of freshly mixed concrete pouring down a chute.

Deciduous. Plants (trees) that shed their leaves annually.

Decomposition. The chemical breakdown of rocks and minerals.

Dendritic (drainage pattern). An arrangement of trunk and tributary streams resembling the structure of a maple tree.

Detritus. *See* rock debris.

Diatomite. A sedimentary rock consisting almost entirely of the siliceous skeletons of single-celled algae.

Dike. A sheet-like body of igneous rock formed by intrusion along a fracture.

Diorite. A coarse-grained intrusive igneous rock about midway between a granite and a gabbro in chemical and mineralogical composition.

Dip. The direction and degree of inclination (from horizontal) of a sedimentary bed or any other geological planar feature.

Dip slope. A smooth, inclined surface formed by the exposed bedding plane of a sedimentary stratum.

Disconformity. An unconformity or break within a sequence of sedimentary beds along which material has been removed by erosion, but with beds on both sides of the break conformable (parallel in bedding).

Disintegration. The physical breakup of rocks and minerals.

Distributaries. Diverging channels in the lower part of a stream where it distributes its water and debris, as on alluvial fans or deltas.

Dome (structural). An upfold in sedimentary rocks from which the beds dip outward in all directions.

Dome (topographic). A roughly circular, upwardly convex landform.

Drowned. Used here to describe the lower part of a stream course invaded by the sea.

Dune. A deposit of wind-blown sand of a size and shape capable of capturing additional sand.

Earthflow. Both a landform and a process involving downslope movement of a discrete mass of relatively incoherent rock or rock debris through internal flow and basal slippage.

Embayment. An indentation along a shoreline, mountain front, or any other natural linear feature.

Epicenter. The spot on the earth's surface directly above the subsurface point at which an earthquake shock originates.

Erosion. The pickup and removal of rock material by any natural process of transportation.

Estuary. An inlet of the sea into land.

Eustatic sea-level change. A worldwide rise or fall of sea level. Most recently caused by formation or melting of glacial ice.

Extrusive rock. Rock expelled onto the earth's surface, usually in molten condition (lava).

Fan. A deposit, usually alluvial, of rock debris at the foot of a steep slope (mountain face) with an apex at the mountain base (canyon mouth) and a radial, fan-like, divergence therefrom.

Fanglomerate. The consolidated deposits of an alluvial fan; a variety of conglomerate which is coarse, ill-sorted, and contains angular stones.

Fault. A fracture along which blocks of the earth's crust have slipped past each other.

Fault plane. The planar surface along which fault displacement has occurred.

Fault ridge. An elevated, elongate block lying between two essentially parallel faults.

Fault scarp. A relatively straight, steep topographic face, possibly thousands of feet high, formed by displacement along a fault, not by subsequent differential erosion.

Fault slice. A narrow segment of rock caught between two essentially parallel, closely adjacent faults.

Fault zone. A zone in the earth's crust consisting of many roughly parallel, overlapping, closely spaced faults and fractures; may be up to several miles wide.

Feldspar. An abundant rock-forming class of minerals composed of aluminum, silicon, oxygen, and one or more of the alkalies, sodium, calcium, and potassium.

Ferro-magnesian mineral. One relatively rich in iron and magnesium.

Flatiron. A landform consisting of a steeply inclined dip slope cut into triangualr shape by transecting canyons.

Flood (stream). A discharge of water overtopping the confines of the normal stream channel.

Flood plain. A strip of relatively smooth land bordering a stream subjected to episodic flooding.

Flute. A small, elongate, scoop-shaped depression created by erosion.

Flute cast. The sediment filling a flute, best seen on the underside of an exposed sedimentary bed.

Fluvial. Features of erosion or deposition created by running water.

Folding. Bending of planar rock units, usually strata, normally by tectonic deformation.

Foliation. A crude banding formed in rocks by metamorphism, less regular than the bedding of sedimentary rocks.

Foot wall. The lower side of an inclined fault.

Foredune. A linear sand-dune ridge formed along the edge of a lake or the sea.

Foreland. An extensive area of land jutting into the sea.

Foreridge. A subsidiary ridge lying in front of a larger mountain mass.

Foreslope (of a beach). That part of the beach facing the ocean.

Formation. A geological formation is a rock unit of distinctive characteristics which formed over a limited span of time and under some uniformity of conditions. To a geologist it is a rock body of some considerable areal extent which can be recognized, named, and mapped.

Fossil landscape. A terrain in which the principal landforms are relict (left over) from an earlier landscape.

Gabbro. A dark, coarse-grained intrusive igneous rock richer in iron, magnesium, and calcium and poorer in silica than granite.

Geophysical exploration (methods). Subsurface exploration of rocks and structures carried on by indirect means such as gravity or magnetic variations.

Geophysics. Study of the earth with particular emphasis on physical principles.

Glacier. A land-bound mass of ice that has moved by processes of internal flowage.

Glaucophane schist. A thinly foliated metamorphic rock containing the mineral glaucophane, a sodium-bearing amphibole.

Gneiss. A coarse-grained metamorphic rock with irregular banding (foliation).

Gorge. A narrow, steep-walled passage cut into rock by a stream.

Gouge. Finely ground rock material within a fault zone.

Graben. A sizable block of the earth's crust dropped down between two faults steeply inclined inward, giving a keystone shape to the block, longer than it is wide.

Granite. A common, coarse-grained, igneous intrusive rock relatively rich in silica, potassium, and sodium.

Granitic. A term commonly used for many coarse-grained igneous intrusive rocks not strictly of granite composition.

Granodiorite. A coarse-grained, igneous intrusive rock intermediate between a granite and a diorite in composition.

Gravel. A natural, unconsolidated accumulation of mixed sand and stones, usually somewhat rounded.

Gravity (or normal) fault. A fault with an inclined plane along which the overhanging block has moved relatively down.

Gravity flow. The mass flow of rock debris downslope by gravity.

Ground water. Water filling pores and other openings in subsurface rock materials within the zone of saturation.

Grus (gruss). Disintegrated granitic rock.

Gulch. Small, narrow, deep ravine, steep-sided and larger than a gully, often short.

Gully. A small erosional valley cut by an ephemeral stream.

Gypsum. A common mineral, hydrated calcium sulphate, usually of sedimentary origin; used as a fertilizer and to make plaster.

Hanging wall. The upper side of an inclined fault.

Headland. The bold tip of a projection of land into the sea.

High-tide bench. A nearly flat erosional bench truncating rock at the base of a sea cliff cut by wave abrasion at high-tide level. (*See* storm-wave platform.)

Hogback. A ridge composed of a resistant layer within steeply tilted eroded strata.

Hoodoos. Pillars and pinnacles, often of fantastic shapes, created by erosion.

Hydrogen sulphide (gas). An ill-smelling gas (H_2S) given off as a common volcanic emanation and from some hot springs.

Ice ages. Those intervals of earth history during which masses of ice (glaciers) of continental proportions formed on land.

Igneous rocks. Rocks formed by crystallization from a molten state.

Immature sand. Sand of varied mineralogical composition, not just quartz.

Impervious. The state of a substance (rock) into which a fluid (water) cannot percolate.

Inclusion. A fragment of older rock inclosed (included) within an igneous rock.

Incompetent. A rock which is relatively weak and responds readily to pressure by crumpling or by flow.

Inlet. A narrow opening through a shoreline bar, or a recess or indentation into a coastline created by marine erosion.

Intercalation. A layer of material laid down or inserted between layers of different material.

Interference pattern. A pattern created by waves on a water surface moving in different directions.

Intermittent stream. One which does not have a continuous or perennial flow.

Intraformational conglomerate (or breccia). Fragments of material derived from a nearby bed incorporated within a layer of sedimentary rock, rounded if conglomerate, angular if breccia.

Intrusive rocks. Rocks which have been intruded or injected into other rock, usually in a molten state.

Inversion. *See* atmospheric inversion.

Joint. A planar fracture in a rock along which no significant slip has occurred.

Jointing. The one or more sets of parallel fractures breaking an otherwise relatively homogeneous rock mass.

Kelp. Seaweed.

Kitchen midden. Literally the refuse pile (largely sea shells) of an ancient Indian settlement.

Lagoon. A shallow body of sea water separated from the ocean by a narrow barrier beach or reef.

Landform. A topographic feature of the land surface displaying distinct and consistent physical characteristics.

Land-laid. Sedimentary material deposited on land.

Landscape. An association of landforms as seen in a single view.

Landslide. A landform developed by rapid, often catastrophic, downslope movement of rock and rock debris primarily by basal slippage.

Lateral fault. One on which the displacement is sidewise rather than up-down.

Lava. The term is used both for molten rock material extruded onto the earth's surface and for the consolidated (crystallized) rock.

Left-lateral fault. One on which the opposing block appears to have moved to the left, no matter which side you stand on.

Leucocratic. Light-colored.

Lignite. A low-grade variety of coal intermediate between peat and bituminous coal.

Limb. One of the two sides of an anticline or syncline.

Limestone. A sedimentary rock composed wholly or almost wholly of the mineral calcite.

Lithology. The nature of a rock as to class, composition, color, texture, and other characteristics.

Live oak (tree). A species of oak that retains green leaves the year round.

Longshore. Used here primarily for the movement of water and debris laterally along a shoreline and for the responsible processes.

Longshore current (marine). A current moving along the shore.

Longshore drift (marine). The slow intermittent movement along shore of transportable materials caused by oblique wave approach and the longshore current.

Magma. Molten rock within the earth's crust.

Mantle rock. The surficial, more or less *in situ*, layer of broken-up and altered rock debris mantling bedrock. (*See* Photo 1-1.)

Marble. Recrystallized limestone or dolomite; a metamorphic rock.

Marine. The ocean environment; marine sediments are those deposited in the ocean.

Mass movements. The movement, usually downslope, of a mass of rock or rock debris by gravity, not transported by some other agent such as ice or water.

Matrix. The fine-grained constituents of a rock in which coarser particles are embedded.

Mélange. A complex mixture of rock types produced by severe deformation.

Mesa. A flat-topped tableland with steep sides.

Mesozoic. One of the eras of the geological time scale (see Appendix A) extending from 70 to 230 million years ago.

Metamorphic rocks. Those which have undergone such marked physical change because of heat or pressure or both as to be distinct from the original rock. The process is *metamorphism*.

Metavolcanic rocks. Formed by metamorphism of volcanic materials.

Mineral. A homogeneous, naturally-occurring, solid substance of inorganic composition, consistent physical properties, and specified chemical composition.

Mineralized. A rock into which a significant amount of mineral matter has been secondarily introduced.

Mio-Pliocene. An interval of time extending from uppermost Miocene into lowermost Pliocene. (See Appendices A and B.)

Mistletoe. A parasitic shrub that grows on some deciduous trees. Great to have around at Christmas time.

Mudflow. A form of mass movement involving the flow of mud, usually containing coarser rock debris, in which instance the term debris flow is equally applicable.

Mudstone. A fine-grained sedimentary rock which is hard to characterize as shale or siltstone because of massiveness or poor sorting.

Mussel. A two-valve shellfish, dark and elongate, that grows prolifically on rocks and pilings at water level along the shore of the ocean.

Nip (marine). A small recess at the base of a

sea cliff caused by wave erosion at high tide (*See* Photo 1-7).

Nodule (nodular). Small, hard, irregular, rounded or tuberous mass within a sedimentary layer.

Normal fault. *See* gravity fault.

Nose. *See* anticlinal nose.

Oblique air photo. One taken with the axis of the camera tilted from vertical. If the horizon shows, it is a high-oblique photo.

Odometer. An instrument for measuring distance.

Outcrop. An exposure of bedrock on the surface.

Outlier. A detached portion of rock that lies separate and out from the main mass of the same rock.

Overturn. A fold in which the beds of one limb are overturned (upside-down) from their normal depositional relationships.

Overturned beds. Sedimentary layers so intensely deformed that older layers lie above younger layers without fault intervention.

Paleozoic. A major era of the geological time scale embracing the interval from 230 to 600 million years. (*See* Appendix A.)

Parting. A plane of separation within a rock mass.

Pediment. A relatively smooth, gently sloping surface produced by erosion at the foot of a steeper face, usually a mountain.

Pegmatite. A very coarse-grained igneous rock formed by the fluids given off in the late stage of crystallization of an igneous body; most often close to granite in composition.

Percolate. The movement of a fluid (water) into the small open spaces within a rock, usually a loose aggregate of grains, such as sand.

Pholad boring. A small hemispherical depression created in seashore stones by the boring of certain shoreline shellfish.

Phosphate rock. A rock, usually sedimentary, relatively rich in phosphate minerals, usually compounds of PO_4 (phosphorous oxide).

Piedmont. Pertaining to areas or features lying at the foot of a mountain or mountain range.

Piracy. *See* stream capture.

Plain. An extensive region of comparatively smooth flatland at low elevation. Can be of either erosional or depositional origin.

Plate tectonics. The movement and interaction of huge plates of crustal material of continental proportions on the earth's surface.

Playa. The flat, smooth floor of a dry lake in desert regions.

Plio-Pleistocene. An interval of time extending from uppermost Pliocene into lowermost Pleistocene. (*See* Appendix A.)

Plug. A small, cylindrical, near-surface, igneous intrusive body.

Plunge. The inclination from horizontal of the long axis of a fold or warp.

Pore. A minute opening within rock, rock detritus, sediment, or soil.

Potassium-argon. A method of absolute dating of rocks and minerals using the ratio of radioactive potassium to its daughter product, the argon 40 isotope.

Precambrian. All rocks older than Paleozoic (*See* Appendix A).

Pumice. Frothy rock glass, so light that it floats.

Pyroclastic. Hot or firey (pyro) fragmental (clastic) debris thrown out of an explosive volcanic vent.

Pyroxene. A common igneous- and metamorphic-rock family of minerals, often green to black, and ranging widely in composition.

Quartz. One of our most common minerals, hard and chemically resistant, composed of silicon and oxygen (SiO_2).

Quartzite. A rock formed by metamorphism of sandstone, which is hard, coherent, and consists of quartz.

Quartz latite porphyry. A fine-grained extrusive or near-surface intrusive igneous rock with scattered larger crystals of feldspar and of acidic composition.

Radioactive. The property of some elements to spontaneously change into other elements with the emission of charged particles, usually accompanied by generation of heat.

Radio-carbon. The radioactive isotope of carbon (^{14}C) which disintegrates at a known rate. It is used to determine geological ages up to about 70,000 years.

Rainbeat. The impact of rain drops on the ground.

Reef. Used here for a prominently projecting ridge or linear outcropping of resistant rock extending down a steep hillside. Has many other meanings.

Refraction (wave, swell). The bending of a wave front as one part advances more rapidly than an adjacent part.

Regression. *See* regressive shoreline.

Regressive shoreline. A shoreline receding gradually seaward owing to a falling of sea level or a rising of the land.

Relief. Topographic relief is the difference in elevation of contiguous parts of a landscape, valley to peak.

Revolution. An episode in earth history during which a large region was subjected to severe tectonic deformation (an episode of mountain building).

Rhyolite. An extrusive igneous rock of granitic composition, fine-grained, often light-colored to red.

Rib. A narrow ridge-like outcropping of resistant rock extending down a steep slope (valley side or hillside).

Rift. Used here for the shallow topographic trench, a mile or two wide, along the trace of a major fault.

Right-lateral fault. One on which the displacement of the opposing block appears to have been to the right, no matter on which side the observer stands.

Rill. A small, shallow, narrow, straight, unbranched channel extending directly down slope eroded by an ephemeral streamlet. Rills are usually multiple and parallel.

Rilled. A slope dissected by many, small, parallel rill channels.

Ring dike. An igneous dike with a ring-like configuration.

Riparian. Pertaining to the banks of a body of water, usually a stream, and commonly applied to stream-side vegetation.

Rip current. A relatively narrow, high-velocity surface current returning water piled up on a shore by waves and currents to the ocean. Miscalled rip *tide*.

Rock. An aggregate of minerals.

Rock debris (detritus). Surficial broken-up rock material.

Rockfall. The relatively free fall of rock masses from steep bedrock faces.

Rock slide. A landslide involving principally rock.

Rock-slide debris. The broken-up rock formed by a rock slide, rockfall or rock avalanche.

Roundstone. A rock fragment rounded by abrasion and wear during movement by currents or waves.

Saddle. A relatively low, broad, open gap or pass across a ridge.

Sag pond. A pond occupying a depression along the trace of a major fault, usually where a block within the zone has sunk.

Sand flow. A mass flowage of loose sand; can occur on steep sand faces (lee side of a dune) or on the floor of the sea.

Sandstone. A sedimentary rock formed by cementation of sand-size particles.

Sandstone dike. A clastic dike in which the material is sand.

Scarp. A straight steep bank or face which can be a few feet to thousands of feet high, like the east face of the Sierra Nevada.

Schist. A finer-grained and more thinly and regularly foliated metamorphic rock than gneiss.

Scour channel. A small shallow channel created on the bed of a stream or the floor of the ocean by current scouring. Usually subsequently filled with sediment.

Sea arch. Opening through a headland (or a stack) created by marine erosion.

Sea cliff. A cliff, bluff or steep slope created by wave erosion cutting back into the land.

Sea-floor spreading. A phenomenon by which new sea floor is formed by upwelling and lateral spreading of material from the earth's mantle.

Sedimentary rocks. A class of rocks of secondary origin, made up of transported and deposited rock and mineral particles and of chemical substances, all derived from weathering.

Sedimentary structures. Largely primary structures within sedimentary rocks formed during their deposition—ripple marks, for example.

Seismology. The science of earthquake phenomena.

Septum. An older mass of metamorphic rock separating two adjacent intrusive igneous bodies.

Serpentine or serpentinite. Used here for a rock composed largely of minerals of the serpentine group, formed chiefly by alteration of igneous rocks rich in iron and magnesium.

Shale. A sedimentary rock consisting largely of very fine mineral particles, laid down in thin layers.

Sheetflow. An overland downslope flow of water in a continuous thin sheet (unchanneled).

Shore. The narrow strip of land bordering a water body over which water is shifted by tides and waves.

Shoreline. The line defined by intersection of water and land along the margin of a water body.

Shoreline processes. Transportation, erosion, and deposition as accomplished largely by waves and currents along a sea or lake shore.

Silica. The chemical compound SiO_2. Common quartz is a variety of silica.

Silicic. Rich in silica (SiO_2). (*See* acidic.)

Silicified. Impregnated with or replaced by silica.

Siltstone. A fine-grained, well-bedded sedimentary rock composed of silt, finer than sand and coarser than clay.

Skin slide. The slippage of a thin layer of water-saturated, weathered mantle rock (soil) on a steep, usually grassy, hillslope.

Slate. A weakly metamorphosed rock derived from shale by compaction with the development of closely spaced, smooth, parallel-fracture surfaces (slaty cleavage).

Slickenside. Polished and scratched (striated) surface created by slippage along a fault plane.

Slide. *See* landslide.

Slope wash. Loose soil and rock debris carried downslope by water in other than channeled form.

Slump. A form of mass movement occurring predominately on a concave slip surface causing rotation of the slumped block.

Soil. A surficial layer of rock debris with characteristics produced by weathering that distinguish it from the parent material.

Soil slip. *See* skin slide.

Sorting. The arrangement of particles by size.

Spanish grant. A large tract of land granted to an individual by the government of Spain within its American provinces.

Spit. A shoreline sandbar partly closing the mouth of a bay or estuary.

Spur. The subordinate ridges extending from the crest of a larger ridge.

Stack. A steep-sided, upstanding offshore rock or islet isolated from land by coastline recession under erosion. (Also has a more general meaning.)

Strand (marine). The narrow strip of land immediately bordering the ocean. Essentially synonymous with beach.

Strata. Layers of a sedimentary rock. Bedded rocks are *stratified*.

Stratigraphic. Pertaining to relationships involving the succession of layers (strata) within sedimentary rocks.

Stratigraphy. The succession and interrelationship of layers within stratified sedimentary rocks.

Stream capture. The diversion of the headwaters of a stream owing to headward growth of an adjacent stream.

Stream gravels. An admixture of larger rock particles within sand, transported and deposited by a stream.

Storm-wave bench. A narrow, near-horizontal platform cut in bedrock at the foot of a sea cliff at the level of high-tide storm-wave activity.

Strike. The compass bearing of a horizontal line in an inclined plane, or the trend of a line formed by intersection of an inclined surface with a horizontal surface.

Stripping. A process of erosion removing overlying beds to expose the bedding plane of an underlying stratum.

Structural trough. A low-lying trough-like feature formed by faulting or folding.

Structurally depressed. A region lower than the surroundings owing to down-faulting, warping, or folding.

Structure. Phenomena that determine the geometrical relationships of rock units, such as folds, faults, and fractures.

Submarine canyon. A canyon carved into the floor of the sea.

Superimposed stream. One which has cut down through an overlying mantle into rocks of different character and structure.

Superimposition. (*See* superimposed stream.)

Surf. That zone along a shore within which breakers are active.

Swale. A local area of slightly lower ground in a near-level region.

Swash. The uprush of water on the foreslope of a beach caused by a breaker.

Syncline. A down-fold in layered rocks which is concave upward. Beds on the flanks are inclined inward.

Talus. Accumulation of angular rock fragments at the base of a cliff.

Tar. A viscous brown-to-black organic liquid, free of water, formed by condensation of hydrocarbon volatiles.

Tectonic. Pertaining to deformation of the earth's crust resulting from forces internal to the earth.

Terrace. A geometrical form consisting of a flat tread and a steep riser or cliff. Stream terraces, lake terraces, marine terraces, and structural terraces are distinguished in geology.

Terrace gravel. Strictly, a deposit of gravel on a terrace surface. More loosely used for any deposit of fluvial (stream-laid) gravel.

Terrain. The tract of ground visible or under observation at any particular time.

Terrane. An area in which a particular rock formation prevails.

Terrestrial. Pertaining to planet Earth. Also used to distinguish between land-laid and marine deposits and environments.

Tertiary. A period of the Cenozoic Era (*See* Appendix A) embracing the time from 70 to 2 million years ago.

Threadflow. Flow of water, on the upper part of a slope, in ill-defined, interlaced, temporary threads between surface irregularities.

Thrust fault. A gently inclined fault along which one block is thrust over another.

Tonalite. A coarse-grained intrusive igneous rock of dioritic composition with a higher than normal content of quartz (a quartz diorite).

Tourmalinized. A rock within which tourmaline has been pervasively formed.

Transgressive shoreline. A shoreline moving gradually inland over land because of rising of sea level or a sinking of the land.

Travertine. A surface accumulation of calcium carbonate formed by deposition from ground or surface waters, commonly porous and cellular.

Trellis (drainage pattern). An arrangement of streams along parallel and perpendicular courses, suggestive of a wallside trellis.

Tuff. *See* volcanic tuff.

Tule. A swamp or marsh plant, more commonly known as cattail.

Turbidite. Sediment (or a sedimentary rock) deposited by a turbidity flow.

Turbidity current (flow). A current created by a mass of water of increased density, owing to suspended fine debris, that undergoes gravity flow within a larger body of water, often the ocean.

Turbidity flow. *See* turbidity current.

Turbulence. A highly confused state of water movement in which different particles of water move in all different directions.

Two-story valley. A younger valley or canyon incised within remnants of an older, wider valley form. (*See* Figure 1-3.)

Unconformity. A surface of erosion separating younger strata from older rocks.

Undertow. The intermittent seaward flow of water along the bottom off a beach.

Vein. A sheet-like deposit of mineral matter along a fracture.

Vertical air photo. One taken with the axis of the camera pointed straight down toward the ground.

Volcanic ash. Fine-grained (less than 1/8 inch diameter) volcanic debris, often glassy, explosively erupted from a volcanic vent.

Volcanic cinders. Like volcanic ash but coarser, 1/8 to 1 inch. Fragments are highly porous.

Volcanic tuff. A compacted deposit consisting of ash, cinders, and occasionally larger fragments of solid volcanic rock. If the latter are numerous, it is known as a tuff-breccia.

Volcanism. The expulsion of volcanic materials (lava, fragments, gas) onto the earth's surface.

Warp. A part of the earth's crust which has been broadly bent.

Water table. The level beneath the ground surface below which all openings in rocks are filled with water.

Wave (marine). An oscillatory movement of water caused by the passage of a traveling wave form.

Wave (or swell) front. The linear line defined by the crest (or trough) of an advancing wave train.

Wave height. The vertical difference between the crest and trough of a wave form.

Wave length (of a swell or wave). The distance from one crest to the next in a train of swells or waves.

Wave (or swell) ray. The line drawn perpendicular to the wave front. It defines the direction toward which the front is moving.

Weathering. The mechanical break up and chemical decomposition of rock materials on or near the earth's surface through interaction with the atmosphere, water, and the biosphere.

Weeping cliff. A steep rock face over which water continually seeps in a thin film.

Whaleback. A large elongate mound or hill having a general smooth rounded surface resembling a whale's back.

Wildfire. A natural fire in forest, chaparral, brush, or grass.

Wool-sack boulders. Large, rounded residual boulders formed on hillslopes underlain by homogeneous massive but jointed rock.

Appendix **D**

Selected References

In no sense is this a comprehensive list, but all of the items cited will provide further references to the pertinent literature, for those who wish to dig more deeply. The references given are principally to publications available through book sellers or government agencies. References to professional journals are avoided as being generally too difficult of access.

All maps and publications of the California Division of Mines and Geology are available through the Publications Office of that organization, P.O. Box 2980, Sacramento, California 95812; or through over-the-counter sale at Junipero Serra Building, 107 S. Broadway, Room 1065, Los Angeles.

Maps and publications of the U.S. Geological Survey are most readily ordered from that organization at the Federal Center, Denver, Colorado 80225. They are also available for over-the-counter sale at 7638 Federal Building, 300 North Los Angeles Street, Los Angeles, California.

Landforms

Bloom, A. L. *The Surface of the Earth.* Englewood Cliffs, N.J.: Prentice-Hall, Inc., 1969.
A compact, clear exposition of processes shaping the earth's surface.

Easterbrook, D. J. *Principles of Geomorphology.* New York: McGraw-Hill Book Co., 1969.
A straightforward modern text on landform development.

Hinds, N. E. A. *Evolution of California Landscape,* Bulletin 158. California Division of Mines and Geology, 1952.
A lavish illustration (photographs) of California regional landscapes.

Shelton, J. S. *Geology Illustrated.* San Francisco: W. H. Freeman and Co., 1966.
The best illustrated basic geology book extant; includes many southern California features but is general in scope.

Geological Map of California

Available in separate sheets for different areas at $1.50 each, plus tax, from California Division of Mines and Geology. Sheets pertinent to coastal southern California, south to north are: San Diego-El Centro, Santa Ana, Long Beach, Los Angeles, Santa Maria, and San Luis Obispo.

Southern California (General)

Emery, K. O. *The Sea off Southern California.* New York, John Wiley and Sons, 1960.
A description of sea-floor features and characteristics.

Jahns, R. H., ed. *Geology of Southern California,* Bulletin 170. California Division of Mines and Geology, 1954.
This is the definitive professional work on the area, a massive compilation of articles, maps, and guidebooks.

Norris, R. M., and Webb, R. W. *Geology of California.* New York: John Wiley and Sons, 1976.

Oakeshott, G. B. *California's Changing Landscapes.* New York: McGraw-Hill Co., 1971.
Both are handsomely illustrated digests of California regional geology prepared by mature professionals widely acquainted with the area. Presentation is simplified and factual.

San Diego Area

Kennedy, M. P., and Peterson, G. L. *Geology of the San Diego Metropolitan Area, California,* Bulletin 200. California Division of Mines and Geology, 1975.
By far the best and most up-to-date single source of geological information on much of the greater San Diego area.

Weber, F. H. *Geology and Mineral Resources of San Diego County, California,* County Report 3. California Division of Mines and Geology.
A compilation of useful information.

Peninsular Ranges Area

Engel, Rene. *Geology of the Lake Elsinore Quadrangle, California,* Bulletin 146. California Division of Mines and Geology, 1959.
Provides geological details on the Elsinore region.

Jahns, R. H. *Geology of the Peninsular Range Province, Southern California and Baja California,* in Chap. II, Bulletin 170. California Division of Mines and Geology, 1954.
The best short summary and overview available.

Laguna-San Joaquin Hills Area

Vedder, J. G. and others. *Geologic Map of the San Joaquin Hills-San Juan Capistrano Area, Orange County, California,* Map OM 193. U.S. Geological Survey, 1957.
A comprehensive, detailed geological map with limited text on stratigraphy.

Los Angeles Area

Yerkes, R. F. and others. *Geology of the Los Angeles Basin, California.* Professional Paper 420-A. U.S. Geological Survey, 1965.
An authoritative professional introduction to this complex area.

Ventura County Area

Weber, F. H. and others. *Geology and Mineral Resources Study of Southern Ventura County, California,* Preliminary Report 14.
Provides details and many references to the heavily inhabited part of Ventura County.

Santa Barbara-Santa Ynez Area

Dibblee, T. W., Jr. *Geology of the Central Santa Ynez Mountains, Santa Barbara County, California,* Bulletin 186. California Division of Mines and Geology, 1966.

Dibblee, T. W., Jr. *Geology of Southwestern Santa Barbara County, California,* Bulletin 150. California Division of Mines and Geology, 1950.
These two bulletins by a premier geological field mapper do the job beautifully.

Vedder, J. G. *Geology, Petroleum Development, and Seismicity of the Santa Barbara Channel Region, California,* Professional Paper 679. U.S. Geological Survey, 1969.
A professional treatment of the Santa Barbara Channel problem giving considerable information concerning the adjacent mainland.

Santa Maria-San Luis Obispo Area

Cooper, William S. *Coastal Dunes of California,* Memoir 104. Boulder, Colorado, Geological Society of America, 1968.

Hall, C. A. *Geology of the Arroyo Grande Quadrangle, San Luis Obispo County, California,* Map Sheet 24. California Division of Mines and Geology, 1974.
An excellent map with limited text extending into the Pismo area.

Woodring, W. P., and Bramlette, M. N. *Geology and Paleontology of the Santa Maria District, California,* Professional Paper 222. U.S. Geological Survey, 1950.
This is the classical professional work on the Santa Maria basin. The geological maps, on a photographic base, are particularly informative and unusual.

INDEX

COALINGA STACKS
3 1965 0000 58419
551.45 SHAR
DISCARD